THE NAVARRE BIBLE: STANDARD EDITION

THE ACTS OF THE APOSTLES

EDITORIAL COMMITTEE

VOLUMES IN THIS SERIES

THE NAVARRE BIBLE

The Acts of the Apostles

in the Revised Standard Version and New Vulgate
with a commentary by members of the
Faculty of Theology of the University of Navarre

FOUR COURTS PRESS • DUBLIN
SCEPTER PUBLISHERS • NEW YORK

Typeset by Carrigboy Typesetting Services for
FOUR COURTS PRESS LTD
7 Malpas Street, Dublin 8, Ireland
www.fourcourtspress.ie
Distributed in North America by
SCEPTER PUBLISHERS, INC.
P.O. Box 211, New York, NY 10018–0004
www.scepterpublishers.org

Nihil obstat: Stephen J. Greene, *censor deputatus*
Imprimi potest: Desmond, Archbishop of Dublin, 2 January 1989

The translation of introductions and commentary was made by Michael Adams.

A catalogue record for this title is available from the British Library.
First edition 1989
Second edition 1992, reprinted many times
Third edition (reset and repaged) 2005
Reprinted 2007; 2012; 2016; 2020

ISBN 978–1–85182–904–0

Library of Congress Cataloging-in-Publication Data [for first volume in this series]

Bible. O.T. English. Revised Standard. 1999.
   The Navarre Bible. – North American ed.
      p. cm
   "The Books of Genesis, Exodus, Leviticus, Numbers, Deuteronomy in the Revised
      Standard Version and New Vulgate with a commentary by members of the
      Faculty of Theology of the University of Navarre."
   Includes bibliographical references.
   Contents: [1] The Pentateuch.
   ISBN 1–889334–21–9 (hardback: alk. paper)
I. Title.
   BS891.A1   1999.P75   99–23033
   221.7'7—dc21   CIP

ACKNOWLEDGMENTS
Quotations from Vatican II documents are based on the translation in *Vatican Council II:
The Conciliar and Post Conciliar Documents*, ed. A. Flannery, OP (Dublin 1981).

The New Vulgate text of the Bible can be accessed via
http://www.vatican.va.archive/bible/index.htm

Printed and bound by CPI Group (UK) Ltd, Croydon, CR0 4YY.

Contents

Preface and Preliminary Notes

The Commentary
The distinguishing feature of the *Navarre Bible* is its commentary on the biblical text. Compiled by members of the Theology faculty of the University of Navarre, Pamplona, Spain, this commentary draws on writings of the Fathers, texts of the Magisterium of the Church, and works of spiritual writers, including St Josemaría Escrivá, the founder of Opus Dei; it was he who in the late 1960s entrusted the faculty at Navarre with the project of making a translation of the Bible and adding to it a commentary of the type found here.

The commentary, which is not particularly technical, is designed to explain the biblical text and to identify its main points, the message God wants to get across through the sacred writers. It also deals with doctrinal and practical matters connected with the text.

The first volume of the *Navarre Bible* (the English edition) came out in 1985—first, twelve volumes covering the New Testament; then seven volumes covering the Old Testament. Many reprints and revised editions have appeared over the past twenty years. All the various volumes are currently in print.

The Revised Standard Version
The English translation of the Bible used in the *Navarre Bible* is the Revised Standard Version (RSV) which is, as its preface states, "an authorized revision of the American Standard Version, published in 1901, which was a revision of the King James Version [the "Authorized Version"], published in 1611".

The RSV of the entire Bible was published in 1952; its Catholic edition (RSVCE) appeared in 1966. The differences between the RSV and the RSVCE New Testament texts are listed in the "Explanatory Notes" in the end-matter of this volume. Whereas the Spanish editors of what is called in English the "Navarrre Bible" made a new translation of the Bible, for the English edition the RSV has proved to be a very appropriate choice of translation. The publishers of the *Navarre Bible* wish to thank the Division of Christian Education of the National Council of the Churches of Christ in the USA for permission to use that text.

The Latin Text
This volume also carries the official Latin version of the New Testament in the *editio typica altera* of the New Vulgate (Vatican City, 1986).

Preface

The headings within the biblical text have been provided by the editors (they are not taken from the RSV). A full list of these headings, giving an overview of the New Testament, can be found at the back of the volume.

An asterisk *inside the biblical text* signals an RSVCE "Explanatory Note" at the end of the volume.

References in the biblical text indicate parallel texts in other biblical books. All these marginal references come from the *Navarre Bible* editors, not the RSV.

Abbreviations

1. BOOKS OF HOLY SCRIPTURE

Acts	Acts of the Apostles	1 Kings	1 Kings
Amos	Amos	2 Kings	2 Kings
Bar	Baruch	Lam	Lamentations
1 Chron	1 Chronicles	Lev	Leviticus
2 Chron	2 Chronicles	Lk	Luke
Col	Colossians	1 Mac	1 Maccabees
1 Cor	1 Corinthians	2 Mac	2 Maccabees
2 Cor	2 Corinthians	Mal	Malachi
Dan	Daniel	Mic	Micah
Deut	Deuteronomy	Mk	Mark
Eccles	Ecclesiastes (Qoheleth)	Mt	Matthew
Esther	Esther	Nah	Nahum
Eph	Ephesians	Neh	Nehemiah
Ex	Exodus	Num	Numbers
Ezek	Ezekiel	Obad	Obadiah
Ezra	Ezra	1 Pet	1 Peter
Gal	Galatians	2 Pet	2 Peter
Gen	Genesis	Phil	Philippians
Hab	Habakkuk	Philem	Philemon
Hag	Haggai	Ps	Psalms
Heb	Hebrews	Prov	Proverbs
Hos	Hosea	Rev	Revelation (Apocalypse)
Is	Isaiah	Rom	Romans
Jas	James	Ruth	Ruth
Jer	Jeremiah	1 Sam	1 Samuel
Jn	John	2 Sam	2 Samuel
1 Jn	1 John	Sir	Sirach (Ecclesiasticus)
2 Jn	2 John	Song	Song of Solomon
3 Jn	3 John	1 Thess	1 Thessalonians
Job	Job	2 Thess	2 Thessalonians
Joel	Joel	1 Tim	1 Timothy
Jon	Jonah	2 Tim	2 Timothy
Josh	Joshua	Tit	Titus
Jud	Judith	Wis	Wisdom
Jude	Jude	Zech	Zechariah
Judg	Judges	Zeph	Zephaniah

2. OTHER ABBREVIATIONS

ad loc.	*ad locum*, commentary on this passage	f	and following (*pl.* ff)
AAS	*Acta Apostolicae Sedis*	ibid.	*ibidem*, in the same place
Apost.	Apostolic	in loc.	*in locum,* commentary on this passage
can.	canon	loc.	*locum*, place or passage
chap.	chapter	par.	parallel passages
cf.	*confer*, compare	Past.	Pastoral
Const.	Constitution	RSV	Revised Standard Version
Decl.	Declaration	RSVCE	Revised Standard Version, Catholic Edition
Dz-Sch	Denzinger-Schönmetzer, *Enchiridion Biblicum* (4th edition, Naples & Rome, 1961)	SCDF	Sacred Congregation for the Doctrine of the Faith
		sess.	session
Enc.	Encyclical	v.	verse (*pl.* vv.)
Exhort.	Exhortation		

"Sources quoted in the Commentary", which appears at the end of this book, explains other abbreviations used.

Introduction to
the Acts of the Apostles

TITLE AND LITERARY GENRE

The usual English title—"Acts of the Apostles"—corresponds to the Latin "Actus" or "Acta Apostolorum" and the Greek "Práxeis Apostolicón". This is the title invariably given the book from the middle of the second century onwards in all Greek manuscripts, in early translations and in references in the works of the Fathers and ecclesiastical writers. It seems likely, however, that the author did not give it this title but that it received it some time after it was written. It is not really an account of the activity of the apostles but rather a description of the early years of Christianity linked to the missionary work of the two most prominent apostles, Peter and Paul.

The Acts of the Apostles seeks to give an account of how the Church was originally established and of the first stage of the spread of the Gospel, after our Lord's ascension. It is a type of history book, the first history of Christianity. However, it does not belong only or primarily to the category of history; it is not a mere chronicle of events; it cannot and should not be separated from the Third Gospel, with which it is in total continuity as history and as theology. It is a book dominated by a religious purpose—to report events which, under the impulse of the Holy Spirit, reveal God's saving plan for mankind.

The sacred author has managed to combine history and theology remarkably well. He does not limit himself to producing a narrative similar in style to profane history; yet neither has he written a sacred book which is totally detached from the cultural environment in which he is living. He is well aware that any proclamation of the Gospel must also be to some degree an account of historical events which truly happened.

The Acts of the Apostles, in relating the beginnings of the Church, aims primarily at strengthening the faith of Christians, assuring them as to the origin and basis of that faith. Secondarily, it discreetly anticipates the kind of writing typical of the apologists of the second and third centuries, by arguing that Christ's disciples had a right to the same freedom and the same respect as the Empire gave to what were called "lawful religions" (particularly Judaism).

Acts portrays Christianity as an outstanding faith, trusting in God and self-assured, which has no time for obscurantism or the kind of secrecy typical of

11

sects, and which is not afraid to debate its principles and convictions with all comers.

The entire narrative is imbued with an extraordinary spiritual joy—a joy which comes from the Holy Spirit, from certainty about the supernatural origin of the Church, from contemplation of the prodigies which God works in support of the preachers of his Gospel, from—essentially—the protection God gives his disciples despite the persecution they undergo.

THEME AND STRUCTURE

The book describes the way Jesus' prediction to his disciples prior to his ascension was fulfilled: "You shall be my witnesses in Jerusalem and in all Judea and Samaria and to the end of the earth" (1:8). Following a fairly precise and detailed chronological order, it covers events over a period of about thirty years—from the death, resurrection and ascension of our Lord until the end of St Paul's imprisonment in Rome about the year 63.

Commentators have suggested different ways of dividing the book up as a guide to understanding it better. From the point of view of God's plans of salvation, which the book reflects, it divides into two sections—before and after the Council of Jerusalem (15:6–29). This assembly at Jerusalem is certainly the theological centre of the book, due to the unique role it played in explaining God's will about the catholic nature of the Church and the primacy of grace over the Mosaic Law, and the impetus it gave to the universal spread of the Gospel.

If we look at the book in terms of the episodes it contains—stages as it were in the history of the preaching of the Gospel—the Acts of the Apostles can be divided into four parts:

Part 1. *Chapters 1–7*. These tell of the life of the early community in Jerusalem. They begin with our Lord's ascension, the sending of the Holy Spirit on Pentecost and the revealing of the supernatural character of the Church that followed on from that. Then comes the account of the growth of the first community around the apostle Peter. Miracles and prodigies accompany the spread of the Gospel. This is followed by persecution by the Jewish establishment, culminating in the martyrdom of Stephen.

Part 2. *Chapters 8–12*. These report the dispersion of the Christians: with the exception of the Twelve, this scattering is the result of persecution and it in turn leads to the Gospel being preached in Judea, Samaria and Syria. The Church begins to open its doors to the Gentiles. We are told of the conversion of the Ethiopian, an official of the court of the queen of that country, and learn that many Samaritans received Baptism. The conversion of Cornelius, a

Gentile—an event of extraordinary significance, with the Gospel breaking down ethnic barriers—is described in great detail. This section ends with the death of James, the brother of John, and the arrest and miraculous release of St Peter.

Part 3. *Chapters 13–20.* This section focuses on the missionary endeavours of Paul, who on his first journey with Barnabas prior to the Council of Jerusalem, and on two other subsequent journeys, brings the Gospel to the pagan world, in keeping with his special vocation as apostle of the Gentiles.

Part 4. *Chapters 21–28.* This section begins in Jerusalem with the imprisonment of Paul, who from this point onwards will, in chains, bear witness to the Gospel up to the time of his stay in Rome. From that city of cities the way lies open for the Gospel to be spread all over the world.

AUTHOR AND DATE OF COMPOSITION

Christian tradition and almost all commentators assert that the book of the Acts of the Apostles was written by the author of the Third Gospel and that that author was St Luke, the companion of St Paul on his second journey and his loyal aide (cf. Acts 16:10ff; Col 4:14; Philem 24). St Luke was also with the apostle from Troas to Jerusalem (cf. Acts 20:5ff) and, later on, from Caesarea to Rome (cf. 27:1ff). He was probably not Jewish by birth. An early tradition, attested by Eusebius of Caesarea, the historian,[1] and by St Jerome,[2] gave Antioch as his birthplace.

There are a number of good reasons for identifying St Luke as the author of Acts. The best internal evidence is found in the passages of the book written in the first person plural (cf. Acts 16:10–17; 20:5–15; 21:1–18; 27:1—28:16). The most obvious interpretation is that these passages were written by a companion of Paul and incorporated into the book without any change in style for the simple reason that the author of this source—which is possibly a travel diary—and the author of the rest of the book were one and the same person. By eliminating everyone mentioned in Acts by name, we are left with St Luke as the only one who could have been Paul's companion in Caesarea and Rome.

The external arguments are mainly the testimony of Christian writers, especially St Irenaeus of Lyons (d. 180), who refers to St Luke as author of the Third Gospel and of the Acts of the Apostles. This is also stated in the Muratorian Canon (end of the second century).

The date of the book can be established by reference to certain factors which place it within a period and help to pin it down more specifically. The

---

1. *Ecclesiastical History*, 3, 4, 6. 2. Cf. *Comm. on Matthew*, preface.

main factors in question are Paul's Roman imprisonment and the destruction of Jerusalem. Clearly St Luke could not have written his work earlier than the year 62 or 63, the date of the apostle's confinement in Rome. Whether it was written before or after Paul's martyrdom is disputed, but that does not affect the choice of the earlier limit. On the other hand, it is virtually certain that Acts was written before the destruction of Jerusalem, that is, before the year 70. It is difficult to conceive how Luke could have written after that date and yet made no reference of any kind to such a tremendous event and one so relevant to the relationship between the nascent Church and Judaism and the temple. The reader of the book has the impression all along that the Holy City is still standing and that the temple is still the centre of Jewish worship. Some authors reach the same conclusion by arguing from the book's silence on the martyrdom of James, and of Peter, who fell victim to Nero's persecution.

We can conclude, then, that the Third Gospel and the Acts of the Apostles, which are two parts of a single work, could have been written over quite a short period of time and were completed prior to the year 70.

The book's dedication to Theophilus tells us—as does every such dedication in ancient writings—that the author has completed his work and made it available to the Christian readership for which he intended it, and indeed to Jewish readership also.

HISTORICAL ACCURACY

The Church has always maintained that the Acts of the Apostles is a true history of events. Luke's evangelizing and theological purpose did not prevent him from collecting, evaluating and interpreting facts with a skill that demonstrates he was an excellent historian. We have to put down to theological prejudice that scepticism expressed by some non-Catholic scholars about the historical value of Acts. These exegetes quite arbitrarily claim that the supernatural events reported in the book are later additions included into the text by an anonymous imaginative writer interested in projecting a particular image of Paul. Nowadays, there is a growing acceptance of the historicity of Acts: many non-Catholic scholars have come to this view through detailed study of the text, and their conviction has led others to tend in the same direction.

Few ancient texts provide such scope for checking their accuracy as Acts does. It is full of references to contemporary Jewish, Greek and Roman history, culture and topography. Everything it recounts is carefully set into an historical framework. Details of time and place are invariably found to be accurate, and the atmosphere of the period imbues the entire book. The writer leads his reader on a tour of the streets, markets, theatres and assemblies of the Ephesus, Thessalonica, Corinth and Philippi of the first century of the Christian era.

The events narrated in Acts invite and permit the scholar to check them for historical accuracy against the letters of St Paul, which deal with the same material, to some degree.

Like all writers of antiquity, the author of Acts focuses his attention on his principal characters and builds the narrative around them. He presents Paul as a fully mature Christian personality from the day of his conversion forward. This understandable simplification does not prevent us, however, from recognizing the Paul of Acts and the Paul of the Letters as being the same person. The Paul of Acts is the real Paul as seen retrospectively by a disciple who is also a friend.

The connexions between Acts and the Letters point to one and the same Paul. His activity as persecutor of the Church is recorded in similar language in Acts (8:3; 9:1) as in Galatians 1:13 and 1 Corinthians 15:9. Galatians 1:17 confirms what Acts says (9:3) about his conversion taking place in Damascus. In Acts 9:23–27 and Galatians 1:18 we are told that Paul made his first journey after his conversion from Damascus to Jerusalem. In Acts 9:30 and Galatians 1:21 we are told about Paul being sent to Tarsus after his stay in Jerusalem. His missionary companions after the split with Barnabas — that is, Silas and Timothy (cf. Acts 15:22, 40; 16:1) — are to be found in the letters written during this period. The itinerary in Acts 16–19 (Philippi – Thessalonica – Athens – Corinth – Ephesus – Macedonia – Achaia) is confirmed by 1 Thess 2:2; 3:1; 1 Cor 2:1; 16:5–9; 2 Cor 12:14ff, Rom 16:1, 23). Only the Letters tell us that Paul was of the tribe of Benjamin (cf. Rom 11:1; Phil 3:5). Acts merely says that his Jewish name was Saul (cf. Acts 7:58; 9:1; 13:9): this ties in, because it would be quite reasonable for parents from that tribe to call a child after the first king of Israel, its most outstanding member (cf. 1 Sam 9:1ff). Many more examples could be given in support of the historical accuracy of the book.

Another source which throws a great deal of light on Luke's narrative is Flavius Josephus' *Jewish Antiquities*, written some twenty years after Acts. Josephus helps us establish the dates of Herod Agrippa I's reign (from the year 41 to 10 March 44), and we can see the agreement between Acts 12 and *Antiquities*, 19, 274–363 on the circumstances of the king's death. Josephus' account also helps explain Luke's references (cf. Acts 5:36–37; *Antiquities*, 20, 169–172) to the Jewish rebels Judas of Galilee and Theudas. Luke's profile of the two governors Felix and Festus and of King Herod Agrippa II is confirmed and developed by Josephus. Another instance of corroboration is that Acts 18:12 describes Gallio as being proconsul of Achaia and this has been confirmed by an inscription found at Delphi, near Corinth.

This historical reliability of Acts only serves to reinforce its validity as a testimony to the faith of that early Church governed by the apostles and guided at every step by the invisible and often visible power of the Holy Spirit: Acts sets an example of faith and doctrine for the Church in every era.

The speeches which the book contains, especially the more important ones of Peter (cf. 2:14ff; 3:12ff; 10:34ff; 11:5ff), Stephen (cf. 7:2ff) and Paul (cf.

13:16ff; 17:22ff; 20:18ff; 22:1ff; 24:10ff; 26:2ff) have been the subject of many detailed studies. Naturally, the actual address in each case would have been longer than the version given in the book, and Luke would have had more to draw on for some than for others. However, the accounts which Luke gives are to be taken as accurate. The addresses can be seen to reflect traditional Jewish styles of quoting and interpreting Holy Scripture and, although similar in structure, there is also quite a variety in them. They obviously reflect the different speakers, locations and audiences, and they give a good idea of the Church's earliest form of preaching.

SOURCES

In line with the style of Jewish and Hellenist writers, St Luke made use of written sources to produce his book. He had not been an eyewitness of everything he reported and he would not have settled for simply word-of-mouth information: he would have used documents of different kinds, such as short narrative accounts, summaries of speeches, notes, travel diaries etc. It is quite likely that for the earlier part of the book he used material collected from the various churches or from the main people involved.

However, the book is so all-of-a-piece that it is difficult to reconstruct, with any accuracy, the sources he would have used. Some commentators suggest that Acts is based on two main groups of documents—a) an Antiochene source, containing information about Stephen, Philip, Barnabas and the early years of St Paul; and b) a collection of accounts of St Peter's activity. But this is only a hypothesis.

Nor is it possible to say whether Luke included all the material available to him or instead operated selectively. He certainly seems to have used his own judgment as to what material to incorporate and what not to, and when to edit, re-use, combine or divide up material made available to him. Whatever his method, he did manage to impose remarkable unity on his work, every page of which evidences the supernatural action of the Spirit of God.

DOCTRINAL CONTENT

Acts is a sort of compendium of the Christian faith in action. St Luke's purpose, which is one of instruction, leads him to put forward all the main truths of the Christian religion and to show the main outlines of the liturgical and sacramental life of the infant Church. His book also gives us accurate insights into the way the Church was structured and managed, and into the attitudes of Christians towards political and social questions of their time.

Its teachings on Christ, the Holy Spirit and the Church merit special attention.

Christology. Teaching on Christ in Acts is based on the Synoptic Gospels, on Jesus' life on earth and his glorification, which are the core of the Gospel message. All aspects of the paschal mystery—Passion, Death, Resurrection and Ascension—are given prominence, and that mystery is shown to fulfil the plans revealed by God in the Old Testament prophecies. Various Christological titles are applied to Jesus which show his divinity and his redemptive mission—titles such as Lord (2:36), Saviour (5:31), Servant of Yahweh (3:13, 16), the Righteous One (7:52), the Holy One (3:14) and especially Christ—the Messiah—which becomes his proper name.

Theology of the Holy Spirit. St Luke stresses the key role of the Holy Spirit in all aspects of the life of the Church. At one and the same time the Spirit of God and the Spirit of Jesus Christ, the Holy Spirit, at Pentecost causes the Church to be made manifest to all the people and enables it to begin its salvific activity. The Spirit is the personal possession and the common inheritance of Christians, and also the source of their joy and spiritual vitality. He endows and supports in a special way those Christians who are ordained to carry out the various sacred ministries; and it is he who guides the Church in its choice of rulers and missionaries and encourages it and protects it in its work of evangelization. This second book by St Luke has rightly been called "the Gospel of the Holy Spirit".

Ecclesiology. Acts is an indispensable source of documentation on the life of the Church in its very earliest period. In it we are shown the Church as the instrument God uses to fulfil the Old Testament promises. The Church is, then, the true Israel, a new people, a worldwide community of people joined by spiritual links, a people which is essentially missionary.

The Church is the outcome of the invisible but real presence of the risen Christ, who is the focus of Christian worship and the only Name by which men can be saved. Jesus' presence is really and truly effected in the "breaking of the bread", that is, in the eucharistic sacrifice, which his disciples already celebrate on Sunday, the first day of the week.

Acts describes the lifestyle of the early Christians in a very direct and moving way. Their life centres on prayer, the Eucharist and the apostles' teaching, and it expresses itself in attitudes and actions of detachment, concord and love. St Luke offers this lifestyle as a kind of model and heritage for future generations of Christians.

Two aspects of Christianity are combined extremely well in this book—expectation of our Lord's second coming (which runs right through the New Testament) and the need to commit oneself, through prayer, work and cheerful sacrifice, to the building up of the Kingdom of God on earth.

Acts also tells us a good deal about the structure of the Church in earliest times and provides us with a most valuable account of the first council of the Church (cf. 15:6ff).

THE ACTS OF THE APOSTLES

The Revised Standard Version, with notes

1 ¹In the first book,* O Theophilus, I have dealt with all that
Jesus began to do and teach, ²until the day when he was taken

---

1:1–5. St Luke is the only New Testament author to begin his book with a prologue, in the style of secular historians. The main aim of this preface is to convey to the reader the profoundly religious character of the book which he is holding in his hands. It is a work which will give an account of events marking the fulfilment of the promises made by the God of Israel, the Creator and Saviour of the world. Under the inspiration of the Holy Spirit, into his book St Luke weaves quotations from the Psalms, Isaiah, Amos and Joel; it both reflects the Old Testament and interprets it in the light of its fulfilment in Jesus Christ.

The prologue refers to St Luke's Gospel as a "first book". It mentions the last events of our Lord's life on earth—the appearances of the risen Christ and his ascension into heaven—and links them up with the account which is now beginning.

St Luke's aim is to describe the origins and the early growth of Christianity, of which the main protagonist of this book, the Holy Spirit, has been the cause. Yet this is not simply an historical record: the Acts of the Apostles, St Jerome explains, "seems to be a straightforward historical account of the early years of the nascent Church. But if we bear in mind it is written by Luke the physician, who is praised in the Gospel (cf. 2 Cor 8:18), we will realize that everything he says is medicine for the ailing soul" (*Epistle* 53, 9).

The spiritual dimension of this book, which is one of a piece with the Third Gospel, nourished the soul of the first generations of Christians, providing them with a chronicle of God's faithful and loving support of the new Israel.

"This book", St John Chrysostom writes at the start of his great commentary, "will profit us no less than the Gospels, so replete is it with Christian wisdom and sound doctrine. It offers an account of the numerous miracles worked by the Holy Spirit. It contains the fulfilment of the prophecies of Jesus Christ recorded in the Gospel; we can observe in the very facts the bright evidence of Truth which shines in them, and the mighty change which is taking place in the apostles: they become perfect men, extraordinary men, now that the Holy Spirit has come upon them. All Christ's promises and predictions—He who believes in me will do these and even greater works, you will be dragged before tribunals and kings and beaten in the synagogues, and will suffer grievous things, and yet you will overcome your persecutors and executioners and will bring the Gospel to the ends of the earth—all this, how it came to pass, may be seen in this admirable book. Here you will see the apostles speeding their way over land and sea as if on wings. These Galileans, once so timorous and obtuse, we find suddenly changed into new men, despising wealth and honour, raised above passion and concupiscence" (*Hom. on Acts*, 1).

St Luke dedicates this book to Theophilus—as he did his Gospel. The dedication suggests that Theophilus was an educated Christian, of an upper-class background, but he may be a fictitious person symbolizing "the beloved of God", which is what the name means. It also may imply that Acts was written quite soon after the Third Gospel.

1:1. "To do and teach": these words very concisely sum up the work of Jesus

Jn 20:22
1 Tim 3:16
Acts 13:31

Lk 24:49
Acts 10:41

Mt 3:11
Lk 3:16
Acts 11:16

up, after he had given commandment through the Holy Spirit to the apostles whom he had chosen. ³To them he presented himself alive after his passion by many proofs, appearing to them during forty days, and speaking of the kingdom of God. ⁴And while staying^a with them he charged them not to depart from Jerusalem, but to wait for the promise of the Father, which, he said, "you heard from me, ⁵for John baptized with water, but before many days you shall be baptized with the Holy Spirit."

Christ, reported in the Gospels. They describe the way in which God's saving revelation operates: God lovingly announces and reveals himself in the course of human history through his actions and through his words. "The economy of revelation is realized by deeds and words, which are intrinsically bound up with each other", Vatican II teaches. "As a result, the works performed by God in the history of salvation show forth and bear out the doctrine and realities signified by the words; the words, for their part, proclaim the works, and bring to light the mystery they contain. The most intimate truth which this revelation gives us about God and the salvation of man shines forth in Christ, who is himself both the mediator and the sum total of Revelation" (*Dei Verbum*, 2).

The Lord "proclaimed the kingdom of the Father both by the testimony of his life and by the power of his word" (Vatican II, *Lumen gentium*, 35). He did not limit himself to speech, to being simply the Teacher whose words opened man's minds to the truth. He was, above all, the Redeemer, able to save fallen man through the divine efficacy of each and every moment of his life on earth.

"Our Lord took on all our weaknesses, which proceed from sin—with the exception of sin itself. He experienced hunger and thirst, sleep and fatigue, sadness and tears. He suffered in every possible way, even the supreme

suffering of death. No one could be freed from the bonds of sinfulness had he who alone was totally innocent not been ready to die at the hands of impious men. Therefore, our Saviour, the Son of God, has left all those who believe in him an effective source of aid, and also an example. The first they obtain by being reborn through grace, the second by imitating his life" (St Leo the Great, *Twelfth homily on the Passion*).

Jesus' redemptive action—his miracles, his life of work, and the mystery of his death, resurrection and ascension, whose depth and meaning only faith can plumb—also constitute a simple and powerful stimulus for our everyday conduct. Faith should always be accompanied by words, by deeds, that is, our humble and necessary cooperation with God's saving plans.

"Don't forget that doing must come before teaching. '*Coepit facere et docere*', the holy Scripture says of Jesus Christ: 'He began to do and to teach.'

"First deeds: so that you and I might learn" (St J. Escrivá, *The Way*, 342).

1:3. This verse recalls the account in Luke 24:13–43 of the appearances of the risen Jesus to the disciples of Emmaus and to the apostles in the Cenacle.

It stresses the figure of *forty* days. This number may have a literal meaning and also a deeper meaning. In Holy Scripture periods of forty days or forty

a. Or *eating*

22

The Ascension

⁶So when they had come together, they asked him, "Lord, will you at this time restore the kingdom of Israel?" ⁷He said to them, "It is not for you to know times or seasons which the Father has fixed by his own authority. ⁸But you shall receive power when the Holy Spirit has come upon you; and you shall be my witnesses in Jerusalem and in all Judea and Samaria and to the end of the

Lk 19:11
Dan 2:22
Mt 24:36
1 Thess 5:1–2

Mt 28:19
Lk 24:47–48
Acts 2:32; 10:39

---

years have a clearly salvific meaning: they are periods during which God prepares or effects important stages in his plans. The great flood lasted forty days (Gen 7:17); the Israelites journeyed in the wilderness for forty years on their way to the promised land (Ps 95:10); Moses spent forty days on Mount Sinai to receive God's revelation of the Covenant (Ex 24:18); on the strength of the bread sent by God Elijah walked forty days and forty nights to reach his destination (1 Kings 19:8); and our Lord fasted in the wilderness for forty days in preparation for his public life (Mt 4:2).

1:5. "You shall be baptized with the Holy Spirit": this book has been well described as the "Gospel of the Holy Spirit". "There is hardly a page in the Acts of the Apostles where we fail to read about the Spirit and the action by which he guides, directs and enlivens the life and work of the early Christian community. It is he who inspires the preaching of St Peter (cf. Acts 4:8), who strengthens the faith of the disciples (cf. Acts 4:31), who confirms with his presence the calling of the Gentiles (cf. Acts 10:44–47), who sends Saul and Barnabas to distant lands, where they will open new paths for the teaching of Jesus (cf. Acts 13:2–4). In a word, his presence and doctrine are everywhere" (St Josemaría Escrivá, *Christ Is Passing By*, 127).

1:6–8. The apostles' question shows that they are still thinking in terms of earthly

restoration of the Davidic dynasty. It would seem that for them—as for many Jews of their time—eschatological hope in the Kingdom extended no further than expectation of world-embracing Jewish hegemony.

"It seems to me", St John Chrysostom comments, "that they had not any clear notion of the nature of the Kingdom, for the Spirit had not yet instructed them. Notice that they do not ask when it shall come but 'Will you at this time restore the Kingdom to Israel?', as if the Kingdom were something that lay in the past. This question shows that they were still attracted by earthly things, though less than they had been" (*Hom. on Acts*, 2).

Our Lord gives an excellent and encouraging reply, patiently telling them that the Kingdom is mysterious in character, that it comes when one least expects, and that they need the help of the Holy Spirit to be able to grasp the teaching they have received. Jesus does not complain about their obtuseness; he simply corrects their ideas and instructs them.

1:8. The outline of Acts is given here: the author plans to tell the story of the growth of the Church, beginning in Jerusalem and spreading through Judea and Samaria to the ends of the earth. This is the geographical structure of St Luke's account. In the Third Gospel Jerusalem was the destination point of Jesus' public life (which began in Galilee); here it is the departure point.

23

Mk 16:19
Lk 24:50–51
Jn 6:62
Eph 4:8–10
1 Pet 3:22
Lk 24:4

Mt 24:30;
25:31; 26:64
Rev 1:7

earth." ⁹And when he had said this, as they were looking on, he was lifted up, and a cloud took him out of their sight. ¹⁰And while they were gazing into heaven as he went, behold, two men stood by them in white robes, ¹¹and said, "Men of Galilee, why do you stand looking into heaven? This Jesus, who was taken up from you into heaven, will come in the same way as you saw him go into heaven."

The apostles' mission extends to the whole world. Underlying this verse we can see not so much a "geographical" dimension as the universalist aspirations of the Old Testament, articulated by Isaiah: "It shall come to pass in the latter days that the mountain of the house of the Lord shall be established as the highest of the mountains, and shall be raised above the hills; and all the nations shall flow to it, and many peoples shall come, and say: 'Come, let us go up to the mountain of the Lord, to the house of the God of Jacob; that he may teach us his ways and that we may walk in his paths.' For out of Zion shall go forth the law, and the word of the Lord from Jerusalem" (Is 2:2–3).

1:9. Jesus' life on earth did not end with his death on the cross but with his ascension into heaven. The ascension, reported here, is the last event, the last mystery of our Lord's life on earth (cf. also Lk 24:50–53)—and also it concerns the origins of the Church. The ascension scene takes place, so to speak, between heaven and earth. "Why did a cloud take him out of the apostles' sight?", St John Chrysostom asks. "The cloud was a sure sign that Jesus had already entered heaven; it was not a whirlwind or a chariot of fire, as in the case of the prophet Elijah (cf. 2 Kings 2:11), but a cloud, which was a symbol of heaven itself" (*Hom. on Acts*, 2). A cloud features in theophanies—manifestations of God—in both the Old Testament (cf. Ex 13:22) and the New (cf. Lk 9:34f).

Our Lord's ascension is one of the actions by which Jesus redeems us from sin and gives us the new life of grace. It is a redemptive mystery. "What we have already taught of the mystery of his death and resurrection the faithful should deem not less true of his ascension. For although we owe our redemption and salvation to the passion of Christ, whose merits opened heaven to the just, yet his ascension is not only proposed to us as a model, which teaches us to look on high and ascend in spirit into heaven, but it also imparts to us a divine virtue which enables us to accomplish what it teaches" (St Pius V, *Catechism*, 1, 7, 9).

Our Lord's going up into heaven is not simply something which stirs us to lift up our hearts—as we are invited to do at the preface of the Mass, to seek and love the "things that are above" (cf. Col 3:1–2); along with the other mysteries of his life, death and resurrection, Christ's ascension *saves* us. "Today we are not only made possessors of paradise", St Leo says, "but we have ascended with Christ, mystically but really, into the highest heaven, and through Christ we have obtained a more ineffable grace than that which we lost through the devil's envy" (*First homily on the Ascension*).

The ascension is the climax of Christ's exaltation, which was achieved in the first instance by his resurrection and which—along with his passion and death—constitutes the paschal mystery. The Second Vatican Council expresses

PART ONE

The Church in Jerusalem

1. THE DISCIPLES IN JERUSALEM

The apostolic college

¹²Then they returned to Jerusalem from the mount called Olivet, which is near Jerusalem, a sabbath day's journey away; ¹³and

---

this as follows: "Christ our Lord redeemed mankind and gave perfect glory to God [...] principally by the paschal mystery of his blessed passion, resurrection from the dead, and glorious ascension" (*Sacrosanctum Concilium*, 5; cf. *Dei Verbum*, 19).

Theology has suggested reasons why it was very appropriate for the glorified Lord to go up into heaven to be "seated at the right hand of the Father". "First of all, he ascended because the glorious kingdom of the highest heavens, not the obscure abode of this earth, presented a suitable dwelling place for him whose body, rising from the tomb, was clothed with the glory of immortality. He ascended, however, not only to possess the throne of glory and the kingdom which he had merited by his blood, but also to attend to whatever regards our salvation. Again, he ascended to prove thereby that his kingdom is not of this world" (St Pius V, *Catechism*, 1, 7, 5; cf. *Summa theologiae*, 3, 57, 6).

The ascension marks the point when the celestial world celebrates the victory and glorification of Christ: "It is fitting that the sacred humanity of Christ should receive the homage, praise and adoration of all the hierarchies of the Angels and of all the legions of the blessed in heaven" (St Josemaría Escrivá, *Holy Rosary*, second glorious mystery).

1:11. The angels are referring to the Parousia—our Lord's second coming, when he will judge the living and the dead. "They said to them, 'What are you doing here, looking into heaven?' These words are full of solicitude, but they do not proclaim the second coming of the Saviour as imminent. The angels simply assert what is most important, that is, that Jesus Christ will come again and the confidence with which we should await his return" (St John Chrysostom, *Hom. on Acts*, 2).

We know for a certainty that Christ will come again at the end of time. We confess this in the Creed as part of our faith. However, we know "neither the day nor the hour" (Mt 25:13) of his coming. We do not need to know it. Christ is always imminent. We must always be on the watch, that is, we should busy ourselves in the service of God and of others, which is where our sanctification lies.

1:13–14. St Luke mentions the twelve apostles by name, with the exception of Judas Iscariot.

This is the first passage which tells of the spiritual life and devout practices of the disciples. Significantly it places the emphasis on prayer, in keeping with our Lord's own practice and with his constant recommendation to his followers (cf. Mt 6:5; 14:23; etc.).

Mt 10:2–4
Lk 6:14–16

when they had entered, they went up to the upper room, where they were staying, Peter and John and James and Andrew, Philip and Thomas, Bartholomew and Matthew, James the son of

Mt 13:55
Lk 8:2–3;
24:10
Acts 12:12

Alphaeus and Simon the Zealot and Judas the son of James. ¹⁴All these with one accord devoted themselves to prayer, together with the women and Mary the mother of Jesus, and with his brethren.*

The election of Matthias

¹⁵In those days Peter stood up among the brethren (the company of persons was in all about a hundred and twenty), and said, ¹⁶"Brethren, the scripture had to be fulfilled, which the Holy Spirit

---

"Prayer is the foundation of the spiritual edifice. Prayer is all-powerful" (St J. Escrivá, *The Way*, 83). It can truly be said that prayer is the bedrock of the Church, which will be made manifest with the coming of the Holy Spirit. The prayer of the disciples, including the women, in the company of Mary would have been a supplication of entreaty and praise and thanksgiving to God. This union of hearts and feelings produced by prayer is a kind of anticipation of the gifts the Holy Spirit will bring.

"We are told this time and again in the passage narrating the lives of the first followers of Christ. 'All these with one accord devoted themselves to prayer' (Acts 1:14). […] Prayer was then, as it is today, the only weapon, the most powerful means, for winning the battles of our interior struggle" (St Josemaría Escrivá, *Friends of God*, 242).

Here we see Mary as the spiritual centre round which Jesus' intimate friends gather: tradition has meditated on this "tableau", and found it to depict our Lady's motherhood over the whole Church, both at its beginning and over the course of the centuries.

On 21 November 1964, at the closing of the third session of Vatican II, Paul VI solemnly proclaimed Mary Mother of the Church: "Our vision of the Church must include loving contemplation of the mar-

vels which God worked in his holy Mother. And knowledge of the true Catholic doctrine about Mary will always be the key to correct understanding of the mystery of Christ and of the Church.

"Reflection on the close ties linking Mary and the Church, so clearly indicated by the present constitution [*Lumen gentium*], allows us to think this is the most appropriate moment to satisfy a desire which, as we pointed out at the end of the last session, many council Fathers have made their own, calling insistently for an explicit declaration during this council of the maternal role which the Blessed Virgin exercises towards the Christian people. To this end we have considered it opportune to dedicate a title in honour of the Virgin which has been proposed in different parts of the Catholic world and which we find particularly touching, for it sums up in a wonderfully succinct way the privileged position which this council has recognized the Blessed Virgin to have in the Church.

"And so, for the glory of the Virgin and for our consolation, we proclaim Mary Most Holy to be the Mother of the Church, that is, Mother of the entire people of God, faithful as well as pastors, who call her loving Mother, and we desire that from now on she be honoured and invoked by the entire people of God under this most pleasing title."

spoke beforehand by the mouth of David, concerning Judas who was guide to those who arrested Jesus. [17]For he was numbered among us, and was allotted his share in this ministry. [18](Now this man bought a field with the reward of his wickedness; and falling headlong[b] he burst open in the middle and all his bowels gushed out. [19]And it became known to all the inhabitants of Jerusalem, so that the field was called in their language Akeldama, that is, Field of Blood.) [20]For it is written in the Book of Psalms,

> 'Let his habitation become desolate,
> and let there be no one to live in it';

and

Lk 22:47
Jn 13:18
Acts 1:20

Mt 27:3–10

Ps 69:25

The text makes reference to Jesus' "brethren", an expression which also appears in the Gospels. Given that the Christian faith teaches us that the Virgin Mary had no children other than Jesus, whom she conceived by the action of the Holy Spirit and without intervention of man, this expression cannot mean that Jesus had blood brothers or sisters.

The explanation lies in the peculiarities of Semitic languages. The word used in the New Testament translates a Hebrew term which applied to all the members of a family group and was used for even distant cousins (cf. Lev 10:4) and for nephews (Gen 13:8). See the note on Mt 12:46–47. In the New Testament then, the word "brethren" has a very wide meaning—as happens, also, for example, with the word "apostle".

At one point Jesus describes those who hear and keep his word as his "brethren" (Lk 8:21), which seems to imply that, in addition to meaning belonging to the same family group, the word "brother" in the New Testament may be a designation for certain disciples who were particularly loyal to our Lord. St Paul, for his part, uses this term for all Christians (cf., e.g., 1 Cor 1:10; etc.), as does St Peter, according to Acts 12:17.

1:15–23. "Peter is the ardent and impetuous apostle to whom Christ entrusted the care of his flock; and since he is first in dignity, he is the first to speak" (St John Chrysostom, *Hom. on Acts*, 3).

Here we see Peter performing his ministry. Events will make for the gradual manifestation of the supreme role of government which Christ entrusted to him. His is a ministry of service—he is the *servus servorum Dei*, the servant of the servants of God—a ministry given to none other, different from all other ministries in the Church. Peter will carry it out in solidarity with his brothers in the Apostolate and in close contact with the whole Church represented here in the one hundred and twenty brethren around him.

This account of Peter with the other apostles and disciples all brought together is described by St John Chrysostom in these words: "Observe the admirable prudence of St Peter. He begins by quoting the authority of a prophet and does not say, 'My own word suffices,' so far is he from any thought of pride. But he seeks nothing less than the election of a twelfth apostle and he presses for this. His entire behaviour shows the degree of his authority and that he understood the apostolic office of government not as a position of honour but as a commitment

b. Or *swelling up*

27

Acts 1:21

Ps 109:8

Jn 15:27

Acts 3:15

Jer 11:20
Lk 16:15
Acts 15:8
Rev 2:23

'His office let another take.'

[21]So one of the men who have accompanied us during all the time that the Lord Jesus went in and out among us, [22]beginning from the baptism of John until the day when he was taken up from us— one of these men must become with us a witness to his resurrection."* [23]And they put forward two, Joseph called Barsabbas, who was surnamed Justus, and Matthias. [24]And they prayed and said,

---

to watch over the spiritual health of those under him.

"The disciples were one hundred and twenty, and Peter asks for one of these. But he it is who proposes the election and exercises the principal authority because he has been entrusted with the care of all" (*Hom. on Acts*, 3).

1:21–22. The apostles are the witnesses *par excellence* of Jesus' public life. The Church is "apostolic" because it relies on the solid testimony of people specially chosen to live with our Lord, witnessing his works and listening to his words. The twelve apostles certify that Jesus of Nazareth and the risen Lord are one and the same person and that the words and actions of Jesus preserved and passed on by the Church are indeed truly reported.

Everyone who maintains unity with the Pope and the bishops in communion with him maintains unity with the apostles and, through them, with Jesus Christ himself. "Orthodox teaching has been conserved by being passed on successively since the time of the apostles and so it has remained up to the present in all the churches. Therefore, only that teaching can be considered true which offers no discord with ecclesiastical and apostolic tradition" (Origen, *De principiis*, Preface, 2). See the note on Acts 1:26.

1:24–26. Verses 24–25 record the first prayer of the Church, which is linked with what we were told in v. 14—"all these with one accord devoted them-

selves to prayer"—and shows the disciples' firm belief that God rules over all things and all events and looks after the Church in a very special way.

The Christian community leaves in God's hands the choice as to who will fill the empty place in the Twelve. It does this by using the traditional Hebrew method of casting lots, the outcome of which will reveal God's will. This method of divining God's will is to be found quite a number of times in the Old Testament (cf. 1 Sam 14:41f); its use was restricted to Levites, to prevent it degenerating into a superstitious practice. In casting lots the Jews used dice, sticks, pieces of paper etc. each bearing the name of a candidate for an office, or of people suspected of having committed some crime etc. Lots were cast as often as necessary to fill the number of places to be filled or the suspected number of criminals.

In this instance they decide to cast lots because they consider that God has already made his choice and all that remains is for him to make his will known: his decision can be ascertained unerringly by using this simple human device. This method of appointing people, borrowed from Judaism, did not continue to be used in the Church for very long.

Now that Matthias has been appointed, the Twelve is complete again. The apostolic college is now ready to receive the Holy Spirit whom Jesus promised to send, and to go on to bear universal witness to the Good News.

28

"Lord, who knowest the hearts of all men, show which one of these two thou hast chosen [25]to take the place in this ministry and apostleship from which Judas turned aside, to go to his own place." [26]And they cast lots for them, and the lot fell on Matthias; and he was enrolled with the eleven apostles.

1 Sam 14:41
Prov 16:33

1:26. St Luke usually applies the term "apostles" only to the Twelve (cf., for example, Acts 6:6), or the Eleven plus Peter, who appears as head of the apostolic college (cf. 2:14). Except in Acts 14:14, Luke never describes St Paul as an apostle—not because he minimizes Paul's role (indeed, half the chapters of Acts deal with Paul) but because he reserves to the Twelve the specific function of being witnesses to our Lord's life on earth.

This apostolic character or apostolicity is one of the marks of the true Church of Christ—a Church built, by the express wish of its Founder, on the solid basis of the Twelve.

The *St Pius V Catechism* (1, 10, 17) teaches that "the true Church is also to be recognized from her origin, which can be traced back under the law of grace to the apostles; for her doctrine is the truth not recently given, nor now first heard of, but delivered of old by the apostles, and disseminated throughout the entire world. [...] That all, therefore, might know which was the Catholic Church, the Fathers, guided by the Spirit of God, added to the Creed the word 'apostolic'. For the Holy Spirit, who presides over the Church, governs her by no other ministers than those of apostolic succession. This Spirit, first imparted to the apostles, has by the infinite goodness of God always continued in the Church."

The principal role of the apostles is to be witnesses to the resurrection of Jesus (cf. 1:22). They perform it through the ministry of the word (6:4), which takes various forms, such as preaching to the people (cf. 2:14–40; 3:12–26; 4:2, 33; 5:20–21), teaching the disciples within the Christian community itself (2:42), and declarations uttered fearlessly against the enemies and persecutors of the Gospel of Jesus (4:5–31; 5:27–41). Like the word of the Lord, that of the apostles is supported by signs and wonders, which render visible the salvation which they proclaim (2:14–21, 43; 3:1–11, 16; 4:8–12, 30; 5:12, 15–16; 9:31–43).

The Twelve also perform a role of government in the Church. When the members of the community at Jerusalem give up their property to help their brothers in need, they lay the money "at the apostles' feet" (4:35). When the Hellenist Christians need to be reassured, the Twelve summon the assembly to establish the ministry of the diaconate (6:2). When Saul goes up to Jerusalem after his conversion, he is introduced to the apostles by Barnabas (9:26–28). The apostles quite evidently exercise an authority given them by our Lord who invested them with untransferable responsibilities and duties connected with service to the entire Church.

The apostles also intervene outside Jerusalem as guarantors of internal and external unity, which also is an essential distinguishing mark of the Church. After Philip baptizes some Samaritans, the apostles Peter and John travel from Jerusalem to give them the Holy Spirit by the laying on of hands (8:14–17).

After the baptism of the pagan Cornelius, the apostles study the situation with Peter, to ascertain more exactly the designs of God and the details of the new

2. PENTECOST

The coming of the Holy Spirit

2 ¹When the day of Pentecost had come, they were all together in one place. ²And suddenly a sound came from heaven like the rush of a mighty wind, and it filled all the house where they

---

economy of salvation (11:1–18). Apropos of the debate in Antioch about the circumcision of baptized pagans, the community decides to consult the apostles (15:2) to obtain a final decision on this delicate matter.

Most of St Luke's attention is concentrated on the figure of Peter, whom he mentions 56 times in Acts. Peter is always the centre of those scenes or episodes in which he appears with other apostles or disciples. In matters to do with the community at Jerusalem Peter acts as the spokesman of the Twelve (2:14, 37; 5:29) and plays a key role in the opening up of the Gospel to pagans.

The college of the twelve apostles, whose head is Peter, endures in the episcopacy of the Church, whose head is the Pope, the bishop of Rome, successor of Peter and vicar of Jesus Christ. The Second Vatican Council proposes this once again when it teaches that the "Lord Jesus, having prayed at length to the Father, called to himself those whom he willed and appointed twelve to be with him, whom he might send to preach the Kingdom of God (cf. Mk 3:13–19; Mt 10:1–42). These apostles (cf. Lk 6:13) he constituted in the form of a college or permanent assembly, at the head of which he placed Peter, chosen from among them (cf. Jn 21:15–17)" (*Lumen gentium*, 19).

"Just as, in accordance with the Lord's decree, St Peter and the rest of the apostles constitute a unique apostolic college, so in like fashion the Roman Pontiff, Peter's successor, and the bishops, the successors of the apostles, are related and united to one another. [...]

"In it the bishops, whilst loyally respecting the primacy and pre-eminence of their head, exercise their own proper authority for the good of their faithful, indeed even for the good of the whole Church, the organic structure and harmony of which are strengthened by the continued influence of the Holy Spirit. The supreme authority over the whole Church, which this college possesses, is exercised in a solemn way in an ecumenical council. [...] And it is the prerogative of the Roman Pontiff to convoke such councils, to preside over them and to confirm them" (ibid., 22).

2:1–13. This account of the Holy Spirit visibly coming down on the disciples who, in keeping with Jesus' instructions, had stayed together in Jerusalem, gives limited information as to the time and place of the event, yet it is full of content. Pentecost was one of the three great Jewish feasts for which many Israelites went on pilgrimage to the Holy City to worship God in the temple. It originated as a harvest thanksgiving, with an offering of first-fruits. Later it was given the additional dimension of commemorating the promulgation of the Law given by God to Moses on Sinai. The Pentecost celebration was held fifty days after the Passover, that is, after seven weeks had passed. The material harvest which the Jews celebrated so joyously became, through God's providence, the symbol of the spiritual harvest which the apostles began to reap on this day.

were sitting. ³And there appeared to them tongues as of fire, distributed and resting on each one of them. ⁴And they were all filled with the Holy Spirit and began to speak in other tongues, as the Spirit gave them utterance.

2:2–3. Wind and fire were elements which typically accompanied manifestations of God in the Old Testament (cf. Ex 3:2; 13:21–22; 2 Kings 5:24; Ps 104:3). In this instance, as Chrysostom explains, it would seem that separate tongues of fire came down on each of them: they were "separated, which means they came from one and the same source, to show that the Power all comes from the Paraclete" (*Hom. on Acts*, 4). The wind and the noise must have been so intense that they caused people to flock to the place. The fire symbolizes the action of the Holy Spirit who, by enlightening the minds of the disciples, enables them to understand Jesus' teachings—as Jesus promised at the Last Supper (cf. Jn 16:4–14); by inflaming their hearts with love he dispels their fear and moves them to preach boldly. Fire also has a purifying effect, God's action cleansing the soul of all trace of sin.

2:4. Pentecost was not an isolated event in the life of the Church, something over and done with. "We have the right, the duty and the joy to tell you that Pentecost is still happening. We can legitimately speak of the 'lasting value' of Pentecost. We know that fifty days after Easter, the apostles, gathered together in the same Cenacle as had been used for the first Eucharist and from which they had gone out to meet the Risen One for the first time, *discover* in themselves the power of the Holy Spirit who descended upon them, the strength of Him whom the Lord had promised so often as the outcome of his suffering on the Cross; and strengthened in this way, they began to

act, that is, to perform their role. [...] Thus is born the *apostolic Church*. But even today—and herein the continuity lies—the Basilica of St Peter in Rome and every Temple, every Oratory, every place where the disciples of the Lord gather, is an extension of that original Cenacle" (John Paul II, Homily, 25 May 1980).

Vatican II (cf. *Ad gentes*, 4) quotes St Augustine's description of the Holy Spirit as the soul, the source of life, of the Church, which was born on the cross on Good Friday and whose birth was announced publicly on the day of Pentecost: "Today, as you know, the Church was fully born, through the breath of Christ, the Holy Spirit; and in the Church was born the Word, the witness to and promulgation of salvation in the risen Jesus; and in him who listens to this promulgation is born faith, and with faith a new life, an awareness of the Christian vocation and the ability to hear that calling and to follow it by living a genuinely human life, indeed a life which is not only human but holy. And to make this divine intervention effective, today was born the apostolate, the priesthood, the ministry of the Spirit, the calling to unity, fraternity and peace" (Paul VI, Address, 25 May 1969).

"Mary, who conceived Christ by the work of the Holy Spirit, the Love of the living God, presides over the birth of the Church, on the day of Pentecost, when the same Holy Spirit comes down on the disciples and gives life to the mystical body of Christians in unity and charity" (Paul VI, Address, 25 October 1969).

Gen 11:1–9

⁵Now there were dwelling in Jerusalem Jews, devout men from every nation under heaven. ⁶And at this sound the multitude came together, and they were bewildered, because each one heard them speaking in his own language. ⁷And they were amazed and wondered, saying, "Are not all these who are speaking Galileans? ⁸And how is it that we hear, each of us in his own native language? ⁹Parthians and Medes and Elamites and residents of Mesopotamia, Judea and Cappadocia, Pontus and Asia, ¹⁰Phrygia and Pamphylia, Egypt and the parts of Libya belonging to Cyrene, and

---

2:5–11. In his account of the events of Pentecost St Luke distinguishes "devout men" (v. 5), Jews and proselytes (v. 11). The first-mentioned were people who were residing in Jerusalem for reasons of study or piety, to be near the only temple the Jews had. They were Jews—not to be confused with "God-fearing men", that is, pagans sympathetic to Judaism, who worshipped the God of the Bible and who, if they became converts and members of the Jewish religion by being circumcised and by observing the Mosaic Law, were what were called "proselytes", whom Luke distinguishes from the "Jews", that is, those of Jewish race.

People of different races and tongues understand Peter, each in his or her own language. They can do so thanks to a special grace from the Holy Spirit given them for the occasion; this is not the same as the gift of "speaking with tongues" which some of the early Christians had (cf. 1 Cor 14), which allowed them to praise God and speak to him in a language which they themselves did not understand.

2:11. When the Fathers of the Church comment on this passage they frequently point to the contrast between the confusion of languages that came about at Babel (cf. Gen 11:1–9)—God's punishment for man's pride and infidelity—and the reversal of this confusion on the day of Pentecost, thanks to the grace of the

Holy Spirit. The Second Vatican Council stresses the same idea: "Without doubt, the Holy Spirit was at work in the world before Christ was glorified. On the day of Pentecost, however, he came down on the disciples that he might remain with them forever (cf. Jn 14:16); on that day the Church was openly displayed to the crowds and the spread of the Gospel among the nations, through preaching, was begun. Finally, on that day was foreshadowed the union of all peoples in the catholicity of the faith by means of the Church of the New Alliance, a Church which speaks every language, understands and embraces all tongues in charity, and thus overcomes the dispersion of Babel" (*Ad gentes*, 4).

Christians need this gift for their apostolic activity and should ask the Holy Spirit to give it to them to help them express themselves in such a way that others can understand their message; to be able so to adapt what they say to suit the outlook and capacity of their hearers, that they pass Christ's truth on: "Every generation of Christians needs to redeem, to sanctify, its own time. To do this, it must understand and share the desires of other men—their equals—in order to make known to them, with a 'gift of tongues', how they are to respond to the action of the Holy Spirit, to that permanent outflow of rich treasures that comes from our Lord's heart. We Christians are called upon to announce, in our

visitors from Rome, both Jews and proselytes, [11]Cretans and Arabians, we hear them telling in our own tongues the mighty works of God." [12]And all were amazed and perplexed, saying to one another, "What does this mean?" [13]But others mocking said, "They are filled with new wine."

1 Cor 14:22–25

Peter's address

[14]But Peter,* standing with the eleven, lifted up his voice and addressed them, "Men of Judea and all who dwell in Jerusalem,

Acts 1:15; 15:17

---

own time, to this world to which we belong and in which we live, the message—old and at the same time new—of the Gospel" (St Josemaría Escrivá, *Christ Is Passing By*, 132).

2:12. The action of the Holy Spirit must have caused such amazement, in both the disciples and those who heard them, that everyone was "beside himself". The apostles were so filled with the Holy Spirit that they seemed to be drunk (cf. Acts 2:13).

"Then Peter stood up with the Eleven and addressed the people in a loud voice. We, people from a hundred nations, hear him. Each of us hears him in his own language—you and I in ours. He speaks to us of Christ Jesus and of the Holy Spirit and of the Father.

"He is not stoned nor thrown into prison; of those who have heard him, three thousand are converted and baptized.

"You and I, after helping the apostles administer baptism, bless God the Father, for his Son Jesus, and we too feel drunk with the Holy Spirit" (St J. Escrivá, *Holy Rosary*, third glorious mystery).

2:13. These devout Jews, from different countries, who happened to be in Jerusalem on the day of Pentecost—many of them living there, for reasons of study or piety, and others who had come up on pilgrimage for these days—listen to the

apostles' preaching because they are impressed by the amazing things they can see actually happening. The same Holy Spirit who acted in our Lord's disciples also moved their listeners' hearts and led them to believe. There were others, however, who resisted the action of grace and looked for an excuse to justify their behaviour.

2:14–36. Even as the Church takes its first steps St Peter can be seen to occupy the position of main spokesman. In his address we can distinguish an introduction and two parts: in the first part (vv. 16–21) he is explaining that the messianic times foretold by Joel have now arrived; in the second (vv. 22–36) he proclaims that Jesus of Nazareth, whom the Jews crucified, is the Messiah promised by God and eagerly awaited by the righteous of the Old Testament; it is he who has effected God's saving plan for mankind.

2:14. In his commentaries St John Chrysostom draws attention to the change worked in Peter by the Holy Spirit: "Listen to him preach and argue so boldly, who shortly before had trembled at the word of a servant girl! This boldness is a significant proof of the resurrection of his Master: Peter preaches to men who mock and laugh at his enthusiasm. [...] Calumny ('they are filled with new wine') does not deter the apostles; sarcasm does not undermine their

let this be known to you, and give ear to my words. [15]For these men are not drunk, as you suppose, since it is only the third hour of the day; [16]but this is what was spoken by the prophet Joel:

Joel 2:28

[17]'And in the last days it shall be, God declares,
that I will pour out my Spirit upon all flesh,
and your sons and your daughters shall prophesy,
and your young men shall see visions,
and your old men shall dream dreams;

Rom 5:5

[18]yea, and on my menservants and my maidservants in
those days
I will pour out my Spirit; and they shall prophesy.

Acts 5:12

[19]And I will show wonders in the heaven above
and signs on the earth beneath,
blood, and fire, and vapour of smoke;

Rev 6:12

[20]the sun shall be turned into darkness
and the moon into blood,
before the day of the Lord comes,
the great and manifest day.

Rom 10:9–13

[21]And it shall be that whoever calls on the name of the Lord
shall be saved.'

Mt 2:23
Jn 3:2; 5:36

[22]"Men of Israel, hear these words: Jesus of Nazareth a man attested to you by God with mighty works and wonders and signs which God did through him in your midst, as you yourselves know—[23]this Jesus, delivered up according to the definite plan and foreknowledge of God, you crucified and killed by the hands

Jn 19:6–11
Acts 3:15

---

courage, for the coming of the Holy Spirit has made new men of them, men who can put up with every kind of human test. When the Holy Spirit enters into hearts he does so to elevate their affections and to change earthly souls, souls of clay, into chosen souls, people of real courage [...]. Look at the harmony that exists among the apostles. See how they allow Peter to speak on behalf of them all. Peter raises his voice and speaks to the people with full assurance. That is the kind of courage a man has when he is the instrument of the Holy Spirit. [...] Just as a burning coal does not lose its heat when it falls on a haystack but instead is enabled to release its heat, so Peter, now that he is in con-

tact with the life-giving Spirit, spreads his inner fire to those around him" (*Hom. on Acts*, 4).

2:17. "In the last days": a reference to the coming of Christ and the era of salvation which follows; and also to the fact that the Holy Spirit, whom God would pour out on men of every nation and era when the Kingdom of the Messiah arrived, would continue to aid his Church until the day of the Last Judgment, which will be heralded by amazing events.

2:22–36. To demonstrate that Jesus of Nazareth is the Messiah foretold by the prophets, St Peter reminds his listeners of our Lord's miracles (v. 22), as well as of

of lawless men. [24]But God raised him up, having loosed the pangs of death, because it was not possible for him to be held by it. [25]For David says concerning him,

'I saw the Lord always before me,
for he is at my right hand that I may not be shaken;
[26]therefore my heart was glad, and my tongue rejoiced;
moreover my flesh will dwell in hope.
[27]For thou wilt not abandon my soul to Hades,
nor let thy Holy One see corruption.
[28]Thou hast made known to me the ways of life;
thou wilt make me full of gladness with thy presence.'

[29]"Brethren, I may say to you confidently of the patriarch David that he both died and was buried, and his tomb is with us to this day. [30]Being therefore a prophet, and knowing that God had sworn with an oath to him that he would set one of his descendants upon his throne, [31]he foresaw and spoke of the resurrection of the Christ, that he was not abandoned to Hades, nor did his flesh see corruption. [32]This Jesus God raised up, and of that we all are witnesses. [33]Being therefore exalted at the right hand of God, and having received from the Father the promise of the Holy Spirit, he has poured out this which you see and hear. [34]For David did not ascend into the heavens; but he himself says,

'The Lord said to my Lord, Sit at my right hand,
[35]till I make thy enemies a stool for thy feet.'

[36]Let all the house of Israel therefore know assuredly that God has made him both Lord and Christ, this Jesus whom you crucified."

Marginal references:
Ps 18:4–5
Acts 13:34
Ps 16:8–11
1 Kings 2:10
2 Sam 7:12
Ps 132:11
Ps 16:10
Acts 5:31
Phil 2:9
Ps 110:1
Mt 22:44

---

his death (v. 23), resurrection (v. 24–32) and glorious ascension (vv. 33–35). His address ends with a brief summing-up (v. 36).

2:32. To proofs from prophecy, very important to the Jews, St Peter adds his own testimony on the resurrection of Jesus, and that of his brothers in the Apostolate.

2:36. During his life on earth Jesus had often presented himself as the Messiah and Son of God. His resurrection and ascension into heaven reveal him as such to the people at large.

In Peter's address we can see an outline of the content of the apostolic proclamation (*kerygma*), the content of Christian preaching, the object of faith. This proclamation bears witness to Christ's death and resurrection and subsequent exaltation; it recalls the main points of Jesus' mission, announced by John the Baptist, confirmed by miracles and brought to fulfilment by the appearances of the risen Lord and the outpouring of the Holy Spirit; it declares that the messianic time predicted by the prophets has arrived, and calls all men to conversion, in preparation for the Parousia, or second coming of Christ in glory.

Many baptisms

³⁷Now when they heard this they were cut to the heart, and said to
Peter and the rest of the apostles, "Brethren, what shall we do?"
³⁸And Peter said to them, "Repent, and be baptized every one of
you in the name of Jesus Christ for the forgiveness of your sins;
and you shall receive the gift of the Holy Spirit. ³⁹For the promise

Mt 3:2
Lk 13:3
Acts 3:19; 8:16
Is 57:19

2:37. St Peter's words were the instrument used by God's grace to move the
hearts of his listeners: they are so
impressed that they ask in all simplicity
what they should do. Peter exhorts them
to be converted, to repent (cf. the note on
3:19). The *St Pius V Catechism* explains
that in order to receive Baptism adults
"need to repent the sins they have committed and their evil past life and to be
resolved not to commit sin henceforth
[...], for nothing is more opposed to the
grace and power of Baptism than the outlook and disposition of those who never
decide to abjure sin" (2, 2, 4).

2:38. "Be baptized in the name of Jesus
Christ": this does not necessarily mean
that this was the form of words the apostles normally used in the liturgy, rather
than the Trinitarian formula prescribed
by Jesus. In the *Didache* (written around
the year 100) it is stated that Baptism
should be given in the name of the Father
and of the Son and of the Holy Spirit, but
this does not prevent it, in other passages,
from referring to "those baptized in the
name of the Lord." The expression "baptized in the name of Christ" means,
therefore, becoming a member of Christ,
becoming a Christian (cf. *Didaché*, 7, 1;
9, 5).

"Like the men and women who came
up to Peter on Pentecost, we too have
been baptized. In baptism, our Father
God has taken possession of our lives,
has made us share in the life of Christ,
and has given us the Holy Spirit" (St J.
Escrivá, *Christ Is Passing By*, 128).

From this point onwards, the Trinity
begins to act in the soul of the baptized
person. "In the same way as transparent
bodies, when light shines on them,
become resplendent and bright, souls ele-
vated and enlightened by the Holy Spirit
become spiritual too and lead others to
the light of grace. From the Holy Spirit
comes knowledge of future events,
understanding of mysteries and of hidden
truths, an outpouring of gifts, heavenly
citizenship, conversation with angels.
From him comes never-ending joy, perseverance in good, likeness to God and—
the most sublime thing imaginable
—becoming God" (St Basil, *On the Holy
Spirit*, 9, 23).

This divinization which occurs in the
baptized person shows how important it
is for Christians to cultivate the Holy
Spirit who has been infused into their
souls, where he dwells as long as he is
not driven out by sin. "Love the third
Person of the most Blessed Trinity.
Listen in the intimacy of your being to
the divine motions of encouragement or
reproach you receive from him. Walk
through the earth in the light that is
poured out in your soul. [...] We can
apply to ourselves the question asked by
the apostle: 'Do you not know that you
are God's temple and that God's Spirit
dwells in you?' (1 Cor 3:16). And we can
understand it as an invitation to deal with
God in a more personal and direct
manner. For some, unfortunately, the
Paraclete is the Great Stranger. He is
merely a name that is mentioned, but not
Someone—not one of the three Persons

is to you and to your children and to all that are far off, every one whom the Lord our God calls to him." [40]And he testified with many other words and exhorted them, saying, "Save yourselves from this crooked generation." [41]So those who received his word were baptized, and there were added that day about three thousand souls.

Acts 3:26; 13:46
Eph 2:13–17

Deut 32:5
Mt 17:17
Lk 9:41
Acts 5:14; 6:7

in the one God—with whom we can talk and with whose life we can live. We have to deal with him simply and trustingly, as we are taught by the Church in its liturgy. Then we will come to know our Lord better, and at the same time, we will realize more fully the great favour that was granted us when we became Christians. We will see all the greatness and truth of this divinization, which is a sharing in God's own life" (St Josemaría Escrivá, *Christ Is Passing By*, 133–134).

2:39. The "promise" of the Holy Spirit applies to both Jews and Gentiles, but in the first instance it concerns the Jews: it is they to whom God entrusted his oracles; theirs was the privilege to receive the Old Testament and to be preached to directly by Jesus himself. St Peter makes it clear that this promise is also made "to all that are far off"—a reference to the Gentiles, as St Paul explains (cf. Eph 2:13–17) and in line with Isaiah's announcement, "Peace, peace, to the far and to the near" (Is 57:19). Cf. Acts 22:21.

2:40. "This crooked generation" is not only that part of the Jewish people who rejected Christ and his teaching, but everyone who is estranged from God (cf. Deut 32:5; Phil 2:15).

2:41. St Luke here concludes his Pentecost account and prepares to move on to a new topic. Before he does so he adds a note, as it were, to say that "about three thousand souls" became Christians as a result of Peter's address.

St Luke often makes reference to the numerical growth of the Church (2:47; 4:4; 5:14; 6:1, 7; 9:31; 11:21, 24; 16:5). Interesting in itself, this growth clearly shows the effectiveness of the Gospel message boldly proclaimed by the apostles. It proves that if the Gospel is preached with constancy and clarity it can take root in any setting and will always find men and women ready to receive it and put it into practice.

"It is not true that everyone today—in general—is closed or indifferent to what our Christian faith teaches about man's being and destiny. It is not true that men in our time are turned only toward the things of this earth and have forgotten to look up to heaven. There is no lack of narrow ideologies, it is true, or of persons who maintain them. But in our time we find both great desires and base attitudes, heroism and cowardice, zeal and disenchantment—people who dream of a new world, more just and more human, and others who, discouraged perhaps by the failure of their youthful idealism, take refuge in the selfishness of seeking only their own security or remaining immersed in their errors.

"To all those men and women, wherever they may be, in their more exalted moments or in their crises and defeats, we have to bring the solemn and unequivocal message of St Peter in the days that followed Pentecost: Jesus is the cornerstone, the Redeemer, the hope of our lives. 'For there is no other name under heaven given among men by which we must be saved' (Acts 4:12)" (*Christ Is Passing By*, 132).

The early Christians

⁴²And they devoted themselves to the apostles' teaching and fellowship, to the breaking of bread and the prayers.

2:42–47. This is the first of the three summaries contained in the early chapters of Acts (cf. 4:32–35 and 5:12–16). In simple words it describes the key elements in the ascetical and liturgical-sacramental life of the first Christians. It gives a vivid spiritual profile of the community which now—after Pentecost extends beyond the Cenacle, a contemplative community, more and more involved in the world around it.

2:42. "The sacred writer", St John Chrysostom observes, "draws attention to two virtues in particular—perseverance and fellowship and tells us that the apostles spent a long period instructing the disciples" (*Hom. on Acts*, 7).

"The apostles' teaching": the instruction normally given new converts. This is not the proclamation of the Gospel to non-Christians but a type of *catechesis* (which became more structured and systematic as time went on) aimed at explaining to the disciples the Christian meaning of Sacred Scripture and the basic truths of faith (out of this grew the credal statements of the Church) which they had to believe and practise in order to attain salvation.

Catechesis—an ongoing preaching and explanation of the Gospel *within* the Church—is a phenomenon to be found even in the very early days of Christianity. "An evangelizer, the Church begins by evangelizing itself. A community of believers, a community of hope practised and transmitted, a community of fraternal love, it has a need to listen unceasingly to what it must believe, to the reasons for its hope, to the new commandment of love" (Paul VI, *Evangelii nuntiandi*, 15).

If catechesis is something which con-

verts and in general all Christians *need*, obviously pastors have a grave duty to provide it. "The whole of the book of the Acts of the Apostles is a witness that they were faithful to their vocation and to the mission they had received. The members of the first Christian community are seen in it as 'devoted to the apostles' teaching and fellowship, to the breaking of bread and the prayers'. Without any doubt we find in that a lasting image of the Church being born of and continually nourished by the word of the Lord, thanks to the teaching of the apostles, celebrating that word in the eucharistic Sacrifice and bearing witness to it before the world in the sign of charity" (John Paul II, *Catechesi tradendae*, 10).

The "fellowship" referred to in this verse is that union of hearts brought about by the Holy Spirit. This profound solidarity among the disciples resulted from their practice of the faith and their appreciation of it as a peerless treasure which they all shared, a gift to them from God the Father through Jesus Christ. Their mutual affection enabled them to be detached from material things and to give up their possessions to help those in need.

The "breaking of bread" refers to the Blessed Eucharist and not just to an ordinary meal. This was a special way the early Christians had of referring to the making and distribution of the sacrament containing the Lord's body. This expression, connected with the idea of a banquet, was soon replaced by that of "Eucharist", which emphasizes the idea of thanksgiving (cf. *Didaché*, 9, 1). From Pentecost onwards the Mass and eucharistic communion form the centre of Christian worship. "From that time on-

⁴³And fear came upon every soul; and many wonders and signs were done through the apostles. ⁴⁴And all who believed were

wards the Church has never failed to come together to celebrate the paschal mystery, reading those things 'which were in all the scriptures concerning him' (Lk 24:27), celebrating the Eucharist in which 'the victory and triumph of his death are again made present' (Council of Trent, *De SS. Eucharistia*, chap. 5), and at the same time giving thanks to God" (Vatican II, *Sacrosanctum Concilium*, 6).

By receiving the Eucharist with a pure heart and clear conscience the disciples obtain the nourishment needed to follow the new life of the Gospel and to be in the world without being worldly. This connexion between the Eucharist and Christian living was something Pope John Paul II vigorously reminded Catholics about when he said in Dublin, "It is from the Eucharist that all of us receive the grace and strength for daily living—to live real Christian lives, in the joy of knowing that God loves us, that Christ died for us, and that the Holy Spirit lives in us.

"Our full participation in the Eucharist is the real source of the Christian spirit that we wish to see in our personal lives and in all aspects of society. Whether we serve in politics, in the economic, cultural, social or scientific fields—no matter what our occupation is—the Eucharist is a challenge to our daily lives.

"Our union with Christ in the Eucharist must be expressed in the truth of our lives today—in our actions, in our behaviour, in our lifestyle, and in our relationships with others. For each one of us the Eucharist is a call to ever greater effort, so that we may live as true followers of Jesus: truthful in our speech, generous in our deeds, concerned, respectful

of the dignity and rights of all persons, whatever their rank or income, self-sacrificing, fair and just, kind, considerate, compassionate and self-controlled. [...] The truth of our union with Jesus Christ in the Eucharist is tested by whether or not we really love our fellow men and women; it is tested by how we treat others, especially our families. [...] It is tested by whether or not we try to be reconciled with our enemies, on whether or not we forgive those who hurt us or offend us" (Homily in Phoenix Park, 29 September 1979).

2:43. The fear referred to here is the religious awe the disciples felt when they saw the miracles and other supernatural signs which the Lord worked through his apostles. A healthy type of fear, denoting respect and reverence for holy things, it can cause a great change of attitude and behaviour in those who experience it.

An outstanding example of this sense of awe is St Peter's reaction at the miraculous catch of fish: "Depart from me, for I am a sinful man, O Lord": as St Luke explains, "he was astonished, and all that were with him, at the catch of fish they had taken" (Lk 5:8–9).

2:44. Charity and union of hearts lead the disciples to sacrifice their own interests to meet the material needs of their poorer brothers and sisters. The sharing of possessions referred to here was not a permanent, "communistic" kind of system. The more well-to-do Christians freely provided for those in need. Each of the disciples retained ownership of such property as he or she had: by handing it over to the community they showed their charity.

"This voluntary poverty and detachment", Chrysostom comments, "cut at

Acts 6:1 together and had all things in common; [45]and they sold their posses-
sions and goods and distributed them to all, as any had need. [46]And
Lk 24:53 day by day, attending the temple together and breaking bread in
Acts 8:8; 16:34 their homes, they partook of food with glad and generous hearts,
Acts 2:21; 13:48 [47]praising God and having favour with all the people. And the Lord
added to their number day by day those who were being saved.

the selfish root of many evils, and the
new disciples showed that they had
understood the Gospel teaching.

"This was not recklessness of the
kind shown by certain philosophers, of
whom some gave up their inheritance
and others cast their gold into the sea:
that was no contempt of riches, but folly
and madness. For the devil has always
made it his endeavour to disparage the
things God has created, as if it were
impossible to make good use of riches"
(*Hom. on Acts*, 7).

A spendthrift who wastes his resources does not have the virtue of detachment; nor can someone be called selfish
because he retains his property, provided
that he uses it generously when the need
arises. "Rather than in not having, true
poverty consists in being detached, in
voluntarily renouncing one's dominion
over things.

"That is why there are poor who are
really rich. And vice-versa" (St Josemaría
Escrivá, *The Way*, 632).

2:46. In the early days of the Church the
temple was a centre of Christian prayer
and liturgy. The first Christians regarded
it as God's house, the House of the
Father of Jesus Christ. Although Christianity involved obvious differences from
Judaism, they also realized that Christ's
message was an extension of Judaism;
for a while, it was quite natural for them
to maintain certain external aspects of the
religion of their forefathers.

In addition to this legitimate religious
instinct to venerate the one, true, loving

God, whom Jews and Christians adore,
St Jerome suggests that prudence may
have dictated this practice: "Because the
early Church was made up of Jews," he
says, "the apostles were very careful not
to introduce any innovations, in order to
avoid any possible scandal to believers"
(*Epistles*, 26, 2).

However, the temple was not the
only place in the Holy City where
Christians met for prayer and worship.
The reference to "breaking bread in their
homes" reminds us that the Christian
community in Jerusalem, as also the
communities later founded by St Paul,
did not yet have a building specially
reserved for liturgical functions. They
met in private houses—presumably in
suitable rooms specially prepared. For
financial as well as policy reasons (persecutions etc.), it was not until the third
century that buildings designed solely for
liturgical purposes began to be erected.

3:1. This was the hour of the evening
sacrifice, which began around three
o'clock and was attended by a large
number of devout Jews. The ritual, which
went on until dusk, was the second sacrifice of the day. The earlier one, on similar lines, began at dawn and lasted until
nine in the morning.

3:2. None of the documents that have come
down to us which describe the temple
mentions a gate of this name. It was probably the Gate of Nicanor (or Corinthian
Gate), which linked the court of the
Gentiles with the court of the women

3. THE APOSTLES' WORK IN JERUSALEM

Curing of a man lame from birth

3 ¹Now Peter and John were going up to the temple at the hour
of prayer, the ninth hour.* ²And a man lame from birth was
being carried, whom they laid daily at the gate of the temple
which is called Beautiful to ask alms of those who entered the
temple. ³Seeing Peter and John about to go into the temple, he

Acts 10:3–30
Jn 9:1
Acts 14:8–10

---

which led on to the court of the Israelites.
It was architecturally a very fine structure
and because of its location it was a very
busy place, which would have made it a
very good place for begging.

3:3–8. The cure of this cripple was the
first miracle worked by the apostles.
"This cure", says St John Chrysostom,
"testifies to the resurrection of Christ, of
which it is an image. [...] Observe that
they do not go up to the temple with the
intention of performing a miracle, so
clear were they of ambition, so closely
did they imitate their Master" (*Hom. on
Acts*, 8).

However, the apostles decide that the
time has come to use the supernatural
power given them by God. What Christ
did in the Gospel using his own divine
power, the apostles now do in his name,
using his power. "The blind receive their
sight, the lame walk, lepers are cleansed,
and the deaf hear, the dead are raised up"
(Lk 7:22). Our Lord now keeps his
promise to empower his disciples to
work miracles—visible signs of the
coming of the Kingdom of God. These
miracles are not extraordinary actions
done casually or suddenly, without his
disciples' involvement: they occur
because our Lord is moved to perform
them by the apostles' faith (faith is an
essential precondition). The disciples are
conscious of having received a gift and
they act on foot of it.

These miracles in the New Testament
obviously occur in situations where grace
is intensely concentrated. However, that
is not to say that miracles do not continue
to occur in the Christian economy of salvation—miracles of different kinds, performed because God is attracted to men
and women of faith. "The same is true of
us. If we struggle daily to become saints,
each of us in his own situation in the
world and through his own job or profession, in our ordinary lives, then I assure
you that God will make us into instruments that can work miracles and, if
necessary, miracles of the most extraordinary kind. We will give sight to the
blind. Who could not relate thousands of
cases of people, blind almost from the
day they were born, recovering their
sight and receiving all the splendour of
Christ's light? And others who were deaf,
or dumb, who could not hear or pronounce
words fitting to God's children ... Their
senses have been purified and now they
hear and speak as men, not animals. *In
nomine Iesu!* In the name of Jesus his
apostles enable the cripple to move and
walk, when previously he had been incapable of doing anything useful; and that
other lazy character, who knew his duties
but didn't fulfil them. ... In the Lord's
name, *surge et ambula!*, rise up and
walk.

"Another man was dead, rotting,
smelling like a corpse: he hears God's
voice, as in the miracle of the son of the

41

Acts 3:16

Is 35:6
Lk 7:22

asked for alms. ⁴And Peter directed his gaze at him, with John, and said, "Look at us." ⁵And he fixed his attention upon them, expecting to receive something from them. ⁶But Peter said, "I have no silver and gold, but I give you what I have; in the name of Jesus Christ of Nazareth, walk." ⁷And he took him by the right hand and raised him up; and immediately his feet and ankles were made strong. ⁸And leaping up he stood and walked and entered the temple with them, walking and leaping and praising God. ⁹And all the people saw him walking and praising God, ¹⁰and recognized him as the one who sat for alms at the Beautiful Gate of the temple; and they were filled with wonder and amazement at what had happened to him.

Jn 10:23
Acts 5:12
Ex 3:6, 15
Is 52:13
Lk 23:22
Jn 18:38; 19:4

Peter's address in the temple

¹¹While he clung to Peter and John, all the people ran together to them in the portico called Solomon's, astounded. ¹²And when

---

widow at Naim: 'Young man, I say to you, rise up' (Lk 7:14). We will work miracles like Christ did, like the first apostles did" (St Josemaría Escrivá, *Friends of God*, 262).

Miracles call for cooperation—*faith*—on the part of those who wish to be cured. The lame man does his bit, even if it is only the simple gesture of obeying Peter and looking at the apostles.

3:11–26. This second address by St Peter contains two parts: in the first (vv. 12–16) the apostle explains that the miracle has been worked in the name of Jesus and through faith in his name; in the second (vv. 17–26) he moves his listeners to repentance—people who were responsible in some degree for Jesus' death.

This discourse has the same purpose as that of Pentecost—to show the power of God made manifest in Jesus Christ and to make the Jews see the seriousness of their crime and have them repent. In both discourses there is reference to the second coming of the Lord and we can clearly see the special importance of tes-

tifying to the resurrection of Jesus; the apostolic college is presented as a witness to that unique event.

3:13. "Servant": the original Greek word (*pais*) is the equivalent of the Latin *puer* (slave, servant) and *filius* (son). By using this word St Peter must have in mind Isaiah's prophecy about the Servant of Yahweh: "Behold, my servant shall prosper, he shall be exalted and lifted up, and shall be very high. As many were astonished at him—his appearance was so marred, beyond human semblance, and his form beyond that of the sons of men—so shall he startle many nations" (52:13–15).

Peter identifies Jesus with the Servant of Yahweh, who, because he was a man of suffering and sorrow, the Jews did not identify with the future Messiah. That Messiah, Jesus Christ, combines in his person suffering and victory.

3:14. St Peter, referring to Jesus, uses terms which Jews can readily understand in a messianic sense. The expression "the Holy One of God" was already used by

Peter saw it he addressed the people, "Men of Israel, why do you wonder at this, or why do you stare at us, as though by our own power or piety we had made him walk? ¹³The God of Abraham and of Isaac and of Jacob, the God of our fathers, glorified his servant^c Jesus, whom you delivered up and denied in the presence of Pilate, when he had decided to release him. ¹⁴But you denied the Holy and Righteous One, and asked for a murderer to be granted to you, ¹⁵and killed the Author of life, whom God raised from the dead. To this we are witnesses. ¹⁶And his name, by faith in his name, has made this man strong whom you see and know; and the faith which is through Jesus^d has given the man this perfect health in the presence of you all.

¹⁷"And now, brethren, I know that you acted in ignorance, as did also your rulers. ¹⁸But what God foretold by the mouth of all the prophets, that his Christ should suffer, he thus fulfilled.

Rom 4:25
Eph 5:2
Mk 1:24
Lk 1:35; 23:25
Jn 6:69; 18:40
Acts 7:52
Rev 3:7

Acts 1:8; 13:31
Heb 2:10

Acts 4:10;
16:18; 19:13–17

Lk 23:34
Acts 13:27
1 Cor 2:8

I Tim 1:13
Lk 18:31;
24:27

Jesus as referring to the Messiah in Mark 1:24 and Luke 4:34. It is reminiscent of Old Testament language (cf. Ps 16:10).

The "Righteous One" also refers to the Messiah, whom the prophets described as a model and achiever of righteousness (cf. Acts 7:52). "Holy", "righteous" and "just" all have similar meaning.

3:15. When St Peter reminds his listeners about their choice of a murderer (Barabbas) in place of Jesus, the Author of Life, we might usefully consider that he was referring not only to physical life but also to spiritual life, the life of grace. Every time a person sins—sin means the death of the soul—this same choice is being made again. "It was he who created man in the beginning, and he left him in the power of his own inclination. If you will, you can keep the commandments, and to act faithfully is a matter of your own choice. He has placed before you fire and water: stretch out your hand for whichever you wish. Before a man are life and death, and whichever he chooses will be given to him" (Sir 15:14–17).

3:16. The original text, structured in a very Jewish way, is difficult to understand. One reason for this is the use of the word "name" instead of simply identifying who the person is. In this passage "name" means the same as "Jesus". Thus the verse can be interpreted in this way: through faith in Jesus, the man lame from birth, whom they know and have seen, has been cured; it is Jesus himself who has worked this complete and instantaneous cure.

3:17–18. The Jewish people acted in ignorance, St Peter says. Indeed, when he was on the cross Jesus had prayed, "Father, forgive them; for they know not what they do" (Lk 23:34). The people did not know that Jesus was the Christ, the Son of God. They let themselves be influenced by their priests. These, who were familiar with the Scriptures, should have recognized him.

God's pardon is offered to one and all. St Peter "tells them that Christ's death was a consequence of God's will and decree. [...] You can see how incomprehensible and profound God's design

c. Or *child* d. Greek *him*

Acts 2:38

2 Pet 3:11–13

Acts 1:11
Rev 10:7

Deut 18:15, 19
Acts 7:37

Lev 23:29

Acts 10:43

Gen 12:3; 22:18
Acts 13:32–34;
26:6–8

[19]Repent therefore, and turn again, that your sins may be blotted out, that times of refreshing may come from the presence of the Lord, [20]and that he may send the Christ appointed for you, Jesus, [21]whom heaven must receive until the time for establishing all that God spoke by the mouth of his holy prophets from of old. [22]Moses said, 'The Lord God will raise up for you a prophet from your brethren as he raised me up. You shall listen to him in whatever he tells you. [23]And it shall be that every soul that does not listen to that prophet shall be destroyed from the people.' [24]And all the prophets who have spoken, from Samuel and those who came afterwards, also proclaimed these days. [25]You are the sons of the prophets and of the covenant which God gave to your fathers,

---

is. It was not just one but all the prophets who foretold this mystery. Yet although the Jews had been, without knowing it, the cause of Jesus' death, that death had been determined by the wisdom and will of God, who used the malice of the Jews to fulfil his designs. The apostle does not say, Although the prophets foretold this death and you acted out of ignorance, do not think you are entirely free from blame; Peter speaks to them gently: 'Repent and turn again.' To what end? 'That your sins may be blotted out'. Not only your murder but all the stains on your souls" (St John Chrysostom, *Hom. on Acts*, 9).

The Second Vatican Council tells us how Christians should treat Jewish people and those who follow other non-Christian religions—with respect and also a prudent zeal to attract them to the faith. "Even though the Jewish authorities and those who followed their lead pressed for the death of Christ (cf. Jn 19:6), neither all Jews indiscriminately at that time, nor Jews today, can be charged with the crimes committed during his passion. It is true that the Church is the new people of God, yet the Jews should not be spoken of as rejected or accursed. [...] Jews for the most part did not accept the Gospel; on the contrary, many opposed the

spreading of it (cf. Rom 11:28–29). Even so, the apostle Paul maintains that the Jews remain very dear to God, for the sake of the patriarchs, since God does not take back the gifts he bestowed or the choice he made" (Vatican II, *Nostra aetate*, 4). We must not forget this special position of the Jewish people (cf. Rom 9:4–5) and the fact that from them came Jesus as far as his human lineage was concerned, and his Mother, the Blessed Virgin Mary, and the apostles—the foundation, the pillars of the Church—and many of the first disciples who proclaimed Christ's Gospel to the world.

Moved by charity, the Church prays to our Lord for the spiritual conversion of the Jewish people: "Christ, God and man, who is the Lord of David and his children, we beseech you that in keeping with the prophecies and promises, Israel recognize you as Messiah" (*Divine Office*, Morning Prayer, 31 December).

3:19. One result of sorrow for sin is a desire to make up for the damage done. On the day of Pentecost many Jews were moved by grace to ask the apostles what they should do to make atonement. Here also St Peter encourages them to change their lives and turn to God. This repentance or conversion which Peter preaches

saying to Abraham, 'And in your posterity shall all the families of the earth be blessed.' [26]God having raised up his servant,[c] sent him to you first, to bless you in turning every one of you from your wickedness."

Gal 3:8

Peter and John are arrested

4 [1]And as they were speaking to the people, the priests and the captain of the temple and the Sadducees came upon them, [2]annoyed because they were teaching the people and proclaiming in Jesus the resurrection from the dead.* [3]And they arrested them and put them in custody until the morrow, for it was already evening. [4]But many of those who heard the word believed; and the number of the men came to about five thousand.

Lk 22:4–52
Acts 5:24

Acts 23:6–8
1 Cor 15:20–23

Acts 2:47

---

is the same message as marked the initial proclamation of the Kingdom (cf. Mk 1:15; 13:1–4). "This means a change of outlook, and it applies to the state of sinful man, who needs to change his ways and turn to God, desirous of breaking away from his sins and repenting and calling on God's mercy" (Paul VI, Homily, 24 February 1971).

On another occasion Paul VI explained that the word "conversion" can be translated normally as "change of heart". "We are called to this change and it will make us see many things. The first has to do with interior analysis of our soul [...]: we should examine ourselves as to what is the main direction our life is taking, what attitude is usually to the fore in the way we think and act, what is our reason of being. [...] Is our rudder fixed so as to bring us exactly to our goal or does its direction need perhaps to be changed? [...] By examining ourselves in this way [...] we will discover sins, or at least weaknesses, which call for penance and profound reform" (Paul VI, General Audience, 21 March 1973).

3:20. A reference to the Parousia or second coming of Christ as Judge of the living and the dead (cf. the note on 1:11).

3:22–24. St Peter wants to show that the Old Testament prophecies are fulfilled in Jesus: he is descended from David (2:30), a prophet (cf. Deut 18:15), who suffered (2:23), who is the cornerstone (4:11) and who rose from the dead and sits in glory at the right hand of the Father (2:25–34).

4:1–4. On the Sadducee sect see the note on Mt 3:7.

In this chapter St Luke reports on the first conflict between the apostles and the Jerusalem authorities. Despite the incident at the end of Peter's address, his words are still an instrument of grace, stirring his listeners to believe and moving them to love.

A large crowd has gathered round Peter after the curing of the cripple, which brings on the scene the "captain of the temple", a priest second in line to the high priest whose function it was to maintain order. The priests St Luke refers to here would have been those who were on for this particular week and were responsible for the day-to-day affairs of the temple.

c. Or *child*

Address to the Sanhedrin

Acts 5:21
Lk 3:2

Mt 21:23
Lk 20:2
Mt 10:19–20

⁵On the morrow their rulers and elders and scribes were gathered together in Jerusalem, ⁶with Annas the high priest and Caiaphas and John and Alexander, and all who were of the high-priestly family. ⁷And when they had set them in the midst, they inquired, "By what power or by what name did you do this?" ⁸Then Peter, filled with the Holy Spirit, said to them, "Rulers of the people and elders, ⁹if we are being examined today concerning a good deed

---

4:5–7. These three groups—rulers, elders, scribes—made up the Sanhedrin, the same tribunal as had recently judged and condemned our Lord (cf. the note on Mt 2:4). Jesus' words are already being fulfilled: "'A servant is not greater than his master.' If they persecuted me, they will persecute you" (Jn 15:20).

Annas was not in fact the high priest at this time, but the title was applied to him along with Caiaphas because of the authority he still wielded: he had been high priest and five of his sons succeeded him in the office, as well as Caiaphas, his son-in-law (cf. Flavius Josephus, *Jewish Antiquities*, 20, 198f).

4:8–12. The apostles' confidence and joy is quite remarkable, as is their outspokenness in asserting that "we cannot but speak of what we have seen and heard" (v. 20). "This is the glorious freedom of the children of God. Christians who let themselves be browbeaten or become inhibited or envious in the face of the licentious behaviour of those who do not accept the Word of God, show that they have a very poor idea of the faith. If we truly fulfil the law of Christ—that is, if we make the effort to do so, for we will not always fully succeed—we will find ourselves endowed with a wonderful gallantry of spirit" (St Josemaría Escrivá, *Friends of God*, 38).

Christians have a duty to confess their faith where silence would mean its implicit denial, disrespect for religion, an offence against God or scandal to their neighbour. Thus Vatican II: "Christians should approach those who are outside wisely, 'in the Holy Spirit, genuine love, truthful speech' (2 Cor 6:6–7), and should strive, even to the shedding of their blood, to spread the light of life with all confidence (cf. Acts 4:29) and apostolic courage. The disciple has a grave obligation to Christ, his Master, to grow daily in his knowledge of the truth he has received from him, to be faithful in announcing it and vigorous in defending it" (*Dignitatis humanae*, 14).

Pope Paul VI asked Catholics to check on any weak points in their faith, including ignorance and human respect, "that is, shame or timidness in professing their faith. We are not speaking of that discretion or reserve which in a pluralist and profane society like ours avoids certain signs of religion when with others. We are referring to weakness, to failure to profess one's own religious ideas for fear of ridicule, criticism or others' reactions [...] and which is a cause—perhaps the main cause—of the abandonment of faith by people who simply conform to whatever new environment they find themselves in" (General Audience, 19 June 1968).

4:8. Even in the very early days of Christianity Jesus' prediction is borne out: "Beware of men; for they will deliver you up to councils [...]. When

done to a cripple, by what means this man has been healed, [10]be it known to you all, and to all the people of Israel, that by the name of Jesus Christ of Nazareth, whom you crucified, whom God raised from the dead, by him this man is standing before you well. [11]This is the stone which was rejected by you builders, but which has become the head of the corner. [12]And there is salvation in no one else, for there is no other name under heaven given among men by which we must be saved."

Acts 3:16

Ps 118:22
Mt 21:42
1 Pet 2:4–7
Mt 1:21
Jn 1:12
Acts 2:21
Lk 21:12–15
Jn 7:15

they deliver you up, do not be anxious how you are to speak or what you are to say; for what you are to say will be given to you in that hour; for it is not you who speak, but the Spirit of your Father speaking through you" (Mt 10:17–20).

4:10. "Whom God raised from the dead": St Peter once again bears witness to the resurrection of Jesus, the central truth of apostolic preaching; he uses here the same words as he did at Pentecost. These are compatible with our holding that Jesus "rose by his own power on the third day" (Paul VI, *Creed of the People of God*, 12). The power by which Christ rose was that of his divine Person, to which both his soul and his body remained joined even after death separated them. "The divine power and operation of the Father and of the Son is one and the same; hence it follows that Christ rose by the power of the Father and by his own power" (St Thomas Aquinas, *Summa theologiae*, 3, 53, 4).

"By the word 'Resurrection'," the *Pius V Catechism* explains, "we are not merely to understand that Christ was raised from the dead, which happened to many others, but that he rose by his own power and virtue, a singular prerogative peculiar to him alone. For it is incompatible with nature and was never given to man to raise himself by his own power, from death to life. This was reserved for the almighty power of God [...]. We sometimes, it is true, read in Scripture

that he was raised by the Father; but this refers to him as man, just as those passages on the other hand, which say that he rose by his own power, relate to him as God" (1, 6, 8).

4:11. St Peter applies the words of Psalm 118:22 to Jesus, conscious no doubt that our Lord had referred to himself as the stone rejected by the builders which had become the cornerstone, the stone which keeps the whole structure together (cf. Mt 21:42 and par.).

4:12. Invocation of the name of Jesus is all-powerful because this is our Saviour's own name (cf. the note on Mt 1:21). Our Lord himself told his apostles this: "If you ask anything of the Father, he will give it to you in my name" (Jn 16:23), and they, trusting in this promise, work miracles and obtain conversions "in the name of Jesus." Today—as ever—the power of this name will work wonders in the souls of those who call upon him. St Josemaría Escrivá gives this advice: "Don't be afraid to call our Lord by his name—Jesus—and to tell him that you love him" (*The Way*, 303); and the Divine Office invites us to pray: "God our Father, you are calling us to prayer, at the same hour as the apostles went up to the Temple. Grant that the prayer we offer with sincere hearts in the name of Jesus may bring salvation to all who call upon that holy name" (Week 1, Monday afternoon).

¹³Now when they saw the boldness of Peter and John, and perceived that they were uneducated, common men, they wondered; and they recognized that they had been with Jesus. ¹⁴But seeing the man that had been healed standing beside them, they had nothing to say in opposition. ¹⁵But when they had commanded them to go aside out of the council, they conferred with one another, ¹⁶saying, "What shall we do with these men? For that a notable sign has been performed through them is manifest to all the inhabitants of Jerusalem, and we cannot deny it. ¹⁷But in order that it may spread no further among the people, let us warn them to speak no more to any one in this name." ¹⁸So they called them and charged them not to speak or teach at all in the name of Jesus. ¹⁹But Peter and John answered them, "Whether it is right in the sight of God to listen to you rather than to God, you must judge;

Jn 11:47

Acts 5:29

4:13. The members of the Sanhedrin are surprised by Peter's confidence and by the way these men, who are not well versed in the Law, are able to use Holy Scripture. "Did not the apostles," Chrysostom asks in admiration, "poor and without earthly weapons, enter into battle against enemies who were fully armed …? Without experience, without skill of the tongue, they fought against experts in rhetoric and the language of the academies" (*Hom. on Acts*, 4).

4:18–20. In one of his homilies John Paul II gives us a practical commentary on this passage, which helps us see the right order of priorities and give pride of place to the things of God: "Whereas the elders of Israel charge the apostles not to speak about Christ, God, on the other hand, does not allow them to remain silent. [...] In Peter's few sentences we find a full testimony to the Resurrection of the Lord. [...] The word of the living God addressed to men obliges us more than any other human commandment or purpose. This word carries with it the supreme eloquence of truth, it carries the authority of God himself. [...]

"Peter and the apostles are before the Sanhedrin. They are completely and absolutely certain that God himself has spoken in Christ, and has spoken definitively through his Cross and Resurrection. Peter and the apostles to whom this truth was directly given—as also those who in their time received the Holy Spirit—must bear witness *to it*.

"*Believing* means accepting with complete conviction the truth that comes from God, drawing support from the grace of the Holy Spirit 'whom God has given to those who obey him' (Acts 5:32) to accept what God has revealed and what comes to us through the Church in its living transmission, that is, in tradition. The organ of this tradition is the teaching of Peter and of the apostles and of their successors.

"Believing means accepting their testimony in the Church, who guards this deposit from generation to generation, and then—basing oneself upon it—expounding this same truth, with identical certainty and interior conviction.

"Over the centuries the sanhedrins change which seek to impose silence, abandonment or distortion of this truth. The *sanhedrins of the contemporary world* are many and of all types. These

²⁰for we cannot but speak of what we have seen and heard." ²¹And when they had further threatened them, they let them go, finding no way to punish them, because of the people; for all men praised God for what had happened. ²²For the man on whom this sign of healing was performed was more than forty years old.

1 Cor 9:16
2 Tim 1:7–8

The Church's thanksgiving prayer

²³When they were released they went to their friends and reported what the chief priests and the elders had said to them. ²⁴And when they heard it, they lifted their voices together to God and said, "Sovereign Lord, who didst make the heaven and the earth and the sea and everything in them, ²⁵who by the mouth of our father David, thy servant,ᶜ didst say by the Holy Spirit,

Ex 20:11
Ps 146:6
Is 37:16
Jer 32:17
Rev 10:6

---

sanhedrins are each and every person who rejects divine truth; they are systems of human thought, of human knowledge; they are the various *conceptions of the world* and also the various programmes of human behaviour; they are also the different *forms of pressure* used by so-called public opinion, mass civilization, media of social communication, which are materialist or secular agnostic or anti-religious; they are, finally, certain contemporary *systems of government* which—if they do not totally deprive citizens of scope to profess the faith—at least limit that scope in different ways, marginalize believers and turn them into second-class citizens ... and against all these modern types of the sanhedrin of that time, the response of faith is always the same: 'We must obey God rather than men' (Acts 5:29)" (Homily, 20 April 1980).

4:24–30. This prayer of the apostles and the community provides Christians with a model of reliance on God's help. They ask God to give them the strength they need to continue to proclaim the Word boldly and not be intimidated by persecution, and they also entreat him to accredit

their preaching by enabling them to work signs and wonders.

The prayer includes some prophetic verses of Psalm 2 which find their fulfilment in Jesus Christ. The Psalm begins by referring to earthly rulers plotting against God and his Anointed. Jesus himself experienced this opposition, as the apostles do now and as the Church does throughout history. When we hear the clamour of the forces of evil, still striving to "burst their bonds asunder, and cast their cords from us" (v. 3), we should put our trust in the Lord, who "has them in derision. [...] He will speak to them in his wrath, and terrify them in his fury" (vv. 4–5); in this way we make it possible for God's message to be heard by everyone: "Now, therefore, O kings, be wise; be warned, O rulers of the earth. Serve the Lord with fear, with trembling kiss his feet ... Blessed are all who take refuge in him" (vv. 10–12).

Meditation on this psalm has been a source of comfort to Christians in all ages, filling them with confidence in the Lord's help: "Ask of me, and I will make the nations your heritage, and the ends of the earth your possession" (v. 8).

c. Or *child*

Ps 2:1–2

'Why did the Gentiles rage,
and the peoples imagine vain things?
²⁶The kings of the earth set themselves in array,
and the rulers were gathered together,
against the Lord and against his Anointed' —ᵉ

Lk 23:12
Mt 3:16
Acts 10:38

²⁷for truly in this city there were gathered together against thy holy servantᶜ Jesus, whom thou didst anoint, both Herod and

Acts 2:23

Pontius Pilate, with the Gentiles, and the peoples of Israel, ²⁸to do whatever thy hand and thy plan had predestined to take place.

Eph 6:19

²⁹And now, Lord, look upon their threats, and grant to thy servantsᶠ to speak thy word with all boldness, ³⁰while thou stretchest out thy hand to heal, and signs and wonders are performed

---

4:31. The Holy Spirit chose to demonstrate his presence visibly in order to encourage the nascent Church. The shaking that happens here was, St John Chrysostom comments, "a sign of approval. It is an action of God to instil a holy fear in the souls of the apostles, to strengthen them against the threats of senators and priests, and to inspire them with boldness to preach the Gospel. The Church was just beginning and it was necessary to support preaching with wonders, in order the better to win men over. It was a need then but later on it does not occur. ... When the earth is shaken, this sometimes is a sign of heaven's wrath, sometimes of favour and providence. At the death of our Saviour the earth shook in protest against the death of its author. ... But the shaking where the apostles were gathered together was a sign of God's goodness, for the result was that they were filled with the Holy Spirit" (*Hom. on Acts*, 11).

4:32–37. Here we are given a second summary of the life of the first Christian community—which, presided over by Peter and the other apostles, was *the Church*, the entire Church of Jesus Christ.

The Church of God on earth was only beginning, all contained within the Jeru-

salem foundation. Now every Christian community—no matter how small it be—which is in communion of faith and obedience with the Church of Rome is the Church.

"The Church of Christ", Vatican II teaches, "is really present in all legitimately organized local groups of the faithful, which, in so far as they are united to their pastors, are also quite appropriately called churches in the New Testament. ... In them the faithful are gathered together through the preaching of the Gospel of Christ, and the mystery of the Lord's Supper is celebrated. ... In each altar community, under the sacred ministry of the bishop, a manifest symbol is to be seen of that charity and 'unity of the mystical body, without which there can be no salvation' (*Summa theologiae*, 3, 73, 3). In these communities, though they may often be small and poor, or existing in the diaspora, Christ is present through whose power and influence the one, holy, catholic and apostolic Church is constituted" (*Lumen gentium*, 26).

4:32. The text stresses the importance of "being one": solidarity, unity, is a virtue of good Christians and one of the marks

e. Or *Christ* f. Or *slaves*

through the name of thy holy servant^c Jesus." ³¹And when they had prayed, the place in which they were gathered together was shaken; and they were all filled with the Holy Spirit and spoke the word of God with boldness.

The way of life of the early Christians

³²Now the company of those who believed were of one heart and soul, and no one said that any of the things which he possessed was his own, but they had everything in common.* ³³And with great power the apostles gave their testimony to the resurrection of the Lord Jesus, and great grace was upon them all. ³⁴There was not a needy person among them, for as many as were possessors

Jn 17:11–21
Phil 1:27
Acts 2:44

Acts 1:8, 22

Deut 15:7–8
Lk 12:33
Acts 9:27

---

of the Church: "The apostles bore witness to the Resurrection not only by word but also by their virtues" (St John Chrysostom, *Hom. on Acts*, 11). The disciples obviously were joyful and self-sacrificed. This disposition, which results from charity, strives to promote forgiveness and harmony among the brethren, all sons and daughters of the same Father. The Church realizes that this harmony is often threatened by rancour, envy, misunderstanding and self-assertion. By asking, in prayers and hymns like *Ubi caritas*, for evil disputes and conflicts to cease, "so that Christ our God may dwell among us", it is drawing its inspiration from the example of unity and charity left it by the first Christian community in Jerusalem.

Harmony and mutual understanding among the disciples both reflects the internal and external unity of the Church itself and helps its practical implementation.

There is only one Church of Jesus Christ because it has only "one Lord, one faith, one baptism" (Eph 4:5), and only one visible head—the Pope—who represents Christ on earth. The model and ultimate source of this unity is the Trinity of divine Persons, that is, "the unity of one

God, the Father and the Son in the Holy Spirit" (Vatican II, *Unitatis redintegratio*, 2). This characteristic work of the Church is visibly expressed: in confession of one and the same faith, in one system of government, in the celebration of the same form of divine worship, and in fraternal concord among all God's family (cf. ibid.).

The Church derives its life from the Holy Spirit; a main factor in nourishing this life and thereby reinforcing the Church's unity is the Blessed Eucharist: it acts in a mysterious but real way, incessantly, to build up the mystical body of the Lord.

God desires all Christians separated from the Church (they have Baptism, and the Gospel truths in varying degrees) to find their way to the flock of Christ—which they can do by spiritual renewal, and prayer, dialogue and study.

4:34–35. St Luke comes back again to the subject of renunciation of possessions, repeating what he says in 2:44 and going on to give two different kinds of example—that of Barnabas (4:36f) and that of Ananias and Sapphira (5:1f).

The disciples' detachment from material things does not only mean that they

c. Or *child*

51

Acts 11:22–30;
12:25; 13:1 — 15:39
1 Cor 9:6

Gal 2:1–13
Col 4:10
of lands or houses sold them, and brought the proceeds of what was sold ³⁵and laid it at the apostles' feet; and distribution was made to each as any had need. ³⁶Thus Joseph who was surnamed by the apostles Barnabas (which means, Son of encouragement), a Levite, a native of Cyprus, ³⁷sold a field which belonged to him, and brought the money and laid it at the apostles' feet.

Deception by Ananias and Sapphira

Acts 4:35, 37

Lk 22:3

Acts 5:11;
19:17

5 ¹But a man named Ananias with his wife Sapphira sold a piece of property, ²and with his wife's knowledge he kept back some of the proceeds, and brought only a part and laid it at the apostles' feet. ³But Peter said, "Ananias, why has Satan filled your heart to lie to the Holy Spirit and to keep back part of the proceeds of the land? ⁴While it remained unsold, did it not remain your own? And after it was sold, was it not at your disposal? How is it that you have contrived this deed in your heart? You have not lied to men but to God." ⁵When Ananias heard these words, he fell down and

---

have a caring attitude to those in need. It also shows their simplicity of heart, their desire to pass unnoticed and the full confidence they place in the Twelve. "They gave up their possessions and in doing so demonstrated their respect for the apostles. For they did not presume to give it into their hands, that is, they did not present it ostentatiously, but left it at their feet and made the apostles its owners and dispensers" (St John Chrysostom, *Hom. on Acts*, 11).

The text suggests that the Christians in Jerusalem had an organized system for the relief of the poor in the community. Judaism had social welfare institutions and probably the early Church used one of these as a model. However, the Christian system of helping each according to his need would have had characteristics of its own, deriving from the charity from which it sprang and as a result of gradual differentiation from the Jewish way of doing things.

4:36–37. Barnabas is mentioned because of his generosity and also in view of his

important future role in the spreading of the Gospel. It will be he who introduces the new convert Saul to the apostles (9:27). Later, the apostles will send him to Antioch when the Christian church begins to develop there (11:22). He will be Paul's companion on his first journey (13:2) and will go up to Jerusalem with him in connexion with the controversy about circumcising Gentile converts (15:2). St Paul praises Barnabas' zeal and selflessness in the cause of the Gospel (cf. 1 Cor 9:6).

5:1–11. Ananias hypocritically pretended that he had given all the money from the sale of the land to the community welfare fund, whereas in fact he kept part of it, and his wife went along with him on that. No one was obliged to sell his property or give it to the apostles: people who did so acted with complete freedom. Ananias was free to sell the land or not, and to give all or part of the proceeds to help needy brethren. But he had no right to disguise his greed as charity and try to deceive God and the Church.

died. And great fear came upon all who heard of it. ⁶The young men rose and wrapped him up and carried him out and buried him.

⁷After an interval of about three hours his wife came in, not knowing what had happened. ⁸And Peter said to her, "Tell me whether you sold the land for so much." And she said, "Yes, for so much." ⁹But Peter said to her, "How is it that you have agreed together to tempt the Spirit of the Lord? Hark, the feet of those that have buried your husband are at the door, and they will carry you out." ¹⁰Immediately she fell down at his feet and died. When the young men came in they found her dead, and they carried her out and buried her beside her husband. ¹¹And great fear came upon the whole church,* and upon all who heard of these things.

1 Cor 10:9; 11:30–32

Lk 1:12

Growth of the Church

¹²Now many signs and wonders were done among the people by the hands of the apostles. And they were all together in Solomon's

Acts 2:19, 46

God punished Ananias and Sapphira, St Ephrem says, "not only because they stole something and concealed it, but because they did not fear and sought to deceive those in whom dwelt the Holy Spirit who knows everything" (*Armenian Commentary on Acts*, ad loc.). By their hypocritical attitude Ananias and Sapphira show their greed and particularly their vainglory. The severe punishment they receive befits the circumstances: the Church was in a foundational period, when people had a special responsibility to be faithful and God was specially supportive.

"This fault could not have been treated lightly", St John Chrysostom explains; "like a gangrene it had to be cut out, before it infected the rest of the body. As it is, both the man himself benefits in that he is not left to advance further in wickedness, and the rest of the disciples, in that they were made more vigilant" (*Hom. on Acts*, 12). Some Fathers (cf. St Augustine, *Sermons*, 148, 1) think that God's punishment was that of physical death, not eternal reprobation.

This episode shows once again how much God detests hypocrisy; and from it we can appreciate the virtue of truthfulness. Veracity inclines people to bring what they say and what they do into line with their knowledge and convictions and to be people of their word. It is closely connected to the virtue of fidelity, which helps one to stay true to promises made (cf. *Summa theologiae*, 2-2, 80, 1). Only the truthful person, the faithful person, can keep the Lord's commandment: "Let what you say be simply 'Yes' or 'No'" (Mt 5:37).

5:12–16. In this third summary (cf. 2:42–47 and 4:32–37) of the lifestyle of the first community St Luke refers particularly to the apostles' power to work miracles. These miracles confirm to the people that the Kingdom of God has in fact come among them. Grace abounds and it shows its presence by spiritual conversions and physical cures. These "signs and wonders" are not done to amaze people or provoke curiosity but to awaken faith.

Portico. [13]None of the rest dared join them, but the people held them in high honour. [14]And more than ever believers were added to the Lord, multitudes both of men and women, [15]so that they even carried out the sick into the streets, and laid them on beds and pallets, that as Peter came by at least his shadow might fall on some of them. [16]The people also gathered from the towns around Jerusalem, bringing the sick and those afflicted with unclean spirits, and they were all healed.

Mk 6:56
Acts 19:11–12

Acts 8:6–7

The apostles are arrested and miraculously freed

Acts 4:1–6;
13:45

[17]But the high priest rose up and all who were with him, that is, the party of the Sadducees, and filled with jealousy [18]they arrested the apostles and put them in the common prison. [19]But at night an angel of the Lord opened the prison doors and brought them out and said, [20]"Go and stand in the temple and speak to the people all the words of this Life."* [21]And when they heard this, they entered the temple at daybreak and taught.

Acts 12:7

Acts 7:38; 13:26
Phil 2:16
1 Jn 1:1
Acts 4:5

Now the high priest came and those who were with him and called together the council and all the senate of Israel, and sent to

---

Miracles always accompany God's revelation to men; they are part of that revelation. They are not simply a bending of the laws of nature: they are a kind of advance sign of the glorious transformation which the world will undergo at the end of time. Thus, just as a sinner, when he repents, obeys God without ceasing to be free, so matter can be changed if its Creator so ordains, without undermining or destroying its own laws.

Miracles are a form of accreditation God gives to the Gospel message: they are actions of God in support of the truth of his messengers' preaching. "If they had not worked miracles and wonders," Origen says, "Jesus' disciples could not have moved their hearers to give up their traditional religion for new teachings and truths, and to embrace, at the risk of their lives, the teachings which were being proclaimed to them" (*Against Celsus*, 1, 46). And St Ephrem comments: "The apostles' miracles made the resurrection and ascension of the Lord credible"

(*Armenian Commentary*, ad loc.).

Through miracles God speaks to the minds and hearts of those who witness them, inviting them to believe but not forcing their freedom or lessening the merit of their faith. The apostles follow in the footsteps of our Lord, who "supported and confirmed his preaching by miracles to arouse the faith of his hearers and give them assurance, not to coerce them" (Vatican II, *Dignitatis humanae*, 11). If people have the right dispositions they will generally have no difficulty in recognizing and accepting miracles. Common sense and religious instinct tell them that miracles are possible, because all things are subject to God; however, prejudice and resistance to conversion and its implications can blind a person and make him deny something which is quite obvious to a man of good will.

"Since the apostles were all together, the people brought them their sick on beds and pallets. From every quarter fresh tribute of wonder accrued to

the prison to have them brought. [22]But when the officers came, they did not find them in the prison, and they returned and reported, [23]"We found the prison securely locked and the sentries standing at the doors, but when we opened it we found no one inside." [24]Now when the captain of the temple and the chief priests heard these words, they were much perplexed about them, wondering what this would come to. [25]And some one came and told them, "The men whom you put in prison are standing in the temple and teaching the people."

The apostles before the Sanhedrin

[26]Then the captain with the officers went and brought them, but without violence, for they were afraid of being stoned by the people.

Lk 20:19; 22:2

[27]And when they had brought them, they set them before the council. And the high priest questioned them, [28]saying, "We strictly charged you not to teach in this name, yet here you have filled Jerusalem with your teaching and you intend to bring this man's blood upon us." [29]But Peter and the apostles answered, "We

Mt 27:25
Acts 4:18

Acts 4:19

---

them—from them that believed, from them that were healed, such was the apostles' boldness of speech and the virtuous behaviour of the believers. Although the apostles modestly ascribe these things to Christ, in whose name they acted, their own life and noble conduct also helped to produce this effect" (St John Chrysostom, *Hom. on Acts*, 12).

5:19. In Holy Scripture we meet angels as messengers of God and also as mediators, guardians and ministers of divine justice. Abraham sent his servant on a mission to his kindred and told him, "The Lord will send his angel before you and prosper your way" (Gen 24:7, 40). Tobit, Lot and his family, Daniel and his companions, Judith etc. also experienced the help of angels. The Psalms refer to trust in the angels (cf. Ps 34:7; 91:11–13) and the continuous help they render men in obedience to God's command.

This episode of the freeing of the apostles is one of the examples the *St*

Pius V Catechism gives to illustrate "the countless benefits which the Lord distributes among men through angels, his interpreters and ministers, sent not only in isolated cases but appointed from our birth to watch over us, and constituted for the salvation of every individual person" (4, 9, 6).

This means, therefore, that the angels should have a place in a Christian's personal piety: "I ask our Lord that, during our stay on this earth of ours, we may never be parted from our divine travelling companion. To ensure this, let us also become firmer friends of the Holy Guardian Angels. We all need a lot of company, company from heaven and company on earth. Have great devotion to the Holy Angels" (St Josemaría Escrivá, *Friends of God*, 315).

5:29. The apostles' failure to obey the Sanhedrin is obviously not due to pride or to their not knowing their place (as citizens they are subject to the Sanhedrin's

Acts 2:23
Gal 3:13

Acts 2:33;
10:43; 13:38

must obey God rather than men. [30]The God of our fathers raised Jesus whom you killed by hanging him on a tree. [31]God exalted him at his right hand as Leader and Saviour, to give repentance to

authority); the Sanhedrin is imposing a ruling which would have them go against God's law and their own conscience.

The apostles humbly and boldly remind their judges that obedience to God comes first. They know that many members of the Sanhedrin are religious men, good Jews who can understand their message; they try not so much to justify themselves as to get the Sanhedrin to react: they are more concerned about their judges' spiritual health than about their own safety. St John Chrysostom comments: "God allowed the apostles to be brought to trial so that their adversaries might be instructed, if they so desired. [...] The apostles are not irritated by the judges; they plead with them compassionately, with tears in their eyes, and their only aim is to free them from error and from divine wrath" (*Hom. on Acts*, 13). They are convinced that "those who fear God are in no danger, only those who do not fear him" (ibid.) and that it is worse to commit injustice than to suffer it. We can see from the apostles' behaviour how deep their convictions run; grace and faith in Jesus Christ have given them high regard for the honour of God. They have begun at last to love and serve God without counting the cost. This is true Christian maturity. "In that cry *Serviam!* [I will serve!] you express your determination to 'serve' the Church of God most faithfully, even at the cost of fortune, of reputation and of life" (St Josemaría Escrivá, *The Way*, 519).

The Church often prays to God to give its children this resilience: they need it because there is always the danger of growing indifferent and of abandoning the faith to some extent. "Lord, fill us with that spirit of courage which gave your martyr Sebastian," his feast's liturgy says, "strength to offer his life in faithful witness. Help us to learn from him to cherish your law and to obey you rather than men" (*Roman Missal*).

A Christian should conform his behaviour to God's law: that law should be his very life. He should obey and love God's commandments as taught by the Church, if he wishes to live a truly human life. The law of God is not something burdensome: it is a way of freedom, as Sacred Scripture is at pains to point out: "The Lord is my portion, I promise to keep thy words. I entreat thy favour with all my heart; be gracious to me according to thy promise. When I think of thy ways, I turn my feet to thy testimonies; I hasten and do not delay to keep thy commandments. Though the cords of the wicked ensnare me, I do not forget thy law. At midnight I rise to praise thee, because of thy righteous ordinances. I am a companion of all who fear thee, of those who keep thy precepts. The earth, O Lord, is full of thy steadfast love; teach me thy statutes" (Ps 119:57–64).

Conscience, which teaches man in the depths of his heart, gradually shows him what the law of God involves: "Man has in his heart a law inscribed by God. His dignity lies in observing this law, and by it he will be judged (cf. Rom 2:15–16). His conscience is man's most secret core, and his sanctuary. There he is alone with God, whose voice echoes in his depths. By conscience, in a wonderful way, that law is made known. [...] The more a correct conscience prevails, the more do persons and groups turn aside from blind choice and try to be guided by the objective standards of moral conduct" (Vatican II, *Gaudium et spes*, 16).

Israel and forgiveness of sins. [32]And we are witnesses to these things, and so is the Holy Spirit whom God has given to those who obey him."

Lk 24:48
Jn 7:39;
15:26–27

Good and evil are facts of life. A person can identify them. There are such things as good actions—and there are evil actions, which should always be avoided. The goodness or badness of human actions is not essentially dependent on the circumstances, although sometimes these can affect it to some extent.

Like the eye, conscience is designed to enable a person to see, but it needs light from outside (God's law and the Church's guidance) to discover religious and moral truths and properly appreciate them. Without that help man simply tires himself out in his search; he seeks only himself and forgets about good and evil, and his conscience becomes darkened by sin and moral opportunism.

"With respect to conscience," Paul VI teaches, "an objection can arise: Is conscience not enough on its own as the norm of our conduct? Do the decalogues, the codes, imposed on us from outside, not undermine conscience […]? This is a delicate and very current problem. Here all we will say is that subjective conscience is the first and immediate norm of our conduct, but it needs light, it needs to see which standard it should follow, especially when the action in question does not evidence its own moral exigencies. Conscience needs to be instructed and trained about what is the best choice to make, by the authority of a law" (General Audience, 28 March 1973).

A right conscience, which always goes hand in hand with moral prudence, will help a Christian to obey the law like a good citizen and also to take a stand, personally or in association with others, against any unjust laws which may be proposed or enacted. The State is not almighty in the sphere of law. It may not order or permit anything it likes; therefore not everything legal is morally lawful or just. Respect due to civil authority—which is part of the Gospel message and has always been taught by the Church—should not prevent Christians and people of good will from opposing legislators and rulers when they legislate and govern in a way that is contrary of the law of God and therefore to the common good. Obviously, this legitimate kind of resistance to authority should always involve the use of lawful methods.

It is not enough for good Christians to profess *privately* the teaching of the Gospel and the Church regarding human life, the family, education, freedom etc. They should realize that these are subjects of crucial importance for the welfare of their country, and they should strive, using all the usual means at their disposal, to see that the laws of the State are supportive of the common good. Passivity towards ideologies and stances that run counter to Christian values is quite deplorable.

5:30. "Hanging him on a tree": this is reminiscent of Deuteronomy 21:23: if a criminal is put to death "and you hang him on a tree, his body shall not remain all night upon the tree, but you shall bury him the same day, for a hanged man is accursed by God." This is a reference to crucifixion, a form of capital punishment which originated in Persia; it was common throughout the East and was later adopted by the Romans.

5:32. God sends the Holy Spirit to those who obey him, and, in turn, the apostles

³³When they heard this they were enraged and wanted to kill them.

Gamaliel's intervention

Acts 22:3

³⁴But a Pharisee in the council named Gamaliel,* a teacher of the law, held in honour by all the people, stood up and ordered the men to be put outside for a while. ³⁵And he said to them, "Men of Israel, take care what you do with these men. ³⁶For before these days Theudas arose, giving himself out to be somebody, and a number of men, about four hundred, joined him; but he was slain and all who followed him were dispersed and came to nothing.

Lk 2:2

³⁷After him Judas the Galilean arose in the days of the census and drew away some of the people after him; he also perished, and all who followed him were scattered. ³⁸So in the present case I tell you, keep away from these men and let them alone; for if this plan or this undertaking is of men, it will fail; ³⁹but if it is of God, you

2 Mac 7:19
Mt 15:13

---

obey the indications of the Spirit with complete docility.

If we are to obey the Holy Spirit and do what he asks us, we need to cultivate him and listen to what he says. "Get to know the Holy Spirit, the Great Stranger, on whom depends your sanctification.

"Don't forget that you are God's temple. The Advocate is in the centre of your soul: listen to him and be docile to his inspirations" (St Josemaría Escrivá, *The Way*, 57).

5:34–39. Gamaliel had been St Paul's teacher (cf. 22:3). He belonged to a moderate grouping among the Pharisees. He was a prudent man, impartial and religiously minded. The Fathers of the Church often propose him as an example of an upright man who is awaiting the Kingdom of God and dares to defend the apostles.

"Gamaliel does not say that the undertaking is of man or of God; he recommends that they let time decide. [...] By speaking in the absence of the apostles he was better able to win over the judges. The gentleness of his word and

arguments, based on justice, convinced them. He was almost preaching the Gospel. Indeed, his language is so correct that he seemed to be saying: Be convinced of it: you cannot destroy this undertaking. How is it that you do not believe? The Christian message is so impressive that even its adversaries bear witness to it" (St John Chrysostom, *Hom. on Acts*, 14).

This commentary seems to be recalling our Lord's words, "He that is not against us is for us" (Mk 9:40). Certainly, Gamaliel's intervention shows that a person with good will can discern God's action in events or at least investigate objectively without prejudging the issue.

The revolts of Theudas and Judas are referred to by Flavius Josephus (cf. *Jewish Antiquities*, 18, 4–10; 20, 169–172), but the dates he gives are vague; apparently these events occurred around the time of Jesus' birth. Both Theudas and Judas had considerable following; they revolted against the chosen people having to pay tribute to foreigners such as Herod and Imperial Rome.

will not be able to overthrow them. You might even be found opposing God!"

The apostles are flogged

⁴⁰So they took his advice, and when they had called in the apostles, they beat them and charged them not to speak in the name of Jesus, and let them go. ⁴¹Then they left the presence of the council, rejoicing that they were counted worthy to suffer dishonour for the name. ⁴²And every day in the temple and at home they did not cease teaching and preaching Jesus as the Christ.

Mt 10:17
Acts 22:19

Mt 5:10–12
1 Pet 4:13–14

Acts 18:5

4. THE "DEACONS". ST STEPHEN

Appointment of the seven deacons

6 ¹Now in these days when the disciples were increasing in number, the Hellenists* murmured against the Hebrews

---

5:40–41. Most members of the Sanhedrin are unimpressed by Gamaliel's arguments; they simply decide to go as far as they safely can: they do not dare to condemn the apostles to death; but, in their stubborn opposition to the Gospel message, they decree that they be put under the lash in the hope that this will keep them quiet. However, it has just the opposite effect.

"It is true that Jeremiah was scourged for the word of God, and that Elijah and and other prophets were also threatened, but in this case the apostles, as they did earlier by their miracles, showed forth the power of God. He does not say that they did not suffer, but that they rejoiced over having to suffer. This we can see from their boldness afterwards: immediately after being beaten they went back to preaching" (St John Chrysostom, *Hom. on Acts*, 14).

The apostles must have remembered our Lord's words, "Blessed are you when men revile you and persecute you and utter all kinds of evil against you falsely on my account. Rejoice and be glad, for

your reward is great in heaven, for so men persecuted the prophets who were before you" (Mt 5:11–12).

5:42. The apostles and the first disciples of Jesus were forever preaching, with the result that very soon all Jerusalem was filled with their teaching (cf. v. 28). These early brethren are an example to Christians in every age: zeal to attract others to the faith is a characteristic of every true disciple of Jesus and a consequence of love of God and love for others: "You have but little love if you are not zealous for the salvation of all souls. You have but poor love if you are not eager to inspire other apostles with your craziness" (St Josemaría Escrivá, *The Way*, 796).

6:1–6. A new section of the book begins at this point. It is introduced by reference to two groups in the early community, identified by their background prior to their conversion—the Hellenists and the Hebrews. From this chapter onwards, Christians are referred to as "disciples";

59

Ex 18:17–23   because their widows were neglected in the daily distribution. ²And the twelve summoned the body of the disciples and said, "It is not right that we should give up preaching the word of God to

in other words this term is no longer applied only to the apostles and to those who were adherents of Jesus during his life on earth: all the baptized are "disciples". Jesus is the Lord of his Church and the Teacher of all: after his ascension into heaven he teaches, sanctifies and governs Christians through the ministry of the apostles, initially, and after the apostles' death, through the ministry of their successors, the Pope and the Bishops, who are aided by priests.

Hellenists were Jews who had been born and lived for a time outside Palestine. They spoke Greek and had synagogues of their own where the Greek translation of Scripture was used. They had a certain amount of Greek culture; the Hebrews would have also had some, but not as much. The Hebrews were Jews born in Palestine; they spoke Aramaic and used the Hebrew Bible in their synagogues. This difference of backgrounds naturally carried over into the Christian community during its early years, but it would be wrong to see it as divisive or to imagine that there were two opposed factions in early Christianity. Before the Church was founded there existed in Jerusalem a well-established Hellenist-Jewish community—an influential and sizeable grouping.

This chapter relates the establishment by the apostles of "the seven": this is the second, identifiable group of disciples entrusted with a ministry in the Church, the first being "the twelve".

Although St Luke does not clearly present this group as constituting a holy "order", it is quite clear that the seven have been given a public role in the community, a role which extends beyond dis-

tribution of relief. We shall now see Philip and Stephen preaching and baptizing—sharing in some ways in ministry of the apostles, involved in "care of souls".

St Luke uses the term *diakonia* (service), but he does not call the seven "deacons". Nor do later ancient writers imply that these seven were deacons (in the later technical sense of the word)—constituting with priests and Bishops the hierarchy of the Church. Therefore, we do not know for certain whether the diaconate as we know it derives directly from the seven. St John Chrysostom, for example, has doubts about this (cf. *Hom. on Acts*, 14). However, it is at least possible that the ministry described here played a part in the instituting of the diaconate proper.

In any event, the diaconate is a form of sacred office of apostolic origin. At ordination deacons take on an obligation to perform—under the direction of the diocesan bishop—certain duties to do with evangelization, catechesis, organization of liturgical ceremonies, Christian initiation of catechumens and neophytes, and Church charitable and social welfare work.

The Second Vatican Council teaches that "at a lower level of the hierarchy are to be found deacons, who receive the imposition of hands 'not unto the priesthood, but unto the ministry'. For, strengthened by sacramental grace they are dedicated to the people of God, in conjunction with the bishop and his body of priests, in the service of the liturgy, of the Gospel and of works of charity. It pertains to the office of a deacon, in so far as it may be assigned to him by the competent authority, to administer Bapt-

serve tables. ³Therefore, brethren, pick out from among you seven   1 Tim 3:8–10
men of good repute, full of the Spirit and of wisdom, whom we
may appoint to this duty. ⁴But we will devote ourselves to prayer

---

ism solemnly, to be custodian and distributor of the Eucharist, in the name of the Church to assist at and to bless marriages, to bring Viaticum to the dying, to read the Sacred Scripture to the faithful, to instruct and exhort the people, to preside over the worship and the prayer of the faithful, to administer sacramentals, and to officiate at funeral and burial services" (*Lumen gentium*, 29).

6:2–4. The Twelve establish a principle which they consider basic: their apostolic ministry is so absorbing that they have no time to do other things. In this particular case an honorable and useful function—distribution of food—cannot be allowed to get in the way of another even more important task essential to the life of the Church and of each of its members. "They speak of it 'not being right' in order to show that the two duties cannot in this case be made compatible" (St John Chrysostom, *Hom. on Acts*, 14).

The main responsibility of the pastors of the Church is the preaching of the word of God, the administration of the sacraments and the government of the people of God. Any other commitment they take on should be compatible with their pastoral work and supportive of it, in keeping with the example given by Christ: he cured people's physical ailments in order to reach their souls, and he preached justice and peace as signs of the Kingdom of God.

"A mark of our identity which no doubt ought to encroach upon and no objection eclipse is this: as pastors, we have been chosen by the mercy of the Supreme Pastor (cf. 1 Pet 5:4), in spite of our inadequacy, to proclaim with authority the Word of God, to assemble the scattered people of God, to nourish this people on the road to salvation, to maintain it in that unity of which we are, at different levels, active and living instruments, and increasingly to keep this community gathered around Christ faithful to its deepest vocation" (Paul VI, *Evangelii nuntiandi*, 68).

A priest should be avid for the word of God, John Paul II emphasizes; he should embrace it in its entirety, meditate on it, study it assiduously and spread it through his example and preaching (cf., e.g., addresses in Ireland and the United States, 1 October and 3 October 1979 respectively). His whole life should be a generous proclamation of Christ. Therefore, he should avoid the temptation to "temporal leadership: that can easily be a source of division, whereas he should be a sign and promoter of unity and fraternity" (To the priests of Mexico, 27 January 1979).

This passage allows us to see the difference between election and appointment to a ministry in the Church. A person can be elected or designated by the faithful; but power to carry out that ministry (which implies a calling from God) is something he must receive through ordination, which the apostles confer. "The apostles leave it to the body of the disciples to select the [seven], in order that it should not seem that they favour some in preference to others" (St John Chrysostom, *Hom. on Acts*, 14). However, those designated for ordination are not representatives or delegates of the Christian community; they are ministers of God. They have received a calling and, by the imposition of hands, God—

Acts 8:5; 21:8 and to the ministry of the word." ⁵And what they said pleased the whole multitude, and they chose Stephen, a man full of faith and of the Holy Spirit, and Philip, and Prochorus, and Nicanor, and Timon, and Parmenas, and Nicolaus, a proselyte of Antioch.
Acts 13:3
1 Tim 4:14
2 Tim 1:6 ⁶These they set before the apostles, and they prayed and laid their hands upon them.
Acts 12:24;
19:20 ⁷And the word of God increased; and the number of the disciples multiplied greatly in Jerusalem, and a great many of the priests were obedient to the faith.

Stephen's arrest

⁸And Stephen, full of grace and power, did great wonders and signs among the people. ⁹Then some of those who belonged to the synagogue of the Freedmen (as it was called), and of the Cyrenians, and of the Alexandrians, and of those from Cilicia and
Lk 21:15
Acts 1:8 Asia, arose and disputed with Stephen. ¹⁰But they could not with-

---

not men—gives them a spiritual power which equips them to govern the Christian community, make and administer the sacraments and preach the Word.

Christian pastoral office, that is, the priesthood of the New Testament in its various degrees, does not derive from family relationship, as was the case with the Levitical priesthood in the Old Testament; nor is it a type of commissioning by the community. The initiative lies with the grace of God, who calls whom he chooses.

6:5. All the people chosen have Greek names. One of them is a "proselyte", that is, a pagan who became a Jew through circumcision and observance of the Law of Moses.

6:6. The apostles establish the seven in their office or ministry through prayer and the laying on of hands. This latter gesture is found sometimes in the Old Testament, principally as a rite of ordination of Levites (cf. Num 8:10) and as a way of conferring power and wisdom on Joshua, Moses' successor as leader of Israel (cf. Num 27:20).

Christians have retained this rite, as can be seen quite often in Acts. Sometimes it symbolizes curing (9:12, 17; 28:8), in line with the example given by our Lord in Luke 4:40. It is also a rite of blessing, as when Paul and Barnabas are sent out on their first apostolic journey (13:3); and it is used as a post-baptismal rite for bringing down the Holy Spirit (8:17; 19:6).

In this case it is a rite for the ordination of ministers of the Church—the first instance of sacred ordination reported by Acts (cf. 1 Tim 4:14; 5:22; 2 Tim 5:22). "St Luke is brief. He does not say how they were ordained, but simply that it was done with prayer, because it was an ordination. The hand of a man is laid [upon the person], but the whole work is of God and it is his hand which touches the head of the one ordained" (St John Chrysostom, *Hom. on Acts*, 14).

The essential part of the rite of ordination of deacons is the laying on of hands; this is done in silence, on the candidate's head, and then a prayer is said to God asking him to send the Holy Spirit to the person being ordained.

stand the wisdom and the Spirit with which he spoke. ¹¹Then they
secretly instigated men, who said, "We have heard him speak
blasphemous words against Moses and God." ¹²And they stirred
up the people and the elders and the scribes, and they came upon
him and seized him, and brought him before the council, ¹³and set
up false witnesses who said, "This man never ceases to speak
words against this holy place and the law; ¹⁴for we have heard
him say that this Jesus of Nazareth will destroy this place, and
will change the customs which Moses delivered to us." ¹⁵And
gazing at him, all who sat in the council saw that his face was like
the face of an angel.

Mt 26:59–66

Mt 10:17

Jer 26:11
Acts 21:28

Mk 14:58

Stephen's address to the Sanhedrin

7 ¹And the high priest said, "Is this so?" ²And Stephen said:
"Brethren and fathers, hear me. The God of glory appeared to
our father Abraham, when he was in Mesopotamia, before he

Acts 24:9

Ps 29:3

6:7. As in earlier chapters, St Luke here refers to the spread of the Church—this time reporting the conversion of "a great many of the priests." Many scholars think that these would have come from the lower ranks of the priesthood (like Zechariah: cf. Lk 1:5) and not from the great priestly families, which were Sadducees and enemies of the new-born Church (cf. 4:1; 5:17). Some have suggested that these priests may have included members of the Qumran sect. However, the only evidence we have to go on is what St Luke says here.

6:8–14. From the text it would appear that Stephen preached mainly among Hellenist Jews; this was his own background. Reference is made to synagogues of Jews of the Dispersion (Diaspora). These synagogues were used for worship and as meeting places. The very fact that these Hellenist Jews were living in the Holy City shows what devotion they had to the Law of their forebears.

No longer is it only the Sanhedrin who are opposed to the Gospel; other Jews have been affected by misunder-

standing and by misrepresentation of the Christian message.

The charge of blasphemy—also made against our Lord—was the most serious that could be made against a Jew. As happened in Jesus' case, the accusers here resort to producing false witnesses, who twist Stephen's words and accuse him of a crime the penalty for which is death.

6:15. St John Chrysostom, commenting on this verse, recalls that the face of Moses, when he comes down from Sinai (cf. Ex 34:29–35), reflected the glory of God and likewise made the people afraid: "It was grace, it was the glory of Moses. I think that God clothed him in this splendour because perhaps he had something to say, and in order that his very appearance would strike terror into them. For it is possible, very possible, for figures full of heavenly grace to be attractive to friendly eyes and terrifying to the eyes of enemies" (*Hom. on Acts*, 15).

7:1–53. Stephen's discourse is the longest one given in Acts. It is a summary of the

Gen 12:1

Gen 11:32;
12:5

Gen 12:7;
13:15; 17:8
Gal 3:16

Gen 15:13–14
Ex 12:40

Ex 3:12

Gen 17:10;
21:4

Gen 37:11, 28
Wis 10:13

Gen 39:21;
41:40–41

Gen 41:54

Gen 42:2

Gen 45:3–16

Gen 46:27

Gen 46:6;
49:33

lived in Haran, ³and said to him, 'Depart from your land and from your kindred and go into the land which I will show you.' ⁴Then he departed from the land of the Chaldeans, and lived in Haran. And after his father died, God removed him from there into this land in which you are now living; ⁵yet he gave him no inheritance in it, not even a foot's length, but promised to give it to him in possession and to his posterity after him, though he had no child. ⁶And God spoke to this effect, that his posterity would be aliens in a land belonging to others, who would enslave them and ill-treat them four hundred years. ⁷'But I will judge the nation which they serve,' said God, 'and after that they shall come out and worship me in this place.' ⁸And he gave him the covenant of circumcision. And so Abraham became the father of Isaac, and circumcised him on the eighth day; and Isaac became the father of Jacob, and Jacob of the twelve patriarchs.

⁹"And the patriarchs, jealous of Joseph, sold him into Egypt; but God was with him, ¹⁰and rescued him out of all his afflictions, and gave him favour and wisdom before Pharaoh, king of Egypt, who made him governor over Egypt and over all his household. ¹¹Now there came a famine throughout all Egypt and Canaan, and great affliction, and our fathers could find no food. ¹²But when Jacob heard that there was grain in Egypt, he sent forth our fathers the first time. ¹³And at the second visit Joseph made himself known to his brothers, and Joseph's family became known to Pharaoh. ¹⁴And Joseph sent and called to him Jacob his father and all his kindred, seventy-five souls; ¹⁵and Jacob went down into Egypt. And he died, himself and our fathers, ¹⁶and they were car-

history of Israel, divided into three periods—of the Patriarchs (vv. 1–16), of Moses (vv. 17–43) and of the building of the temple (vv. 44–50). It ends with a short section (vv. 51–53) where he brings his argument together.

One thing that stands out is that Stephen does not defend himself directly. He answers his accusers with a Christian vision of salvation history, in which the temple and the Law have already fulfilled their purpose. He tells them that he continues to respect the Mosaic Law and the temple, but that as a Christian his idea of God's law is more universal and more profound, his concept of the temple more

spiritual (for God can be worshipped anywhere in the world). This approach, which respects and perfects the religious values of Judaism (because it probes their true meaning and brings them to fulfilment), is reinforced by the way he presents the figure of Moses. Stephen shows Moses as a "type" of Christ: Christ is the new Moses. Small elucidations of the Greek text of the Old Testament help in this direction: expressions like "they refused" or "deliverer" (v. 35) are not applied to Moses in the books of the Old Testament, but they are used here to suggest Christ. The Israelites' rebellious and aggressive treatment of Moses, who had

ried back to Shechem and laid in the tomb that Abraham had bought for a sum of silver from the sons of Hamor in Shechem. [1]

[17]"But as the time of the promise drew near, which God had granted to Abraham, the people grew and multiplied in Egypt [18]till there arose over Egypt another king who had not known Joseph. [19]He dealt craftily with our race and forced our fathers to expose their infants, that they might not be kept alive. [20]At this time Moses was born, and was beautiful before God. And he was brought up for three months in his father's house; [21]and when he was exposed, Pharaoh's daughter adopted him and brought him up as her own son. [22]And Moses was instructed in all the wisdom of the Egyptians, and he was mighty in his words and deeds.

[23]"When he was forty years old, it came into his heart to visit his brethren, the sons of Israel. [24]And seeing one of them being wronged, he defended the oppressed man and avenged him by striking the Egyptian. [25]He supposed that his brethren understood that God was giving them deliverance by his hand, but they did not understand. [26]And on the following day he appeared to them as they were quarrelling and would have reconciled them, saying, 'Men, you are brethren, why do you wrong each other?' [27]But the man who was wronging his neighbour thrust him aside, saying, 'Who made you a ruler and a judge over us? [28]Do you want to kill me as you killed the Egyptian yesterday?' [29]At this retort Moses fled, and became an exile in the land of Midian, where he became the father of two sons.

[30]"Now when forty years had passed, an angel appeared to him in the wilderness of Mount Sinai, in a flame of fire in a bush.

1 Gen 50:13

Ex 1:7

Ex 1:10–22

Ex 2:2
Heb 11:23

Ex 2:5, 10

Lk 24:19

Ex 2:11

Ex 2:12

Ex 2:13

Ex 2:14
Lk 12:14

Ex 2:15, 22;
18:3

Ex 3:1–2
Deut 33:16

---

a mission from God, is being repeated—much more seriously—in their rejection of the Gospel.

St John Chrysostom expands on the last words of the discourse in this way: "Is it to be wondered that you do not know Christ, seeing that you did not know Moses, and God himself, who was manifested by such wonders? [...] 'You always resist the Holy Spirit'. [...] When you received commandments, you neglected them; when the temple already stood, you worshipped idols" (*Hom. on Acts*, 17). Despite the vigour of his reproaches, Chrysostom has to point out Stephen's meekness: "he did

not abuse them; all he did was remind them of the words of the Prophets" (ibid.).

St Ephrem, however, stresses other aspects of Stephen's prayer: "Since he knew that the Jews were not going to take his words to heart and were only interested in killing him, full of joy in his soul [...] he censured their hardness of heart. [...] He discussed circumcision of the flesh, to exalt instead circumcision of the heart which sincerely seeks God, against whom they were in rebellion. In this way he added his own accusations to those of the prophet" (*Armenian Commentary*, ad loc.).

Ex 3:4
Ex 3:6
Mt 22:32

Ex 2:5

Ex 3:7–10

Ex 2:14

Ex 7:3; 14:21
Num 14:33

Deut 18:15
Acts 3:22

Ex 19:3
Deut 4:10; 9:10
Gal 3:19
Heb 2:2

Num 14:3

Ex 32:1, 23

Ex 32:4–6

Jer 19:13
Amos 5:25–27

[31]When Moses saw it he wondered at the sight; and as he drew near to look, the voice of the Lord came, [32]'I am the God of your fathers, the God of Abraham and of Isaac and of Jacob.' And Moses trembled and did not dare to look. [33]And the Lord said to him, 'Take off the shoes from your feet, for the place where you are standing is holy ground. [34]I have surely seen the ill-treatment of my people that are in Egypt and heard their groaning, and I have come down to deliver them. And now come, I will send you to Egypt.'

[35]"This Moses whom they refused, saying, 'Who made you a ruler and a judge?' God sent as both ruler and deliverer by the hand of the angel that appeared to him in the bush. [36]He led them out, having performed wonders and signs in Egypt and at the Red Sea, and in the wilderness for forty years. [37]This is the Moses who said to the Israelites, 'God will raise up for you a prophet from your brethren as he raised me up.' [38]This is he who was in the congregation in the wilderness with the angel who spoke to him at Mount Sinai, and with our fathers; and he received living oracles to give to us. [39]Our fathers refused to obey him, but thrust him aside, and in their hearts they turned to Egypt, [40]saying to Aaron, 'Make for us gods to go before us; as for this Moses who led us out from the land of Egypt, we do not know what has become of him.' [41]And they made a calf in those days, and offered a sacrifice to the idol and rejoiced in the works of their hands. [42]But God turned and gave them over to worship the host of heaven, as it is written in the book of the prophets:

'Did you offer to me slain beasts and sacrifices,
forty years in the wilderness, O house of Israel?
[43]And you took up the tent of Moloch,
and the star of the god Rephan,

7:42–43. "The host of heaven": Scripture normally uses this expression to refer to the stars, which were worshipped in some ancient religions. God sometimes allowed the Israelites to forget him and worship false gods.

The quotation from "the book of the prophets" to which Stephen refers is from Amos 5:25–27 (which in Acts is taken from the Septuagint Greek). It is not easy to work out what Amos means. We know from the Pentateuch that the Israelites a number of times offered sac-rifices to Yahweh when they were in Sinai during the Exodus (cf. Ex 24:4–5; chap. 29; Lev chaps. 8–9; Num chap. 7), but all these sacrifices were offered at the foot of Mount Sinai, before they started out on their long pilgrimage through the wilderness, before they reached the promised land. Perhaps St Stephen is referring to those long years (about forty years) during which nothing is said in the Old Testament about their offering sacrifice to Yahweh. Even during the Exodus—a period when God frequently

the figures which you made to worship;
and I will remove you beyond Babylon.'

⁴⁴"Our fathers had the tent of witness in the wilderness, even as
he who spoke to Moses directed him to make it, according to the
pattern that he had seen. ⁴⁵Our fathers in turn brought it in with
Joshua when they dispossessed the nations which God thrust out
before our fathers. So it was until the days of David, ⁴⁶who found
favour in the sight of God and asked leave to find a habitation for
the God of Jacob. ⁴⁷But it was Solomon who built a house for
him. ⁴⁸Yet the Most High does not dwell in houses made with
hands; as the prophet says,

⁴⁹'Heaven is my throne,
and earth my footstool.
What house will you build for me, says the Lord,
or what is the place of my rest?
⁵⁰Did not my hand make all these things?'

⁵¹"You stiff-necked people, uncircumcised in heart and ears,
you always resist the Holy Spirit. As your fathers did, so do you.
⁵²Which of the prophets did not your fathers persecute? And they
killed those who announced beforehand the coming of the
Righteous One, whom you have now betrayed and murdered,
⁵³you who received the law as delivered by angels and did not
keep it."

Ex 25:40
Heb 8:5
Josh 3:14; 18:1
2 Sam 7:2
Ps 132:5
1 Kings 6:1
Is 66:1
Acts 17:24
Heb 9:11, 24

Ex 33:3
Is 63:10
Jer 4:4; 6:10;
9:26
Mt 23:31
Acts 3:14
Acts 7:38

Martyrdom of St Stephen

⁵⁴Now when they heard these things they were enraged, and they
ground their teeth against him. ⁵⁵But he, full of the Holy Spirit,
gazed into heaven and saw the glory of God, and Jesus standing
at the right hand of God; ⁵⁶and he said, "Behold, I see the heavens
opened, and the Son of man standing at the right hand of God."

Dan 7:13
Lk 22:69

---

showed his special favour—the Israelites strayed from Yahweh.

7:55–56. "It is clear", St Ephrem comments, "that those who suffer for Christ enjoy the glory of the whole Trinity. Stephen saw the Father and Jesus at his side, because Jesus appears only to his own, as was the case with the apostles after the Resurrection. While the champion of the faith stood there helpless in the midst of those who had killed the Lord, just at the point when the first

martyr was to be crowned, he saw the Lord, holding a crown in his right hand, as if to encourage him to conquer death and to show that he inwardly helps those who are about to die on his account. He therefore reveals what he sees, that is, the heavens opened, which were closed to Adam and only opened to Christ at the Jordan, but open now after the Cross to all those who share Christ's sufferings, and in the first instance open to this man. See how Stephen reveals why his face was lit up: it was because he was on the

67

Acts 22:20

Ps 31:5
Lk 23:46
Lk 23:34

⁵⁷But they cried out with a loud voice and stopped their ears and rushed together upon him. ⁵⁸Then they cast him out of the city and stoned him; and the witnesses laid down their garments at the feet of a young man named Saul. ⁵⁹And as they were stoning Stephen, he prayed, "Lord Jesus, receive my spirit." ⁶⁰And he knelt down and cried with a loud voice, "Lord, do not hold this sin against them." And when he had said this, he fell asleep. ¹ᵃAnd Saul was consenting to his death.

point of contemplating this wondrous mission. That is why he took on the appearance of an angel—so that his testimony might be more reliable" (*Armenian Commentary*, ad loc.).

7:57–59. The cursory trial of Stephen ends without any formal sentence of death: this Jewish tribunal was unable to pass such sentences because the Romans restricted its competence. In any event no sentence proves necessary: the crowd becomes a lynching party; it takes over and proceeds to stone Stephen, with the tacit approval of the Sanhedrin.

Tradition regards Stephen as the first Christian martyr, an example of fortitude and suffering for love of Christ. "Could you keep all God's commandments," St Cyprian asks, "were it not for the strength of patience? That was what enabled Stephen to hold out: in spite of being stoned he did not call down vengeance on his executioners, but rather forgiveness. ... How fitting it was for him to be Christ's first martyr, so that by being, through his glorious death, the model of all the martyrs that would come after him, he should not only be a preacher of the Lord's Passion, but should also imitate it in his meekness and immense patience" (*De bono patientiae*, 16).

Martyrdom is a supreme act of bravery and of true prudence, but to the world it makes no sense. It is also an expression of humility, because a martyr does not act out of bravado or overweening self-confidence; he is a weak man like anyone else, but God's grace gives him the strength he needs. Although martyrdom is something which happens rarely, it does show Christians what human nature can rise to if God gives it strength, and it establishes a standard, both real and symbolic, for the behaviour of every disciple of Christ.

"Since all the virtues and the perfection of all righteousness are born of love of God and one's neighbour," St Leo says, "in no one is this love more worthily found than in the blessed martyrs, who are nearest to our Lord in terms of imitation of both his charity and his Passion.

"The martyrs have been of great help to others, because the Lord has availed of the very strength as he granted them to ensure that the pain of death and the cruelty of the Cross do not frighten any of his own, but are seen as things in which man can imitate him ... .

"No example is more useful for the instruction of the people of God than that of the martyrs. Eloquence is effective for entreating, argument for convincing; but examples are worth more than words, and it is better to teach by deeds than by speech" (*Hom. on the feast of St Laurence*).

The Second Vatican Council has reminded us of the excellence of martyrdom as a form of witness to the faith. Although there are heroic ways of imitat-

PART TWO

The Church spreads beyond Jerusalem

5. THE CHURCH IN SAMARIA

Persecution of the Church

8 ¹ᵇAnd on that day a great persecution arose against the church in Jerusalem; and they were all scattered throughout the

Jn 16:2
Acts 7:58;
11:19; 26:10

---

ing and following our Lord which do not involve the drama of bloodshed and death, all Christians should realize that confession of the faith in this way is not a thing of the past and is sometimes necessary.

"Since Jesus, the Son of God, showed his love by laying down his life for us, no one has greater love than he who lays down his life for him and for his brothers (cf. 1 Jn 3:16; Jn 15:13). Some Christians have been called from the beginning, and will always be called, to give this greatest testimony of love to all, especially to persecutors. Martyrdom makes the disciple like his Master. [...] Therefore, the Church considers it the highest gift and supreme test of love. And although it is given to few, all must be prepared to confess Christ before men and to follow him along the way of the Cross amidst the persecutions which the Church never lacks. Likewise the Church's holiness is fostered [...] by the manifold counsels which the Lord proposes to his disciples in the Gospel" (Vatican II, *Lumen gentium*, 42).

The Liturgy of the Church sums up the asceticism and theology of martyrdom in the preface for Christian martyrs: "Your holy martyr followed the example of Christ, and gave his life for the glory of your name. His death reveals your

power shining through our human weakness. You choose the weak and make them strong in bearing witness to you."

Like Jesus, Stephen dies commending his soul to God and praying for his persecutors. At this point St Luke brings in Saul, who cooperates in the proceedings by watching the executioners' clothes; Saul will soon experience the benefit of Stephen's intercession. "If Stephen had not prayed to God, the Church would not have had Paul" (St Augustine, *Sermons*, 315, 7).

Stephen has died, but his example and teaching continue to speak across the world.

8:1. Stephen's death signals the start of a violent persecution of the Christian community and Hellenist members in particular.

A new situation has been created. "Far from diminishing the boldness of the disciples, Stephen's death increased it. Christians were scattered precisely in order to spread the word further afield" (St John Chrysostom, *Hom. on Acts*, 18). This scattering of the disciples is not simply flight from danger. It originates in danger, but they avail of it to serve God and the Gospel. "Flight, so far from implying cowardice, requires often greater courage than not to flee. It is a great

Acts 9:1; 22:4
Gal 1:13
1 Cor 15:9
1 Tim 1:13

region of Judea and Samaria, except the apostles. [2]Devout men buried Stephen, and made great lamentation over him. [3]But Saul laid waste the church, and entering house after house, he dragged off men and women and committed them to prison.

[4]Now those who were scattered went about preaching the word.

Philip's preaching in Samaria

Acts 6:5

[5]Philip went down to a city of Samaria, and proclaimed to them

trial of heart. Death is an end of all trouble; he who flees is ever expecting death, and dies daily. [...] Exile is full of miseries. The afterconduct of the saints showed they had not fled for fear. [...] How would the Gospel ever have been preached throughout the world, if the apostles had not fled? And, since their time, those, too, who have become martyrs, at first fled; or, if they advanced to meet their persecutors, it was by some secret suggestion of the Divine Spirit. But, above all, while these instances abundantly illustrate the rule of duty in persecution, and the temper of mind necessary in those who observe it, we have that duty itself declared in a plain precept by no other than our Lord: 'When they shall persecute you in this city,' He says, 'flee into another'" (Ven. John Henry Newman, *Historical Sketches*, 2, 7).

8:4. "Observe how, in the middle of misfortune, the Christians keep up their preaching instead of neglecting it" (St John Chrysostom, *Hom. on Acts*, 18). Misfortune plays its part in the spread of the Gospel. God's plans always exceed man's calculations and expectations. An apparently mortal blow for the Gospel in fact plays a decisive role in its spread. What comes from God cannot be destroyed; its adversaries in fact contribute to its consolidation and progress. "The religion founded by the mystery of the cross of Christ cannot be destroyed by any form of cruelty. The Church is not dimin-

ished by persecutions; on the contrary, they make for its increase. The field of the Lord is clothed in a richer harvest. When the grain which falls dies, it is reborn and multiplied" (St Leo the Great, *Hom. on the feast of St Peter and St Paul*).

The disciples are disconcerted to begin with, but then they begin to have a better understanding of God's providence. They may well have been reminded of Isaiah's words: "My thoughts are not your thoughts, neither are your ways my ways" (55:8), and of the promises of a heavenly Father, who arranges all events to the benefit of his elect.

The different periods of Church history show certain similarities, and difficulties caused by hidden or overt enemies never create totally new situations. Christians always have good reason to be optimistic—with an optimism based on faith, self-sacrifice and prayer. "Christianity has been too often in what seemed deadly peril that we should fear for it any new trial now. So far is certain; on the other hand, what is uncertain [...] is the particular mode by which, in the event, Providence rescues and saves His elect inheritance. Sometimes our enemy is turned into a friend; sometimes he is despoiled of that special virulence of evil which was so threatening; sometimes he falls to pieces himself; sometimes he does just so much as is beneficial, and then is removed. Commonly the Church has nothing more to do than to go on in

the Christ. [6]And the multitudes with one accord gave heed to what was said by Philip, when they heard him and saw the signs which he did. [7]For unclean spirits came out of many who were possessed, crying with a loud voice; and many who were paralyzed or lame were healed. [8]So there was much joy in that city.

Mt 8:29
Mk 16:17

Jn 4:38-41

Simon the magician

[9]But there was a man named Simon who had previously practised magic in the city and amazed the nation of Samaria, saying that he

---

her own proper duties, in confidence and peace; to stand still and to see the salvation of God" (Ven. J.H. Newman, *Biglietto Speech*, 1879).

Those who do not know Christ may resist the Gospel, but that resistance makes good Christians spiritually stronger and helps to purify the Church. "The storm of persecution is good. What is the loss? What is already lost cannot be lost. When the tree is not torn up by the roots—and there is no wind or hurricane that can uproot the tree of the Church—only the dry branches fall. And they ... are well fallen" (St Josemaría Escrivá, *The Way*, 685).

8:5. This is not Philip the apostle (1:13) but one of the seven deacons appointed to look after Christians in need (6:5). The Gospel is proclaimed to the Samaritans —who also were awaiting the Messiah. This means that it now spreads beyond the borders of Judea once and for all, and our Lord's promise (Acts 1:8) is fulfilled: "you shall be my witnesses in Jerusalem and in all Judea and Samaria."

The despised Samaritans became the first to benefit from the Gospel's determination to spread all over the world. We can sense St Luke's pleasure in reporting its proclamation to the Samaritans; earlier he already showed them in a favourable light: he is the only Evangelist to recount the parable of the Good Samaritan (cf. Lk 10:30–37) and to men-

tion that the leper who came back to thank Jesus after being cured was a Samaritan (cf. Lk 17:16). On the Samaritans in general, see the note on Jn 4:20.

8:9–13. Simon the magician is an imposter who pretends to have spiritual powers and who trades on the credulity and superstition of his audience.

St Luke uses this episode to show the difference between the genuine miracles performed by the apostles in the name of Jesus and using Jesus' authority, and the real or apparent wonders worked by a charlatan: "As in the time of Moses, so now the distinction is made between different kinds of prodigies. Magic was practised, but it was easy to see the difference between it and genuine miracles. [...] Unclean spirits, in great numbers, went out of possessed people, protesting as they went. This showed that they were being expelled. Those who practised magic did just the opposite: they reinforced the bonds that bound the possessed" (St John Chrysostom, *Hom. on Acts*, 18).

The power which Peter and John have is different from Simon Magus'. Further on (vv. 15–17), St Luke contrasts the magician and his desire to make money, and the apostles who are themselves poor but who enrich others with the Spirit. The apostles do not perform miracles through powers which they

71

himself was somebody great. [10]They all gave heed to him, from the least to the greatest, saying, "This man is that power of God which is called Great." [11]And they gave heed to him, because for a long time he had amazed them with his magic. [12]But when they

Mt 28:19

believed Philip as he preached good news about the kingdom of God and the name of Jesus Christ, they were baptized, both men and women. [13]Even Simon himself believed, and after being baptized he continued with Philip. And seeing signs and great miracles performed, he was amazed.

Peter and John in Samaria

Acts 11:1–22

[14]Now when the apostles at Jerusalem heard that Samaria had received the word of God, they sent to them Peter and John, [15]who

---

have in their personal control; they always perform them by virtue of God's power, which they obtain by means of prayer. The miracles which Christians work are accompanied by prayer and never involve conjuring or spells. Luke makes the same point when recounting the episodes of Elymas (13:6ff), the diviner in Philippi (16:16ff) and the sons of Sceva (19:13ff).

Magic (occultism) and superstition (attempting to obtain supernatural effects using methods which cannot produce them) are a symptom of debased religion. Man has a natural obligation to be religious—to seek God, worship him and atone to him for sin. However, natural religion needs to be corrected, purified and filled out by supernatural revelation, whereby God seeks man out, raises him up and guides him on his way. Left to its own devices, natural religion can easily deviate and become useless or even harmful.

8:10. "That power of God which is called Great": it is not very clear what this means. It may mean that the Samaritans called that divine power "the Great" which they regarded as being the strongest. Another interpretation is that

the Greek adjective *megale*, great, is not a Greek word, but a transcription of an Aramaic word meaning "Revealing". Whichever interpretation is correct, Simon Magus claimed to have this divine power.

8:14–17. Here we see the apostles exercising through Peter and John the authority they have over the entire Church. The two apostles proceed to confirm the disciples recently baptized by Philip: we may presume that in addition to laying their hands on them to communicate the Holy Spirit, the apostles made sure that they had a correct grasp of the central points of the Gospel message. At this time the apostles constituted the spiritual centre of the Church and took an active interest in ensuring that the new communities were conscious of the links—doctrinal and affective—that united them to the mother community in Jerusalem.

This passage bears witness to the existence of Baptism and the gift of the Holy Spirit (or Confirmation) as two distinct sacramental rites. The most important effects Christian Baptism has are the infusion of initial grace and the remission of original sin and any personal sin; it is the first sacrament a person receives,

came down and prayed for them that they might receive the Holy
Spirit; [16]for it had not yet fallen on any of them, but they had only
been baptized in the name of the Lord Jesus. [17]Then they laid their
hands on them and they received the Holy Spirit.

Acts 2:38
Acts 19:2–6
1 Tim 4:14

The sin of simony

[18]Now when Simon saw that the Spirit was given through the
laying on of the apostles' hands, he offered them money, [19]saying,
"Give me also this power, that any one on whom I lay my hands
may receive the Holy Spirit." [20]But Peter said to him, "Your silver
perish with you, because you thought you could obtain the gift of
God with money!* [21]You have neither part nor lot in this matter,
for your heart is not right before God. [22]Repent therefore of this

Mt 10:8

Heb 12:15

---

which is why it is called the "door of the Church".

There is a close connexion between Baptism and Confirmation, so much so that in the early centuries of Christianity, Confirmation was administered immediately after Baptism. There is a clear distinction between these two sacraments of Christian initiation, which helps us understand the different effects they have. A useful comparison is the difference, in natural life, between conception and later growth (cf. St Pius V, *Catechism*, 2, 3, 5). "As nature intends that all her children should grow up and attain full maturity [...], so the Catholic Church, the common mother of all, earnestly wishes that, in those whom she has regenerated by Baptism, the perfection of Christian manhood be completed" (ibid., 2, 3, 17).

"The nature of the sacrament of Confirmation," John Paul II explains, "grows out of this endowment of strength which the Holy Spirit communicates to each baptized person, to make him or her—as the well-known language of the Catechism puts it—a perfect Christian and soldier of Christ, ready to witness boldly to his resurrection and its redemptive power: 'You shall be my witnesses' (Acts 1:8)" (Homily, 25 May 1980). "All

Christians, incorporated into Christ and his Church by Baptism, are consecrated to God. They are called to profess the faith which they have received. By the sacrament of Confirmation they are further endowed by the Holy Spirit with special strength to be witnesses of Christ and sharers in his mission of salvation" (Homily in Limerick, 1 October 1979). "This is a sacrament which in a special way associates us with the mission of the apostles, in that it inserts each baptized person into the apostolate of the Church" (Homily in Cracow, 10 June 1979). In the sacrament of Confirmation divine grace anticipates the aggressive and demoralizing temptations a young Christian man or woman is likely to experience, and reminds them of the fact that they have a vocation to holiness; it makes them feel more identified with the Church, their Mother, and helps them live in accordance with their Catholic beliefs and convictions. From their formative years Christ makes them defenders of the faith.

8:18–24. Simon's disgraceful proposition—offering the apostles money in exchange for the power to transmit the Holy Spirit—gave rise to the term "simony", that is, trading in sacred

Deut 29:18

wickedness of yours, and pray to the Lord that, if possible, the intent of your heart may be forgiven you. [23]For I see that you are in the gall of bitterness and in the bond of iniquity." [24]And Simon answered, "Pray for me to the Lord, that nothing of what you have said may come upon me."

Jn 4:35
Acts 1:8

[25]Now when they had testified and spoken the word of the Lord, they returned to Jerusalem, preaching the gospel to many villages of the Samaritans.

---

things. Simony is the sin of buying or selling, in exchange for money or some other temporal thing, something spiritual—a sacrament, an indulgence, an ecclesiastical office etc. It is sinful because it degrades something supernatural, which is essentially a free gift, by using it unlawfully to obtain material benefit.

However, there is no simony involved in ministers of sacred worship accepting reasonable alms, in cash or kind, for their maintenance. Jesus teaches that the apostle deserves to receive wages (cf. Lk 10:7), and St Paul says that those who proclaim the Gospel should get their living from it (cf. 1 Cor 9:14). An example of valid earnings is the alms or stipend given to a minister to say Mass for one's intention: it is not given as payment for spiritual benefit, but as a contribution to the priest's keep.

The Church has striven and warned against its ministers falling into the sin of simony (cf. 1 Pet 5:2; 2 Pet 2:3), often recalling what our Lord said to his disciples in this connexion: "Heal the sick, raise the dead, cleanse lepers, cast out demons. You have received without pay, give without pay" (Mt 10:8), and particularly setting before them the wonderful example Jesus himself gave, in the way he lived and in the manner of his death.

Our Lord has left us a supreme example of disinterest and uprightness of intention in the service of men—by living and dying on our behalf, asking

nothing in exchange except the just response his love merits.

A pastor of souls would be guilty of a serious sin if through his ministry he sought financial gain, social prestige, esteem, honours or political leadership. Instead of being a pastor he would be a mercenary, a hireling, who in time of real danger would only think of himself, leaving the faithful to fend for themselves (cf. Jn 10:12).

8:26–40. The baptism of the Ethiopian official marks an important step in the spread of Christianity. St Luke's account underlines the importance of Sacred Scripture, and its correct interpretation, in the work of evangelization. This episode encapsulates the various stages in apostolate: Christ's disciple is moved by the Spirit (v. 29) and readily obeys his instruction; he bases his preaching on Sacred Scripture—as Jesus did in the case of the disciples of Emmaus—and then administers Baptism.

8:27. Ethiopia: the kingdom of Nubia, whose capital was Meroe, to the south of Egypt, below Aswan, the first cataract on the Nile (part of modern Sudan). Candace, or Kandake, is not the name of an individual; it was the dynastic name of the queens of that country, a country at that time ruled by women (cf. Eusebius, *Ecclesiastical History*, 2, 1, 13).

The term "eunuch", like its equivalent in Hebrew, was often used indepen-

Philip baptizes an Ethiopian official

²⁶But an angel of the Lord said to Philip, "Rise and go toward the south^g to the road that goes down from Jerusalem to Gaza." This is a desert road. ²⁷And he rose and went. And behold, an Ethiopian, a eunuch, a minister of Candace the queen of the Ethiopians, in charge of all her treasure, had come to Jerusalem to worship ²⁸and was returning; seated in his chariot, he was reading the prophet Isaiah. ²⁹And the Spirit said to Philip, "Go up and join this chariot." ³⁰So Philip ran to him, and heard him reading Isaiah the prophet, and asked, "Do you understand what you are reading?" ³¹And he said, "How can I, unless some one guides me?" And he

Ps 68:31
Is 56:3–7

Rom 10:14

---

dently of its original physiological meaning and could refer to any court official (cf., e.g., Gen 39:1; 2 Kings 25:19). This particular man was an important official, the equivalent of a minister of finance. We do not know if he was a member of the Jewish race, a proselyte (a Jew not by race but by religion) or—perhaps—a God-fearer (cf. the note on Acts 2:5–11).

8:28. "Consider," St John Chrysostom says, "what a good thing it is not to neglect reading Scripture even when one is on a journey. ... Let those reflect on this who do not even read the Scriptures at home, and, because they are with their wife, or are fighting in the army, or are very involved in family or other affairs, think that there is no particular need for them to make the effort to read the divine Scriptures. [...] This Ethiopian has something to teach us all—those who have a family life, members of the army, officials, in a word, all men, and women too (particularly those women who are always at home), and all those who have chosen the monastic way of life. Let all learn that no situation is an obstacle to reading the word of God: this is something one can do not only when one is alone at home but also in the public square, on a journey, in the company of

others, or when engaged in one's occupation. Let us not, I beg you, neglect to read the Scriptures" (*Hom. on Acts*, 35).

8:29–30. The fact that they are alone, that the road is empty, makes it easier for them to have a deep conversation and easier for Philip to explain Christian teaching. "I think so highly of your devotion to the early Christians that I will do all I can to encourage it, so that you—like them—will put more enthusiasm each day into that effective apostolate of discretion and friendship" (St J. Escrivá, *The Way*, 971). This was in fact one of the characteristic features of the kind of apostolate carried out by our first brothers and sisters in the faith as they spread gradually all over the Roman empire. They brought the Christian message to the people around them—the sailor to the rest of the crew, the slave to his fellow slaves, soldiers, traders, housewives. ... This eager desire of theirs to spread the Gospel showed their genuine conviction and was an additional proof of the truth of the Christian message.

8:31. "How can I understand it, unless some one guides me?": to a Jew of this period the very idea of a Messiah who suffers and dies at the hands of his ene-

g. Or *at noon*

Is 53:7–8
Lk 18:31 invited Philip to come up and sit with him. [32]Now the passage of the scripture which he was reading was this:
"As a sheep led to the slaughter
or a lamb before its shearer is dumb,
so he opens not his mouth.
[33]In his humiliation justice was denied him.
Who can describe his generation?
For his life is taken up from the earth."

mies was quite repugnant. This explains why the Ethiopian has difficulty in understanding this passage—and, indeed, the entire song of the Servant of Yahweh, from which it comes (cf. Is 53).

Sometimes it is difficult to understand a passage of Scripture; as St Jerome comments: "I am not (to speak in passing of myself) more learned or more holy than that eunuch who travelled to the temple from Ethiopia, that is, from the end of the earth: he left the royal palace and such was his desire for divine knowledge that he was even reading the sacred words in his chariot. And yet ... he did not realize whom he was venerating in that book. Philip comes along, he reveals to him Jesus hidden and as it were imprisoned in the text [...], and in that very moment he believes, is baptized, is faithful and holy. [...] I tell you this to show you that, unless you have a guide who goes ahead of you to show you the way, you cannot enter the holy Scriptures" (*Letters*, 53, 5–6).

This guide is the Church; God, who inspired the sacred books, has entrusted their interpretation to the Church. Therefore, the Second Vatican Council teaches that "If we are to derive their true meaning from the sacred texts," attention must be devoted "not only to their content but to the unity of the whole of Scripture, the living tradition of the entire Church, and the analogy of faith. [...] Everything to do with the interpretation of Scripture is ultimately subject to the

judgment of the Church, which exercises the divinely conferred communion and ministry of watching over and interpreting the Word of God" (Vatican II, *Dei Verbum*, 12).

8:35. "The eunuch deserves our admiration for his readiness to believe," St John Chrysostom comments. "He has not seen Jesus Christ nor has he witnessed any miracle; what then is the reason for his change? It is because, being observant in matters of religion, he applies himself to the study of the sacred books and makes them his book of meditation and reading" (*Hom. on Acts*, 19).

8:36. "What is to prevent my being baptized?": the Ethiopian's question reminds us of the conditions necessary for receiving Baptism. Adults should be instructed in the faith before receiving this sacrament; however, a period of "Christian initiation" is not required if there is a good reason, such as danger of death.

The Church's Magisterium stresses the obligation to baptize children without delay. "The fact that children are incapable of making a personal profession of faith does not deter the Church from conferring this sacrament on them; what it does is baptize them in its own faith. This teaching was already clearly expressed by St Augustine: 'Children are presented for the reception of spiritual grace, not so much by those who carry them in their arms—although also by them, if they are

76

[34]And the eunuch said to Philip, "About whom, pray, does the prophet say this, about himself or about some one else?" [35]Then Philip opened his mouth, and beginning with this scripture he told him the good news of Jesus. [36]And as they went along the road they came to some water, and the eunuch said, "See, here is water! What is to prevent my being baptized?"[h] [38]And he commanded the chariot to stop, and they both went down into the water, Philip and the eunuch, and he baptized him. [39]And when

Lk 24:27

Acts 10:47;
11:17

good members of the Church—as by the universal society of saints and faithful. [...] It is Mother Church herself who acts in her saints, because the whole Church begets each and all' (*Letters*, 98, 5; cf. *Sermons*, 176, 2). St Thomas Aquinas, and after him most theologians, take up the same teaching: the child who is baptized does not believe for itself, by a personal act of faith, but rather through others 'by the faith of the Church which is communicated to the child' (*Summa theologiae*, 3, 69, 6, ad 3; cf. 68, 9, ad 3). This same teaching is expressed in the new rite of Baptism, when the celebrant asks the parents and godparents to profess the faith of the Church 'in which the children are being baptized'" (*Instruction on Infant Baptism*, 20 October 1980).

The Instruction goes on to say that "it is true that apostolic preaching is normally addressed to adults, and that the first to be baptized were adults who had been converted to the Christian faith. From what we read in the New Testament we might be led to think that it deals only with adults' faith. However, the practice of Baptism of infants is based on an ancient tradition of apostolic origin, whose value must not be underestimated; furthermore, Baptism has never been administered without faith: in the case of infants the faith that intervenes is the Church's own faith. Besides, according to the Council of Trent's teaching on the sacraments, Baptism is not only a sign of faith: it is also the cause of faith" (ibid).

Christian parents have a duty to see that their children are baptized quickly. The *Code of Canon Law* specifies that "parents are obliged to see that their infants are baptized within the first few weeks. As soon as possible after the birth, indeed often before it, they are to approach the parish priest to ask for the sacrament for their child, and to be themselves duly prepared for it" (can. 867).

8:37. This verse, not to be found in some Greek codexes or in the better translations, was probably a gloss which later found its way into the text. In the Vulgate it is given in this way: "*Dixit autem Philippus: Si credis ex toto corde, licet. Et respondens ait: Credo, Filium Dei esse Jesum Christum*" (see RSV note below) This very ancient gloss, inspired by baptismal liturgy, helps to demonstrate that faith in Christ's divine worship was the nucleus of the creed a person had to subscribe to in order to be baptized. On this occasion Philip, guided by the Holy Spirit, lays down no further condition and he immediately proceeds to baptize the Ethiopian.

8:39. St John Chrysostom pauses to note that the Spirit takes Philip away without

h. Other ancient authorities add all or most of verse 37, *And Philip said, "If you believe with all your heart, you may." And he replied, "I believe that Jesus Christ is the Son of God."*

1 Kings 18:12
Lk 24:31–32

Acts 21:8

they came up out of the water, the Spirit of the Lord caught up Philip; and the eunuch saw him no more, and went on his way rejoicing. [40]But Philip was found at Azotus, and passing on he preached the gospel to all the towns till he came to Caesarea.

---

giving him time to rejoice with the man he has just baptized: "Why did the Spirit of the Lord bear him away? Because he had to go on to preach in other cities. We should not be surprised that this happened in a divine rather than a human way" (*Hom. on Acts*, 19).

The official "went on his way rejoicing" that God had made him his son through Baptism. He had received the gift of faith, and with the help of divine grace he was ready to live up to all the demands of that faith, even in adverse circumstances: quite probably he would be the only Christian in all Ethiopia.

Faith is a gift of God and is received as such at Baptism; but man's response is necessary if this gift is not to prove fruitless.

Baptism is one of the sacraments which imprints an indelible mark on the soul and which can be received only once. However, a baptized person needs to be continually renewing his commitment; this is not something to be done only during the Easter liturgy: in his everyday activity he should be striving to act like a son of God.

It is natural and logical for the Ethiopian to be so happy, for Baptism brings with it many graces. These St John Chrysostom lists, using quotations from the Gospels and from the letters of St Paul: "The newly baptized are free, holy, righteous, sons of God, heirs of heaven, brothers and co-heirs of Christ, members of his body, temples of God, instruments of the Holy Spirit. ... Those who yesterday were captives are today free men and citizens of the Church. Those who yesterday were in the shame of sin are now safe in righteousness; not alone are they free, they are holy" (*Baptismal Catechesis*, 3, 5).

9:1–3. The Roman authorities recognized the moral authority of the Sanhedrin and even permitted it to exercise a certain jurisdiction over members of Jewish communities outside Palestine—as was the case with Damascus. The Sanhedrin even had the right to extradite Jews to Palestine (cf. 1 Mac 15:21).

Damascus was about 230–250 kilometres (150 miles) from Jerusalem, depending on which route one took. Saul and his associates, who would probably have been mounted, would have had no difficulty in doing the journey in under a week. This apparition took place towards the end of the journey, when they were near Damascus.

9:2. "The Way": the corresponding word in Hebrew also means religious behaviour. Here it refers to both Christian lifestyle and the Gospel itself; indirectly it means all the early followers of Jesus (cf. Acts 18:25f; 19:9, 23; 22:4) and all those who come after them and are on the way to heaven; it reminds us of Jesus' words, "The gate is narrow and the way is hard, that leads to life, and those who find it are few" (Mt 7:14).

9:3–19. This is the first of the three accounts of the calling of Saul—occurring probably between the years 34 and 36—that are given in the Acts of the Apostles (cf. Acts 22:5–16; 26:10–18); where important events are concerned, St Luke does not mind repeating himself.

6. THE CONVERSION OF ST PAUL

Saul on his way to Damascus

9 ¹But Saul, still breathing threats and murder against the disciples of the Lord, went to the high priest ²and asked him for
letters to the synagogues at Damascus, so that if he found any
belonging to the Way, men or women, he might bring them bound
to Jerusalem. ³Now as he journeyed he approached Damascus,

Acts 22:5–16;
26:10–18
Gal 1:12–17

Acts 8:3

Once again the Light shines in the darkness (cf. Jn 1:5). It does so here in a spec-
tacular way and, as in every conversion,
it makes the convert see God, himself
and others in a new way.

However, the episode on the road to
Damascus is not only a conversion. It
marks the beginning of St Paul's vocation: "What amazes you seems natural to
me: that God has sought you out in the
practice of your profession!

"This is how he sought the first, Peter
and Andrew, James and John, beside
their nets, and Matthew, sitting in the
custom-house.

"And—wonder of wonders!—Paul,
in his eagerness to destroy the seed of
Christianity" (St Josemaría Escrivá, *The
Way*, 799).

The background to St Luke's concise
account is easy to fill in. There would
have been no Hellenist Christians left in
Jerusalem: they had fled the city, some
going as far afield as Phoenicia, Cyprus
and Antioch. Many had sought refuge in
Damascus, and Saul must have realized
that their evangelizing zeal would win
many converts among faithful Jews in
that city. Saul genuinely wanted to serve
God, which explains his readiness to
respond to grace. Like most Jews of his
time, he saw the Messiah as a political
liberator, a warrior-king, a half-heavenly,
half-earthly figure such as described in
the apocryphal *Book of Enoch*, 46: "It is
impossible to imagine how even his
glance terrifies his enemies. Wherever he

turns, everything trembles; wherever his
voice reaches everything is overwhelmed
and those who hear it are dissolved as
wax in fire." A hero of this type does not
fall into the power of his enemies, much
less let them crucify him; on the contrary,
he is a victor, he annihilates his enemies
and establishes an everlasting kingdom
of peace and justice. For Saul, Jesus'
death on a cross was clear proof that he
was a false messiah; and the whole
notion of a brotherhood of Jews and
Gentiles was inconceivable.

He has almost reached Damascus
when a light flashes; he is thrown onto
the ground and hears a voice from
heaven calling his name twice, in a tone
of sad complaint.

Saul surrenders unconditionally and
places himself at the Lord's service. He
does not bemoan his past life; he is ready
to start anew. No longer is the Cross a
"scandal": it has become for him a sign
of salvation, the "power of God", a
throne of victory, whose praises he will
sing in his epistles. Soon St Paul will
learn more about this Way and about all
that Jesus did and taught, but from this
moment onwards, the moment of his
calling, he realizes that Jesus is the risen
Messiah, in whom the prophecies find
fulfilment; he believes in the divinity of
Christ: he sees how different his idea of
the Messiah was from the glorified, pre-
existing and eternal Son of God; he
understands Christ's mystical presence in
his followers: "Why do you persecute

1 Cor 15:8

and suddenly a light from heaven flashed about him. [4]And he fell to the ground and heard a voice saying to him, "Saul, Saul, why do you persecute me?" [5]And he said, "Who are you, Lord?" And he said, "I am Jesus, whom you are persecuting;* [6]but rise and enter the city, and you will be told what you are to do." [7]The men

Dan 10:7

who were travelling with him stood speechless, hearing the voice but seeing no one. [8]Saul arose from the ground; and when his eyes were opened, he could see nothing; so they led him by the hand and brought him into Damascus. [9]And for three days he was without sight, and neither ate nor drank.

Ananias baptizes Saul

1 Sam 3:4

[10]Now there was a disciple at Damascus called Ananias. The Lord said to him in a vision, "Ananias." And he said, "Here I am,

---

me?" In other words, he realizes that he has been chosen by God, called by God, and he immediately places himself at his service.

9:4. This identification of Christ and Christians is something which the apostle will later elaborate on when he speaks of the mystical body of Christ (cf. Col 1:18; Eph 1:22f).

St Bede comments as follows: "Jesus does not say, 'Why do you persecute my members?', but, 'Why do you persecute me?', because he himself still suffers affronts in his body, which is the Church. Similarly Christ will take account of the good actions done to his members, for he said, 'I was hungry and you gave me food ...' (Mt 25:35), and explaining these words he added, 'As you did it to one of the least of these my brethren, you did it to me' (Mt 25:40)" (*Super Act. expositio*, ad loc.).

9:5–6. In the Vulgate and in many other translations these words are added between the end of v. 5 and the start of v. 6: "It is hard for thee to kick against the goad. And he, trembling and astonished, said: Lord, what wilt thou have me to

do? And the Lord said to him". These words do not seem to be part of the original sacred text but rather a later explanatory gloss; for this reason the New Vulgate omits them. (The first part of the addition comes from Paul's address in Acts 26:14.)

9:6. The calling of Saul was exceptional as regards the manner in which God called him; but the effect it had on him was the same as what happens when God gives a specific calling to the apostolate to certain individual Christians, inviting them to follow him more closely. Paul's immediate response is a model of how those who receive these specific callings should act (all Christians, of course, have a common calling to holiness and apostolate that comes with Baptism).

Paul VI describes in this way the effects of this specific kind of vocation in a person's soul: "The apostolate is [...] an inner voice, which makes one both restless and serene, a voice that is both gentle and imperious, troublesome and affectionate, a voice which comes unexpectedly and with great events and then, at a particular point, exercises a strong attraction, as it were revealing to us our

Lord." [11]And the Lord said to him, "Rise and go to the street called Straight, and inquire in the house of Judas for a man of Tarsus named Saul; for behold, he is praying, [12]and he has seen a man named Ananias come in and lay his hands on him so that he might regain his sight." [13]But Ananias answered, "Lord, I have heard from many about this man, how much evil he has done to thy saints* at Jerusalem; [14]and here he has authority from the chief priests to bind all who call upon thy name." [15]But the Lord said to him, "Go, for he is a chosen instrument of mine to carry my name before the Gentiles and kings and the sons of Israel; [16]for I will show him how much he must suffer for the sake of my name." [17]So Ananias departed and entered the house. And laying his hands on him he said, "Brother Saul, the Lord Jesus who

1 Cor 1:2

1 Cor 4:9–13
2 Cor 11:23–28
2 Tim 2:11–12

Acts 15:8;
22:14–16

---

life and our destiny. It speaks prophetically and almost in a tone of victory, which eventually dispels all uncertainty, all timidity and all fear, and which facilitates—making it easy, desirable and pleasant—the response of our whole personality, when we pronounce that word which reveals the supreme secret of love: Yes; Yes, Lord, tell me what I must do and I will try to do it, I will do it. Like St Paul, thrown to the ground at the gates of Damascus: What would you have me do?

"The roots of the apostolate run deep: the apostolate is vocation, election, interior encounter with Christ, abandonment of one's personal autonomy to his will, to his invisible presence; it is a kind of substitution of our poor, restless heart, inconstant and at times unfaithful yet hungry for love, for his heart, the heart of Christ which is beginning to pulsate in the one who has been chosen. And then comes the second act in the psychological drama of the apostolate: the need to spread, to do, to give, to speak, to pass on to others one's own treasure, one's own fire. [...]

"The apostolate becomes a continuous expansion of one's soul, the exuberance of a personality taken over by Christ and animated by his Spirit; it becomes a

need to hasten, to work, to do everything one can to spread the Kingdom of God, to save other souls, to save all souls" (Homily, 14 October 1968).

9:11. Straight Street runs through Damascus from east to west and can still be identified today.

9:13. Ananias refers to Christ's followers as "saints"; this was the word normally used to describe the disciples, first in Palestine and then in the world at large. God is *the* Holy One (cf. Is 6:3); as the Old Testament repeatedly says, those who approach God and keep his commandments share in this holiness: "The Lord said to Moses, 'Say to all the congregation of the people of Israel, You shall be holy; for I the Lord your God am holy'" (Lev 19:1–2).

The use of this term is an example of the spiritual sensitivity of our first brothers and sisters in the faith: "What a moving name—saints!—the early Christians used to address each other! ...

"Learn to be a brother to your brothers" (St J. Escrivá, *The Way*, 469).

9:15–16. Our Lord calls St Paul his "vessel of election", which is a Hebraic-

Tob 11:10–15   appeared to you on the road by which you came, has sent me that
you may regain your sight and be filled with the Holy Spirit."
[18]And immediately something like scales fell from his eyes and he
regained his sight. Then he rose and was baptized, [19]and took food
and was strengthened.

Paul begins his apostolate

Gal 1:16   For several days he was with the disciples at Damascus. [20]And in
the synagogues immediately he proclaimed Jesus, saying, "He is
the Son of God." [21]And all who heard him were amazed, and said,
"Is not this the man who made havoc in Jerusalem of those who
called on this name? And he has come here for this purpose, to
Acts 18:5, 28   bring them bound before the chief priests." [22]But Saul increased
all the more in strength, and confounded the Jews who lived in
Damascus by proving that Jesus was the Christ.

---

ism equivalent to "chosen instrument", and he tells Ananias how much the apostle will have to suffer on his account. A Christian called to the apostolate is also, by virtue of this divine vocation, an instrument in the hands of God; to be effective he must be docile: he must let God use him and must do what God tells him.

The task God has given him is far beyond Paul's ability—"to carry my name before the Gentiles and kings and the sons of Israel". In Acts we will see how Paul fulfils his mission, with the help of God's grace and suffering a great deal on account of his name. Down through the centuries, in diverse circumstances, those whom the Lord elects to carry out specific missions will also be able to perform them if they are good instruments who allow grace to act in them and who are ready to suffer for their ideals.

9:19. In spite of the exceptional manner in which God called St Paul, he desired him to mature in the normal way—to be instructed by others and learn God's will

through them. In this case he chose Ananias to confer Baptism on Paul and teach him the basics of the Christian faith.

In Ananias we can see a trace of the role of the spiritual director or guide in Christian asceticism. There is a principle which states that "no one can be a good judge in his own case, because everyone judges according to his own inclinations" (cf. Cassian, *Collationes*, 16, 11). A person guiding a soul has a special "grace of state" to make God's will known to him; and even if the guide makes a mistake, the person who is being guided will—if obedient—always do the right thing, always do God's will. In this connexion St Vincent Ferrer says: "Our Lord Jesus Christ, without whom we can do nothing, will not give his grace to him who, though he has access to an expert guide, rejects this precious means of sanctification, thinking that he can look after on his own everything that touches on his salvation. He who has a director, whom he obeys in everything, will reach his goal more easily and more quickly than if he acted as his own guide, even if he

Paul flees from Damascus

[23]When many days had passed, the Jews plotted to kill him, [24]but their plot became known to Saul. They were watching the gates day and night, to kill him; [25]but his disciples took him by night and let him down over the wall, lowering him in a basket.

2 Cor 11:32–33

Barnabas and Paul in Jerusalem

[26]And when he had come to Jerusalem he attempted to join the disciples; and they were all afraid of him, for they did not believe that he was a disciple. [27]But Barnabas took him, and brought him to the apostles, and declared to them how on the road he had seen the Lord, who spoke to him, and how at Damascus he had preached boldly in the name of Jesus. [28]So he went in and out among them at Jerusalem, [29]preaching boldly in the name of the Lord. And he spoke and disputed against the Hellenists; but they were seeking to kill him. [30]And when the brethren knew it, they brought him down to Caesarea, and sent him off to Tarsus.

Gal 1:18f

Acts 11:25
Gal 1:21

be very intelligent and have the very best of spiritual books" (*Treatise on the Spiritual Life*, 2, 1).

On the spiritual guidance of ordinary Christians, who seek holiness and carry out apostolate in the context of everyday life, St Escrivá, writes: "A director—you need one, so that you can give yourself to God, and give yourself fully ... by obedience. You need a director who understands your apostolate, who knows what God wants: that way he will second the work of the Holy Spirit in your soul, without taking you from your place, filling you with peace, and teaching you how to make your work fruitful" (*The Way*, 62).

9:20–23. In his letter to the Galatians (cf. Gal 1:16f) St Paul tells of how he went into Arabia after his conversion and then returned to Damascus. He spent almost three years away, and it was on his return that he preached the divinity of Jesus, using all his energy and learning, now placed at the service of Christ. This surprised and confounded the Jews, who immediately began to take action against him.

9:25. In 2 Corinthians 11:32f St Paul tells of how he fled, after King Aretas tried to seize him at the instigation of the Jews of Damascus.

9:26. This is the first time Paul presents himself in Jerusalem after his conversion. He went up to see Peter, with whom he spent fifteen days (cf. Gal 1:18), and put himself at Peter's disposal; and to check that his teaching was in line with that of the apostles.

Barnabas (see the note on 4:36–37) dispelled the Jerusalem community's initial understandable suspicion of their one-time persecutor. They had been only too well aware of his determination to suppress the Church and had not yet heard about his preaching in Damascus.

During his short stay in Jerusalem Paul preached boldly his faith in the divinity of Jesus and met the same kind of opposition as he did in Damascus.

9:30. For the second time St Paul has to flee for his life. Commenting on this episode, St John Chrysostom explains

Growth of the Church

Acts 2:46

³¹So the church throughout all Judea and Galilee and Samaria had peace and was built up; and walking in the fear of the Lord and in the comfort of the Holy Spirit it was multiplied.

7. ST PETER'S ACTIVITY

Curing of a paralyzed man at Lydda

Acts 8:4

³²Now as Peter went here and there among them all, he came down also to the saints that lived at Lydda. ³³There he found a man named Aeneas, who had been bedridden for eight years and

---

that, in addition to grace, human resourcefulness has a part to play in apostolic activity. "The disciples were afraid that the Jews would do to Saul what they had done to St Stephen. This may be why they sent him to preach the Gospel in his homeland, where he would be safer. In this action of the apostles you can see that God does not do everything directly, by means of his grace, and that he frequently lets his disciples act in line with the rule of prudence" (*Hom. on Acts*, 20).

Chrysostom also sees in Paul's earlier flight from Damascus an example of prudent conduct: "Despite his great desire to be with God, he first had to carry out his mission for the salvation of souls. [...] Jesus Christ does not preserve his apostles from dangers: he lets them confront them, because he wants men to use the resources of prudence to escape from them. Why does he arrange things in this way? In order to have us understand that the apostles are also men and that grace does not do everything in its servants. Otherwise, would people not have seen them as inert and lifeless things? That is why the apostles did many things by following the dictates of prudence. Let us follow their example and use all our natural abilities to work with grace for the salvation of our brethren" (ibid.).

9:31. St Luke breaks his narrative to give an over-view of the steady progress of the Church as a whole and of the various communities that have grown up as a result of the Christians' flight from Jerusalem (cf. Acts 2:41, 47; 4:4; 5:14; 6:1, 7; 11:21, 24; 16:5). He emphasizes the peace and consolation the Holy Spirit has brought them. This note of justified optimism and trust in God confirms that God is with his Church and that no human force can destroy it (cf. 5:39).

9:32. Acts now turns to St Peter's apostolic activity in Palestine. Lydda (cf. 9:32–35), Joppa (cf. 9:36–43) and Maritime Caesarea (cf. 10:24–28; 12:19) were some of the cities in which the head of the apostles preached the Good News.

"St Luke goes on to speak about Peter and his visits to the faithful. He does not want to give the impression that fear is the reason for Peter's leaving Jerusalem, and so he first gives an account of the situation of the Church, after indicating, previously, that Peter had stayed in Jerusalem during the persecution. [...] Peter acts like a general reviewing his troops to see that they are properly trained and in good order, and to discover where his presence is most needed. We see him going in all direc-

was paralyzed. ³⁴And Peter said to him, "Aeneas, Jesus Christ heals you; rise and make your bed." And immediately he rose. ³⁵And all the residents of Lydda and Sharon saw him, and they turned to the Lord.

Acts 3:7

Peter raises Tabitha to life

³⁶Now there was at Joppa a disciple named Tabitha, which means Dorcas or Gazelle. She was full of good works and acts of charity. ³⁷In those days she fell sick and died; and when they had washed her, they laid her in an upper room. ³⁸Since Lydda was near Joppa, the disciples, hearing that Peter was there, sent two men to him entreating him, "Please come to us without delay."

Lk 12:33

---

tions and we find him in all parts. If he makes this present journey it is because he thinks that the faithful are in need of his teaching and encouragement" (St John Chrysostom, *Hom. on Acts*, 21).

The last report Acts gives of St Peter deals with his intervention at the Council of Jerusalem (chap. 15).

9:33–35. St Peter takes the initiative; he does not wait for the paralyzed man to seek his help. We are told about the man being sick for eight years, to show how difficult he was to cure—and yet through the power of Jesus Christ he is cured "immediately". "Why did Peter not wait for the man to show his faith? Why did he not first ask him if he wanted to be cured? Surely because it was necessary to impress the people by means of this miracle" (St John Chrysostom, *Hom. on Acts*, 21). However, the conversion of the people of Lydda and Sharon was also the result of Peter's work: miracles are not designed to make life easier for the apostles; their tireless preaching is by no means secondary or superfluous.

9:36–43. Joppa (Jaffa, today virtually part of Tel Aviv) is mentioned in the writings of Tell-el-Amarna where it is called Iapu. Its people were converted to

Judaism in the time of Simon Maccabeus (*c*.140 BC).

The miracle of the raising of Tabitha by Peter is the first one of its kind reported in Acts. Here, as in the Gospel, miracles are performed to awaken faith in those who witness them with good dispositions and a readiness to believe. In this case the miracle is a kindness God shows Tabitha to reward her virtues, and an encouragement to the Christians of Joppa.

"In the Acts of the Apostles," St Cyprian writes, "it is clear that alms not only free us from spiritual death, but also from temporal death. Tabitha, a woman who did many 'good works and acts of charity,' had taken ill and died: and Peter was sent for. No sooner had he arrived, with all the diligence of his apostolic charity, than he was surrounded by widows in tears ... , praying for the dead woman more by gestures than by words. Peter believed that he could obtain what they were asking for so insistently and that Christ's help would be available in answer to the prayers of the poor in whose persons he himself had been clothed. [...] And so it was: he did come to Peter's aid, to whom he had said in the Gospel that he would grant everything asked for in his name. For this reason he

85

Mk 5:40

Lk 7:15
Acts 3:7

Acts 10:6

³⁹So Peter rose and went with them. And when he had come, they took him to the upper room. All the widows stood beside him weeping, and showing coats and garments which Dorcas made while she was with them. ⁴⁰But Peter put them all outside and knelt down and prayed; then turning to the body he said, "Tabitha, rise." And she opened her eyes, and when she saw Peter she sat up. ⁴¹And he gave her his hand and lifted her up. Then calling the saints and widows he presented her alive. ⁴²And it became known throughout all Joppa, and many believed in the Lord. ⁴³And he stayed in Joppa for many days with one Simon, a tanner.

---

stops the course of death and the woman returns to life, and to the amazement of all she revives, restoring her risen body to the light of day. Such was the power of works of mercy, of good deeds" (*De opere et eleemosynis*, 6).

9:43. Tanning was a permitted trade, but observant Jews regarded it as unclean because it involved contact with dead animals (cf. Lev 11:39: "If any animal of which you may eat dies, he who touches its carcass shall be unclean until the evening").

By staying with Simon the tanner, St Peter shows that these Jewish prohibitions and standards no longer oblige in conscience. The freedom of the Gospel takes over and the only reason why one might sometimes observe them would be out of charity, to avoid giving scandal.

10:1–48. The conversion of the pagan Cornelius is one of the high points of Acts. It is an extremely important event because it demonstrates the fact that the Gospel is addressed to all men and shows that the power of the Holy Spirit knows no limits.

Up to this point the Gospel has been preached only to Jews. Its extension to the Samaritans was seen as an announcement of salvation to people who had at one time formed part of the chosen people. By preaching only to Jews, the

disciples were having regard to the fact that the people of Israel were the only people chosen by God to be bearers of the divine promises: as such, they had a right to be the first to receive the definitive message of salvation. Our Lord himself had acted on this principle, and he had told his disciples to preach only "to the lost sheep of the house of Israel" (Mt 10:6; cf. 15:24).

The apostles had not yet asked themselves whether this preferential right of the Jewish people to receive the Gospel proclamation implied a certain exclusive right. Now God steps in to make Peter realize that the Good News is meant for all: it is his desire that all men be saved and therefore the Christians need to shed the narrow ideas of Judaism as regards the scope of salvation.

Peter is surprised to learn this, but he is completely docile to the voice of God and now begins to play an active part in the fulfilment of the divine promises. "God had previously foretold", St Cyprian writes, "that in the fulness of time many more faithful worshippers would adhere to him, people from every nation, race and city; that they would receive mercy through the divine gifts which the Jews had lost through not appreciating their own religion" (*Quod idola dii non sint*, 11).

St Luke describes the conversion of Cornelius at great length and in great

The vision of the centurion Cornelius

10 [1]At Caesarea there was a man named Cornelius, a centurion of what was known as the Italian Cohort, [2]a devout man who feared God with all his household, gave alms liberally to the people, and prayed constantly to God. [3]About the ninth hour of the day he saw clearly in a vision an angel of God coming in and saying to him, "Cornelius." [4]And he stared at him in terror, and said, "What is it, Lord?" And he said to him, "Your prayers and your alms have ascended as a memorial before God. [5]And now send men to Joppa, and bring one Simon who is called Peter;

Lk 7:5

Acts 9:10
Tob 12:12
Lk 1:12
Rev 8:3–4

detail, deliberately repeating parts of the story to make sure that its key features are fully grasped. His whole account shows how important it is that pagans can and in fact do enter the Church without first being Jews.

Cornelius is regarded as the first pagan convert to Christianity. We do not know if the baptism of the Ethiopian, narrated in chapter 8, occurred after that of Cornelius or if the Ethiopian was in fact a pagan (cf. the note on Acts 8:27); but in any case that was an isolated, marginal event which does not affect the solemn character of the Roman centurion's conversion, which affects the core of the economy of salvation.

10:1. Maritime Caesarea, where Cornelius was living, should not be confused with Caesarea Philippi, where our Lord promised the primacy to Peter (cf. Mt 16:13–20). Maritime Caesarea was the seat of the Roman governor and was situated on the coast, about 100 kilometres (60 miles) from Jerusalem. It had a Roman garrison made up of auxiliaries, that is, not of legionaries.

10:2. Cornelius was a religious man, one who "feared God". "God-fearing men" or "God-fearers" was a special expression used to describe people who worshipped the God of the Bible and practised the Law of Israel without being formal con-

verts to Judaism (cf. the note on Acts 2:5–11).

He was not a proselyte and therefore had not been circumcised (cf. Acts 11:3). "Do not imagine that grace was given them [Cornelius and the Ethiopian] because of their high rank: God forbid! It was because of their piety. Scripture mentions their distinguished stations to show the greatness of their piety; for it is more remarkable when a person in a position of wealth and power is such as these were" (St John Chrysostom, *Hom. on Acts*, 22).

In religious terms Cornelius was rather like the centurion in Capernaum, whose faith Jesus praises in St Luke's Gospel (7:1ff). Some authors think that Cornelius was a member of the Roman *gens* of that name and that St Luke, who, in writing Acts, had Roman readers in mind, takes special pleasure in recounting the story of Cornelius.

10:4. "Prayers and alms" were regarded by Jews and Christians as works pleasing to God and an expression of genuine piety. Cornelius' true devotion brings God's grace and mercy upon himself and his household. "Do you see how the work of the Gospel begins among the Gentiles? Through a devout man, whose deeds have made him worthy of this favour" (*Hom. on Acts*, 22).

The habitual practice of almsgiving—the epitome of many virtues—is

⁶he is lodging with Simon, a tanner, whose house is by the seaside." ⁷When the angel who spoke to him had departed, he called two of his servants and a devout soldier from among those that waited on him, ⁸and having related everything to them, he sent them to Joppa.

Peter's vision

⁹The next day, as they were on their journey and coming near the city, Peter went up on the housetop to pray, about the sixth hour. ¹⁰And he became hungry and desired something to eat; but while they were preparing it, he fell into a trance ¹¹and saw the heaven opened, and something descending, like a great sheet, let down by four corners upon the earth. ¹²In it were all kinds of animals and reptiles and birds of the air. ¹³And there came a voice to him, "Rise, Peter; kill and eat." ¹⁴But Peter said, "No, Lord; for I have

Ezek 4:14

---

highly praised in the Old Testament. "Give alms from your possessions," says the Book of Tobit, " ... so you will be laying up a good treasure for yourself against the day of necessity. For charity delivers from death and keeps you from entering the darkness; and for all who practise it charity is an excellent offering in the presence of the Most High" (4:7, 9–11; cf. 12:9). Almsgiving is an excellent work of mercy which sanctifies the giver and denotes God's preferential love for him.

"Give, and it will be given to you" (Lk 6:38): these words of Christ, which his disciples should keep before their minds, are echoed in Christian writings down the ages. "Give to everyone what he asks you for, and do not claim it back, for it is the Father's wish that you give to all from the gifts you yourself have received. Blessed is he who, in accord with God's command, gives alms to the needy" (*Didache*, 1, 5)

Generous alms to help those in need, and contributions to the upkeep of the Church, its ministers and its works of zeal, are the responsibility of all Christians. It is not a matter of giving whatever

one has left over. Obviously, people to whom God has given wealth and resources in plenty have to give more alms. The fact that they are well-to-do is a sign of the will of God, and he expects them to be ready to meet the reasonable needs of their neighbours.

A Christian who does not understand this obligation or is reluctant to meet it runs the risk of becoming like that rich man (cf. Lk 16:19ff) who was so selfish and so attached to his wealth that he failed to realize that the Lord had placed Lazarus at his gate for him to help him.

" '*Divitiae, si affluant, nolite cor apponere*. Though riches may increase keep your heart detached.' Strive, rather, to use them generously. And, if necessary, heroically. Be poor of spirit" (St Josemaría Escrivá, *The Way*, 636).

"True detachment leads us to be very generous with God and with our fellow men. It makes us actively resourceful and ready to spend ourselves in helping the needy. A Christian cannot be content with a job that only allows him to earn enough for himself and his family. He will be big-hearted enough to give others a helping hand both out of charity and as a

never eaten anything that is common or unclean." [15]And the voice came to him again a second time, "What God has cleansed, you must not call common." [16]This happened three times, and the thing was taken up at once to heaven.*

Mt 15:11
Rom 14:14
1 Tim 4:4

[17]Now while Peter was inwardly perplexed as to what the vision which he had seen might mean, behold, the men that were sent by Cornelius, having made inquiry for Simon's house, stood before the gate [18]and called out to ask whether Simon who was called Peter was lodging there. [19]And while Peter was pondering the vision, the Spirit said to him, "Behold, three men are looking for you. [20]Rise and go down, and accompany them without hesitation; for I have sent them." [21]And Peter went down to the men and said, "I am the one you are looking for; what is the reason for your coming?" [22]And they said, "Cornelius, a centurion, an upright and God-fearing man, who is well spoken of by the whole

Acts 13:2

---

matter of justice" (St Josemaría Escrivá, *Friends of God*, 126).

"As a memorial": in the Old Testament certain sacrifices are described as "memorial"—that is, offered to remind God, to have him be considerate towards the offerer (cf. Lev 2:1–3; Tob 12:12).

10:14. This imperious commandment to eat unclean food is something the apostle initially cannot understand. He reacts like a good Jew who loves and observes the divine law he has learned from his youth, including the regulations referring to food and the distinction between clean and unclean. But now he is invited to rise above so-called legal uncleanness.

Peter's humble attitude to what he is told during the vision enables him to take in God's will and realize that Jewish ritual precepts are not necessary for Christians. He does not arrive at this insight by a process of reasoning: rather, he obeys the voice of God; virtuous obedience, not simple human logic, causes him to change his attitude.

Peter's docility to the Holy Spirit gradually leads him to realize, first, that the regulations forbidding Jews to eat certain kinds of meat do not apply to Christians.

This simple and very important discovery, which he could not have made without special divine intervention, leads him to another even more important one: he now sees the full significance of all Jesus' teaching and realizes that in God's salvific plans Jews and pagans are equals.

Restrictions concerning food had led observant Jews to avoid sitting down to table with pagans. Food regulations and contact with Gentiles were very closely connected with one another and were subject to rigorous prohibition. Once the distinction between clean and unclean food was done away with, there would be no obstacle to communication with pagans: it would become quite clear what it meant in practice to say that the Lord "is not partial" (Deut 10:17), is no respecter of persons, and that having a clean heart is what really matters.

10:20. "Notice that the Holy Spirit does not say, 'Here is the explanation of the vision you have received' but 'I have sent them', to show thereby that obedience is called for and that it is not a

Jewish nation, was directed by a holy angel to send for you to come to his house, and to hear what you have to say." ²³So he called them in to be his guests.

Peter in the house of Cornelius

The next day he rose and went off with them, and some of the brethren from Joppa accompanied him. ²⁴And on the following day they entered Caesarea. Cornelius was expecting them and had

Mt 8:8

called together his kinsmen and close friends. ²⁵When Peter entered, Cornelius met him and fell down at his feet and wor-

Acts 14:15
Rev 19:10

shipped him. ²⁶But Peter lifted him up, saying, "Stand up; I too am a man." ²⁷And as he talked with him, he went in and found

---

matter of asking questions. This sufficed for Peter to realize he had to listen to the Holy Spirit" (St John Chrysostom, *Hom. on Acts*, 22).

10:24. Cornelius, in his zeal, calls in his family and friends to listen to the saving word of God. The group he assembles represents the pagan world which has for centuries been waiting for Christ without knowing it. "I was ready to be sought by those who did not ask for me; I was ready to be found by those who did not seek me" (Is 65:1).

This episode, in which Cornelius the Roman officer plays the leading role, has a much wider significance. His conversion means that the Jews are not the only heirs of the promises: it shows that the Gospel brings a universal remedy to solve a universal need. "Cornelius was such a servant of God that an angel was sent to him, and to his merits must be attributed the mysterious event through which Peter was to rise above the restrictions of circumcision. ... Once the apostle baptized him, the salvation of the Gentiles had begun" (St Jerome, *Epistles*, 79, 2).

10:25–26. It is difficult at first for pagans to realize what is happening when God manifests himself to them, makes

his will known and confers his gifts upon them through the medium of other men: their first reaction is to think that these must be celestial beings or gods in human form (cf. 14:11), until it is quite clear that they are men of flesh and blood. That is how it is: men and women are the defective but essential instruments whom God normally uses to make known his plans of salvation. God in his providence acts in this way, first in the Old Testament and particularly in the New Testament; a prime example is to be seen in the Christian priesthood.

"Every high priest [is] chosen from among men" (Heb 5:1) to be sent back to his brethren as a minister of intercession and forgiveness. "He must therefore be a member of the human race, for it is God's desire that man have one of his like to come to his aid" (St Thomas Aquinas, *Commentary on Heb*, 5, 1).

It has been said that everything about the Gospel of Jesus Christ is quite excellent, except the persons of his ministers—because these priests, who have been consecrated by a special sacrament, are also sons of Adam, and they still have the weak nature of sons of Adam even after being ordained.

"Most strange is this in itself [...] but not strange, when you consider it is the appointment of an all-merciful God; not

many persons gathered; ²⁸and he said to them, "You yourselves   Gal 2:12
know how unlawful it is for a Jew to associate with or to visit any
one of another nation; but God has shown me that I should not
call any man common or unclean. ²⁹So when I was sent for, I
came without objection. I ask then why you sent for me."

³⁰And Cornelius said, "Four days ago, about this hour, I was
keeping the ninth hour of prayer in my house; and behold, a man
stood before me in bright apparel, ³¹saying, 'Cornelius, your
prayer has been heard and your alms have been remembered
before God. ³²Send therefore to Joppa and ask for Simon who is
called Peter; he is lodging in the house of Simon, a tanner, by the
seaside.' ³³So I sent for you at once, and you have been kind

strange in him. [...] The priests of the New Law are men, in order that they may 'condole with those who are in ignorance and error, because they too are encompassed with infirmity' (Heb 5:2)" (St J. H. Newman, *Discourses addressed to Mixed Congregations*).

If priests were not men of flesh and blood, they would not feel for others, who are made of the same stuff; they would not understand their weakness. But in fact they do share the human condition and do experience the same temptations.

10:28. "The apostle did not wish it to appear that he was doing something prohibited out of consideration for Cornelius. Peter desires to make it plain that the Lord is the only reason for his action. That is why he reminds them that contact with pagans and even entering their houses is forbidden" (St John Chrysostom, *Hom. on Acts*, 23).

Peter justifies his actions, which are not in line with the way a strict Jew would act, by saying that he is obeying God's will, made known to him only a short while before. The Gospel no longer recognizes any distinction between clean and unclean people. All are equal in the sight of God if they listen to his word with a pure heart and repent their sins.

10:33. Grace disposes Cornelius to accept Peter's words as coming from God. The centurion was a man of good will and upright conscience, who worshipped God according to his lights. Prior to meeting Peter, he is an example of the religious person who sincerely seeks the truth and is therefore on the way to ensuring his eternal destiny. The Second Vatican Council teaches that "those who, through no fault of their own, do not know the Gospel of Christ or his Church, but who nevertheless seek God with a sincere heart, and, moved by grace, try in their actions to do his will as they know it through the dictates of their conscience—those too may achieve eternal salvation" (*Lumen gentium*, 16).

However, the spiritual blessings given to Cornelius and those with him go further than this: they actually prepare them to enter the Church. When God gives initial graces to people who are not yet Christians, he wishes them to attain the fullness of grace, which they will find in the Catholic Church. "This is God's intention, this is what he does. If he did not despise the Magi, the Ethiopian, the thief or the courtesan, how much less will he despise those who practise righteousness and desire it" (St John Chrysostom, *Hom. on Acts*, 23).

enough to come. Now therefore we are all here present in the sight of God, to hear all that you have been commanded by the Lord."

Peter preaches to Cornelius

Deut 0:17
Rom 2:11
Gal 2:6
1 Pet 1:17

Is 56:7
Rom 15:16

Is 52:7

Is 61:1
Mt 3:16
Acts 4:27

Acts 1:8

1 Cor 15:4
Lk 24:43
Jn 14:22

Acts 17:31
2 Tim 4:1
1 Pet 4:5

³⁴And Peter opened his mouth and said: "Truly I perceive that God shows no partiality, ³⁵but in every nation any one who fears him and does what is right is acceptable to him. ³⁶You know the word which he sent to Israel, preaching good news of peace by Jesus Christ (he is Lord of all), ³⁷the word which was proclaimed throughout all Judea, beginning from Galilee after the baptism which John preached: ³⁸how God anointed Jesus of Nazareth with the Holy Spirit and with power; how he went about doing good and healing all that were oppressed by the devil, for God was with him. ³⁹And we are witnesses to all that he did both in the country of the Jews and in Jerusalem. They put him to death by hanging him on a tree; ⁴⁰but God raised him on the third day and made him manifest; ⁴¹not to all the people but to us who were chosen by God as witnesses, who ate and drank with him after he rose from the dead. ⁴²And he commanded us to preach to the people, and to

10:34–43. Peter's short address is his first to non-Jews. It begins with the central idea that God is impartial: he wants all men to be saved through the proclamation of the Gospel (vv. 34–36). This is followed by a summary of Jesus' public life (vv. 37–41) and, finally, the statement (the first time it appears in Acts) that Jesus Christ has been made Judge of the living and the dead (v. 42). As in all Christian preaching to Gentiles, proofs from Scripture take a secondary place (v. 43).

10:34. This verse refers to 1 Samuel 16:7, where the Lord, in connexion with the anointing of David as king of Israel, tells the prophet, "Do not look on his appearance or on the height of his stature, because I have rejected him; for the Lord sees not as man sees; man looks on the outward appearance, but the Lord looks on the heart." When God calls and offers salvation to his elect, he does not

judge as men do. With him distinctions regarding social class, race, sex or education do not count.

Here St Peter proclaims that the Old Testament prophecies about the Jews and the Gentiles forming one single nation (Is 2:2–4; Joel 2:28; Amos 9:12; Mich 4:1) and Jesus' words calling everyone to enter his Kingdom (cf. Mt 8:11; Mk 16:15–16; Jn 10:16) should be interpreted literally.

10:40. Peter's summary of the Gospel of Jesus (vv. 37–41) reaches its climax with his statement that "God raised him on the third day." This had become the usual way of referring to our Lord's resurrection (cf. 1 Cor 15:4); see the note on Acts 4:10.

10:42. This verse refers to Christ's role as Judge: he has been made supreme Judge over all mankind and will deliver his judgment at his second coming

testify that he is the one ordained by God to be judge of the living and the dead. ⁴³To him all the prophets bear witness that every one who believes in him receives forgiveness of sins through his name."

Is 33:24
Jer 31:34

The baptism of Cornelius and his household

⁴⁴While Peter was still saying this, the Holy Spirit fell on all who heard the word. ⁴⁵And the believers from among the circumcised who came with Peter were amazed, because the gift of the Holy Spirit had been poured out even on the Gentiles. ⁴⁶For they heard them speaking in tongues and extolling God. Then Peter declared, ⁴⁷"Can any one forbid water for baptizing these people who have received the Holy Spirit just as we have?" ⁴⁸And he commanded them to be baptized in the name of Jesus Christ. Then they asked him to remain for some days.

Acts 11:15;
15:8

Acts 2:4–11;
19:6

Acts 8:36; 11:17

In Jerusalem Peter justifies his conduct

11 ¹Now the apostles and the brethren who were in Judea heard that the Gentiles also had received the word of God. ²So when Peter went up to Jerusalem, the circumcision party crit-

---

(Parousia). "The Sacred Scriptures inform us that there are two comings of the Son of God: the one when he assumed human flesh for our salvation in the womb of a virgin; the other when he shall come at the end of the world to judge all mankind" (*St Pius V Catechism*, 1, 8, 2).

Christ's coming as Judge means that men will appear before him twice, to render an account of their lives—of their thoughts, words, deeds and omissions. The first judgment will take place "when each of us departs this life; for then he is instantly placed before the judgment-seat of God, where all that he has ever done or spoken or thought during his life shall be subjected to the most rigid scrutiny. This is called the particular judgment. The second occurs when on the same day and in the same place all men shall stand together before the tribunal of their Judge […], and this is called the general judgment" (ibid., 1, 8, 3).

10:44–48. This scene is reminiscent of Pentecost. There the Holy Spirit came down on the first disciples, Jews all of them. Now he is given to Gentiles, unexpectedly and irresistibly. It is as if the Lord wanted to confirm to Peter everything he had so far revealed to him about the admission of Cornelius to the Church. The centurion and his family are baptized on Peter's instructions, without first becoming Jews through circumcision.

11:1–18. Some members of the Jerusalem community are shocked to learn that Peter has eaten with people who are legally unclean and has allowed them to be baptized without first being circumcised.

"The circumcision party" refers, therefore, to those Christians who are scandalized by the Gospel's attitude to the ritual prohibitions and ethnic exclusiveness of the Mosaic Law.

The apostle's address has a positive effect and sets their minds at ease. This

Acts 10:28, 48
Eph 2:11

Acts 10:9–48

icized him, ³saying, "Why did you go to uncircumcised men and eat with them?" ⁴But Peter began and explained to them in order: ⁵"I was in the city of Joppa praying; and in a trance I saw a vision, something descending, like a great sheet, let down from heaven by four corners; and it came down to me. ⁶Looking at it closely I observed animals and beasts of prey and reptiles and birds of the air. ⁷And I heard a voice saying to me, 'Rise, Peter; kill and eat.' ⁸But I said, 'No, Lord; for nothing common or unclean has ever entered my mouth.' ⁹But the voice answered a second time from heaven, 'What God has cleansed you must not call common.' ¹⁰This happened three times, and all was drawn up again into heaven. ¹¹And that very moment three men arrived at the house in which we were, sent to me from Caesarea. ¹²And the Spirit told me to go with them, making no distinction. These six brethren also accompanied me, and we entered the man's house. ¹³And he told us how he had seen the angel standing in this house and saying, 'Send to Joppa and bring Simon called Peter; ¹⁴he will declare to you a message by which you will be saved, you and all

attitude of the disciples, who are interested only in the will of God and the spread of the Gospel, shows how ready they are to accept instruction: their initial reserve was quite conscientious. Peter once again describes the vision he received (10:9–23), to show that if he had not baptized Cornelius he would have been disobeying God.

This account of the vision differs slightly from his earlier one, the main addition being in vv. 15–16, which connect the coming of the Holy Spirit at Pentecost (2:1ff) with his descent on the Gentile converts in Caesarea (10:44).

Unfortunately the stubborn Judaizing tendencies exhibited by some members of the infant Church took a long time to disappear, as is dramatically borne out in some of St Paul's letters: he refers to "false brethren secretly brought in, who slipped in to spy on our freedom which we have in Jesus Christ, that they might bring us into bondage" (Gal 2:4) and warns Christians to be on their guard against fanatics of the Law of Moses

who are self-serving and "want to pervert the gospel of Christ" (Gal 1:7).

11:19–30. This account links up with Acts 8:1–4, which describes the flight of Christians from Jerusalem due to the first persecution following on the martyrdom of St Stephen. We are now told about the spread of the Gospel to Antioch on the Orontes, the capital of the Roman province of Syria. Antioch was the first major city of the ancient world where the word of Jesus Christ was preached. It was the third city of the empire, after Rome and Alexandria, with a population of about half a million and a sizeable Jewish colony, and was a very important cultural, economic and religious centre.

In Antioch the Gospel is proclaimed not only to Jews and proselytes. These Hellenist Jews from Jerusalem preach the Gospel to all and sundry as part of their ordinary everyday activity. St Luke does not give us any names: the preachers are ordinary Christians. "Notice", says St John Chrysostom, "that it is grace which

your household.' [15]As I began to speak, the Holy Spirit fell on them just as on us at the beginning. [16]And I remembered the word of the Lord, how he said, 'John baptized with water, but you shall be baptized with the Holy Spirit.' [17]If then God gave the same gift to them as he gave to us when we believed in the Lord Jesus Christ, who was I that I could withstand God?" [18]When they heard this they were silenced. And they glorified God, saying, "Then to the Gentiles also God has granted repentance unto life."

Acts 1:5

Acts 15:8–9;
10:47

Acts 14:27

Beginning of the Church in Antioch

[19]Now those who were scattered because of the persecution that arose over Stephen travelled as far as Phoenicia and Cyprus and Antioch, speaking the word to none except Jews. [20]But there were some of them, men of Cyprus and Cyrene, who on coming to Antioch spoke to the Greeks[i] also, preaching the Lord Jesus. [21]And the hand of the Lord was with them, and a great number that believed turned to the Lord. [22]News of this came to the ears of the church in Jerusalem, and they sent Barnabas to Antioch.

Acts 8:1–4

Acts 2:47

Acts 4:36; 8:14

does everything. And also reflect on the fact that this work is begun by unknown workers and only when it begins to prosper do the apostles send Barnabas" (*Hom. on Acts*, 25).

The Christian mission at Antioch played a key part in the spread of Christianity. Evangelization of non-Jews becomes the norm; it is not just something which happens in a few isolated cases. Nor is it limited to "God-fearers"; it extends to all the Gentiles. The centre of gravity of the Christian Church begins to move from Jerusalem to Antioch, which will become the springboard for the evangelization of the pagan world.

11:20. The title "Lord", often applied to Jesus in the New Testament and in the early Church, is a confession of faith in his divinity. To say "Jesus is Lord" (1 Cor 12:3; Rom 10:9) is the same as saying that Jesus Christ is God. It means that he is worshipped as the only Son of the Father and as sovereign of the Church,

and receives the cult of *latria* which is rendered to God alone.

This acclamation of Jesus as Lord shows that from the very beginning the young Christian communities knew that he had dominion over all mankind and was not just the Messiah of one nation.

11:22–26. The community at Jerusalem, where the apostles were based, felt responsible for everything that happened in the Christian mission-field. This was why they sent Barnabas to oversee developments in Antioch. He was a man whom the apostles trusted, noted for his virtue (he was mentioned in Acts 4:36).

No doubt it was because of all the work opening before the preachers of the Gospel that Barnabas sought out Paul, who had returned to Tarsus after his conversion and his visit to Jerusalem (9:30). Barnabas probably knew that the future apostle was the very man he needed to join him in the work of evangelization about to be undertaken by the Antiochene

i. Other ancient authorities read *Hellenists*

95

Acts 13:43; 14:22

Acts 6:5

Acts 9:30

Acts 26:28

1 Pet 4:16

²³When he came and saw the grace of God, he was glad; and he exhorted them all to remain faithful to the Lord with steadfast purpose; ²⁴for he was a good man, full of the Holy Spirit and of faith. And a large company was added to the Lord. ²⁵So Barnabas went to Tarsus to look for Saul; ²⁶and when he had found him, he brought him to Antioch. For a whole year they met with[j] the church, and taught a large company of people; and in Antioch the disciples were for the first time called Christians.

church. Barnabas' sense of responsibility and his zeal to find labourers for the Lord's harvest (cf. Mt 9:38) lead to the first of the great missionary journeys, in which Paul's vocation finds full scope.

11:26. We do not exactly know who first began to describe the disciples as "Christians". In any event the fact that they were given a name shows that everyone recognized them as an identifiable group. The name also suggests that the term *Christos* —Messiah, Anointed—is no longer regarded simply as a messianic title but also as a proper name.

Some Fathers of the Church see this name as further indication that people do not become disciples of the Lord through human causes. "Although the holy apostles were our teachers and have given us the Gospel of the Saviour, it is not from them that we have taken our name: we are *Christians* through Christ and it is for him that we are called in this way" (St Athanasius, *Oratio I contra arianos*, 2).

11:27. This is the first reference to prophets in the first Christian communities (cf. 13:1). As was the case with the Old Testament prophets, these prophets of the early Church receive special illumination from God—charisms—to speak in his name under the inspiration of the Holy Spirit. Their function is not only to predict future events (cf. 11:28; 21:11)

but to show the way the divine promises and plans contained in Sacred Scripture have been fulfilled.

Acts refers to prophets a number of times. In addition to Agabus, it describes as prophets Judas and Silas (15:32) and the daughters of Philip the deacon (21:9). We also know that Paul had the gift of prophecy (cf. 1 Cor 12–14). In the infant Church the prophetic office was subordinate to the apostolic ministry and was exercised under the control of the apostles in the service and building up of the Christian community. "And God has appointed in the church first apostles, second prophets, third teachers" (1 Cor 12:28).

The gift of prophecy in the sense of a special charism as found in the early years of the Church is not to be found in later times. But the gifts of the Holy Spirit are still to be found in all the members of the mystical body of Christ, varying with the ecclesial role which each person has.

The hierarchy of the Church, with the Pope as its head, has the prophetic mission of unerringly proclaiming true teaching within and without the Church.

"The holy People of God", Vatican II teaches, "shares also in Christ's prophetic office: it spreads abroad a living witness to him, especially by a life of faith and love. [...] The whole body of the faithful, who have an anointing that comes from

j. Or *were guests of*

Antioch helps the Church in Judea

[27]Now in these days prophets came down from Jerusalem to Antioch. [28]And one of them named Agabus stood up and foretold by the Spirit that there would be a great famine over all the world; and this took place in the days of Claudius. [29]And the disciples determined, every one according to his ability, to send relief to the brethren who lived in Judea; [30]and they did so, sending it to the elders by the hand of Barnabas and Saul.

Acts 13:1; 15:32

Acts 21:10

Gal 2:10

Acts 12:25

---

the holy one (cf. 1 Jn 2:20, 27) cannot err in matters of belief. This characteristic is shown in the supernatural appreciation of the faith [*sensus fidei*] of the whole people, when, 'from the bishops to the last of the faithful' (St Augustine, *De praed. sanct.*, 14, 27) they manifest a universal consent in matters of faith and morals. By this appreciation of the faith, aroused and sustained by the Spirit of truth, the People of God, guided by the sacred teaching authority [*magisterium*], and obeying it, receives not the mere word of men, but truly the word of God (cf. 1 Thess 2:13), the faith once for all delivered to the saints (cf. Jude 3). The People unfailingly adheres to this faith, penetrates it more deeply with right judgment, and applies it more fully in daily life.

"It is not only through the sacraments and the ministrations of the Church that the Holy Spirit makes holy the People, leads them and enriches them with his virtues. Allotting his gifts according as he wills (cf. 1 Cor 12:11), he also distributes special graces among the faithful of every rank. By these gifts he makes them fit and ready to undertake various tasks and offices for the renewing and building up of the Church" (*Lumen gentium*, 12).

11:28–29. During the reign of Claudius (41–54), the empire suffered a severe food crisis. This famine, which afflicted Greece, Syria and Palestine as well as Rome during the years AD 47–49, would have been the one which Agabus foretold.

This imminent food shortage is what leads the prosperous Antiochene community to send aid to the mother community in Jerusalem. Like their first brothers in the faith (cf. 4:34), the disciples in Antioch show their charity and concern for their fellow-Christians and prove that they have the true Christian spirit.

11:30. This journey may be the same one as mentioned in 15:2 (cf. Gal 2:1–10). The money which Paul and Barnabas bring to Jerusalem on this occasion should not be confused with the results of the big collection organized later (cf. 24:17).

It is the elders of the community who receive and organize the distribution of the collection. These "elders" or presbyters—the traditional Jewish name for those in charge of the community—seem to have been aides of the apostles. We are not told about how they were instituted, but they appear a number of times in Acts (15:2 — 16:4; 21:18), they perform functions which are somewhat different from those of the Twelve, and they take part in the Council of Jerusalem.

Paul and Barnabas appoint elders and put them in charge of the churches they found during their first great missionary journey (cf. 14:23), and in the epistles to Timothy (5:17–19) and Titus (1:5) those entrusted with an established ministry in each community are described as elders.

Apparently, at the start the terms "bishop" and "elder" (cf. 10:17, 28; 1 Tim 3:2; Tit 1:7) were used interchange-

Persecution by Herod. Peter's arrest and miraculous deliverance

Mt 20:22–23

Jas 5:16

Acts 5:18–23;
16:25–40

12 [1]About that time Herod the king laid violent hands upon some who belonged to the church.* [2]He killed James the brother of John with the sword; [3]and when he saw that it pleased the Jews, he proceeded to arrest Peter also. This was during the days of Unleavened Bread. [4]And when he had seized him, he put him in prison, and delivered him to four squads of soldiers to guard him, intending after the Passover to bring him out to the people. [5]So Peter was kept in prison; but earnest prayer for him was made to God by the church.

[6]The very night when Herod was about to bring him out, Peter was sleeping between two soldiers, bound with two chains, and

ably and then later on came to refer to the two highest levels of the hierarchy. By the second century the meaning of each term was clearly fixed. The difference consists in this: bishops have the fullness of the sacrament of Order (cf. Vatican II, *Lumen gentium*, 11), and presbyters, "true priests of the New Testament [...] after the image of Christ" (ibid., 28), carry out pastoral ministry as co-workers of their bishops and in communion with them.

The New Testament texts use the term "priest" only to refer to the ministers of the Old Law (cf. Mt 8:4; 20:18; Heb 7:23) and as a title belonging to Jesus Christ, the only true Priest (cf. Heb 4:15; 5:5; 8:1; 9:11), from whom all lawful priesthood derives. In general, the early Church avoids, where possible, the use of terminology which might imply that it was simply one more among the many religions in the Greco-Roman world.

12:1–19. This is an account of persecution of the Church by Herod Agrippa (37–44), which took place before the visit of Paul and Barnabas to the Holy City (cf. 11:30).

The information given in this chapter about the latest persecution of the Jerusalem community—more severe and

more general than the earlier crises (cf. 5:17f; 8:1)—gives an accurate picture of the situation in Palestine and describes events in chronological sequence. Prior to this the Roman governors more or less protected the rights of the Jerusalem Christians. Now Agrippa, in his desire to ingratiate himself with the Pharisees, abandons the Christians to the growing resentment and hatred the Jewish authorities and people feel towards them.

This chapter brings to an end, so to speak, the story of the first Christian community in Jerusalem. From now on, attention is concentrated on the church of Antioch. The last stage of the Palestinian Judeo-Christian church, under the direction of James "the brother of the Lord", will not experience the expansion enjoyed by other churches, due to the grave turn which events take in the Holy Land.

12:1. This Herod is the third prince of that name to appear in the New Testament. He was a grandson of Herod the Great, who built the new temple of Jerusalem and was responsible for the massacre of the Holy Innocents (cf. Mt 2:16); he was also a nephew of Herod Antipas, the tetrarch of Galilee at the time of our Lord's death. Herod Agrippa I was a favourite of

sentries before the door were guarding the prison; [7]and behold, an
angel of the Lord appeared, and a light shone in the cell; and he
struck Peter on the side and woke him, saying, "Get up quickly."
And the chains fell off his hands. [8]And the angel said to him,
"Dress yourself and put on your sandals." And he did so. And he
said to him, "Wrap your mantle around you and follow me." [9]And
he went out and followed him; he did not know that what was
done by the angel was real, but thought he was seeing a vision.
[10]When they had passed the first and the second guard, they came
to the iron gate leading into the city. It opened to them of its own
accord, and they went out and passed on through one street; and
immediately the angel left him. [11]And Peter came to himself, and
said, "Now I am sure that the Lord has sent his angel and rescued

1 Kings 19:5

Acts 10:17

---

the emperor Caligula, who gradually gave
him more territory and allowed him to
use the title of king. Agrippa I managed
to extend his authority over all the territory his grandfather had ruled: Roman
governors had ruled Judea up to the year
41, but in that year it was given over to
Herod. He was a sophisticated type of
person, a diplomat, so bent on consolidat-
ing his power that he had become a
master of intrigue and a total opportunist.
For largely political motives he practised
Judaism with a certain rigour.

12:2. James the Greater would have been
martyred in the year 42 or 43. He was the
first apostle to die for the faith and the only
one whose death is mentioned in the New
Testament. The Liturgy of the Hours says
of him: "The son of Zebedee and the
brother of John, he was born in Bethsaida.
He witnessed the principal miracles performed by our Lord and was put to death
by Herod around the year 42. He is held
in special veneration in the city of
Compostela, where a famous church is
dedicated to his name."

"The Lord permits this death," St
John Chrysostom observes, "to show his
murderers that these events do not cause
the Christians to retreat or desist" (*Hom.
on Acts*, 26).

12:5. "Notice the feelings of the faithful
towards their pastors. They do not riot or
rebel; they have recourse to prayer,
which can solve all problems. They do
not say to themselves: We do not count,
there is no point in our praying for him.
Their love led them to pray and they did
not think along those lines. Have you
noticed what these persecutors did without intending to? They made (their vic-
tims) more determined to stand the test,
and (the faithful) more zealous and
loving" (*Hom. on Acts*, 26).

St Luke, whose Gospel reports our
Lord's words on perseverance in prayer
(cf. 11:11–13; 18:1–8), here stresses that
God listens to the whole community's
prayer for Peter. He plans in his providence to save the apostle for the benefit
of the Church, but he wants the outcome
to be seen as an answer to the Church's
fervent prayer.

12:7–10. The Lord comes to Peter's help
by sending an angel, who opens the prison
and leads him out. This miraculous freeing
of the apostle is similar to what happened
at the time of Peter and John's detention
(5:19f) and when Paul and Silas are
imprisoned in Philippi (16:19ff).

This extraordinary event, which must
be understood exactly as it is described,

me from the hand of Herod and from all that the Jewish people were expecting."

Acts 12:25;
13:5, 13; 15:37
Col 4:10
Philem 24
2 Tim 4:11
1 Pet 5:13

[12]When he realized this, he went to the house of Mary, the mother of John whose other name was Mark, where many were gathered together and were praying. [13]And when he knocked at the door of the gateway, a maid named Rhoda came to answer. [14]Recognizing Peter's voice, in her joy she did not open the gate but ran in and told that Peter was standing at the gate. [15]They said to her, "You are mad." But she insisted that it was so. They said, "It is his angel!" [16]But Peter continued knocking; and when they opened, they saw him and were amazed. [17]But motioning to them with his hand to be silent, he described to them how the Lord had

Acts 15:13;
21:18
Gal 1:19

---

shows the loving care God takes of those whom he entrusts with a mission. They must strive to fulfil it, but they will "see" for themselves that he guides their steps and watches over them.

12:12. John Mark was Barnabas' cousin (cf. Col 4:10). He will accompany Barnabas and Paul on the first missionary journey (cf. 13:5) up to when they enter the province of Asia (cf. 13:13). Despite Paul's not wanting to have him on the second journey (cf. 15:37–39), we find him later again as a co-worker of the Apostle (cf. Col 4:10; 2 Tim 4:11) and also as a disciple and helper of Simon Peter (1 Pet 5:13). Church tradition credits him with the authorship of the Second Gospel.

"The house of Mary": this may have been the same house as the Cenacle, where Jesus celebrated his Last Supper with his disciples. See Introduction in *St Mark* (2009), pp. 41–42.

12:15. The first Christians had a very lively faith in the guardian angels and their God-given role of assisting men. In the Old Testament God reveals the existence of angels; on various occasions we see them playing an active part (cf., for example, Gen 48:16; Tob 5:21; etc.). In the apocryphal books of the Old Testament and in writings composed between the two Testaments (which flourished around the time of Christ's life on earth) there are many references to angels. Our Lord spoke about them often, as we can see from the Gospels.

"In many parts of Sacred Scripture it is said that each of us has an angel. Our Lord affirms this when he speaks about children: 'in heaven their angels always behold the face of my Father' (Mt 18:10). And Jacob refers to the angel 'who freed him from all evil'. On this occasion the disciples thought that the angel of the apostle Peter was approaching" (St Bede, *Super Act. expositio,* ad loc.).

The first Christians' behaviour in adversity and their trust in God's help are an enduring example. "Drink at the clear fountain of the Acts of the Apostles. In the twelfth chapter, Peter, freed from prison by the ministry of angels, comes to the house of the mother of Mark. Those inside will not believe the servant girl, who says that Peter is at the door. '*Angelus ejus est!* It must be his angel!' they said. See on what intimate terms the early Christians were with their guardian angels. And what about you?" (St Josemaría Escrivá, *The Way,* 570).

12:17. After Peter and the other apostles leave Jerusalem, the community in that city is governed by James the Less, the

brought him out of the prison. And he said, "Tell this to James and to the brethren." Then he departed and went to another place.

[18]Now when day came, there was no small stir among the soldiers over what had become of Peter. [19]And when Herod had sought for him and could not find him, he examined the sentries and ordered that they should be put to death. Then he went down from Judea to Caesarea, and remained there.

Death of Herod

[20]Now Herod was angry with the people of Tyre and Sidon; and they came to him in a body, and having persuaded Blastus, the king's chamberlain, they asked for peace, because their country

---

"brother" of the Lord; even before that he was a prominent figure in the Jerusalem church. According to Flavius Josephus, this James was stoned to death by order of the Sanhedrin (cf. *Jewish Antiquities*, 20, 200).

We do not know where Peter went after leaving Jerusalem—probably to Antioch or Rome. He was certainly in Antioch at one stage (cf. Gal 2:11), but it may not have been at this point. Tradition does state that Peter had his see in Antioch for a period. We do know that he was present at the Council of Jerusalem. In any event he ultimately settled in Rome.

According to St Jerome, Peter arrived in Rome in the second year of Claudius' reign (43) and had his see there for twenty-five years, up to the fourteenth year of Nero's reign, that is, 68 (cf. *On Famous Men*, 1).

12:20–23. Herod Agrippa I must have died in Caesarea in the year 44 during the games in honour of Claudius. St Luke's brief account agrees with that of Josephus. "When at daybreak of the second day he made his way to the theatre", the Jewish historian writes, "and the rays of the sun made his garments look like silver and made him look splendid, his sycophants acclaimed him as a god and

said, 'Up to this we regarded you as a man, but from now on we shall revere you as one who is more than mortal.' The king accepted this blasphemous flattery: he made no comment. But immediately he began to feel terrible stomach pains and he was dead within five days" (*Jewish Antiquities*, 19, 344–346).

The painful and unexpected death of this king who had persecuted the Church recalls the death of King Antiochus Epiphanes (cf. 2 Mac 9:5ff), another declared enemy of God's elect and of divine Law: "The all-seeing God of Israel struck him with an incurable and unseen blow."

Not content with persecuting the Church, Agrippa attributes to himself glory which belongs only to God; his evil life eventually provokes God to judge him in this way. "The hour of judgment has not yet come, but God wounds the most blameworthy of all, as an object lesson for others" (St John Chrysostom, *Hom. on Acts*, 27).

Agrippa's persecution of the Church and of Christians was the logical result of his failure to acknowledge God as lord of all: Agrippa sees him as a kind of rival. In his pride, he refuses to admit his human limitations and dependence on God; and he goes further and attacks God's work and God's servants. Human

depended on the king's country for food. [21]On an appointed day Herod put on his royal robes, took his seat upon the throne, and made an oration to them. [22]And the people shouted, "The voice of a god, and not of man!" [23]Immediately an angel of the Lord smote him, because he did not give God the glory; and he was eaten by worms and died.

Ezek 28:2

Dan 5:20
2 Mac 9:5, 28

Barnabas and Paul return

Acts 6:7
Acts 11:29;
12:12

[24]But the word of God grew and multiplied. [25]And Barnabas and Saul returned from[k] Jerusalem when they had fulfilled their mission, bringing with them John whose other name was Mark.

---

dignity is only possible if God's majesty is positively asserted and adored: in that recognition and service man's true wisdom lies.

"'*Deo omnis gloria*. All glory to God.' It is an emphatic confession of our nothingness. He, Jesus, is everything. We, without him, are worth nothing: nothing.

"Our vainglory would be just that: vain glory; it would be sacrilegious robbery. There should be no room for that 'I' anywhere" (St Josemaría Escrivá, *The Way*, 780).

12:24. St Luke contrasts the failure and downfall of the Church's persecutors with the irresistible progress of the Word of God.

12:25. They "returned from Jerusalem": following the best Greek manuscripts, the reading accepted by the New Vulgate is "returned to Jerusalem" (cf. RSV note). However, it does not seem to fit in with the end of chapter 11 and the beginning of chapter 13. Therefore, from very early on many Greek manuscripts and translations (including the Sixto-Clementine edition of the Vulgate) read "returned from Jerusalem". It is not clear

which is correct; the Navarre Spanish follows the New Vulgate.

13:1. From this point onwards Luke's account centres on the church of Antioch. This was a flourishing community, with members drawn from all sectors of society. In some respects its organization structure was like that of the Jerusalem church; in others, not. It clearly had ordained ministers who were responsible for its government, who preached and administered the sacraments; alongside these we find prophets (cf. 11:27) and teachers, specially trained members of the community.

In the early Church "teachers" were disciples well versed in Sacred Scripture who were given charge of catechesis. They instructed the catechumens and other Christians in the basic teaching of the Gospel as passed on by the apostles, and some of them had a capacity for acquiring and communicating to others an extensive and profound knowledge of the faith.

Teachers do not necessarily have to be priests or preachers. Preaching was usually reserved to ordained ministers; teachers had an important position in the Church: they were responsible for on-

---

k. Other ancient authorities read *to*

PART THREE

The spread of the Church among the Gentiles. Missionary journeys of St Paul

8. ST PAUL'S FIRST APOSTOLIC JOURNEY

Paul and Barnabas are sent on a mission

13 ¹Now in the church at Antioch there were prophets and teachers, Barnabas, Symeon who was called Niger, Lucius of Cyrene, Manaen a member of the court of Herod the tetrarch, and Saul. ²While they were worshipping the Lord and fasting, the

Acts 4:36;
11:20, 27

Gal 1:15

going doctrinal and moral education and were expected faithfully to hand on the same teaching as they themselves had received. A virtuous life and due learning would have protected them against any temptation to invent new teachings or go in for mere speculation not based on the Gospel (cf. 1 Tim 4:7; 6:20; Tit 2:1).

The *Letter to Diognetus* describes the ideal Christian teacher: "I do not speak of passing things nor do I go in search of new things, but, like the disciple of the apostles that I am, I become a teacher of peoples. I do nothing but hand on what was given me by those who made themselves worthy disciples of the truth" (11, 1).

13:2–3. "Worship" of the Lord includes prayer, but it refers primarily to the celebration of the Blessed Eucharist, which is at the centre of all Christian ritual. This text indirectly establishes a parallel between the Mass and the sacrificial rite of the Mosaic Law. The Eucharist provides a Christian with the nourishment he needs, and its celebration "causes the Church of God to be built up and grow in stature" (Vatican II, *Unitatis redintegratio*, 15). Significantly, the Eucharist is

associated with the start of this new stage in the expansion of the Church.

Paul and Barnabas receive a missionary task directly from the Holy Spirit, and by an external sign—the laying on of hands—the Antiochene community prays God to go with them and bless them. In his promotion of the spread of the Church the Holy Spirit does not act at a distance, so to speak. Every step in the progress of the Church in the world is rightly attributed to the initiative of the Paraclete. It is as if God were repeatedly ratifying his salvific plans to make it perfectly plain that he is ever-faithful to his promises. "The mission of the Church is carried out by means of that activity through which, in obedience to Christ's command and moved by the grace and love of the Holy Spirit, the Church makes itself fully present to all men and people" (Vatican II, *Ad gentes*, 5).

The dispatch of Paul and Barnabas is inspired by the Holy Spirit, but it is also an ecclesial act: the Church gives them this charge, specifying God's plans and activating the personal vocation of the two envoys.

The Lord, "who had set me apart before I was born, and had called me by

Acts 6:6

Holy Spirit said, "Set apart for me Barnabas and Saul for the work to which I have called them." ³Then after fasting and praying they laid their hands on them and sent them off.

Paul and Barnabas in Cyprus

Acts 12:12

⁴So, being sent out by the Holy Spirit, they went down to Seleucia; and from there they sailed to Cyprus. ⁵When they arrived at

---

his grace [sent me] in order that I might preach him among the Gentiles" (Gal 1:15–16), now arranges, through the Church, for this mission to begin.

Fasting and prayer are the best preparation for the spiritual enterprise on which Paul and Barnabas are about to embark. "First, prayer; then, atonement; in the third place, very much 'in the third place', action" (St Josemaría Escrivá, *The Way*, 82). They know very well that their mission is not man-made and that it will produce results only with God's help. The prayer and penance which accompany apostolate are not just aimed at obtaining graces from God for others: the purpose of this prayer and fasting is to purify hearts and lips, so that the Lord will be at their side and ensure that none of their words "fall to the ground" (1 Sam 3:19).

13:4–14:28. This first missionary journey took Paul, accompanied by Barnabas, to Cyprus and central Galatia, in Asia Minor. He left Antioch in the spring of 45 and returned almost four years later, after preaching Christ to both Jews and Gentiles wherever he went.

St Luke's account, which covers chapters 13 and 14, is sketchy but accurate. At Seleucia (the port of Antioch, about 35 kilometres or 22 miles from the city) they embarked for Cyprus, the largest island in the eastern Mediterranean, where Barnabas came from. They disembarked at Salamis, the island's main city and port. There they went to the Jewish synagogues on a series of sabbaths.

In v. 6 it says that they crossed the island to Paphos, which is on the extreme west. This would have taken them several months because, although it is only 150 kilometres as the crow flies, there were many towns with Jewish communities, and since they had to stay in each for a number of sabbaths their progress would have been slow. We are told nothing about the result of this work of evangelizing en route from Salamis to Paphos, but the indications are that it was fruitful, because Barnabas will later go back to Cyprus, accompanied by Mark (cf. 15:39), to consolidate the work done on this first mission. New Paphos was where the proconsul resided.

From there they went on board ship again and travelled north, probably disembarking, after a short crossing, at Attalia. After a few miles they reached Perga in Pamphylia, a barren, inhospitable region at the base of the Taurus mountains, where Mark took leave of his companions.

Going from Perga to Pisidian Antioch (v. 14) meant a difficult journey of about 160 kilometres over mountain roads. This other Antioch was 1,200 metres above sea level and would have had a sizeable Jewish community, connected with the trade in hides. The busy commercial life of the region helped the spread of the Christian message (v. 49). Paul addressed his preaching to the Gentiles because of the hostility of many Jews.

Salamis, they proclaimed the word of God in the synagogues of
the Jews. And they had John to assist them. ⁶When they had gone
through the whole island as far as Paphos, they came upon a certain magician, a Jewish false prophet, named Bar-Jesus. ⁷He was
with the proconsul, Sergius Paulus, a man of intelligence, who
summoned Barnabas and Saul and sought to hear the word of
God. ⁸But Elymas the magician (for that is the meaning of his   2 Tim 3:8

The apostles were expelled and they headed for Iconium, about 130 kilometres south east, where they stayed some months and then left because of disturbances created by both Gentiles and Jews: they had to flee to the region of Lycaonia, to two minor cities, Lystra and Derbe. There were very few Jews in Lystra, and no synagogue, and therefore Paul preached to the local people, in the open air; but some Jews, who had arrived from Antioch and Iconium, stoned him and left him for dead. Possibly with the help of Timothy (cf. 16:1) they managed to reach Derbe, where they made many disciples, and then set out on the journey home, retracing their steps through Lystra, Iconium and Pisidian Antioch. Things had quieted down, the local magistrates were new, and with a little prudence everything worked out quite well. The new disciples were confirmed in the faith, and priests, elders, were appointed to each local church. Paul and Barnabas then went back to Pamphylia and Attalia, where they took a ship for Antioch, arriving probably well into the year 49.

13:5. In each city he visits, Paul usually begins his preaching of the Gospel in the local synagogue. This is not simply a tactic: it is in line with what he knows is God's plan of salvation. Like Jesus, he feels obliged to proclaim the Kingdom first to "Israelites [for] to them belong the sonship, the glory, the covenants, the giving of the law, the worship, and the promises; to them belong the patriarchs,

and of their race, according to the flesh, is the Christ" (Rom 9:4–5). The Jews have a right to be the first to have the Gospel preached to them, for they were the first to receive the divine promises (cf. 13:46).

Although many Jews choose not to listen to or understand the word of God, there are many who do accept the Gospel for what it is—the fulness of the Old Testament. All over the Diaspora thousands of men and women like Simeon and Anna, who were awaiting the Kingdom and serving the God of their forefathers with fasting and prayer (cf. Lk 2:25, 37), will receive the light of the Holy Spirit enabling them to recognize and accept Paul's preaching as coming from God.

It is true that the many Jewish communities established in the main cities of the Roman empire often hindered the spread of the Gospel; yet their very existence played a providential part in its progress.

13:6–7. Since the year 22 Cyprus had been a senatorial province and, as such, was governed by a proconsul. Sergius Paulus was the brother of the philosopher Seneca, Nero's tutor. He is described here as "a man of intelligence", in other words, he was a man of upright conscience and with the right disposition to listen to the word of God. The proconsul's discernment helps him resist and reject the evil influence of the false prophet Bar-Jesus.

name) withstood them, seeking to turn away the proconsul from the faith. [9]But Saul, who is also called Paul, filled with the Holy Spirit, looked intently at him [10]and said, "You son of the devil, you enemy of all righteousness, full of all deceit and villainy, will you not stop making crooked the straight paths of the Lord? [11]And now, behold, the hand of the Lord is upon you, and you shall be blind and unable to see the sun for a time." Immediately mist and darkness fell upon him and he went about seeking people to lead him by the hand. [12]Then the proconsul believed, when he saw what had occurred, for he was astonished at the teaching of the Lord.

Jn 8:44

Jn 9:39

Lk 4:32

Paul and Barnabas cross into Asia Minor

Acts 15:38

[13]Now Paul and his company set sail from Paphos, and came to Perga in Pamphylia. And John left them and returned to Jerusalem; [14]but they passed on from Perga and came to Antioch of Pisidia.

13:9. Here we learn, in an aside, that Saul has changed his name and now calls himself Paul. He did not do this at God's bidding, as in the case of Abraham (cf. Gen 17:5) or that of Peter (cf. Mt 16:18), to show that God had given him a new charge or mission. He was simply following the eastern custom of using a Roman name when it suited. Paul is the Roman name for Saul, and from now on he uses it instead of Saul.

"From his own experience," St Bede says, "the apostle knew that the mind can raise itself to the light from the darkness of the eyes" (*Super Act. expositio*, ad loc.).

The punishment of Elymas does influence Sergius Paulus' conversion, but it is not crucial to it. What convinces the proconsul is the consistency and sublimity of Christian teaching, which speaks for itself to people of good will.

13:11. Paul's punishment of Bar-Jesus, Elymas, is one of the few punitive miracles in the New Testament; in fact his purpose is not so much to punish the false prophet as to convert him. "Paul chooses to convert him by means of a miracle similar to that by which he himself was converted. The words 'for a time' is not the word of one who punishes but of one who converts. If it had been the word of one who punishes it would have left him blind for ever. He punishes him only for a time, and also to win over the proconsul" (St John Chrysostom, *Hom. on Acts*, 28).

13:15. Sabbath services in synagogues went right back to the post-exilic period (after the Babylonian captivity, which lasted from 586 to 539 BC), and by now they had a very settled form. They consisted of readings from Sacred Scripture, preaching and public prayers. No one was especially appointed to preside over these services; the president or ruler of the synagogue could ask any member of the community to take the ceremony (cf. 18:8); he supervised the preparations and made sure that everything was done properly.

Preaching in the synagogue of Antioch of Pisidia

And on the sabbath day they went into the synagogue and sat down. [15]After the reading of the law and the prophets, the rulers of the synagogue sent to them, saying, "Brethren, if you have any word of exhortation for the people, say it." [16]So Paul stood up, and motioning with his hand said:*

"Men of Israel, and you that fear God, listen. [17]The God of this people Israel chose our fathers and made the people great during their stay in the land of Egypt, and with uplifted arm he led them out of it. [18]And for about forty years he bore with[m] them in the wilderness. [19]And when he had destroyed seven nations in the land of Canaan, he gave them their land as an inheritance, for about four hundred and fifty years. [20]And after that he gave them judges until Samuel the prophet. [21]Then they asked for a king; and God gave them Saul the son of Kish, a man of the tribe of Benjamin, for forty years. [22]And when he had removed him, he raised up David to be their king; of whom he testified and said, 'I

Acts 15:21

Ex 3–15
Is 1:2

Deut 1:31

Deut 7:1
Josh 14:2

Gen 15:13
Ex 12:40
Judg 2:16
1 Sam 3:20
1 Sam 8:10
Ps 89:20
Is 44:28

13:16–41. Paul's address here is an excellent example of the way he used to present the Gospel to a mixed congregation of Jews and proselytes. He lists the benefits conferred by God on the chosen people from Abraham down to John the Baptist (vv. 16–25); he then shows how all the messianic prophecies were fulfilled in Jesus (vv. 26–37), and, by way of conclusion, states that justification comes about through faith in Jesus, who died and then rose from the dead (vv. 38–41).

This address contains all the main themes of apostolic preaching, that is, God's saving initiative in the history of Israel (vv. 17–22); reference to the Precursor (vv. 24–25); the proclamation of the Gospel or *kerygma* in the proper sense (vv. 26b–31a); mention of Jerusalem (v. 31b); arguments from Sacred Scripture (vv. 33–37) complementing apostolic teaching and tradition (vv. 38–39); and a final exhortation, eschatological in character, announcing the future

(vv. 40–41). In many respects this address is like those of St Peter (cf. 2:14ff; 3:12ff), especially where it proclaims Jesus as Messiah and in its many quotations from Sacred Scripture, chosen to show that the decisive event of the resurrection confirms Christ's divinity.

Paul gives a general outline of salvation history and then locates Jesus in it as the expected Messiah, the point at which all the various strands in that history meet and all God's promises are fulfilled. He shows that all the steps which lead up to Jesus Christ, even the stage of John the Baptist, are just points on a route. Earlier, provisional, elements must now, in Christ, give way to a new, definitive situation.

"You that fear God" (v. 26): see the notes on Acts 2:5–11 and 10:2.

13:28. Paul does not back off from telling his Jewish listeners about the cross, the painful death freely undergone by the innocent Jesus. They naturally

---

m. Other ancient authorities read *cared for* (Deut 1:31)

have found in David the son of Jesse a man after my heart, who
will do all my will.' ²³Of this man's posterity God has brought to
Israel a Saviour, Jesus, as he promised. ²⁴Before his coming John
had preached a baptism of repentance to all the people of Israel.
²⁵And as John was finishing his course, he said, 'What do you
suppose that I am? I am not he. No, but after me one is coming,
the sandals of whose feet I am not worthy to untie.'

²⁶"Brethren, sons of the family of Abraham, and those among
you that fear God, to us has been sent the message of this salvation. ²⁷For those who live in Jerusalem and their rulers, because
they did not recognize him nor understand the utterances of the
prophets which are read every sabbath, fulfilled these by con-
demning him. ²⁸Though they could charge him with nothing
deserving death, yet they asked Pilate to have him killed. ²⁹And
when they had fulfilled all that was written of him, they took him
down from the tree, and laid him in a tomb. ³⁰But God raised him
from the dead; ³¹and for many days he appeared to those who
came up with him from Galilee to Jerusalem, who are now his

Margin references: 2 Sam 7:12; Lk 3:3; Mt 3:11; Jn 1:20–27; Acts 3:17; Mt 27:22–23; Mt 27:59–60; Acts 5:30; Acts 1:3; 3:15; 10:40

---

find it shocking and hurtful, but it is true and it is what brings salvation. "When I came to you, brethren," he says on another occasion, "I did not come proclaiming to you the testimony of God in lofty words or wisdom. For I decided to know nothing among you except Jesus Christ and him crucified" (1 Cor 2:1f).

Sometimes human logic cannot understand how Jesus could have died in this way. But the very fact that he did is evidence of the divine character of the Gospel and supports belief in the Christian faith. With the help of grace man can in some way understand the Lord making himself "obedient unto death, even death on a cross" (Phil 2:8). He can discover some of the reasons why God decided on this superabundant way of redeeming man. "It was very fitting," St Thomas Aquinas writes, "that Christ should die on a cross. First, to give an example of virtue. [...] Also, because this kind of death was the one most suited to atoning for the sin of the first man. ... It was fitting for Christ, in order

to make up for that fault, to allow himself be nailed to the wood, as if to restore what Adam had snatched away. [...] Also, because by dying on the cross Jesus prepares us for our ascent into heaven. [...] And because it also was fitting for the universal salvation of the entire world" (*Summa theologiae*, 3, 46, 4).

Through Jesus' death on the cross we can see how much God loved us and consequently we can feel moved to love him with our whole heart and with all our strength. Only the cross of our Lord, an inexhaustible source of grace, can make us holy.

13:29–31. The empty tomb and the appearances of the risen Jesus to his disciples are the basis of the Church's testimony to the resurrection of the Lord, and they demonstrate that he did truly rise. Jesus predicted that he would rise on the third day after his death (cf. Mt 12:40; 16:21; 17:22; Jn 2:19). Faith in the Resurrection is supported by the fact of

witnesses to the people. [32]And we bring you the good news that   Acts 13:23
what God promised to the fathers, [33]this he has fulfilled to us their
children by raising Jesus; as also it is written in the second psalm,
> 'Thou art my Son,   Ps 2:7
> today I have begotten thee.'

[34]And as for the fact that he raised him from the dead, no more to
return to corruption, he spoke in this way,   Is 55:3
> 'I will give you the holy and sure blessings of David.'

[35]Therefore he says also in another psalm,   Ps 16:10
> 'Thou wilt not let thy Holy One see corruption.'

[36]For David, after he had served the counsel of God in his own   1 Kings 2:10
generation, fell asleep, and was laid with his fathers, and saw cor-   Acts 2:29
ruption; [37]but he whom God raised up saw no corruption. [38]Let it
be known to you therefore, brethren, that through this man for-   Rom 3:20
giveness of sins is proclaimed to you, [39]and by him every one that   Acts 15:11
believes is freed from everything from which you could not be   Rom 10:4
Heb 10:1–4
freed by the law of Moses. [40]Beware, therefore, lest there come
upon you what is said in the prophets:

---

the empty tomb (because it was impossible for our Lord's body to have been stolen) and by his many appearances, during which he conversed with his disciples, allowed them to touch him, and ate with them (cf. Mt 28; Mk 16; Lk 24; Jn 20–21). In his First Letter to the Corinthians (15:3–6) Paul says that "[what I preached was] that Christ died for our sins in accordance with the scriptures, that he was buried, that he was raised on the third day in accordance with the scriptures, and that he appeared to Cephas, then to the twelve. Then he appeared to more than five hundred brethren."

13:32–37. Paul gives three pertinent quotations from Scripture—Ps 2:7 ("Thou art my Son"), Is 55:3 ("I will give you the holy and sure blessings of David") and Ps 16:10 ("thy Holy One"). All refer to aspects of the Lord's resurrection. Taken together, they help support and interpret one another, and to someone familiar with the Bible and with ways of interpreting it then current they reveal the full

meaning of the main texts concerning the promises made to David. Paul's interpretation of Psalms 2 and 16 gets beneath the surface meaning of the texts and shows them to refer to the messianic king who, since he is born of God, will never experience the corruption of the grave.

13:38–39. This passage is reminiscent of Paul's teaching on justification as given in his Letter to the Romans. There we read that God "justifies him who has faith in Jesus" (3:26). The Council of Trent explains that "when the apostle says that man is justified by faith ..., these words must be taken in the sense that [...] 'faith is the beginning of salvation' (St Fulgentius, *De fide ad Petrum*, 1), the basis and root of all justification, without which 'it is impossible to please God' (Heb 11:6)" (*De Iustificatione*, chap. 8).

Once he has received faith, man with the help of grace can address God freely, can accept as true everything that God has revealed, can recognize that he is a

Hab 1:5
> [41] 'Behold, you scoffers, and wonder, and perish;
> for I do a deed in your days,
> a deed you will never believe, if one declares it to you.'"

[42] As they went out, the people begged that these things might
Acts 11:23 be told them the next sabbath. [43] And when the meeting of the synagogue broke up, many Jews and devout converts to Judaism followed Paul and Barnabas, who spoke to them and urged them to continue in the grace of God.

Paul and Barnabas preach to the pagans

[44] The next sabbath almost the whole city gathered together to hear the word of God. [45] But when the Jews saw the multitudes, they were filled with jealousy, and contradicted what was spoken by
Mt 10:6 Paul, and reviled him. [46] And Paul and Barnabas spoke out boldly, saying, "It was necessary that the word of God should be spoken first to you. Since you thrust it from you, and judge yourselves unworthy of eternal life, behold, we turn to the Gentiles. [47] For so
Is 49:6 the Lord has commanded us, saying,

> 'I have set you to be a light for the Gentiles,
> that you may bring salvation to the uttermost parts
> of the earth.'"

---

sinner, can trust in God's mercy and—ready at last to receive Baptism—can decide to keep the commandments and begin to live a new life (cf. ibid., chap. 6).

However, what brings about justification—by eliminating sin and sanctifying the person—is sanctifying grace, with the virtues and gifts that come in its train.

13:45. The opposition of these Jews, who in their jealousy contradict what Paul says, will from now be the typical attitude of the synagogue to the Gospel. It emerges everywhere the apostle goes, with the exception of Beroea (cf. 17:10–12).

13:46. Paul may have been hoping that Christianity would flourish on the soil of Judaism, that the Jews would peacefully and religiously accept the Gospel as the natural development of God's plans. His experience proved otherwise: he encountered the terrible mystery of the infidelity of most of the chosen people, his own people.

Even if Israel had been faithful to God's promises, it would still have been necessary to preach the Gospel to the Gentiles. The evangelization of the pagan world is not a consequence of Jewish rejection of the Word; it is required by the universal character of Christianity. To all men Christianity is the only channel of saving grace; it perfects the Law of Moses and reaches out beyond the ethnic and geographical frontiers of Judaism.

13:47. Paul and Barnabas quote Isaiah 49:6 in support of their decision to preach to the Gentiles. The text referred to Christ, as Luke 2:32 confirms. But now Paul and Barnabas apply it to themselves because the Messiah is "light for the Gentiles" through the preaching of the apostles, for they are conscious of speaking in Christ's

⁴⁸And when the Gentiles heard this, they were glad and glori-
fied the word of God; and as many as were ordained to eternal life
believed. ⁴⁹And the word of the Lord spread throughout all the
region. ⁵⁰But the Jews incited the devout women of high standing
and the leading men of the city, and stirred up persecution against
Paul and Barnabas, and drove them out of their district. ⁵¹But they
shook off the dust from their feet against them, and went to Icon-
ium. ⁵²And the disciples were filled with joy and with the Holy
Spirit.

Rom 8:28–30
Mt 10:14
Acts 18:6

Iconium evangelized. Persecution

14 ¹Now at Iconium they entered together into the Jewish syn-
agogue, and so spoke that a great company believed, both
of Jews and of Greeks. ²But the unbelieving Jews stirred up the
Gentiles and poisoned their minds against the brethren. ³So they
remained for a long time, speaking boldly for the Lord, who bore
witness to the word of his grace, granting signs and wonders to be
done by their hands. ⁴But the people of the city were divided;
some sided with the Jews, and some with the apostles. ⁵When an
attempt was made by both Gentiles and Jews, with their rulers, to
molest them and to stone them, ⁶they learned of it and fled to

Acts 13:14, 44
1 Thess 2:14
Mk 16:17–20
Heb 2:4
2 Tim 3:11

---

name and on his authority. Therefore, probably here "the Lord" refers not to God the Father but to Christ.

13:51. "They shook the dust from their feet": a traditional expression; the Jews regarded as unclean the dust of anywhere other than the holy land of Palestine. Our Lord extended the meaning of the phrase when he told the disciples he was sending them out to preach, "If any one will not receive you or listen to your words, shake off the dust from your feet" (Mt 10:14; cf. Lk 9:5). This gesture of Paul and Barnabas echoes what Jesus said and amounted to "closing the case" or putting on record the unbelief of the Jews.

14:4. "He who is not with me is against me," our Lord says in the Gospel (Mt 12:30). The Word of God is a direct, personal call to which man cannot adopt an indifferent or passive attitude. He has to

take sides, whether he likes it or not; and in fact he does take sides. Many people who persecute or criticize the Church and Christians are often trying to justify their own personal infidelity and resistance to God's grace.

St Luke here describes Paul and Barnabas as "apostles" (cf. 14:14). Even though Paul is not one of the group of "the Twelve", for whom Luke usually reserves the name of apostles, he is regarded as and regarded himself as an apostle by virtue of his unique vocation (cf. 1 Cor 15:9; 2 Cor 11:5) and was tireless in preaching to the Gentiles. When the writings of the Fathers mention "the apostle" without being any more specific than that, they mean St Paul, because he is the apostle most quoted and commented on, due to his many letters.

14:6. Lystra was a Roman colony; Timothy grew up there (cf. 16:1–2).

111

Mt 10:23
Acts 11:19–20

Lystra and Derbe, cities of Lycaonia, and to the surrounding country; [7]and there they preached the gospel.

Curing of a cripple at Lystra

Acts 3:2; 9:33

[8]Now at Lystra there was a man sitting, who could not use his feet; he was a cripple from birth, who had never walked. [9]He listened to Paul speaking; and Paul, looking intently at him and seeing that he had faith to be made well, [10]said in a loud voice, "Stand upright on your feet." And he sprang up and walked. [11]And when the crowds saw what Paul had done, they lifted up their voices, saying in Lycaonian, "The gods have come down to us in the likeness of men!" [12]Barnabas they called Zeus, and Paul, because he was the chief speaker, they called Hermes. [13]And the priest of Zeus, whose temple was in front of the city, brought oxen and garlands to the gates and wanted to offer sacrifice with the people. [14]But when the apostles Barnabas and Paul heard of it,

Mt 9:28

Acts 28:6

14:8–10. "Just as the lame man whom Peter and John cured at the gate of the temple prefigured the salvation of the Jews, so too this cripple represents the Gentile peoples distanced from the religion of the Law and the temple, but now brought in through the preaching of the apostle Paul" (St Bede, *Super Act. expositio*, ad loc.).

We are told that Paul realized the man "had faith to be made well". The man is sure that he is going to be cured of his infirmity and he seems to be hoping also that Paul will cure his soul. Paul responds to the man's faith and, as our Lord did in the case of the paralytic in Capernaum (cf. Mk 2:1ff), he enables him to walk and cleanses his soul of sin.

14:11–13. Astonished by the miracle, the pagans of Lystra are reminded of an ancient Phrygian legend according to which Zeus and Hermes (Mercury) once visited the area in the guise of travellers and worked wonders for those who gave them hospitality. They think this is a repeat and therefore prepare to give Paul and Barnabas honours, thinking they are gods in human form (cf. 10:26).

14:14. Jews rent their garments to symbolize their feelings of shock at something they heard and to reject it out of hand. However, sometimes they did it only as a matter of form and not for genuine religious reasons (cf. Mt 26:65). By rending their garments Paul and Barnabas dramatically display their deepest convictions and religious feelings against the slightest sign of idolatry.

14:15–18. The apostles not only prevent any idolatry being offered them: they try to explain why they act in this way; they tell the Lystrans about the living God, the Creator of all things, who in his providence watches over mankind.

"Throughout history even to the present day, there is found among peoples a certain awareness of a hidden power, which lies behind the course of nature and the events of human life. At times there is even a recognition of a supreme being, or even a Father. This awareness and recognition results in a way of life that is imbued with a deep religious sense" (Vatican II, *Nostra aetate*, 2).

In this short exhortation (which antic-

they tore their garments and rushed out among the multitude, crying, [15]"Men, why are you doing this? We also are men, of like nature with you, and bring you good news, that you should turn from these vain things to a living God who made the heaven and the earth and the sea and all that is in them. [16]In past generations he allowed all the nations to walk in their own ways; [17]yet he did not leave himself without witness, for he did good and gave you from heaven rains and fruitful seasons, satisfying your hearts with food and gladness." [18]With these words they scarcely restrained the people from offering sacrifice to them.

*Acts 10:26;
17:22–30*

*Jer 5:24
Ps 147:8*

Paul is stoned

[19]But Jews came there from Antioch and Iconium; and having persuaded the people, they stoned Paul and dragged him out of the city, supposing that he was dead. [20]But when the disciples gathered about him, he rose up and entered the city; and on the next day he went on with Barnabas to Derbe.

2 Cor 11:25

---

ipates some of the themes of Paul's address in Athens: cf. 17:22–31), the apostles use religious concepts accepted by pagans, trying to bring out their full meaning. They invite their listeners to give up idolatry and turn to the living God, of whom they have a vague knowledge. They speak to them, therefore, about a true God, who transcends man but is ever concerned about him. Everyday experience—the course of history, the changing seasons, and the fulfilment of noble human yearnings—demonstrates the providence of a God who invites people to find him in his works.

This first "natural" encounter with God, presaging future and greater revelations, stirs their consciences to interior conversion, that is, to change their lives and turn away from any action which deprives them of spiritual peace and prevents them from knowing God.

Acknowledging that God exists involves all kinds of practical consequences and is the foundation of the new type of life which the Gospel proposes and makes possible. When a person truly and sincerely recognizes his Creator as

speaking to him through external things and in the intimacy of his conscience, he has taken a huge step in his spiritual life: he has controlled his tendency to assert moral autonomy and false independence and has taken the path of obedience and humility. It becomes easier for him to recognize and accept supernatural revelation under the inspiration of grace.

14:19. Paul mentions this stoning in his Second Letter to the Corinthians. "Five times I have received at the hands of the Jews the forty lashes less one. Three times I have been beaten with rods; once I was stoned" (11:24f).

14:20–22. "If you accept difficulties with a faint heart, you lose your joy and your peace, and you run the risk of not deriving any spiritual profit from the trial" (St J. Escrivá, *The Way*, 696).

St Paul is not cowed by persecution and physical suffering. He knows that this crisis is the prelude to abundant spiritual fruit, and in fact many people in this region do embrace the Gospel.

Even though St Luke records the

113

Return journey to Antioch

Mt 28:19
²¹When they had preached the gospel to that city and had made many disciples, they returned to Lystra and to Iconium and to Mt 10:22 Antioch, ²²strengthening the souls of the disciples, exhorting them Acts 11:23
1 Thess 3:3 to continue in the faith, and saying that through many tribulations Heb 10:36 we must enter the kingdom of God. ²³And when they had Acts 13:3 appointed elders for them in every church, with prayer and fasting, they committed them to the Lord in whom they believed.

²⁴Then they passed through Pisidia, and came to Pamphylia. ²⁵And when they had spoken the word in Perga, they went down Acts 13:1 to Attalia; ²⁶and from there they sailed to Antioch, where they had been commended to the grace of God for the work which they had

---

progress and success of the word of God, he also shows that its preachers certainly encounter the cross (cf. 13:14, 50). The Gospel meets with acceptance everywhere—and also with opposition. "Where there are many laurels", St Ambrose says, "there is fierce combat. It is good for you to have persecutors: that way you attain more rapid success in your enterprises" (*Expositio in Ps 118*, 20, 43).

The apostles have no difficulty in pointing to events to show the disciples that suffering and difficulties form part of Christian living.

"Cross, toil, anguish: such will be your lot as long as you live. That was the way Christ went, and the disciple is not above his master" (St J. Escrivá, *The Way*, 699). "Each one of us has at some time or other experienced that serving Christ our Lord involves suffering and hardship; to deny this would imply that we had not yet found God. [...] Far from discouraging us, the difficulties we meet have to spur us on to mature as Christians. This fight sanctifies us and gives effectiveness to our apostolic endeavours" (St Josemaría Escrivá, *Friends of God,* 28 and 216).

14:23. The appointment of elders in each church means that certain Christians were invested with a ministry of government and religious worship, by a liturgical rite of ordination. These have a share in the hierarchical and priestly ministry of the apostles, from whom their own ministry derives.

"The ministry of priests [...]", Vatican II teaches, "shares in the authority by which Christ himself builds up and sanctifies and rules his Body" (*Presbyterorum ordinis*, 2). The ministerial office of priests is essential to the life of every Christian community, which draws its strength from the word of God and the sacraments. Their priesthoood, derived from our Lord, is essentially different from what is called the "priesthood common to all the faithful".

A man becomes a priest of the New Testament through a special calling from God. "Our vocation," John Paul II told a huge gathering of priests in Philadelphia, "is a gift from the Lord Jesus himself. It is a personal, individual calling: we have been called by our name, just as Jeremiah was" (Homily, 4 October 1979).

The priestly life is a sublime vocation which cannot be delegated or transferred to anyone else. It is a lifelong vocation and means that one has to give himself entirely to God—and this he can do, with the help of grace, because "we do not claim back our gift once given. It cannot be that God, who gave us the impulse to say Yes, should now desire to hear us say No. ...

fulfilled. [27]And when they arrived, they gathered the church Acts 14:3; 15:4 together and declared all that God had done with them, and how he had opened a door of faith to the Gentiles. [28]And they remained no little time with the disciples.

9. THE COUNCIL OF JERUSALEM

Dissension at Antioch; Judaizers

15 [1]But some men came down from Judea and were teaching the brethren, "Unless you are circumcised according to the Gen 17:10
Gal 2:12

"It should not surprise the world that God's calling through the Church should continue, offering us a celibate ministry of love and service according to our Lord Jesus Christ's example. This calling from God touched the very depths of our being. And after centuries of experience the Church knows how appropriate it is that priests should respond in this specific way in their lives, to demonstrate the totality of the Yes they have said to our Lord" (ibid.).

"Since he wishes that no one be saved who has not first believed (cf. Mk 16:16), priests, like the co-workers of the bishops that they are, have as their first duty to proclaim to all men the Gospel of God" (Vatican II, *Presbyterorum ordinis*, 4). To carry out his mission well, a priest needs to be in contact with our Lord all the time—"a personal, living encounter—with eyes wide open and a heart beating fast—with the risen Christ" (John Paul II, Homily in Santo Domingo Cathedral, 26 January 1979).

Reminding priests of their special duty to be witnesses to God in the modern world, John Paul II invites them not only to bear in mind the Christian people, from whom they come and whom they must serve, but also people at large; they should not hide the fact that they are priests: "Do not help the trends towards 'taking God off the streets' by yourselves adopting secular modes of dress and

behaviour" (Address at Maynooth University, 1 October 1979).

14:24–26. Paul and Barnabas return to Syrian Antioch, taking in the cities they have visited—in reverse order: Derbe, Lystra, Icononium, Pisidian Antioch and Perga. At the port of Attalia they take a ship for Syria and arrive shortly afterwards in Antioch. Their journey, which began around the year 45, has taken four years.

Despite the animosity and persecution they experienced in these cities, the two missionaries do not avoid returning. They want to complete arrangements for the government of the new churches and to consolidate the faith of the disciples. The possible risks involved do not cause them any concern.

"Whosoever would save his life will lose it; and whoever loses his life for my sake and the gospel's will save it" (Mk 8:35). "These are mysterious and paradoxical words," John Paul II writes. "But they cease to be mysterious if we strive to put them into practice. Then the paradox disappears and we can plainly see the deep simplicity of their meaning. To all of us this grace is granted in our priestly life and in our zealous service" (*Letter to all priests*, 8 April 1979, 5).

15:1–35. This chapter is the centre of Acts, not just because it comes right in

Gal 2:1–2 custom of Moses, you cannot be saved." ²And when Paul and
Barnabas had no small dissension and debate with them, Paul and
Barnabas and some of the others were appointed to go up to
Jerusalem to the apostles and the elders about this question.

Paul and Barnabas go to Jerusalem

³So, being sent on their way by the church, they passed through
both Phoenicia and Samaria, reporting the conversion of the
Acts 14:27 Gentiles, and they gave great joy to all the brethren. ⁴When they
came to Jerusalem, they were welcomed by the church and the
apostles and the elders, and they declared all that God had done
with them. ⁵But some believers who belonged to the party of the

---

the middle of the book but also because it covers the key event as far as concerns the universality of the Gospel and its unrestricted spread among the Gentiles. It is directly linked to the conversion of the pagan Cornelius; here, with the help of the Holy Spirit, all the consequences of that event are drawn out. Christians with a Pharisee background — "certain men [who] came from James" (Gal 2:12) — arriving in Antioch, assert categorically that salvation is impossible unless a person is circumcised and practises the Law of Moses. They accept (cf. 11:18) that Gentile converts can be baptized and become part of the Church; but they do not properly understand the economy of the Gospel, that it is the *new* way; they think that the Mosaic rites and precepts are all still necessary for attaining salvation. The need arises, therefore, for the whole question to be brought to the apostles and elders in Jerusalem, who form the government of the Church.

15:2. Paul and Barnabas are once again commissioned by the Antiochene community to go to Jerusalem (cf.11:30). Paul says in Galatians 2:2 that this journey to the Holy City was due to a special revelation. Possibly the Holy Spirit inspired him to volunteer for it. "Paul," St Ephrem writes, "so as not to change

without the apostles' accord anything which they would allow to be done perhaps because of the weakness of the Jews, makes his way to Jerusalem to see to the setting aside of the Law and of circumcision in the presence of the disciples: without the apostles' support they [Paul and Barnabas] do not want to set them aside" (*Armenian Commentary on Acts*, ad loc.).

15:4. This does not mean that all the members of the Church were present to receive Paul: the whole Church was morally present in those brethren who attended the gathering and particularly in the apostles and elders.

15:5. "Party": the Greek and the New Vulgate both literally say "heresy". However, in this context the word is not pejorative. It is a correct use of language in view of the religious exclusivity and separateness practised by the Pharisees: they saw themselves as, and in fact were, the rightful representatives of post-exilic Judaism (cf. the note on Acts 13:15). The Pharisees mentioned here were Christians who in practice still lived like Jews.

15:6–21. The hierarchical Church, consisting of the apostles and elders or priests, now meets to study and decide whether

Pharisees rose up, and said, "It is necessary to circumcise them, and to charge them to keep the law of Moses."

Peter's address to the council

⁶The apostles and the elders were gathered together to consider this matter. ⁷And after there had been much debate, Peter rose and said to them, "Brethren, you know that in the early days God made choice among you, that by my mouth the Gentiles should hear the word of the gospel and believe.⁸And God who knows the heart bore witness to them, giving them the Holy Spirit just as he did to us; ⁹and he made no distinction between us and them, but cleansed their hearts by faith. ¹⁰Now therefore why do you make

Acts 2:14

Acts 10:44; 11:15

Mt 11:30; 23:4
Gal 5:1

baptized Gentiles are obliged or not to be circumcised and to keep the Old Law. This is a question of the utmost importance to the young Christian Church and the answer to it has to be absolutely correct. Under the leadership of St Peter, the meeting deliberates at length, but it is not going to devise a new truth or new principles: all it does is, with the aid of the Holy Spirit, to provide a correct interpretation of God's promises and commandments regarding the salvation of men and the way in which Gentiles can enter the New Israel.

This meeting is seen as the first general council of the Church, that is, the prototype of the series of councils of which the Second Vatican Council is the most recent. Thus, the Council of Jerusalem displays the same features as the later ecumenical councils in the history of the Church: a) it is a meeting of the rulers of the entire Church, not of ministers of one particular place; b) it promulgates rules which have binding force for all Christians; c) the content of its decrees deals with faith and morals; d) its decisions are recorded in a written document—a formal proclamation to the whole Church; e) Peter presides over the assembly.

According to the *Code of Canon Law* (can. 338–341) ecumenical councils are assemblies—summoned and presided over by the Pope—or bishops and some

others endowed with jurisiction; decisions of these councils do not oblige unless they are confirmed and promulgated by the Pope. This assembly at Jerusalem probably took place in the year 49 or 50.

15:7–11. Peter's brief but decisive contribution follows on a lengthy discussion which would have covered the arguments for and against the need for circumcision to apply to Gentile Christians. St Luke does not give the arguments used by the Judaizing Christians (these undoubtedly were based on a literal interpretation of the compact God made with Abraham— cf. Gen 17—and on the notion that the Law was perennial).

Once again, Peter is a decisive factor in Church unity. Not only does he draw together all the various legitimate views of those trying to reach the truth on this occasion: he points out where the truth lies. Relying on his personal experience (what God directed him to do in connexion with the baptism of Cornelius: cf. chap. 10), Peter sums up the discussion and offers a solution which coincides with St Paul's view of the matter: it is grace and not the Law that saves, and therefore circumcision and the Law itself have been superseded by faith in Jesus Christ. Peter's argument is not based on

Gal 2:15–21;
3:22–26
Eph 2:1–10

trial of God by putting a yoke upon the neck of the disciples which neither our fathers nor we have been able to bear? [11]But we believe that we shall be saved through the grace of the Lord Jesus, just as they will."

James' speech

[12]And all the assembly kept silence; and they listened to Barnabas and Paul as they related what signs and wonders God had done Acts 12:17
Gal 2:9 through them among the Gentiles. [13]After they finished speaking, James replied, "Brethren, listen to me. [14]Symeon has related how God first visited the Gentiles, to take out of them a people for his name. [15]And with this the words of the prophets agree, as it is written,

Amos 9:11–12

[16]'After this I will return,
And I will rebuild the dwelling of David, which has fallen;

---

the severity of the Old Law or the practical difficulties Jews experience in keeping it; his key point is that the Law of Moses has become irrelevant; now that the Gospel has been proclaimed the Law is not necessary for salvation: he does not accept that it is necessary to obey the Law in order to be saved. Whether one can or should keep the Law for other reasons is a different and secondary matter.

As a gloss on what Peter says, St Ephrem writes that "everything which God has given us through faith and the Law has been given by Christ to the Gentiles through faith and without observance of the Law" (*Armenian Commentary on Acts,* ad loc.).

15:11. St Paul makes the same point to the Galatians: "We ourselves, who are Jews by birth and not Gentile sinners, yet who know that a man is not justified by works of the law but through faith in Jesus Christ, even we have believed in Christ Jesus, in order to be justified by faith in Christ, and not by works of the law, because by works of the law shall no one be justified" (2:15f)."No one can be sanctified after sin," St Thomas Aquinas,

says, "unless it be through Christ. [...] Just as the ancient fathers were saved by faith in the Christ to come, so we are saved by faith in the Christ who was born and suffered" (*Summa theologiae,* 3, 61, 3 and 4).

"That thing is absolutely necessary without which no one can attain salvation: this is the case with the grace of Christ and with the sacrament of Baptism, by which a person is reborn in Christ" (ibid., 84, 5).

15:13–21. James the Less, to whose authority the Judaizers had appealed, follows what Peter says. He refers to the apostle by his Semitic name—Symeon— and accepts that he has given a correct interpretation of what God announced through the prophets. In saying that God had "visited the Gentiles, to take out of them a people for his name" he seems to be giving up the Jewish practice of using "people" to refer to the Israelites (Ex 19:9; Deut 7:6; 14:2) as distinct from the Gentiles. Again the central message of Paul, that baptized pagans also belong to the people of the promise: "You are no longer strangers and sojourners, but you

I will rebuild its ruins,
and I will set it up,
[17]that the rest of men may seek the Lord,
and all the Gentiles who are called by my name,
[18]says the Lord, who has made these things known from of old.'
[19]Therefore my judgment is that we should not trouble those of
the Gentiles who turn to God, [20]but should write to them to
abstain from the pollutions of idols and from unchastity and from
what is strangled[n] and from blood. [21]For from early generations
Moses has had in every city those who preach him, for he is read
every sabbath in the synagogues."

Gen 9:4
Lev 17:11
1 Cor 8:10

Acts 13:27

The council's decision

[22]Then it seemed good to the apostles and the elders, with the
whole church, to choose men from among them and send them to

---

are fellow citizens with the saints and members of the household of God" (Eph 2:19).

James' concurrence with what Peter says and the fact that both are in agreement with the basic principles of Paul's preaching indicate that the Holy Spirit is at work, giving light to all to understand the true meaning of the promise contained in Scripture. "As I see it, the richness of these great events cannot be explained unless it be with help from the same Holy Spirit who was their author" (Origen, *In Ex hom.*, 4, 5).

James immediately goes on to propose that the meeting issue a solemn, formal statement which proclaims the secondary character of the Law and at the same time makes allowance for the religious sensitivity of Jewish Christians by prohibiting four things—1) the eating of meat from animals used in sacrifices to idols; 2) avoidance of fornication, which goes against the natural moral order; 3) eating meat which has blood in it; and 4) eating food made with the blood of animals.

These prohibitions are laid down in Leviticus and to be understood properly they must be read in the light of Leviticus. The Jews considered that if

they ate meat offered to idols this implied in some way taking part in sacrilegious worship (Lev 17:7–9). Although St Paul makes it clear that Christians were free to act as they pleased in this regard (cf. 1 Cor 8–10), he will also ask them not to scandalize "the weak".

Irregular unions and transgressions in the area of sexual morality are mentioned in Leviticus 18:6ff; some of the impediments will later be included in Church marriage law.

Abstention from blood and from the meat of strangled animals (cf. Lev 17:10ff) was based on the idea that blood was the container of life and as such belonged to God alone. A Jew would find it almost impossible to overcome his religious and cultural repugnance at the consumption of blood.

15:22–29. The decree containing the decisions of the Council of Jerusalem incorporating St James' suggestions makes it clear that the participants at the Council are conscious of being guided in their conclusions by the Holy Spirit and that in the last analysis it is God who has decided the matter.

Antioch with Paul and Barnabas. They sent Judas called Barsabbas, and Silas, leading men among the brethren, [23]with the following letter: "The brethren, both the apostles and the elders, to the brethren who are of the Gentiles in Antioch and Syria and Cilicia, greeting. [24]Since we have heard that some persons from us have troubled you with words, unsettling your minds, although we gave them no instructions, [25]it has seemed good to us in assembly to choose men and send them to you with our beloved Barnabas and Paul, [26]men who have risked their lives for the sake of our Lord Jesus Christ. [27]We have therefore sent Judas and Silas, who themselves will tell you the same things by word of mouth. [28]For it has seemed good to the Holy Spirit and to us to lay upon you no greater burden than these necessary things: [29]that you abstain from what has been sacrificed to idols and from blood and from what is strangled[n] and from unchastity. If you keep yourselves from these, you will do well. Farewell."

Acts 15:1

Acts 21:13

"We should take," Melchor Cano writes in the sixteenth century, "the same road as the apostle Paul considered to be the one best suited to solving all matters to do with the doctrine of the faith. [...] The Gentiles might have sought satisfaction from the Council because it seemed to take from the freedom granted them by Jesus Christ, and because it imposed on the disciples certain ceremonies as necessary, when in fact they were not, since faith is the key to salvation. Nor did the Jews object by invoking Sacred Scripture against the Council's decision on the grounds that Scripture seems to support their view that circumcision is necessary for salvation. So, by respecting the Council they gave us all the criteria which should be observed in all later times that is, to place full faith in the authority of synods confirmed by Peter and his legitimate successors. They say, It has seemed good to the Holy Spirit and to us; thus, the Council's decision is the decision of the Holy Spirit himself" (*De locis*, 5, 4).

It is the apostles and the elders, with the whole Church, who designate the people who are to publish the Council's decree, but it is the hierarchy which formulates and promulgates it. The text contains two parts—one dogmatic and moral (v. 28) and the other disciplinary (v. 29). The dogmatic part speaks on imposing no burden other than what is essential and therefore declares that pagan converts are free of the obligation of circumcision and of the Mosaic Law but are subject to the Gospel's perennial moral teaching on matters to do with chastity. This part is permanent: because it has to do with a necessary part of God's salvific will it cannot change. The disciplinary part of the decree lays down rules of prudence which can change, which are temporary. It asks Christians of Gentile background to abstain—out of charity towards Jewish Christians—from what has been sacrificed to idols, from blood and from meat of animals killed by strangulation. The effect on the decree means that the disciplinary rules contained in it, although they derive from the Mosaic

---

n. Other early authorities omit *and from what is strangled*

Reception of the council's decree

[30]So when they were sent off, they went down to Antioch; and having gathered the congregation together, they delivered the letter. [31]And when they read it, they rejoiced at the exhortation. [32]And Judas and Silas, who were themselves prophets, exhorted the brethren with many words and strengthened them. [33]And after they had spent some time, they were sent off in peace by the brethren to those who had sent them.[o] [35]But Paul and Barnabas remained in Antioch, teaching and preaching the word of the Lord, with many others also.

Acts 11:27

Acts 14:28

10. ST PAUL'S SECOND APOSTOLIC JOURNEY

Silas, Paul's new companion

[36]And after some days Paul said to Barnabas, "Come, let us return and visit the brethren in every city where we proclaimed the word

---

Law, no longer oblige by virtue of that law but rather by virtue of the authority of the Church, which has decided to apply them for the time being. What matters is not what Moses says but what Christ says through the Church. The Council "seems to maintain the Law in force", writes St John Chrysostom, "because it selects various prescriptions from it, but in fact it suppresses it, because it does not accept *all* its prescriptions. It had often spoken about these points, it sought to respect the Law and yet establish these regulations as coming not from Moses but from the apostles" (*Hom. on Acts*, 33).

15:34. This verse is not to be found in the more important manuscripts and is not in the New Vulgate. It did appear in the Sixto-Clementine edition of the Vulgate. It was probably a gloss added for clarification and not a part of the authentic text of Acts.

15:35. It was probably during this period

that the incident took place in Antioch when St Paul publicly taxed St Peter with drawing back and separating himself from Gentile Christians, "fearing the circumcision party" (cf. Gal 2:11–14).

15:36–39. Paul and Barnabas part company because of a disagreement over Mark. "Paul sterner, Barnabas kinder, each holds on to his point of view. The argument shows human weakness at work" (St Jerome, *Dialogus adversus pelagianos*, 2, 17). At any event, both apostles are acting in good conscience and God amply blesses their new missionary journeys. "The gifts of the two men differ," Chrysostom comments, "and clearly this difference is itself a gift. [...] Now and then one hears an argument, but even that is part of God's providence, and all that happens is that each is put in the place which suits him best. ...

"Observe that there is nothing wrong in their separating if this means that they can evangelize all the Gentiles. If they go different ways, in order to teach and con-

---

o. Other ancient authorities insert verse 34, *But it seemed good to Silas to remain there*

Acts 12:12
Acts 13:13
Col 4:10
2 Tim 4:11

of the Lord, and see how they are." ³⁷And Barnabas wanted to take with them John called Mark. ³⁸But Paul thought best not to take with them one who had withdrawn from them in Pamphylia, and had not gone with them to the work. ³⁹And there arose a sharp contention, so that they separated from each other; Barnabas took Mark with him and sailed away to Cyprus, ⁴⁰but Paul chose Silas and departed, being commended by the brethren to the grace of the Lord. ⁴¹And he went through Syria and Cilicia, strengthening the churches.

---

vert people, there is nothing wrong about that. What should be emphasized is not their difficulties but what unites them. [...] If only all our divisions were motivated by zeal for preaching!" (*Hom. on Acts*, 34).

This disagreement does not mean that the two disciples have become estranged. Paul always praised Barnabas and Mark for their zeal (cf. 1 Cor 9:6; Gal 2:9) and later on he was happy to have Mark work with him (cf. Col 4:10).

15:40—18:23. The original purpose of this second apostolic journey is to re-visit the brethren in the cities evangelized during the first journey and to confirm them in the faith. Once again the journey begins at Antioch and it will end there in the spring of 53.

St Paul is now acting on his own initiative: he has not been commissioned by any community to undertake this journey. He takes with him Silas, a Christian from Jerusalem and a Roman citizen, who like Paul has two names—Silas and Silvanus. This is the same Silvanus as mentioned in 2 Cor 1:19; 1 Thess 1:1; 2 Thess 1:1; and 1 Pet 5:12.

The account takes up almost three chapters of Acts, up to 18:23, at which point St Luke moves directly into his account of the apostle's third journey.

Paul sets out early in the year 50, with no fixed itinerary, heading for the as yet unevangelized cities which he aims to

visit. The two apostles go to Derbe from Cilicia, Paul's native region, following the line of the Taurus mountains and the plain of Lycaonia. They then go on to Lystra, where Timothy lives, and he joins them as they make their way to Iconium and Pisidian Antioch. The Holy Spirit then instructs them to go north into Phrygia and Galatia, where Paul is taken ill: this illness must have held them up for some months; after evangelizing the Galatians the Spirit directs them to Macedonia and they make for Troas to take ship. St Luke, whom the apostle will later call "the beloved physician" (Col 4:14), must have joined them at this point. The sea journey from Troas to Neapolis is 230 kilometres (150 miles) and half-way across lay the island of Samothrace, where they briefly stopped. About 15 kilometres north of Neapolis lay Philippi, a Roman colony where the events described in chapter 16 take place. From there they went to Thessalonica, the seat of government of the Roman province of Macedonia. Due to disturbances they had to leave there and go to Beroea, and some of the disciples brought the apostle as far as Athens. The last part of chapter 17 describes what happenes in Athens.

The next city to be evangelized was Corinth, where St Paul stayed over a year and a half; at the end of his stay he decided to go to Jerusalem before returning to Antioch. On his way there he made a short stop at Ephesus, where he left

Timothy joins Paul

16 ¹And he came also to Derbe and to Lystra. A disciple was there, named Timothy, the son of a Jewish woman who was a believer; but his father was a Greek. ²He was well spoken of by the brethren at Lystra and Iconium. ³Paul wanted Timothy to accompany him; and he took him and circumcised him because of the Jews that were in those places, for they all knew that his father was a Greek.

Phil 2:19–22
2 Tim 1:5

Tour of the churches of Asia Minor

⁴As they went on their way through the cities, they delivered to them for observance the decisions which had been reached by the

Acts 15:23–29

Priscilla and Aquila, who had travelled with him from Corinth.

The whole journey lasted three years, in the course of which St Paul suffered illnesses, the lash, imprisonment and persecution, and won for Christ disciples in more than ten cities of Asia Minor and Europe and numerous other places on his route.

16:1–3. At Lystra, a city which he evangelized during his first journey (cf. 14:6), Paul meets a young Christian, Timothy, of whom he had received good reports. His Jewish mother Eunice and his grandmother Lois were Christians, and Timothy had received the faith from them.

Paul's apostolic plans for Timothy, and the fact that, despite being Jewish through his mother, he had not been circumcised, lead him to circumcise him: everyone in the city knew he was a Jew and those who practised the Mosaic Law might easily have regarded him as an apostate from Judaism, in which case he would be unlikely to be an effective preacher of the Gospel to Jews.

"He took Timothy," St Ephrem comments, "and circumcised him. Paul did not do this without deliberation: he always acted prudently; but given that Timothy was being trained to preach the

Gospel to Jews everywhere, and to avoid their not giving him a good hearing because he was not circumcised, he decided to circumcise him. In doing this he was not aiming to show that circumcision was necessary—he had been the one most instrumental in eliminating it—but to avoid putting the Gospel at risk" (*Armenian Commentary on Acts*, ad loc.).

In the case of Titus, St Paul did not have him circumcised (cf. Gal 2:3–5), which showed that he did not consider circumcision to be a matter of principle; it is simply for reasons of pastoral prudence and common sense that he has Timothy circumcised. Titus was the son of Gentile parents; to have circumcised him—at a point when Paul was fighting against Judaizers—would have meant Paul giving up his principles. However, the circumcision of Timothy, which takes place later, is in itself something that has no relevance from the Christian point of view (cf. Gal 5:6, 15).

Timothy became one of Paul's most faithful disciples, a most valuable associate in his missionary work (cf. 17:14ff; 18:5; 19:22; 20:4; 1 Thess 3:2; Rom 16:21) and the recipient of two of the apostle's letters.

16:4. The text suggests that all Christians accepted the decisions of the Council of

123

Acts 2:41
apostles and elders who were at Jerusalem. [5]So the churches were strengthened in the faith, and they increased in numbers daily.

Acts 18:23
Gal 4:13–15
[6]And they went through the region of Phrygia and Galatia, having been forbidden by the Holy Spirit to speak the word in Asia. [7]And when they had come opposite Mysia, they attempted to go into Bithynia, but the Spirit of Jesus did not allow them; [8]so, passing by Mysia, they went down to Troas. [9]And a vision appeared to Paul in the night: a man of Macedonia was standing beseeching him and saying, "Come over to Macedonia and help us." [10]And when he had seen the vision, immediately we sought to go on into Macedonia, concluding that God had called us to preach the gospel to them.*

Jerusalem in a spirit of obedience and joy. They saw them as being handed down by the Church through the apostles and as providing a satisfactory solution to a delicate problem. The disciples accept these commandments with internal and external assent: by putting them into practice they showed their docility. Everything which a lawful council lays down merits and demands acceptance by Christians, because it reflects, as the Council of Trent teaches, "the true and saving doctrine which Christ taught, the apostles then handed on, and the Catholic Church, under the inspiration of the Holy Spirit, ever maintains; therefore, no one should subsequently dare to believe, preach or teach anything different"(De iustificatione, preface).

John Paul II called on Christians to adhere sincerely to conciliar directives when he exhorted them in Mexico City to keep to the letter and the spirit of Vatican II: "Take in your hands the documents of the Council. Study them with loving attention, in a spirit of prayer, to discover what the Spirit wished to say about the Church" (Homily in Mexico Cathedral, 26 January 1979).

16:6. In Galatia Paul had the illness which he refers to in Galatians 4:13: "You know it was because of a bodily ailment that I preached the gospel to you at first"; his apostolic zeal makes him turn his illness, which prevented him from moving on, to good purpose.

16:7. We are not told how the Holy Spirit prevented Paul from going to Bithynia. It could have been through an interior voice or through some person sent by God.

Some Greek codexes and a few translations say simply "Spirit" instead of "Spirit of Jesus", but really the two mean the same: cf. Phil 1:19; Rom 8:9; 1 Pet 1:11.

16:9. This vision probably took place in a dream: Acts tells us of a number of instances where God made his will known in that way (cf. 9:10,12; 10:3, 17; 18:9; 22:17). Paul and his companions were convinced he had received a message from God.

The vision is quite right to describe the preaching of the Gospel as help for Macedonia: it is the greatest help, the greatest benefit, a person or a country could be given, an immense grace from God and a great act of charity on the part of the preacher, preparing his listeners, as he does, for the wonderful gift of faith.

16:10. The conviction that Paul and his companions have about what they must

Macedonia

[11]Setting sail therefore from Troas we made a direct voyage to Samothrace, and the following day to Neapolis, [12]and from there to Philippi, which is the leading city of the district[x] of Macedonia, and a Roman colony.

The conversion of Lydia

We remained in this city some days; [13]and on the sabbath day we went outside the gate to the riverside, where we supposed there was a place of prayer;* and we sat down and spoke to the women who had come together. [14]One who heard us was a woman named Lydia, from the city of Thyatira, a seller of purple goods, who was

Acts 13:5–14

---

do is the way every Christian, called as he is at Baptism, should feel about his vocation to imitate Christ and therefore be apostolic.

"All Christians", John Paul II teaches, "incorporated into Christ and his Church by baptism, are consecrated to God. They are called to profess the faith which they have received. By the sacrament of confirmation, they are further endowed by the Holy Spirit with special strength to be witnesses of Christ and sharers in his mission of salvation. Every lay Christian is therefore an extraordinary work of God's grace and is called to the heights of holiness. Sometimes, lay men and women do not seem to appreciate to the full the dignity and the vocation that is theirs as lay people. No, there is no such thing as an 'ordinary layman', for all of you have been called to conversion through the death and resurrection of Jesus Christ. As God's holy people you are called to fulfil your role in the evangelization of the world. Yes, the laity are 'a chosen race, a holy priesthood', also called to be 'the salt of the earth' and 'the light of the world'. It is their specific vocation and mission to express the Gospel in their lives and thereby to insert the Gospel as a leaven into the reality of

the world in which they live and work" (Homily in Limerick, 1 October 1979).

Now the narrative moves into the first person plural (16:10–17; 20:5–8; 13–15; 21:1–18; 27:1—28:16). The author includes himself among St Paul's companions, as an eyewitness of what he reports. Luke must have joined the missionaries at Troas and then stayed behind in Philippi.

16:12. Philippi was a prosperous city, founded by the father of Alexander the Great (in the fourth century BC). Nearby, in 42 BC, there took place the battle in which those who assassinated Julius Caesar were defeated. Octavius raised Philippi to the status of a *colonia* and endowed it with many privileges.

Very few Jews lived in the city, as can be seen from the fact that it had no synagogue (for there to be a synagogue there had to be at least ten Jewish men living in a place). The text refers only to a group of women who met on the riverside to pray—a location probably chosen for the purpose of ritual purification.

16:14. Lydia was probably a surname taken from the region this woman came from. She was not a Jew by birth but a

x. The Greek text is uncertain

Acts 10:44–48

a worshipper of God. The Lord opened her heart to give heed to what was said by Paul. [15]And when she was baptized, with her household, she besought us, saying, "If you have judged me to be faithful to the Lord, come to my house and stay." And she prevailed upon us.

Curing of a possessed girl. Imprisonment of Paul

Acts 19:15–24

[16]As we were going to the place of prayer, we were met by a slave girl who had a spirit of divination and brought her owners much

Mt 8:29

gain by soothsaying. [17]She followed Paul and us, crying, "These men are servants of the Most High God, who proclaim to you the

Mk 16:17

way of salvation." [18]And this she did for many days. But Paul was

---

"God-fearer" (cf. the note on Acts 2:5–11). God chose her from this group of women to enlighten her with the light of faith, opening her heart to understand the words of the apostle. Origen explains that "God opens our mouth, our ears and our eyes to make us say, hear and see divine things" (*In Ex hom.*, III, 2). This shows that we can and ought to address God using the words of the Church's liturgy: "Open my lips, Lord, to bless your holy name; clean my heart of all evil thoughts; enlighten my understanding and inflame my will ... so that I merit to be admitted to your presence" (*Divine Office*, introductory prayer).

When Christians address God, they ask him for the grace to pray well—not only at times of prayer but also in the course of everyday activities: "Lord, be the beginning and end of all that we do and say. Prompt our actions with your grace, and complete them with your all-powerful help" (ibid., morning prayer, Monday, first week).

This episode shows faith to be a gift from God, stemming from his goodness and wisdom: for "no one can give his assent to the Gospel message in a truly salvific way except it be by the light and inspiration of the Holy Spirit: he it is who gives to all the power necessary for affirming and believing the truth" (Vatican I, *Dei Filius*, chap. 3).

16:15. St Luke's succinct account shows that Lydia's good dispositions allow St Paul's preaching to bear fruit very quickly. Her whole family receives Baptism and she insists on the apostles' staying in her house. "Look at her wisdom, how full of humility her words are: 'If you have judged me to be faithful to the Lord.' Nothing could be more persuasive. Who would not have been softened by these words. She did not simply request or entreat: she left them free to decide and yet by her insistence obliged them to stay at her house. See how she straightaway bears fruit and accounts her calling a great gain" (St John Chrysostom, *Hom. on Acts*, 35).

It is worth reflecting on the fact that Christianity began in Europe through this lady's response to God's calling. Lydia set about her mission to Christianize the whole world from within, starting with her own family. Commenting on the role of women in the spread of Christianity, St Josemaría Escrivá says: "The main thing is that like Mary, who was a woman, a virgin and a mother, they live with their eyes on God, repeating her words *'fiat mihi secundum verbum tuum'* (Lk 1:38), 'let it be done to me according to your word'. On these words depends the faithfulness to one's personal vocation—which is always

annoyed, and turned and said to the spirit, "I charge you in the name of Jesus Christ to come out of her." And it came out that very hour.

¹⁹But when her owners saw that their hope of gain was gone, they seized Paul and Silas and dragged them into the market place before the rulers; ²⁰and when they had brought them to the magistrates they said, "These men are Jews and they are disturbing our city. ²¹They advocate customs which it is not lawful for us Romans to accept or practise." ²²The crowd joined in attacking them; and the magistrates tore the garments off them and gave orders to beat them with rods. ²³And when they had inflicted

2 Cor 11:25
Phil 1:30
1 Thess 2:2

---

unique and non-transferable—which will make us all cooperators in the work of salvation which God carries out in us and in the entire world" (*Conversations*, 112).

16:16–18. This slave girl must have been possessed by the devil; the devil knows the present and the past and he is so intelligent that he is good at divining the future (cf. St Thomas, *Summa theologiae*, 1, 57, 3). In Greek mythology Python was a serpent which uttered the Delphic oracles (hence *spiritus pythonis*, "a spirit of divination").

St Paul did not believe in Python but he did believe in the devil. "An unclean spirit is unworthy to proclaim the word of the Gospel; that is why (Paul) commands him to desist and to come out of the girl, for demons ought to confess God in fear and trembling, and not praise him with joy" (St Bede, *Super Act. expositio*, ad loc.).

Jesus addressed demons in the same kind of way (cf. Mk 1:24–27). St Ephrem comments: "The apostles were displeased to be honoured and praised by the evil spirit, just as our Lord rejected the devil who proclaimed him to the Jews. In like manner St Paul upbraids him, because he was motivated by deception and malice" (*Armenian Commentary on Acts*, ad loc.).

16:19–40. This is the first time St Paul comes into conflict with Gentiles. As might be expected, the incident does not take the form of a riot, as happened in cities of Asia Minor (13:50; 14:5, 19), but of a civil suit before local magistrates. The people who bring the charge say nothing about their real reason—loss of profit. They accuse Paul of two things. Their first charge is disturbance of the peace. The second seems to be based on regulations forbidding Roman citizens to practise alien cults, especially where these conflict with Roman custom. They see Paul's exorcism and his preaching as an attempt to propagate what they see as an unacceptable religion. It may well be that the charge also had to do with specific prohibitions on the propagation of Judaism to non-Jews. However, there is no hard evidence that any such prohibition existed; therefore, the charge against Paul must have been based on regulations in the colony separating Roman from alien religious practices.

16:21. For St Luke "Roman" means the same as "Roman citizen" (cf. 16:37–38; 22:25–29; 23:27–28): he is using legal terminology of the time.

16:23. St Paul refers specifically to this punishment in 1 Thessalonians 2:2. It was one of the three beatings mentioned in 2 Corinthians 11:25.

many blows upon them, they threw them into prison, charging the jailer to keep them safely. [24]Having received this charge, he put them into the inner prison and fastened their feet in the stocks.

Baptism of the jailer

Col 3:16

[25]But about midnight Paul and Silas were praying and singing hymns to God, and the prisoners were listening to them, [26]and

Acts 12:6–11

suddenly there was a great earthquake, so that the foundations of the prison were shaken; and immediately all the doors were opened and every one's fetters were unfastened. [27]When the jailer

Acts 12:19

woke and saw that the prison doors were open, he drew his sword and was about to kill himself, supposing that the prisoners had escaped. [28]But Paul cried with a loud voice, "Do not harm yourself, for we are all here." [29]And he called for lights and rushed in, and trembling with fear he fell down before Paul and Silas, [30]and

---

16:24. St John Chrysostom, reflecting on the punishment Paul and Silas underwent, sees them as sitting or lying on the ground, covered with wounds caused by the beating. He contrasts this suffering with the way many people avoid anything which involves effort, discomfort or suffering: "How we should weep over the disorders of our time! The apostles were subjected to the worst kinds of tribulation, and here we are, spending our time in search of pleasure and diversion. This pursuit of leisure and pleasure is the cause of our ruin. We do not see the value of suffering even the least injury or insult for love of Jesus Christ.

"Let us remember the tribulations the saints experienced; nothing alarmed them or scared them. Severe humiliations made them tough, enabled them to do God's work. They did not say, If we are preaching Jesus Christ, why does he not come to our rescue?" (*Hom. on Acts*, 35).

16:25. Paul and Silas spend the night praying and singing hymns. Commenting on this passage St John Chrysostom exhorts Christians to do the same and to sanctify night-time rest: "Show by your

example that the night-time is not just for recovering the strength of your body: it is also a help in sanctifying your soul. [...] You do not have to say long prayers; one prayer, said well, is enough. [...] Offer God this sacrifice of a moment of prayer and he will reward you" (*Hom. on Acts*, 36).

St Bede notes the example Paul and Silas give Christians who are experiencing trials or temptations: "The piety and energy which fires the heart of the apostles expresses itself in prayer and brings them to sing hymns even in prison. Their praise causes the earth to move, the foundations to quake, the doors to open and even their fetters to break. Similarly, that Christian who rejoices when he is happy, let him rejoice also in his weakness, when he is tempted, so that Christ's strength comes to his aid. And then let him praise the Lord with hymns, as Paul and Silas did in the darkness of their prison, and sing with the psalmist, 'Thou does encompass me with deliverance' (Ps 32:7)" (*Super Act. expositio*, ad loc.).

16:30–34. This incident so affects the jailer with religious awe that he comes to

brought them out and said, "Men, what must I do to be saved?" [31]And they said, "Believe in the Lord Jesus, and you will be saved, you and your household." [32]And they spoke the word of the Lord to him and to all that were in his house. [33]And he took them the same hour of the night, and washed their wounds, and he was baptized at once with all his family. [34]Then he brought them up into his house, and set food before them; and he rejoiced with all his household that he had believed in God.

Acts 8:38
Acts 8:39

Release from jail and departure from Philippi

[35]But when it was day, the magistrates sent the police, saying, "Let those men go." [36]And the jailer reported the words to Paul, saying, "The magistrates have sent to let you go; now therefore come out and go in peace." [37]But Paul said to them, "They have beaten us publicly, uncondemned, men who are Roman citizens,

Acts 22:35

---

be converted. He has been helped to react in this way as a result of listening to the prayers and hymns of the apostles: "Notice how the jailer reveres the apostles. He opens his heart to them, when he sees the doors of the prison open. He lights the way further with his torch, but it is another kind of torch that lights up his soul. [...] Then he cleans their wounds, and his soul is cleansed from the filth of sin. On offering them material food, he receives in return a heavenly one. [...] His docility shows that he sincerely believed that all his sins had been forgiven" (St John Chrysostom, *Hom. on Acts*, 36).

A person can meet up with God in all kinds of unexpected situations—in which case he or she needs to have the same kind of docility as the jailer in order to receive the grace of God through the channels which God has established, normally the sacraments.

16:33. As happened with Lydia and her family, the jailer's household is baptized along with him. Noting that these families probably included children and infants, the Magisterium finds support here for its teaching that baptism of children is a practice which goes right back to apostolic times and is, as St Augustine says, "a tradition received from the apostles" (cf. *Instruction on Infant Baptism*, 20 October 1980, 4).

16:35. "Magistrates": in the Roman empire a *praetor* was a magistrate with jurisdiction either in Rome or in the provinces. The "police" (*lictores*) were officials who walked in front of higher magistrates bearing the insignia of Roman justice.

16:37-39. St Paul decides to let it be known that he is a Roman citizen. He probably said nothing about this earlier to avoid giving his fellow Jews the impression that he was not proud to be a Jew or gave more importance to his Roman citizenship.

Ancient Roman law forbade beating of Roman citizens; from the beginning of the Empire it was allowed—once a person had been tried and found guilty.

The magistrates' fear was very much in line with attitudes at the time: very few people had the privilege of Roman citizenship, and the provincial authorities

Acts 22:29

and have thrown us into prison; and do they now cast us out secretly? No! let them come themselves and take us out." [38]The police reported these words to the magistrates, and they were afraid when they heard that they were Roman citizens; [39]so they came and apologized to them. And they took them out and asked them to leave the city. [40]So they went out of the prison, and visited Lydia; and when they had seen the brethren, they exhorted them and departed.

---

were responsible for the protection of the rights of Romans.

St Paul chooses what he considers to be the appropriate time to claim his rights as a citizen, doing so to protect the cause of the Gospel. Some might consider his action haughty or self-assertive; but in fact he is only doing what duty dictates, uncomfortable though it makes him. In this particular situation the dignity of the word of God requires that he claim his rights. Paul sets an example to every Christian by showing him or her the line that should be taken in the interest of the common good. Sometimes charity requires that we do not exercise our rights; but at other times that would mean one was being irresponsible and unjust.

"That false humility is laziness. Such 'humbleness' is a handy way of giving up rights that are really duties" (St Josemaría Escrivá, *The Way*, 603).

In the ecclesial sphere every Christian has a right—which he or she may not renounce—to receive the help necessary for salvation, particularly Christian doctrine and the sacraments. He has a right to follow the spirituality of his choice and to do apostolate, that is, to make the Gospel known without let or hindrance. He is free to associate with others, in keeping with whatever Church law lays down; and others have a duty to respect his right to freely choose his state, his right to his good name and his right to follow his own liturgical rite (Latin, Maronite, etc.).

In the civil sphere citizens have rights which the State should recognize: for example, a right not to be discriminated against on religious grounds, a right to education in line with their legitimate beliefs and to be protected in their married and family life. They also have a right to engage in public affairs, that is, to vote, to occupy public office and to have some influence on legislation. These political rights can easily become serious obligations.

"Lay people", Vatican II teaches, "ought to take on themselves as their distinctive task this renewal of the temporal order. Guided by the light of the Gospel and the mind of the Church, prompted by Christian love, they should act in this domain in a direct way and in their own specific manner. As citizens among citizens they must bring to their cooperation with others their own special competence, and act on their own responsibility; everywhere and always they have to seek the justice of the Kingdom of God. The temporal order is to be renewed in such a way that, while its own principles are fully respected, it is harmonized with the principles of the Christian life and adapted to the various conditions of times, places and peoples" (*Apostolicam actuositatem*, 7).

"It is their duty to cultivate a properly informed conscience and to impress the divine law on the affairs of the earthly city" (*Gaudium et spes*, 43).

Difficulties with Jews in Thessalonica

17 ¹Now when they had passed through Amphipolis and Apollonia, they came to Thessalonica, where there was a synagogue of the Jews. ²And Paul went in, as was his custom, and for three weeksᵖ he argued with them from the scriptures, ³explain-

1 Thess 2:2

Lk 4:16
Acts 16:13

16:40. The last verb seems to imply that St Luke stayed behind in Philippi. Before leaving, Paul and Silas go to Lydia's house to encourage the Christians of Philippi: the treatment they have received and now the fact that they are to leave the city have not weakened their hope in God. When things go wrong, either for himself or others, and a Christian feels disconcerted, he should try to see the situation in a supernatural light and should realize that God's strength more than makes up for human weakness.

"The experience of our weakness and of our failings, the painful realization of the smallness and meanness of some who call themselves Christians, the apparent failure or aimlessness of some works of apostolate, all these things, which bring home to us the reality of sin and human limitation, can still be a trial of our faith. Temptation and doubt can lead us to ask: Where are the strength and power of God? When that happens we have to react by practising the virtue of hope with greater purity and forcefulness, and by striving to be more faithful" (St J. Escrivá, *Christ Is Passing By*, 128).

17:1. Thessalonica was the seat of the Roman governor of the province of Macedonia; it was about 150 kilometres (90 miles) from Philippi. It had been founded in the fourth century BC and declared a "free city" by Augustus in 42 BC. It had a Jewish community, as can be seen from the fact that there was a synagogue.

In all, Paul must have stayed many weeks in this city, in the course of which

he received donations from the Christians of Philippi (cf. Phil 4:16) and had to work to keep himself (cf. 1 Thess 2:9). It was a period of difficulties and joys, as he recalled later: "You yourselves know how you ought to imitate us; we were not idle when we were with you, we did not eat any one's bread without paying, but with toil and labour we worked night and day, that we might not burden any of you" (2 Thess 3:7–8).

Paul seems to have stayed with a prominent citizen called Jason (v. 5). It is not known whether Jason was a Jew or a Gentile; he probably had been converted to Christianity by Paul's teaching.

17:2. Chrysostom draws our attention to the ordinary everyday work of the preacher who, trusting in the power of God's word, engages in a peaceful war of words in which he patiently strives to persuade others of the truth: "His preaching was based on the Scriptures. That was the way Christ preached: wherever he went he explained the Scriptures. When people oppose Paul and call him an imposter, he speaks to them about the Scriptures. For a person who tries to convince others by miracles quite rightly becomes the object of suspicion, whereas he who uses the Scriptures to win people over is not treated with suspicion. St Paul often converted people simply through his preaching. [...] God did not allow them to work too many miracles, for to win without miracles is more wonderful than all possible miracles. God rules without resorting to miracles: that is his

p. Or *sabbaths*

Lk 24:25–27; 46–47
Acts 18:5
Acts 17:12

1 Thess 2:14

Acts 24:5

Lk 23:2
Jn 19:12–15

ing and proving that it was necessary for the Christ to suffer and to rise from the dead, and saying, "This Jesus, whom I proclaim to you, is the Christ." ⁴And some of them were persuaded, and joined Paul and Silas; as did a great many of the devout Greeks and not a few of the leading women. ⁵But the Jews were jealous, and taking some wicked fellows of the rabble, they gathered a crowd, set the city in an uproar, and attacked the house of Jason, seeking to bring them out to the people. ⁶And when they could not find them, they dragged Jason and some of the brethren before the city authorities, crying, "These men who have turned the world upside down have come here also, ⁷and Jason has received them; and they are all acting against the decrees of Caesar, saying that there is another king, Jesus." ⁸And the people and the city authorities were disturbed when they heard this. ⁹And when they had taken security from Jason and the rest, they let them go.

usual policy. And so the apostles did not devote much energy to working miracles, and Paul himself says, 'We preach Christ crucified [rather than provide wisdom or signs]' (1 Cor 1:23)" (*Hom. on Acts*, 37).

17:3. St Luke, who has already reported at length one discourse of Paul to Jews (cf. 13:16ff), limits himself here to giving a very short summary of his preaching in the synagogue of Thessalonica. Paul develops his argument by using quotations from Scripture (probably Ps 2; 16; 110; Is 53) whose meaning he reveals to his listeners: Jesus must be the Messiah expected by Israel; the Messiah had to suffer and then rise from the dead.

What Paul proclaims here is essentially the same as what he says in 1 Corinthians 15:3–5, which is a passage based on very ancient traditions: it is very reasonable to suppose that the apostle is reiterating accepted Christian teaching that Jesus was the Messiah and the Redeemer of man.

17:5–9. Once again Paul's preaching provokes the Jews to jealousy. They see many Gentiles following him who other-

wise might have become converts to Judaism. However, the main motive for their opposition is not religious zeal. There is an element of malice here; their sense of guilt over resisting the grace of the Gospel plays a part in their behaviour. "God opens the lips of those who utter divine words," Origen writes, "and I fear that it is the devil who opens other people's" (*In Ex hom.*, 3, 2).

St Luke calls the city magistrates "politarchs". This was unknown as a term for civic officials in non-Roman cities of Macedonia; but recently discovered inscriptions have shown it to be correct. As a "free city", Thessalonica had a popular assembly empowered to investigate charges.

The Jews bring a religious charge against Paul, but they disguise it in the form of two secular charges. They accuse him of causing a civil disturbance and, by saying that he is proposing "another king", they accuse him also of high treason. These are exactly the same crimes as were alleged against our Lord (cf. Lk 23:2; Jn 19:12).

His accusers have clearly twisted Paul's teaching: he would certainly have

Reception in Beroea

[10]The brethren immediately sent Paul and Silas away by night to Beroea; and when they arrived they went into the Jewish synagogue. [11]Now these Jews were more noble than those in Thessalonica, for they received the word with all eagerness, examining the scriptures daily to see if these things were so. [12]Many of them therefore believed, with not a few Greek women of high standing as well as men. [13]But when the Jews of Thessalonica learned that the word of God was proclaimed by Paul at Beroea also, they came there too, stirring up and inciting the crowds. [14]Then the brethren immediately sent Paul off on his way to the sea, but Silas and Timothy remained there. [15]Those who conducted Paul brought him as far as Athens; and receiving a command for Silas and Timothy to come to him as soon as possible, they departed.

Jn 5:39

Paul in Athens

[16]Now while Paul was waiting for them at Athens, his spirit was provoked within him as he saw that the city was full of idols. [17]So

spoken of Jesus as Lord, but not in the sense of predicting the establishment of an earthly religion.

The magistrates listen to the charges but they accept Jason's security and the charges fail to lead to a conviction.

17:11. The Jews of Beroea were the only ones not to reject Paul's teaching. They immediately began a search of the Scriptures, which led them to discover the truth of the Gospel. They were clearly very upright people who practised both the letter and the spirit of the law of God. "In order to study and understand the Scriptures," St Athanasius says, "one needs to live a clean life and have a pure soul" (*De incarnatione contra arianos*, 57).

The same preaching has different effects on different people. "It is a fact that the teaching of the truth is differently received depending on the listeners' dispositions. The Word shows everyone what is good and what is bad; if a person is predisposed to do what is proclaimed

to him, his soul is in the light; if he is not and he has not decided to fix his soul's gaze on the light of truth, then he will remain in the darkness of ignorance" (St Gregory of Nyssa, *On the Life of Moses*, 2, 65).

As St John of the Cross says, "to seek God one needs to have a heart which is naked and strong, free from all good and evil things that are not simply God" (*Spiritual Canticle*, stanza 3).

17:16–21. St Paul's missionary activity in Athens shows us the Gospel's first encounter with Hellenist paganism, both popular and intellectual. This is an important episode in the spread of the Christian message because it shows us the capacity of Gospel preaching to adapt itself to different outlooks, different cultures, while still remaining completely faithful to itself.

The Athens visited by St Paul was no longer the brilliant intellectual capital it had been in the time of Plato and Aristotle. It was in decline, culturally and

Acts 14:7-17 he argued in the synagogue with the Jews and the devout persons, and in the market place every day with those who chanced to be there. [18]Some also of the Epicurean and Stoic philosophers met him. And some said, "What would this babbler say?" Others said, "He seems to be a preacher of foreign divinities"—because he preached Jesus and the resurrection. [19]And they took hold of him and brought him to the Areopagus, saying, "May we know what this new teaching is which you present? [20]For you bring some

politically, but it still retained traces of its former glory. Here the philosophical currents of the day still had their spokesmen, and intellectual debate was always welcomed.

St Paul presents the Gospel to these pagan philosophers as "true philosophy" without in any sense taking from its transcendental, supernatural character. The point at which they coincide is this: philosophy is the science of life; it is a legitimate search for the answer to profound questions about human existence. Paul tries to lead them beyond mere intellectual curiosity, in a genuine search for perennial truth, which is religious in character. He supports the philosophers in their criticism of superstition, but points out that they have to go farther than just censuring aberrations of that kind.

Paul is well aware that preaching Christ crucified is "a stumbling block to Jews and folly to Gentiles" (1 Cor 1:23). However, this conviction does not prevent his feeling and expressing respect for pagan thought and religion, which he sees as providing a groundwork for the Gospel. In Paul's address we can see the first signs of the Church's and Christians' ongoing recognition of the value, albeit limited, of secular culture. "There are in profane culture", St Gregory of Nyssa writes, "aspects which should not be rejected when the time comes to grow in virtue. Natural moral philosophy can, in fact, be the companion of one who wants

to lead a higher life [...], provided that its fruit does not carry any alien contamination" (*On the Life of Moses*, 2, 37).

Two centuries before Gregory, St Justin Martyr wrote about the merits and defects of pagan philosphy and the relative truth it contains: "I declare that I prayed and strove with all my might to be known as a Christian, not because the teachings of Plato are completely different from those of Christ, but because they are not in all respects the same; neither are those of other writers, Stoics, the poets and the historians. For each discoursed rightly, seeing through his participation in the seminal divine Word what related to it. But they that have uttered contrary opinions clearly do not have sound knowledge and irrefutable wisdom. Whatever has been uttered aright by any man in any place belongs to Christians; for, next to God, we worship and love the Word which is from the unbegotten and ineffable God. [...] All the profane authors were able to see the truth clearly, through the seed of reason [*logos*, word], implanted in them" (*Apology*, 2, 13, 2–3).

17:16. Paul's religious zeal makes him indignant at the failure to recognize the truth, the depraved forms of religious worship and the wretched spiritual situation of people who do not know God.

His devout, serene reaction brings him immediately to tell them about the true God and enlighten their darkened minds.

strange things to our ears; we wish to know therefore what these things mean." [21]Now all the Athenians and the foreigners who lived there spent their time in nothing except telling or hearing something new.

Paul's speech in the Areopagus

[22]So Paul, standing in the middle of the Areopagus, said: "Men of Athens, I perceive that in every way you are very religious. [23]For

---

17:17. As usual Paul preaches in the synagogue, but he also addresses anyone in the market place who is ready to listen to what he has to say. The verb St Luke uses really means "preach", not "argue" (cf. 20:7, 9).

"Market place": *Agora* was the Greek name for the main city square. The people used to foregather in the Agora to debate the political questions of the day; it was also used for other activities, including trading. The Agora in Athens was particularly famous from very early on: it was the centre of Athenian democracy, but it was also used for informal, everyday affairs.

17:18. Epicurean philosophers followed the teachings of Epicurus (341–270 BC), which tended to be rather materialistic. They spoke of there being no gods, or at least they regarded the gods as taking no interest in the doings of men. Epicurean ethics stressed the importance of pleasure and a life of ease and tranquillity.

The Stoics, who followed Zeno of Citium (340–265 BC), saw the *logos* as the cause which shapes, orders and directs the entire universe and the lives of those who inhabit it. The *logos* is the Reason for everything that exists, the ultimate principle, immanent in things; this is a pantheistic concept of the world. Stoic ethics stress individual responsibility and self-sufficiency; but although this philosophy speaks a great deal about freedom it sees Fate as playing a decisive role.

"Babbler": the Greek word does have a rather derogatory meaning and is used mainly to refer to people who never open their mouths without uttering clichés.

These people seem to take "Resurrection" as a proper name of some god accompanying Jesus.

17:19. The word "areopagus" can refer to a hill where the Athenians used to meet and also to a session of a tribunal or city council gathered together to listen to Paul's teaching. It is not clear from the text which meaning applies.

17:22–33. Of all Paul's addresses reported in Acts, this address in the Areopagus is his longest to a pagan audience (cf. 14:15ff). It is a highly significant one, paralleling in importance his address to the Jews of Pisidian Antioch (cf. 13:16ff). It is the first model we have of Christian apologetic method, which tends to stress the reasonableness of Christianity and the fact that it has no difficulty in holding its own with the best in human thought.

The speaker is clearly the same person as wrote the first three chapters of the Epistle to the Romans, someone with a lot of experience of preaching the Gospel; his method consists in first talking about the one, true, living God and then proclaiming Jesus Christ, the divine Saviour of all men (cf. 2 Tim 1:9–10).

After an introduction designed to catch the attention of listeners and highlight the central theme (vv. 22ff), the

135

as I passed along, and observed the objects of your worship, I found also an altar with this inscription, 'To an unknown god.' What therefore you worship as unknown, this I proclaim to you. ²⁴The God who made the world and everything in it, being Lord

Is 42:5
Acts 14:15

---

address can be divided into three parts: 1) God is the Lord of the world; he does not need to live in temples built by men (vv. 24f); 2) man has been created by God and is dependent on him for everything (vv. 26f); 3) there is a special relationship between God and man; therefore, idolatry is a grave sin (vv. 28f). Then, in his conclusion, Paul exhorts his listeners to accept the truth about God, and to repent, bearing in mind the Last Judgment (vv. 30f).

The terminology Paul uses comes mainly from the Greek translation of the Old Testament—the Septuagint. Biblical beliefs are expressed in the language of the Hellenistic culture of the people.

17:22–24. "To an unknown God": St Paul praises the religious feelings of the Athenians, which lead them to offer worship to God. But he goes on to point out that their form of religion is very imperfect because they do not know enough about God and about the right way to worship him; nor does their religion free them from their sins or help them live in a way worthy of human dignity. Religious Athenians, he seems to say somewhat ironically, are in fact superstitious, and they do not know the one true God and his ways of salvation.

Paul criticizes pagan religion and points out its limitations, but he does not totally condemn it. He regards it as a basis to work on: at least it means that his listeners accept the possibility of the existence of a true God as yet unknown to them. They are predisposed to receive and accept the supernatural revelation of God in Christ. Revelation does not

destroy natural religion: rather, it purifies it, completes it and raises it up, enabling a naturally religious person to know the mystery of God, One and Triune, to change his life with the help of the grace of Christ and to attain the salvation he needs and yearns for.

17:23. "Those who acted in accordance with what is universally, naturally and eternally good were pleasing to God and will be saved by Christ [...], just like the righteous who preceded them" (St Justin, *Dialogue with Tryphon*, 45). The Church's esteem for the positive elements in pagan religions leads her to preach to all men the fulness of truth and salvation which is to be found only in Jesus Christ. "The Catholic Church rejects nothing of what is true and holy in these religions. She has a high regard for the manner of life and conduct, the precepts and doctrines which, although differing in many ways from her own teaching, nevertheless often reflect a ray of that truth which enlightens all men. Yet she proclaims, and is in duty bound to proclaim without fail, Christ who is 'the way, and the truth, and the life' (Jn 14:6). In him, in whom God reconciled all things to himself, men find the fulness of their religious life" (Vatican II, *Nostra aetate*, 2).

17:24. Paul's language is in line with the way God is described in the Old Testament as being Lord of heaven and earth (cf. Is 42:5; Ex 20:21). The apostle speaks of God's infinite majesty: God is greater than the universe, of which he is the creator. However, Paul does not mean

of heaven and earth, does not live in shrines made by man, [25]nor is he served by human hands, as though he needed anything, since

Ps 50:8–11

to imply that it is not desirable for God to be worshipped in sacred places designed for that purpose.

His words seem to echo those of Solomon at the dedication of the first temple: "Behold, heaven and the highest heaven cannot contain thee; how much less this house which I have built!" (1 Kings 8:27).

Any worship rendered to God should be "in spirit and truth" (Jn 4:24). But the Lord has desired to dwell in a special way and to receive homage in temples built by men. "The worship of God", St Thomas Aquinas writes, "regards both God who is worshipped and men who perform the worship. God is not confined to any place, and therefore it is not on his account that a tabernacle or temple has to be made. Worshippers, as corporeal beings, need a special tabernacle or temple set up for the worship of God; and this for two reasons. First, that the thought of its being appointed to the worship of God might instil a greater sense of reverence; second, that the way it is arranged and furnished might signify in various respects the excellence of Christ's divine or human nature. [...] From this it is clear that the house of the sanctuary was not set up to receive God as if dwelling there, but that his name might dwell there, that is, in order that the knowledge of God might be exhibited there" (*Summa theologiae*, 1–2, 102, 4, ad 1).

17:25. The idea that God does not need man's service and does not depend on man for his well-being and happiness is to be often found in the prophetical books. "Now in Babylon you will see", Jeremiah proclaims, "gods made of silver and gold and wood, which are carried on men's shoulders and inspire fear in the heathen. [...] Their tongues are smoothed by the craftsmen, and they themselves are overlaid with gold and silver; but they are false and cannot speak. [...] When they have been dressed in purple robes, their faces are wiped because of the dust from the temple, which is thick upon them. Like a local ruler the god holds a sceptre, though unable to destroy any one who offends it. [...] Having no feet, they are carried on men's shoulders, revealing to mankind their worthlessness. And those who serve them are ashamed because through them these gods are made to stand, lest they fall to the ground" (Bar 6:4, 8, 12–14, 26–27).

This does not mean that the Lord does not want men to respond to the love-offering which he makes them. "Hear, O heavens," Isaiah prophesies, "and give ear, O earth; for the Lord has spoken: 'Sons have I reared and brought up, but they have rebelled against me. The ox knows its owner, and the ass its master's crib; but Israel does not know, my people does not understand'" (1:2–3).

In addition to being offensive and senseless, sin implies indifference and ingratitude towards God, who, in an excess of love, is tireless in seeking man's friendship. "When Israel was a child, I loved him, and out of Egypt I called my son," we read in the prophet Hosea. "The more I called them, the more they went from me. [...] Yet it was I who taught Ephraim to walk, I took them up in my arms; but they did not know that I healed them. I led them with cords of compassion, with the bands of love" (11:1–4).

Deut 32:8
2 Mac 7:23

Deut 4:29
Is 55:6
Rom 1:19

he himself gives to all men life and breath and everything. [26]And he made from one every nation of men to live on all the face of the earth, having determined allotted periods and the boundaries of their habitation, [27]that they should seek God, in the hope that they might feel after him and find him. Yet he is not far from each one of us, [28]for

---

By far the greatest sign of God's love for men is the Redemption, and the sacraments of the Church, through which the fruits of the Redemption reach us. His love is expressed in a special way in the Blessed Eucharist, which provides the Christian with nourishment and is where Jesus wishes us to adore him and keep him company.

17:26. "From one": St Paul is referring to the text of Genesis 2:7: "then the Lord God formed man of dust from the ground, and breathed into his nostrils the breath of life"; in other words, he is speaking of the first progenitor of the human race. The expression "from one" should not be interpreted as meaning from *one principle* but from *one man*.

17:27–28. St Paul is speaking about the absolute nearness of God and his mysterious but real presence in every man and woman. St Augustine echoes this teaching when he exclaims, "Yet all the time you were within me, more inward than the most inward place of my heart, and loftier than the highest" (*Confessions*, 3, 6, 11).

Merely to exist, man needs God, his Creator. He also needs him if he is to continue in existence, to live and act. He needs him if he is to think and love. And in particular he needs him in order to love goodness and be good. It is correct to say that God is in us. This intimate union of God and man does not in any way take from the fact that there is a perfect distinction and radical difference between God, who is infinite, and man, who is finite and limited.

"Men, who are incapable of existing of themselves," St Athanasius writes, "are to be found confined by place and dependent on the Word of God. But God exists of himself, he contains all things and is contained by none. He is to be found within everything as far as his goodness and power is concerned, and he is outside of everything as far as his own divine nature is concerned" (*De decretis nicaenae synodi*, 11).

Christian spirituality has traditionally seen in these ideas an invitation to seek God in the depth of one's soul and to always feel dependent upon him.

"Consider God", says St John of Avila, "who is the existence of everything that exists, and without whom there is nothing: and who is the life of all that lives, and without whom there is death; and who is the strength of all that has capacity to act, and without whom there is weakness; and who is the entire good of everything that is good, without whom nothing can have the least little bit of good in it" (*Audi, filia*, chap. 64).

St Francis de Sales writes: "Not only is God in the place where you are, but he is in a very special manner in your heart and in the depth of your soul, which he quickens and animates with his divine presence, since he is there as the heart of your heart, and the spirit of your soul; for, as the soul, being spread throughout the body, is present in every part of it, and yet resides in a special manner in the heart, so God, being present in all things,

'In him we live and move and have our being';
as even some of your poets have said,
    'For we are indeed his offspring.'
[29]Being then God's offspring, we ought not to think that the Deity   Acts 19:26
is like gold, or silver, or stone, a representation by the art and   Rom 1:22–23
imagination of man. [30]The times of ignorance God overlooked,   Rom 3:25–26

---

is present nevertheless in a special manner in our spirit and therefore David called God 'the rock of his heart' (Ps 73:26); and Paul said that 'we live and move and have our being in God' (Acts 17:28). By reflecting on this truth, you will stir up in your heart a great reverence for God, who is so intimately present there" (*Introduction to the Devout Life*, 2, chap. 2).

This quotation—in the singular—is from the Stoic poet Aratus (3rd century BC). The plural in the quotation may refer to a similar verse in the hymn to Zeus written by Cleanthes (also 3rd century).

"The devil spoke words of Scripture but our Saviour reduced him to silence", St Athanasius comments. "Paul cites secular authors, but, saint that he is, he gives them a spiritual meaning" (*De synodis*, 39). "We are rightly called 'God's offspring', not the offspring of his divinity but created freely by his spirit and re-created through adoption as sons" (St Bede, *Super Act. expositio*, ad loc.).

17:29. If men are God's offspring, and are in some way like him, clearly an inanimate representation cannot contain the living God. Men have God's spirit and therefore they should recognize that God is spiritual. However, material representations of God do serve a useful purpose, due to the fact that human knowledge begins from sense experience. Visual images help us to realize that God is present and they help us to adore him. Veneration of images—as encouraged by the Church—is, therefore, quite different

from idolatry: an idolator thinks that God dwells in the idol, that he acts only through the idol, and in some cases he actually thinks that the idol is God.

17:30. St Paul now moves on from speaking about natural knowledge of God to explaining the knowledge of God that comes from faith.

Although man can know God by using his reason, the Lord has chosen to make known the mysteries of his divine life in a supernatural way, in order to make it easier for man to attain salvation. "The Church maintains and teaches that God, the beginning and end of all things, can be known with certainty, by the natural light of human reason, from created things. [...] However, it pleased him in his wisdom and goodness to reveal himself to mankind and to make known the eternal decrees of his will in another, supernatural way" (Vatican I, *Dei Filius*, chap. 2).

"It was also necessary for man to be instructed by divine revelation concerning those truths concerning God, which human reason is able to discover, for these truths, attained by human reason, would reach man through the work of a few, after much effort and mixed in with many errors; yet the entire salvation of man, which lies in God, depends on knowledge of these truths. So, for salvation to reach men more rapidly and more surely, it was necessary for them to be instructed by divine revelation concerning the things of God" (St Thomas Aquinas, *Summa theologiae*, 1, 1, 1).

Lk 24:47
Acts 10:42
1 Pet 4:5
but now he commands all men everywhere to repent, [31]because he has fixed a day on which he will judge the world in righteousness by a man whom he has appointed, and of this he has given asssurance to all men by raising him from the dead."

Supernatural revelation assures man of easily attained, certain knowledge of divine mysteries; it also includes some truths—such as the existence of God—which unaided human reason can discover (cf. Rom 1:20).

"It pleased God, in his goodness and wisdom", Vatican II teaches, "to reveal himself and to make known the mystery of his will (cf. Eph 1:9). His will was that men should have access to the Father, through Christ, the Word made flesh, in the Holy Spirit, and thus become sharers in the divine nature (cf. Eph 2:18; 2 Pet 1:4). By this revelation, then, the invisible God (cf. Col 1:15; 1 Tim 1:17), from the fulness of his love, addresses men as his friends (cf. Ex 33:11; Jn 15:14–15), and moves among them in order to invite and receive them into his own company" (*Dei Verbum*, 2).

The knowledge of the triune God and his saving will which supernatural revelation offers men is not just theoretical or intellectual knowledge: it has the aim of converting man and leading him to repent and to change his life. It is, therefore, a calling from God; and God expects man to make a personal response to that call. " 'The obedience of faith' (Rom 16:26; cf. Rom 1:5; 2 Cor 10:5–6) must be given to God as he reveals himself. By faith man freely commits his entire self to God, making 'the full submission of his intellect and will to God who reveals' (Vatican I, *Dei Filius*, chap. 3), and willingly assenting to the Revelation given by him. Before this faith can be exercised, man must have the grace of God to move and assist him; he must have the interior

helps of the Holy Spirit, who moves the heart and converts it to God" (Vatican II, *Dei Verbum*, 5).

This practical knowledge of the living and true God revealed in Christ is in fact the only way for man to know himself, despise his faults and sins, and find hope in divine mercy. It is a self-knowledge—given by God—which enables the repentant sinner to begin a new life and work freely with God at his own sanctification: "As I see it, we shall never succeed in knowing ourselves unless we seek to know God," St Teresa writes. "Let us think of his greatness and then come back to our own baseness; by looking at his purity we shall see our foulness; by meditating on his humility, we shall see how far we are from being humble" (*Interior Castle*, 1, 2, 9).

17:31. On Jesus Christ as Judge of all, see the note on Acts 10:42.

17:32. When St Paul begins to tell the Athenians about Jesus' resurrection from the dead, they actually begin to jeer. For pagans, the notion of resurrection from the dead was absurd, something they were not prepared to believe. If the apostle speaks in this way, the reason is that the truths of the Christian faith all lead into the mystery of the Resurrection; even though he may have anticipated his listeners' reaction, he does not avoid telling them about this truth, which forms the bedrock of our faith. "See how he leads them," Chrysostom points out,"to the God who takes care of the world, who is kind, merciful, powerful and wise: all these attributes of the Creator

[32]Now when they heard of the resurrection of the dead, some mocked; but others said, "We will hear you again about this." [33]So Paul went out from among them. [34]But some men joined him and believed, among them Dionysius the Areopagite and a woman named Damaris and others with them.

---

are confirmed in the Resurrection" (*Hom. on Acts*, 38).

The apostle fails to overcome the rationalist prejudices of most of his audience. Here we have, as it were, an application of what he wrote later to the Corinthians: "The Greeks seek wisdom, but we preach Christ crucified ..., folly to the Gentiles" (1 Cor 1:22f), the reason being that if people do not have an attitude and disposition of faith, then reason goes out of control and haughtily rejects mysteries. If the human mind is made the measure of all things, it will despise and reject anything it does not understand — including things which are beyond human understanding. The mysteries God has revealed to man cannot be grasped by unaided human reason; they have to be accepted on faith. What moves the mind to accept these mysteries is not the evidence they contain but the authority of God, who is infallible truth and cannot deceive or be deceived. The act of faith, although strictly speaking an act of the assenting mind, is influenced by the will; the desire to believe presupposes that one loves him who is proposing the truth to be believed.

17:34. "Those careful to live an upright life do not take long to understand the word; but the same does not go for others" (*Hom. on Acts*, 39).

Among the few converts in Athens St Luke mentions Damaris. She is one of the many women who appear in Acts — which clearly shows that the preaching of the Gospel was addressed to everyone without distinction. In all that they did

the apostles followed their Master's example, who in spite of the prejudices of his age proclaimed the Kingdom to women as well as men.

St Luke told us about the first convert in Europe being a woman (cf. 16:14ff). Something similar happened in the case of the Samaritans: it was a woman who first spoke to them about the Saviour (cf. Jn 4). In the Gospels we see how attentive women are to our Lord — standing at the foot of the cross or being the first to visit the tomb on Easter Sunday. And there is no record of women being hypocritical or hating Christ or abandoning him out of cowardice.

St Paul has a deep appreciation of the role of the Christian woman — as mother, wife and sister — in the spreading of Christianity, as can be seen from his letters and preaching. Lydia in Philippi, Priscilla and Chloe in Corinth, Phoebe in Cenchrae, the mother of Rufus — who was also a mother to him — and the daughters of Philip (Acts 21:9): these are some of the women to whom Paul was ever-grateful for their help and prayers.

"Women are called to bring to the family, to society and to the Church, characteristics which are their own and which they alone can give — their gentle warmth and untiring generosity, their love for detail, their quick-wittedness and intuition, their simple and deep piety, their constancy..." (St J. Escrivá, *Conversations*, 87). The Church looks to women to commit themselves and bear witness to human values and to where human happiness lies: "Women have received from God", John Paul II says,

Paul in Corinth, with Aquila and Priscilla

Rom 16:3
1 Cor 16:19
2 Tim 4:19

18 ¹After this he left Athens and went to Corinth. ²And he found a Jew named Aquila, a native of Pontus, lately come from Italy with his wife Priscilla, because Claudius had com-

---

"a natural charism of their own, which features great sensitivity, a fine sense of balance, a gift for detail and a providential love for life-in-the-making, life in need of loving attention. These are qualities which make for human maturity" (Address, 7 December 1979).

When these qualities, with which God has endowed feminine personality, are developed and brought into play, woman's "life and work will be really constructive, fruitful and full of meaning, whether she spends the day dedicated to her husband and children or whether, having given up the idea of marriage for a noble reason, she has given herself fully to other tasks.

"Each woman in her own sphere of life, if she is faithful to her divine and human vocation, can and, in fact, does achieve the fulness of her feminine personality. Let us remember that Mary, Mother of God and Mother of men, is not only a model but also a proof of the transcendental value of an apparently unimportant life" (*Conversations*, 87).

18:1–11. St Paul must have arrived in Corinth very discouraged by what happened in Athens, and very short of money. Some time later he wrote: "And I was with you in weakness and in much fear and trembling; and my speech and my message were not in plausible words of wisdom, but in demonstration of the Spirit and power, that your faith might not rest in the wisdom of men but in the power of God." (1 Cor 2:3–5). He would never forget his experience in the Areopagus before the Athenians, who "were friends of new speeches, yet who paid no heed to them or what they said; all they wanted was to have something new to talk about" (St John Chrysostom, *Hom. on Acts*, 39).

Corinth was a very commercial cosmopolitan city located on an isthmus between two gulfs (which are now joined). Ships came to Corinth from all over the world. Low moral standards, concentration on money-making and voluptuous worship of Aphrodite meant that Corinth did not seem the best ground for sowing the word of God; but the Lord can change people's hearts, especially if he has people as obedient and zealous as Paul, Silvanus, Timothy and the early Christians in general. The Athenians' intellectual pride proved to be a more formidable obstacle than the Corinthians' libertarian lifestyle.

Christians should not soft-pedal if they find themselves in situations where paganism and loose living seem to be the order of the day: indeed this should only spur them on. When addressing his Father at the Last Supper Jesus prayed "I do not pray that thou shouldst take them out of the world, but that thou shouldst keep them from the evil one" (Jn 17:15).

18:2. This married couple were probably already Christians when they arrived in Corinth. Since they came from Rome, the indications are that there was a community of Christians in the capital from very early on. Aquila and Priscilla (the diminutive of Prisca) proved to be of great help to Paul from the very beginning of his work in Corinth.

Later on they both must have returned to Rome (cf. Rom 16:3); and it may

manded all the Jews to leave Rome. And he went to see them; ³and because he was of the same trade he stayed with them, and

Acts 20:34
1 Cor 4:12

---

well be that apostolic considerations dictated their movements, as would be the case with countless Christians after them. "The Christian family's faith and evangelizing mission also possesses this Catholic missionary inspiration. The sacrament of marriage takes up and re-proposes the task of defending and spreading the faith, a task which has its roots in Baptism and Confirmation and makes Christian married couples and parents witnesses of Christ 'to the end of the earth' (Acts 1:8) [...]

"Just as at the dawn of Christianity Aquila and Priscilla were presented as a missionary couple (cf. Acts 18; Rom 16:3f), so today the Church shows forth her perennial newness and fruitfulness by the presence of Christian couples who [...] work in missionary territories, proclaiming the Gospel and doing service to their fellowmen for the love of Jesus Christ" (John Paul II, *Familiaris consortio*, 54).

The edict of Claudius (41–54) expelling the Jews from Rome was issued before the year 50. It is referred to by Suetonius, the Roman historian, but the details of the decree are not known. We do know that Claudius had protected Jews on a number of occasions. He gave them the right to appoint the high priest and to have charge of the temple. Apparently, conflict between Jews and Christians in Rome led him to expel some Jews from the city, on a temporary basis, or at least to advise them to leave.

18:3. St Paul earns his living and manages to combine this with all his preaching of the Gospel. "This teaching of Christ on work," John Paul II writes, "based on the example of his life during his years in Nazareth, finds a particularly lively echo in the teaching of the apostle Paul. Paul boasts of working at his trade (he was probably a tentmaker: cf. Acts 18:3), and thanks to that work he was able even as an apostle to earn his own bread" (*Laborem exercens*, 26).

During this stay of a year and a half in Corinth St Paul wrote some rather severe letters to the Thessalonians, pointing out to them the need to work: "If any one will not work, let him not eat. [...] We command and exhort [idlers] in the Lord Jesus Christ to do their work in quietness and to earn their own living" (2 Thess 3:10, 12). St John Chrysostom, commenting on this passage of Acts, says that "Work is man's natural state. Idleness is *against his nature*. God has placed man in this world to work, and the natural thing for the soul is to be active and not passive" (*Hom. on Acts*, 35).

Taking Christ's own example, St J. Escrivá points out that "Work is one of the highest human values and the way in which men contribute to the progress of society. But even more, it is a way to holiness" (*Conversations*, 24). In Jesus' hands, "a professional occupation, similar to that carried out by millions of people all over the world, was turned into a divine task. It became a part of our redemption, a way to salvation" (ibid., 55).

In fact, it is in work, in the middle of ordinary activity, that most people can and should find Christ. "God is calling you to serve him in and from the ordinary, material and secular activities of human life. He waits for us everyday [...] in all the immense panorama of work" (ibid., 114). Man thereby finds God in the most visible, material things,

they worked, for by trade they were tentmakers. ⁴And he argued in the synagogue every sabbath, and persuaded Jews and Greeks.

Preaching to Jews and Gentiles

Acts 17:14–15 ⁵When Silas and Timothy arrived from Macedonia, Paul was occupied with preaching, testifying to the Jews that the Christ was
Acts 13:46–51; Jesus. ⁶And when they opposed and reviled him, he shook out his
20:26; 28:28 garments and said to them, "Your blood be upon your heads! I am

and Christians can avoid the danger of what might be called "a double life: on one side, an interior life, a life of relation with God; and on the other, a separate and distinct professional, social and family life, full of small earthly realities" (ibid.).

Like most people Paul spent part of his day working to earn his living. When engaged in work he was still the apostle of the Gentiles chosen by God, and his very work spoke to his companions and friends. We should not think that there was any split between his on-going personal relationship with God, and his apostolic activity or his work—or that he did not work in a concentrated or exemplary manner.

18:4. It is easy to imagine the hope and eagerness Paul felt when preaching the Gospel to his fellow Jews. He knew from experience the difficulties they had about recognizing Jesus as the Messiah and accepting the Good News. Paul feels both joy and sorrow: he is happy because the moment has arrived for the sons of Abraham to receive the Gospel as is their right by inheritance; but he also realizes that although it brings salvation to some, it spells rejection for those who refuse to accept it.

Origen spoke in similar terms: "I experience anxiety to speak and anxiety not to speak. I wish to speak for the benefit of those who are worthy, so that I may not be taken to task for refusing the

word of truth to those who have the ability to grasp it. But I am afraid to speak in case I address those who are unworthy, because it means I am giving holy things to dogs and casting pearls before swine." Only Jesus was capable of distinguishing, among his listeners, those who were without from those who were within: he spoke in parables to the outsiders and explained the parables to those who entered with him into the house" (*Dialogue with Heraclides*, 15).

18:6. The blindness of the Jews once again causes Paul great sadness; here is further evidence of the mysterious resistance to faith of so many of the chosen people. As he did in Pisidian Antioch (cf. 13:51), the apostle shakes the dust from his clothes to show his break from the Jews of Corinth: their apparent fidelity to the religion of their forefathers disguises their proud rejection of God's promises.

He finds himself confronted by the great enigma of salvation history, in which God dialogues with human freedom. As St Justin writes, "The Jews, in truth, who had the prophecies and always looked for the coming of Christ, not only did not recognize him, but, far beyond that, even mistreated him. But the Gentiles, who had never even heard anything of Christ until his apostles went from Jerusalem and preached about him and gave them the prophecies, were filled with joy and faith, and turned away from their idols, and dedicated themselves to

innocent. From now on I will go to the Gentiles." [7]And he left there and went to the house of a man named Titius[q] Justus, a worshipper of God; his house was next door to the synagogue. [8]Crispus, the ruler of the synagogue, believed in the Lord, together with all his household; and many of the Corinthians hearing Paul believed and were baptized. [9]And the Lord said to Paul one night in a vision, "Do not be afraid, but speak and do not be

1 Cor 1:14

1 Cor 2:3

the Unbegotten God through Christ" (*Apology*, 1, 49, 5).

Paul's words on this occasion are addressed to the Jews of Corinth, not to Jews elsewhere. For a long time past he has directed his preaching to Gentiles as well as Jews. The phrase "From now on I will go to the Gentiles" does not mean that he will no longer address Jews, for in the course of his apostolic work he continues to evangelize Jews as well as Gentiles (cf. Acts 18:19; 28:17).

18:7. Titus Justus had a Roman name and was a Gentile, but the fact that he lived next door to the synagogue and, in particular, the Greek term used to identify him as a "worshipper" of God, indicates that he was a convert to Judaism. Cf. the note on Acts 2:5–11.

18:9. In this vision, given him to strengthen his resolve, Paul sees the Lord, that is, Jesus. The brief message he receives is reminiscent of the language God uses when he addresses the prophets and just men of the Old Testament (cf. Ex 3:12; Josh 1:5; Is 41:10). The words "Do not be afraid" occur often in divine visions and are designed to allay the impact of God's overpowering presence (cf. Lk 1:30).

In this case, the words are meant to allay Paul's premonitions about the severe treatment his opponents will hand out to him in Corinth. The vision once

again indicates the graces which the Lord is bestowing on him to support his intense contemplative life, which is also a life of action in the service of Jesus and the Gospel.

"I tell you," St Teresa of Avila writes, "those of you whom God is not leading by this road [of contemplation], that, as I know from what I have seen and been told by those who are following this road, they are not bearing a lighter cross than you; you would be amazed at all the ways and manners in which God sends them crosses. I know about both types of life and I am well aware that the trials given by God to contemplatives are intolerable; and they of such a kind that, were he not to feed them with consolations, they could not be borne. It is clear that, since God leads those whom he most loves by the way of trials, the more he loves them, the greater will be their trials; and there is no reason to suppose that he hates contemplatives, since with his own mouth he praises them and calls them his friends.

"To suppose that he would admit to his close friendship people who are free from all trials is ridiculous. [...] I think, when those who lead an active life occasionally see contemplatives receiving consolations, they suppose that they never experience anything else. But I can assure you that you might not be able to endure their sufferings for as long as a day" (*Way of Perfection*, chap. 18).

q. Other early authorities read *Titus*

Is 41:10; 43:5
Jer 1:8
Jn 10:16
silent; [10]for I am with you, and no man shall attack you to harm you; for I have many people in this city." [11]And he stayed a year and six months, teaching the word of God among them.

Paul before Gallio

[12]But when Gallio was proconsul of Achaia, the Jews made a united attack upon Paul and brought him before the tribunal, [13]saying, "This man is persuading men to worship God contrary Acts 25:18–19 to the law." [14]But when Paul was about to open his mouth, Gallio said to the Jews, "If it were a matter of wrongdoing or vicious crime, I should have reason to bear with you, O Jews; [15]but since Jn 18:21
Acts 23:29 it is a matter of questions about words and names and your own law, see to it yourselves; I refuse to be a judge of these things." [16]And he drove them from the tribunal. [17]And they all seized Sosthenes, the ruler of the synagogue, and beat him in front of the tribunal. But Gallio paid no attention to this.

18:10. God has foreseen the people who are going to follow the call of grace. From this it follows that the Christian has a serious obligation to preach the Gospel to as many people as he can. This preaching has a guaranteed effectiveness, as can be seen from its capacity to convert men and women of every race, age, social condition etc. The Gospel is for all. God offers it, through Christians, to the rich and the poor, to the educated and the uneducated. Any person can accept this invitation to grace: "Not only philosophers and scholars believed in Christ [...], but also workmen and people wholly uneducated, who all scorned glory, and fear, and death" (St Justin, *Apology*, 1, 10, 8).

18:12. Gallio was a brother of the Stoic philosopher Seneca. He had been adopted in Rome by Lucius Iunius Gallio, whose name he took. From an inscription at Delphi (reported in 1905) we learn that Gallio began his proconsulship of Achaia, of which Corinth was the capital, in July 51. Paul must have appeared before Gallio around the end of 52. This is one of the best-established dates we have for the apostle.

18:17. It is not quite clear what happened. Sosthenes may have been assaulted by the citizens of Corinth who were using the incident to vent their anti-Jewish feelings. But it is more likely that Sosthenes was in sympathy with the Christians and that the Jews were venting their frustration on him. In 1 Corinthians 1:1 a Christian called Sosthenes appears as co-author (amanuensis) of the letter; some commentators identify him with the ruler of the synagogue in this episode.

18:18. The vow taken by a "Nazirite" (one "consecrated to God") is described in the sixth chapter of the Book of Numbers. Among other things it involved not cutting one's hair (to symbolize that one was allowing God to act in one) and not drinking fermented drinks (meaning a resolution to practise self-denial). It is not clear whether it was Paul or Aquila who had taken the vow; apparently the vow ended at Cenchreae,

Return to Antioch via Ephesus

[18]After this Paul stayed many days longer and then took leave of the brethren and sailed for Syria, and with him Priscilla and Aquila. At Cenchreae he cut his hair, for he had a vow. [19]And they came to Ephesus, and he left them there; but he himself went into the synagogue and argued with the Jews. [20]When they asked him to stay for a longer period, he declined; [21]but on taking leave of them he said, "I will return to you if God wills," and he set sail from Ephesus.

[22]When he had landed at Caesarea, he went up and greeted the church, and then went down to Antioch.

Acts 21:24

Acts 19:8

Acts 21:15

11. ST PAUL'S THIRD APOSTOLIC JOURNEY

Galatia and Phrygia

[23]After spending some time there he departed and went from place to place through the region of Galatia and Phrygia, strengthening all the disciples.

1 Cor 3:6
Tit 3:13

---

for the devotee's hair was cut there. For more information, see the note on Acts 21:23–24.

18:19. Ephesus was the capital of proconsular Asia and one of the most flourishing cities of the empire. Its most famous building, the Artemision, or temple of Diana Artemis, was one of the wonders of the ancient world. The city's huge theatre had a capacity for 23,000 spectators. On this journey St Paul did not stay long in Ephesus—perhaps only long enough for the ship to unload and load. However, Ephesus will be the centre of his next missionary journey.

18:23—21:26. Paul's third apostolic journey starts, like the earlier ones, from Antioch, but it ends with his imprisonment in Jerusalem (Acts 21:27ff). It was a long journey, but Luke devotes most attention to events in Ephesus.

To begin with Paul tours the cities he already evangelized in Galatia and

Phrygia: this would have taken him from the last months of 53 to early 54. Then he goes to Ephesus, where he stays for almost three years and meets up with all kinds of contradictions (cf. 2 Cor 1:8), as he describes it in his letter to the Corinthians in spring 57: "To the present hour we hunger and thirst, we are ill-clad and buffeted and homeless. … We have become, and are now, as the refuse of the world, the offscouring of all things" (1 Cor 4:11, 13). Despite this, or perhaps because of it, his apostolate was very fruitful and the Christian message spread through all proconsular Asia, to important cities like Colossae, Laodicae, Hierapolis etc. and to countless towns; as he put it in a letter to the Corinthians (1 Cor 16:9), "a wide door for effective work has opened to me".

The apostle had to leave Ephesus on account of the revolt of the silversmiths, moving on towards Macedonia and Achaia to visit the churches he founded

147

Apollos in Ephesus and Corinth

Acts 19:3

2 Cor 3:1
Col 4:10

24Now a Jew named Apollos, a native of Alexandria, came to Ephesus. He was an eloquent man, well versed in the scriptures. 25He had been instructed in the way of the Lord; and being fervent in spirit, he spoke and taught accurately the things concerning Jesus, though he knew only the baptism of John. 26He began to speak boldly in the synagogue; but when Priscilla and Aquila heard him, they took him and expounded to him the way of God more accurately. 27And when he wished to cross to Achaia, the brethren encouraged him, and wrote to the disciples to receive him. When he arrived, he greatly helped those who through grace

on his second journey—Philippi, Thessalonica and Corinth. He stayed there the three months of the winter of 57/58. On his return journey (to Jerusalem, to bring money collected) he went via Macedonia to avoid a Jewish plot. He embarked at Neapolis (the port near Philippi), stopping off at Troas, Miletus (where he met with the elders from Ephesus whom he had called to come to him), Tyre and Caesarea, and managing to reach Jerusalem in time for the Passover.

18:24. Priscilla and Aquila knew how valuable a man with Apollos' qualities would be if he were to dedicate himself to the Lord's service; so they took the initiative and spoke to him. St J. Escrivá sees this episode as a good lesson about boldness in speaking about God, as "an event that demonstrates the wonderful apostolic zeal of the early Christians. Scarcely a quarter of a century had passed since Jesus had gone up to heaven and already his fame had spread to many towns and villages. In the city of Ephesus a man arrived, Apollos by name, 'an eloquent man, well versed in the scriptures'. ... A glimmer of Christ's light had already filtered into the mind of this man. He had heard about our Lord and he passed the news on to others. But he still had some way to go. He needed to know more if he was to acquire the fulness of

the faith and so come to love our Lord truly. A Christian couple, Aquila and Priscilla, hear him speaking; they are not inactive or indifferent. They do not think: 'This man already knows enough; it's not our business to teach him.' They were souls who were really eager to do apostolate and so they approached Apollos and 'took him and expounded to him the way of God more accurately'" (*Friends of God*, 270).

This was the kind of zeal the first Christians had; a little later on St Justin wrote: "We do our very best to warn them [Jews and heretics], as we do you, not to be deluded, for we know full well that whoever can speak out the truth and fails to do so shall be condemned by God" (*Dialogue with Tryphon*, 82, 3).

18:27. God uses people, in this case Apollos, to channel his grace to the faithful. They are instruments of his; they preach his word and reap an apostolic harvest, but it is God himself who makes the harvest grow, by providing his grace. "It depends not upon man's will or exertion, but upon God's mercy" (Rom 9:16). "It is not we who save souls and move them to do good. We are quite simply instruments, some more, some less worthy, for fulfilling God's plans for salvation. If at any time we were to think that we ourselves were the authors of the

had believed, ²⁸for he powerfully confuted the Jews in public, showing by the scriptures that the Christ was Jesus.

Acts 9:22

Disciples of John the Baptist at Ephesus

19 ¹While Apollos was at Corinth, Paul passed through the upper country and came to Ephesus. There he found some disciples. ²And he said to them, "Did you receive the Holy Spirit when you believed?" And they said, "No, we have never even heard that there is a Holy Spirit." ³And he said, "Into what then were you baptized?" They said, "Into John's baptism." ⁴And Paul said, "John baptized with the baptism of repentance, telling the people to believe in the one who was to come after him, that is,

Jn 7:39
Acts 8:15–17

Mt 3:6–11
Acts 13:24

good we do, then our pride would return, more twisted than ever. The salt would lose its flavour, the leaven would rot and the light would turn to darkness" (*Friends of God*, 250).

Hence the importance of supernatural resources in apostolic activity: building is in vain if God does not support it (cf. Ps 127:1). "It's useless to busy yourself in as many external works if you lack Love. It's like sewing with a needle and no thread" (St J. Escrivá, *The Way*, 967).

19:1–7. This presence in Ephesus of a group of disciples who had received only John's baptism is open to various interpretations. The text seems to imply that they were not, properly speaking, Christians but people who followed the Baptist's teaching and whom Paul regarded as incipient Christians, to the point of calling them disciples. We say this because in the New Testament being a Christian is always connected with receiving Baptism and having the Holy Spirit (cf. Jn 3:5; Rom 8:9; 1 Cor 12:3; Gal 3:2; Acts 11:16; etc.).

19:2. Leaving aside questions as to the origin and composition of this group of disciples, their simple statement about knowing nothing about the Holy Spirit

and his part in fulfilling the messianic promises points to the need to preach Christian doctrine in a systematic, gradual and complete way.

Christian catechesis, John Paul II reminds us, "must be systematic, not improvised but programmed to reach a precise goal; it must deal with essentials, without any claim to tackle all disputed questions or to transform itself into theological research or scientific exegesis; it must nevertheless be sufficiently complete, not stopping short at the initial proclamation of the Christian mystery such as we have in the *kerygma*; it must be an integral Christian initiation, open to all the other factors of Christian life" (*Catechesi tradendae*, 21).

19:3–4. "The whole teaching and work of John," St Thomas Aquinas writes, "was in preparation for Christ, as the helper and under-craftsman are responsible for preparing the materials for the form which the head-craftsman produces. Grace was to be conferred on men through Christ: 'Grace and truth have come through Jesus Christ' (Jn 1:17). And therefore, the baptism of John did not confer grace, but only prepared the way for grace in a threefold way—in one way, by John's teaching, which led men

Jesus." [5]On hearing this, they were baptized in the name of the
Lord Jesus. [6]And when Paul had laid his hands upon them, the
Holy Spirit came on them; and they spoke with tongues and
prophesied. [7]There were about twelve of them in all.

Acts 8:15–17;
11:15–16

Paul's preaching and miracles at Ephesus

[8]And he entered the synagogue and for three months spoke boldly,
arguing and pleading about the kingdom of God; [9]but when some

to faith in Christ; in another way, by
accustoming men to the rite of Christ's
Baptism; and in a third way, through
penance, which prepared men to receive
the effect of Christ's Baptism" (*Summa
theologiae*, 3, 38, 3).

19:5. "They were baptized in the name
of the Lord Jesus": the view of most commentators is that this does not mean that
the Trinitarian formula which appears in
Matthew 28:19 (cf. the note on Acts 2:38)
("in the name of the Father and of the Son
and of the Holy Spirit") was not used.
The reference here may simply be a way
of distinguishing Christian Baptism from
other baptismal rites which were features
of Judaism in apostolic times—particularly John the Baptist's rite. Besides,
Christian Baptism was administered on
Jesus Christ's instructions (cf. Mt 28:19),
in union with him and using his power:
Jesus' redemptive action is initiated by
the Father and expresses itself in the full
outpouring of the Holy Spirit.

19:6. This passage speaks of the laying
on of hands, something distinct from
Baptism, as seen already in Acts 8:14–
17, whereby the Holy Spirit is received.
This is the sacrament which will come to
be called Confirmation and which has
been conferred, from the beginnings of
the Church, as one of the sacraments of
Christian initiation.

Referring to Confirmation, John Paul
II has said: "Christ's gift of the Holy

Spirit is going to be poured out upon you
in a particular way. You will hear the
words of the Church spoken over you,
calling upon the Holy Spirit to confirm
your faith, to seal you in his love, to
strengthen you for his service. You will
then take your place among fellow-
Christians throughout the world, full citizens now of the People of God. You will
witness to the truth of the Gospel in the
name of Jesus Christ. You will live your
lives in such a way as to make holy all
human life. Together with all the confirmed, you will become living stones in
the cathedral of peace. Indeed you are
called by God to be instruments of his
peace [...].

"You, too, are strengthened inwardly
today by the gift of the Holy Spirit, so
that each of you in your own way can
carry the Good News to your companions and friends. [...] The same Holy
Spirit comes to you today in the sacrament of Confirmation, to involve you
more completely in the Church's fight
against sin and in her mission of foster-
ing holiness. He comes to dwell more
fully in your hearts and to strengthen you
for the struggle with evil. [...] The world
of today needs you, for it needs men and
women who are filled with the Holy
Spirit. It needs your courage and hopeful-
ness, your faith and your perseverance.
The world of tomorrow will be built by
you. Today you receive the gift of the
Holy Spirit so that you may work with
deep faith and with abiding charity, so

were stubborn and disbelieved, speaking evil of the Way before the congregation, he withdrew from them, taking the disciples with him, and argued daily in the hall of Tyrannus.[r] [10]This continued for two years, so that all the residents of Asia heard the word of the Lord, both Jews and Greeks.

[11]And God did extraordinary miracles by the hands of Paul,   Acts 14:3

---

that you may help to bring to the world the fruits of reconciliation and peace. Strengthened by the Holy Spirit and his manifold gifts […], strive to be unselfish try not to be obsessed with material things" (Homily at Coventry Airport, 30 May 1982).

As is the case with Baptism and Holy Orders, Confirmation imprints an indelible mark or character on the soul.

19:8–10. This summarized account of Paul's activity in Ephesus is filled out by the account we are given of the apostle's farewell to the elders of that city (cf. 20:18–35) and by information contained in his letters to the Corinthians. Paul made Ephesus the base for his missionary work in the surrounding region, for which he counted on help from Timothy, Erastus, Gaius, Titus and Epaphras of Colossae.

During his stay in Ephesus he wrote 1 Corinthians and the Letter to the Galatians.

19:8. Paul returns to the synagogue where he taught previously (cf. 18:19–21); the Jews' resistance and lack of understanding do not lessen his zeal.

19:9. The obstinacy of some of the Jews eventually obliges Paul to leave the synagogue. He now moves to the school of Tyrannus—who must have been a Christian or at least someone sympathetic to the Gospel. Paul may well have presented himself to the inhabitants of the

city as a teacher of "philosophy," in the meaning of that word then current—the science of living.

The text also shows that Christians already had developed the practice of meeting in private houses to hear the word of God, thus avoiding any need to go to the synagogue.

19:10. To these "two years" should be added the three months Paul spent preaching in the synagogue (cf. v. 8), which means that he spent about two and a quarter years in Ephesus altogether. This ties in with what he says in his farewell remarks (20:31): "For three years ...": at that time parts of years were regarded as full years.

The region evangelized by Paul and his helpers was not the whole province of proconsular Asia but the cities of Smyrna, Pergamon, Thyatira, Sardis, Philadelphia, Laodicea, Colossae and Hierapolis, all of which looked to Ephesus as their centre.

19:11–16. Here we have another reference to miracles worked by Paul (cf. 13:11; 14:10)—the signs which he himself tells us accompanied his preaching (cf. 2 Cor 12:12; Rom 15:19).

St Luke here contrasts the spiritual vitality and the divine character of Paul's message with the falsity and uselessness of magic. Genuine Christian preaching is on a completely different plane from that of opponents or imitators of the Gospel. The author of Acts seems to be anticipating the objections of people who will

r. Other ancient authorities add *from the fifth hour to the tenth*

151

Mk 6:56
Lk 8:44–47
Acts 5:15

Mk 9:38

Lk 4:41
Acts 16:17

[12]so that handkerchiefs or aprons were carried away from his body to the sick, and diseases left them and the evil spirits came out of them. [13]Then some of the itinerant Jewish exorcists undertook to pronounce the name of the Lord Jesus over those who had evil spirits, saying, "I adjure you by the Jesus whom Paul preaches." [14]Seven sons of a Jewish high priest named Sceva were doing this. [15]But the evil spirit answered them, "Jesus I know, and Paul I know; but who are you?" [16]And the man in whom the evil spirit was leaped on them, mastered all of them, and overpowered them, so that they fled out of that house naked and wounded.

Books of magic burned

Lk 5:26
Acts 3:10

[17]And this became known to all residents of Ephesus, both Jews and Greeks; and fear fell upon them all; and the name of the Lord Jesus was extolled. [18]Many also of those who were now believers came, confessing and divulging their practices. [19]And a number of

argue that there was a certain amount of magic in the apostles' miracles. Origen dealt with similar objections in his reply to the pagan Celsus: "Did the disciples of Jesus learn to do miracles and thereby convince their hearers, or did they not do any. It is quite absurd to say that they did not do any miracles of any kind, and that, in blind faith … they went off everywhere to propagate a new teaching; for what would have kept their spirits up when they had to teach something which was so completely new. But if they did also work miracles, how on earth could these magicians have faced so many dangers to spread a teaching which explicitly forbade the use of magic?" (*Against Celsus*, 1, 38).

In religions of ancient times there were lots of exorcists like the sons of Sceva. This man, probably a member of an important priestly family, gave himself the title of high priest to help promote and gain credence for the magic-making his family went in for. Many magicians, fortune-tellers and exorcists were ready to invoke any and every God. For example, there were pagans who used the different names of Yahweh, and we have evidence in the form of a magician's papyrus which reads, "I abjure you by Jesus, the God of the Jews."

In this instance the evil spirit turns on the seven brothers, showing that "the Name does nothing unless it be spoken with faith" (St John Chrysostom, *Hom. on Acts*, 41).

"For the preacher's instruction to exercise its full force", writes St John of the Cross, "there must be two kinds of preparation—that of the preacher and that of the hearer; for, as a rule, the benefit derived from instruction depends on the preparation of the teacher. For this reason it is said, Like master, like pupil. For, when in the Acts of the Apostles those seven sons of that chief priest of the Jews used to cast out devils in the same way as St Paul did, the devil rose up against them […] and then, attacking them, stripped and wounded them. This was only because they had not the proper preparation" (*Ascent of Mount Carmel*, 3, chap. 45).

Paul's actions and their good effects, in contrast with the signs the agents of

those who practised magic arts brought their books together and burned them in the sight of all; and they counted the value of them and found it came to fifty thousand pieces of silver. [20]So the word of the Lord grew and prevailed mightily.

Acts 6:7

Paul's plans for further journeys

[21]Now after these events Paul resolved in the Spirit to pass through Macedonia and Achaia and go to Jerusalem, saying, "After I have been there, I must also see Rome." [22]And having sent into Macedonia two of his helpers, Timothy and Erastus, he himself stayed in Asia for a while.

Acts 23:11

Rom 15:22–23

1 Cor 4:17

---

superstition try to perform, fill many of the Ephesians with holy fear and bring about their conversion. "The sight of events like this can indeed cause conviction and faith in those who love the truth, who are not swayed by opinions and who do not let their evil passions gain the upper hand" (St Justin, *Apology*, 1, 53, 12).

19:12. From the very beginning Christians had great respect for and devotion to relics—not only the mortal remains of the saints but also their clothes or things they had used or things which had touched their tombs.

19:17–19. This fear which overtook the believers marked the start of their spiritual recovery. Fear of the Lord is a gift of the Holy Spirit, which inspires reverence towards God and fear of offending him, and helps us avoid evil and do good. It inspires the respect, admiration, obedience and love of one who wishes to please his Father.

Fear of offending God leads the people of Ephesus to be done with anything that distances them from him, in particular magical arts. Books on magic —each often only a few pages of manuscript—were common in ancient times; they were also worth a lot of money: firstly because of the much sought-after magical formulae they contained, and secondly because they were often very ornately produced.

The attitude of these Christians— inspired by the Holy Spirit—towards things which might lead them to offend God is to avoid them completely. "We Christians have a commitment of love to the call of divine grace, which we have freely accepted, an obligation which urges us to fight tenaciously. We know that we are as weak as other people, but we cannot forget that if we use the resources available to us, we will become salt and light and leaven of the world; we will be the consolation of God" (St Josemaría Escrivá, *Christ Is Passing By*, 74).

19:21–22. Paul's decision to go back to Macedonia and Achaia is another example of the way God encourages the apostle to build up the churches he earlier established in these regions. Paul will also use this visit to collect the donations set aside for the Jerusalem community.

His planned visit to Rome should not be seen in terms of a vague desire to go there some time, but as something he feels he really needs to do, something God wants him to do.

The silversmiths' riot in Ephesus

Acts 16:16

Acts 17:29

Acts 20:4; 27:2

23About that time there arose no little stir concerning the Way. 24For a man named Demetrius, a silversmith, who made silver shrines of Artemis, brought no little business to the craftsmen. 25These he gathered together, with the workmen of like occupation, and said, "Men, you know that from this business we have our wealth. 26And you see and hear that not only at Ephesus but almost throughout all Asia this Paul has persuaded and turned away a considerable company of people, saying that gods made with hands are not gods. 27And there is danger not only that this trade of ours may come into disrepute but also that the temple of the great goddess Artemis may count for nothing, and that she may even be deposed from her magnificence, she whom all Asia and the world worship."

28When they heard this they were enraged, and cried out, "Great is Artemis of the Ephesians!" 29So the city was filled with the confusion; and they rushed together into the theatre, dragging with them Gaius and Aristarchus, Macedonians who were Paul's companions in travel. 30Paul wished to go in among the crowd, but the disciples would not let him; 31some of the Asiarchs also,

19:23. St Luke describes Christianity and the Church as the "Way" (cf. Acts 9:2; 22:4; 24:14, 22). This term was probably fairly widely used, with this meaning, by Christians of the period. It has Jewish roots and refers to a moral and religious lifestyle and even a set of moral criteria. In the Book of Acts (and among the first Christians) the word "way", then, often implies that "following Christ", embracing his religion, is not just one way of salvation among many, but the only way that God offers man; in certain passages of Acts it is referred to as *the* Way (cf. 9:2). Sometimes *the* Way is equivalent to *the* Church of Christ, outside of which there is no redemption.

"The preaching of the Gospel is rightly called 'way', for it is the route that truly leads to the Kingdom of heaven" (St John Chrysostom, *Hom. on Acts*, 41).

19:24. Artemis was the Greek name of the goddess the Romans called Diana, but through syncretism it was identified with an oriental goddess of fertility. A statue of Diana was worshipped in the *Artemision*. Feast-days of Artemis were celebrated with disgraceful orgies, for which people flocked into Ephesus from the surrounding region. Demetrius and his fellow-craftsmen did good business selling little statuettes of Diana which many visitors took home as souvenirs and cult objects.

19:26. Demetrius fairly accurately gives the gist of a central point of Paul's preaching against idolatry (cf. 17:29). Christians spoke out against the false gods of paganism, using arguments and passages from the Old Testament in the same way as Jewish apologists did (cf. Is 44:9–20; 46:1–7; Wis 13:10–19).

19:29. What started off as a meeting of craftsmen to discuss a threat to their business has become a huge popular gather-

who were friends of his, sent to him and begged him not to venture into the theatre. [32]Now some cried one thing, some another; for the assembly was in confusion, and most of them did not know why they had come together. [33]Some of the crowd prompted Alexander, whom the Jews had put forward. And Alexander motioned with his hand, wishing to make a defence to the people. [34]But when they recognized that he was a Jew, for about two hours they all with one voice cried out, "Great is Artemis of the Ephesians!" [35]And when the town clerk had quieted the crowd, he said, "Men of Ephesus, what man is there who does not know that the city of the Ephesians is temple keeper of the great Artemis, and of the sacred stone* that fell from the sky?[s] [36]Seeing then that these things cannot be contradicted, you ought to be quiet and do nothing rash. [37]For you have brought these men here who are neither sacrilegious nor blasphemers of our goddess. [38]If therefore Demetrius and the craftsmen with him have a complaint against any one, the courts are open, and there are proconsuls; let them bring charges against one another. [39]But if you seek anything further,[t] it shall be settled in the regular assembly. [40]For we are in danger of being charged with rioting today, there being no cause

Acts 16:20

Acts 18:12

---

ing. The Ephesians flock into the city's theatre, which was where all huge meetings usually took place. They do not really seem to know very much about what is going on; but we can detect a certain amount of anti-Jewish feeling. They were more familiar with Judaism than with the new Christian religion, and this may have led them to blame the Jews for the threat to their pagan practices and beliefs.

Aristarchus was from Thessalonica (cf. Acts 20:4). He accompanied St Paul on his journey to Rome and during his imprisonment there (cf. Acts 27:2 and Col 4:10). Gaius may have been the same Christian as is referred to in Acts 20:4.

19:30–31. As in other similar situations, Paul wants to use the opportunity to justify his actions and speak to the people about the faith he preaches and is proud to acknowledge. However, he goes along

with the disciples' advice and decides that it would be imprudent to enter the theatre. Given the hysteria of the crowd he probably realizes that it would be counterproductive to appear before them.

The Asiarchs, as the magistrates of Ephesus were called, presided over meetings of the provincial assembly of Asia. Paul was apparently on friendly terms with them.

19:33–34. Alexander, a Jew, feels called to explain to those present that the Jews and their religion were not responsible for the events which led the people to assemble; but in fact this only causes further provocation.

19:35–40. The town clerk's sober remarks, especially his reference to legal channels, show him to be admirably impartial. He probably has some impression of the merits of the Christian mes-

s. The meaning of the Greek is uncertain   t. Other ancient authorities read *about their own matters*

155

that we can give to justify this commotion." [41]And when he had said this, he dismissed the assembly.

Paul goes into Macedonia and begins his return journey

Acts 14:22;
16:40

20 [1]After the uproar ceased, Paul sent for the disciples and having exhorted them took leave of them and departed for Macedonia. [2]When he had gone through these parts and had given them much encouragement, he came to Greece. [3]There he spent three months, and when a plot was made against him by the Jews as he was about to set sail for Syria, he determined to return through Macedonia. [4]Sopater of Beroea, the son of Pyrrhus, accompanied him; and of the Thessalonians, Aristarchus and Secundus; and Gaius of Derbe, and Timothy; and the Asians, Tychicus and Trophimus. [5]These went on and were waiting for us at Troas, [6]but we sailed away from Philippi after the days of Unleavened Bread, and in five days we came to them at Troas, where we stayed for seven days.

1 Cor 16:5–6

---

sage; anyone, indeed, who looks at Christianity calmly and closely cannot fail to be impressed by it.

20:1. This verse connects up with 19:22, at which point the narrative branched off to deal with the riot of the silversmiths. Paul's exhortations to the disciples of Ephesus must have been on the same lines as his address in vv. 18–35.

This journey to Macedonia is probably the same one as mentioned in 2 Corinthians 2:12–13: "When I came to Troas to preach the gospel of Christ, a door was opened for me in the Lord; but my mind could not rest because I did not find my brother Titus there. So I took leave of them and went on to Macedonia."

20:2. From here Paul wrote 2 Corinthians, which was delivered by Titus.

20:3. During his stay in Corinth Paul wrote and despatched his letter to the Romans.

We know nothing else about this Jewish plot which caused Paul to change

his plans. Possibly some Jews, pilgrims to Jerusalem on the same boat as Paul, were planning to deal with him during the sea journey.

20:4. Paul has now set out on his last journey to Jerusalem. The seven brethren who travelled with him were presumably delegates of the churches appointed to help him bring the monies collected for the support of the Christians in Jerusalem.

20:5. The narrative changes again into the first person plural. Luke joined Paul at Philippi and will stay with him from now on. "We" means "Paul and I"; we have no reason to think that it includes other people.

20:6. The Azymes or days of the Unleavened Bread are the week when the Passover is celebrated. The Christian Easter and the Jewish Passover fell on the same days. See also the notes on Mt 26:2 and 26:17.

20:7. This is the first reference in Acts to the Christian custom of meeting on the first day of the week to celebrate the Eucharist

Celebration of the Eucharist. Eutychus' fall and recovery

[7]On the first day of the week, when we were gathered together to break bread,* Paul talked with them, intending to depart on the morrow; and he prolonged his speech until midnight. [8]There were many lights in the upper chamber where we were gathered. [9]And a young man named Eutychus was sitting in the window. He sank into a deep sleep as Paul talked still longer; and being overcome by sleep, he fell down from the third storey and was taken up dead. [10]But Paul went down and bent over him, and embracing him said, "Do not be alarmed, for his life is in him." [11]And when Paul had gone up and had broken bread and eaten, he conversed with them a long time, until daybreak, and so departed. [12]And they took the lad away alive, and were not a little comforted.

Acts 2:42

1 Kings 17:17–24

From Troas to Miletus

[13]But going ahead to the ship, we set sail for Assos, intending to take Paul aboard there; for so he had arranged, intending himself

---

(cf. 2:42; 1 Cor 10:16). "In una autem sabbatorum: that is," St Bede comments, "on the Lord's Day, the first day after the sabbath, when we gather to celebrate our mysteries" (*Super Act. expositio*, ad loc.).

"We call this food," St Justin explains, "the Eucharist, of which only he can partake who has acknowledged the truth of our teachings, who has been cleansed by baptism for the remission of his sins and for his regeneration, and who regulates his life upon the principles laid down by Christ" (*Apology*, 1, 66, 1).

Christian writers have pointed to the profound connexion between the Eucharist and that true brotherhood which God lays as a duty on, and grants as a gift to, Christ's disciples. St Francis de Sales writes: "How the greatness of God has lowered itself on behalf of each and every one of us—and how high he desires to raise us! He desires us to be so perfectly united to him as to make us one with him. He has desired this in order to teach us that, since we have been loved with an equal love whereby he embraces us all in the most blessed Sacrament, he

desires that we love one another with that love which tends towards union, and to the greatest and most perfect form of union. We are all nourished by the same bread, that heavenly bread of the divine Eucharist, the reception of which is called communion, and which symbolizes that unity that we should have one with another, without which we could not be called children of God" (*Sermon on the third Sunday of Lent*).

20:8–12. This is the only miracle recounted in Acts where Paul raises someone from the dead. St Bede sees in it a certain spiritual symbolism: "The restoring of this young man to life is brought about in the course of preaching. Thereby Paul's preaching is confirmed by the kindness of the miracle and the teaching; the effort involved in the long vigil is repaid with interest; and all those present are reminded vividly of their departed Master" (*Super Act. expositio*, ad loc.).

20:13–16. The various little details given by Luke suggest that he very likely kept

157

to go by land. [14]And when he met us at Assos, we took him on board and came to Mitylene. [15]And sailing from there we came the following day opposite Chios; the next day we touched at Samos; and[u] the day after that we came to Miletus. [16]For Paul had decided to sail past Ephesus, so that he might not have to spend time in Asia; for he was hastening to be at Jerusalem, if possible, on the day of Pentecost.

Acts 18:21

Farewell address to the elders of Ephesus

[17]And from Miletus he sent to Ephesus and called to him the elders of the church. [18]And when they came to him he said to them:

1 Thess 1:5

---

a diary which he later used when writing his book.

20:16. The Law laid down that all Jews should go up to Jerusalem three times a year, for the feasts of the Passover, Pentecost and Tabernacles (cf. Deut 16:16). St Paul's desire is to press on to Jerusalem to hand over the collection and to establish contact with the many Jews who would gather in the city for the festival.

20:18–35. Paul's address to the elders of Ephesus is his third great discourse related in Acts (the others being his address to Jews in Pisidian Antioch—13:16ff—and to pagans at Athens—17:22ff). It is, as it were, an emotional farewell to the churches which he had founded.

The address divides into two parts. The first (vv. 18–27) is a brief resume of Paul's life of dedication to the church of Ephesus, which he founded and directed, with hints of the difficulties which he expects to meet in the immediate future. Two parallel sections (vv. 18–21 and 26–27) frame the central passage of this section (vv. 22–25).

In the second section the apostle speaks movingly about the mission and role of elders. Two series of recommendations (vv. 28–31 and 33–35) hinge on the central verse (v. 32).

The pathos, vigour and spiritual depth of the discourse clearly show that it is Paul who is speaking. Here we have the Paul of the letters addressing a community which has already been evangelized, and inviting them to get to know their faith better and practise it better.

20:18–20. Paul is not embarrassed to set himself as an example of how to serve God and the disciples in the cause of the Gospel (cf. 1 Cor 11:1). He has worked diligently, out of love for Jesus Christ and the brethren, doing his duty, conscious that this kind of patient, persevering work is the way of perfection and holiness that God expects him to follow.

The Apostle has learned to imitate Christ both in his public life and in the long years of his hidden life, ever deepening in his love. In this connexion, St Francis de Sales writes: "Those are spiritually greedy who never have enough of exercises of devotion, so keen are they, they say, to attain perfection; as if perfection consisted in the amount of things we do and not in the perfection with which we do them. [...] God has not made perfection to lie in the number of acts we do to please him, but in the way in which we

---

u. Other ancient authorities add *after remaining at Trogyllium*

"You yourselves know how I lived among you all the time from the first day that I set foot in Asia, [19]serving the Lord with all humility and with tears and with trials which befell me through the plots of the Jews; [20]how I did not shrink from declaring to you anything that was profitable, and teaching you in public and from house to house, [21]testifying both to Jews and to Greeks of repentance to God and of faith in our Lord Jesus Christ. [22]And now, behold, I am going to Jerusalem, bound in the Spirit, not knowing

2 Cor 11:23–31
Phil 2:3

2 Tim 4:2

---

do them: that way is to do the little we have to do according to our calling, that is, to do it in love, through love and for love" (*Sermon on the first Sunday of Lent*).

St Catherine of Siena understood our Lord to say to her something along the same lines: "I reward every good which is done, great or small, according to the measure of the love of him who receives the reward" (*Dialogue*, chap. 68).

As in his letters, Paul associates the idea of service with humility (cf. 2 Cor 10:1; 1 Thess 2:6), tears (cf. Rom 9:2; Phil 3:18) and fortitude to keep on working despite persecution (cf. 2 Cor 11:24; 1 Thess 2:14–16). The apostle's true treasure is humility, for it allows him to discover his shortcomings and at the same time teaches him to rely on God's strength. As St Teresa says, "The truly humble person will have a genuine desire to be thought little of, and condemned unjustly, even in serious matters. For, if she desires to imitate the Lord, how can she do so better than in this? And no bodily strength is necessary here, nor the aid of anyone but God" (*Way of Perfection*, 15, 2).

20:21. This very brief summary of Paul's preaching to Jews and pagans mentions repentance and faith as inseparable elements in the new life Jesus confers on Christians. "It is good to know", Origen writes, "that we will be judged at the divine judgment seat not on our faith alone, as if we had not to answer for our conduct; nor on our conduct alone, as if our faith were not to be scrutinized. What justifies is our uprightness on both scores, and if we are short on either we shall deserve punishment" (*Dialogue with Heraclides*, 8).

The presence of grace and faith in the soul equips it to fight the Christian fight, which ultimately leads to rooting out sins and defects. "From the very day faith enters your soul," Origen also says, "battle must be joined between virtues and vices. Prior to the onslaught of the Word, vices were at peace within you, but from the moment the Word begins to judge them one by one, a great turmoil arises and a merciless war begins. 'For what partnership have righteousness and iniquity?' (2 Cor 6:14)" (*In Ex hom.*, 3, 3).

20:22. The apostle is convinced that God is guiding his steps and watching over him like a father; but he is also unsure about what lies ahead: this uncertainty about the future is part of the human condition. "Grace does not work on its own. It respects men in the actions they take, it influences them, it awakens and does not entirely dispel their restlessness" (St John Chrysostom, *Hom. on Acts*, 37).

"The true minister of Christ is concious of his own weakness and labours in humility. He searches to see what is well-pleasing to God (cf. Eph 5:10) and, bound as it were in the Spirit (cf. Acts

159

Acts 21:4–11
Acts 26:16–18
2 Tim 4:7

Acts 18:6

what shall befall me there; [23]except that the Holy Spirit testifies to me in every city that imprisonment and inflictions await me. [24]But I do not account my life of any value nor as precious to myself, if only I may accomplish my course and the ministry which I received from the Lord Jesus, to testify to the gospel of the grace of God. [25]And now, behold, I know that all you among whom I have gone about preaching the kingdom will see my face no more. [26]Therefore I testify to you this day that I am innocent of

---

20:22), he is guided in all things by the will of him who wishes all men to be saved. He is able to discover and carry out that will in the course of his daily routine" (Vatican II, *Presbyterorum ordinis*, 15).

20:23. "No man, whether he be a Christian or not, has an easy life. To be sure, at certain times it seems as though everything goes as we planned. But this generally lasts for only a short time. Life is a matter of facing up to difficulties and of experiencing in our hearts both joy and sorrow. It is in this forge that a person can acquire fortitude, patience, magnanimity and composure [...].

"Naturally, the difficulties we meet in our daily lives will not be as great or as numerous as St Paul encountered. We will, however, discover our own meanness and selfishness, the sting of sensuality, the useless, ridiculous smack of pride, and many other failings besides: so very many weaknesses. But are we to give in to discouragement? Not at all. Together with St Paul, let us tell our Lord, 'For the sake of Christ, I am content with weakness, insults, hardships, persecutions and calamities; for when I am weak, then I am strong' (2 Cor 12:10)" (St Josemaría Escrivá, *Friends of God*, 77 and 212).

20:24. Paul has come to love Jesus Christ so much that he gives himself no importance: he sees his life as having no

meaning other than that of doing what God wants him to do (cf. 2 Cor 4:7; Phil 1:19–26; Col 1:24). He sees holiness as a constant, uninterrupted striving towards his encounter with the Lord; and all the great Fathers of the Church have followed him in this: "On the subject of virtue," St Gregory of Nyssa, for example, writes, "we have learned from the apostle himself that the only limit to perfection of virtue is that there is no limit. This fine, noble man, this divine apostle, never ceases, when running on the course of virtue, to 'strain forward to what lies ahead' (Phil 3:13). He realizes it is dangerous to stop. Why? Because all good, by its very nature, is unlimited: its only limit is where it meets its opposite: thus, the limit of life is death, of light darkness, and in general of every good its opposite. Just as the end of life is the beginning of death, so too if one ceases to follow the path of virtue one is beginning to follow the path of vice" (*On the Life of Moses*, 1, 5).

20:26. "He considers himself innocent of the blood of the disciples because he has not neglected to point out to them their defects" (St Bede, *Super Act. expositio, ad loc.*) Paul not only preached the Gospel to them and educated them in the faith: he also corrected their faults, putting into practice the advice he gave to the Galatians: "if a man is overtaken in any trespass, you who are spiritual should restore him in a spirit of gentleness. Look

the blood of all of you, ²⁷for I did not shrink from declaring to you the whole counsel of God. ²⁸Take heed to yourselves and to all the flock, in which the Holy Spirit has made you guardians, to feed the church of the Lord^v which he obtained with his own blood.^{w} ²⁹I know that after my departure fierce wolves will come in among you, not sparing the flock; ³⁰and from among your own selves will arise men speaking perverse things, to draw away the disciples after them. ³¹Therefore be alert, remembering that for

1 Tim 4:16
1 Pet 2:9; 5:2

Mt 7:15
Jn 10:12

2 Pet 2:1–2
1 Jn 2:19

1 Thess 2:11
1 Pet 5:8–9

---

to yourself, lest you too be tempted" (Gal 6:1). "A disciple of Christ will never treat anyone badly. Error he will call error, but the person in error he will correct with kindness. Otherwise he will not be able to help him, to sanctify him" (St J. Escrivá, *Friends of God*, 9).

20:28. Using a metaphor often found in the New Testament to describe the people of God (Ps 100:3; Is 40:11; Jer 13:17), Paul describes the Church as a flock and its guardians or bishops (*episcopos*) as shepherds. "The Church is a sheepfold, the sole and necessary gateway to which is Christ (Jn 10:1–10). It is also a flock, of which God foretold that he would himself be the shepherd (cf. Is 40:11; Ezek 34:11f), and whose sheep, although watched over by human shepherds, are nevertheless at all times led and brought to pasture by Christ himself, the Good Shepherd and prince of shepherds (cf. Jn 10:11; 1 Pet 5:4), who gave his life for his sheep (cf. Jn 10:11–16)" (Vatican II, *Lumen gentium*, 6).

In the early days of the Church the terms "priest" and "bishop" had not yet become defined: they both refer to sacred ministers who have received the sacrament of priestly Order.

The last part of the verse refers to Christ's sacrifice: through his redeeming action, the Church has become God's special property. The price of redemption

was the blood of Christ. Paul VI says that Christ, the Lamb of God, took to "himself the sins of the world, and he died for us, nailed to the Cross, saving us by his redeeming blood" (*Creed of the People of God*, 12).

The Council of Trent speaks of this when it presents the Redemption as an act of "his beloved Only-begotten, our Lord Jesus Christ, who ... merited justification for us by his most holy Passion on the wood of the Cross and made satisfaction for us to God the Father" (*De Iustificatione*, 7).

20:30. Errors derive not only from outsiders: they are also the product of members of the Church who abuse their position as brethren and even as pastors, leading the people astray by taking advantage of their good will. "It is of this that John writes, 'They went out from us, but they were not of us' [1 Jn 2:19]" (St Bede, *Super Act. expositio*, ad loc.).

20:31. "Here he shows that he actually taught them and did not proclaim the teaching once only, just to ease his conscience" (St John Chrysostom, *Hom. on Acts*, 44). Paul did not avoid the pastoral work which fell to him; he set an example of what a bishop should be. "Those who rule the community must perform worthily the tasks of government. [...] There is a danger that some who concern

v. Other ancient authorities read *of God*   **w.** Or *with the blood of his Own*

three years I did not cease night or day to admonish every one
with tears. ³²And now I commend you to God and to the word of
his grace, which is able to build you up and to give you the inheritance among all those who are sanctified. ³³I coveted no one's
silver or gold or apparel. ³⁴You yourselves know that these hands
ministered to my necessities, and to those who were with me.*
³⁵In all things I have shown you that by so toiling one must help
the weak, remembering the words of the Lord Jesus, how he said,
'It is more blessed to give than to receive.'"

³⁶And when he had spoken thus, he knelt down and prayed
with them all. ³⁷And they all wept and embraced Paul and kissed
him, ³⁸sorrowing most of all because of the word he had spoken,
that they should see his face no more. And they brought him to
the ship.

Deut 33:3
Eph 2:20–22

Mt 10:8

Acts 18:3
1 Cor 4:12
1 Thess 2:9

Acts 21:5

Rom 16:16
1 Pet 5:14

Acts 20:25

PART FOUR

St Paul, in imprisonment, bears witness to Christ

12. ST PAUL IN JERUSALEM

From Miletus to Caesarea

21 ¹And when we had parted from them and set sail, we came by a straight course to Cos, and the next day to Rhodes,

themselves with others and guide them towards eternal life may ruin themselves without realizing it. Those who are in charge must work harder than others, must be humbler than those under them, must in their own lives give an example of service, and must regard their subjects as a deposit which God has given them in trust" (St Gregory of Nyssa, *De instituto christiano*).

20:32. "It is not right for Christians to give such importance to human action

that they think all the laurels depend on their efforts: their expectation of reward should be subject to the will of God" (ibid.).

20:33–35. "The teachings of the apostle of the Gentiles [...] have key importance for the morality and spirituality of human work. They are an important complement to the great though discreet gospel of work that we find in the life and parables of Christ, in what Jesus 'did and taught'" (John Paul II, *Laborem exercens*, 26).

and from there to Patara.[x] [2]And having found a ship crossing to Phoenicia, we went aboard, and set sail. [3]When we had come in sight of Cyprus, leaving it on the left we sailed to Syria, and landed at Tyre; for there the ship was to unload its cargo. [4]And having sought out the disciples, we stayed there for seven days. Through the Spirit they told Paul not to go* on to Jerusalem. [5]And when our days there were ended, we departed and went on our journey; and they all, with wives and children, brought us on our way till we were outside the city; and kneeling down on the beach we prayed and bade one another farewell. [6]Then we went on board the ship, and they returned home.

[7]When we had finished the voyage from Tyre, we arrived at Ptolemais; and we greeted the brethren and stayed with them for one day. [8]On the morrow we departed and came to Caesarea; and

Acts 20:23; 21:11

Acts 20:36

Acts 6:5; 8:40

This saying of our Lord (v. 35) is not recorded in the Gospels.

20:36. For Christians every situation is suitable for prayer: "The Christian prays everywhere", Clement of Alexandria writes, "and in every situation, whether it be when taking a walk or in the company of friends, or while he is resting, or at the start of some spiritual work. And when he reflects in the interior of his soul and invokes the Father with unspeakable groanings" (*Stromata*, 7, 7).

20:37. They kiss Paul to show their affection for him and how moved they are. This is not the liturgical "kiss of peace". In the East kisses are a common expression of friendship and good manners—like handshaking in the West.

21:4. These Christians of Tyre were the fruit of earlier evangelization (cf. 11:19). The Spirit gave them foreknowledge of the "imprisonment and afflictions" (20:23) awaiting Paul in Jerusalem. It was only natural for them to try to dissuade him from going—a sign of Christian fraternity and mutual affection.

Without losing our serenity we too should be concerned about our brothers' and sisters' physical and spiritual health: "I am glad that you feel concern for your brothers: there is no better proof of your mutual love. Take care, however, that your concern does not degenerate into anxiety" (St J. Escrivá, *The Way*, 465).

21:5. "Kneeling down on the beach we prayed": every place is suitable for raising one's heart to God and speaking to him. "Each day without fail we should devote some time especially to God, raising our minds to him, without any need for the words to come to our lips, for they are being sung in our heart. Let us give enough time to this devout practice; at a fixed hour, if possible. Before the Tabernacle, close to him who has remained there out of Love. If this is not possible, we can pray anywhere because our God is ineffably present in the heart of every soul in grace" (St Josemaría Escrivá, *Friends of God*, 249).

21:8. Philip was one of the seven Christians ordained deacons to serve the needy, as described in 6:5. He played an

x. Other ancient authorities add *and Myra*

163

Acts 2:17

we entered the house of Philip the evangelist, who was one of the seven, and stayed with him. ⁹And he had four unmarried daughters, who prophesied.

The prophet Agabus

Acts 11:27–28
Acts 21:31–33

¹⁰While we were staying for some days, a prophet named Agabus came down from Judea. ¹¹And coming to us he took Paul's girdle and bound his own feet and hands, and said, "Thus says the Holy Spirit, 'So shall the Jews at Jerusalem bind the man who owns this girdle and deliver him into the hands of the Gentiles.'" ¹²When we heard this, we and the people there begged him not to go up to Jerusalem. ¹³Then Paul answered, "What are you doing, weeping and breaking my heart? For I am ready not only to be imprisoned but even to die at Jerusalem for the name of the Lord

important part in the evangelization of Samaria (cf. 8:5ff), opposed Simon the magician (cf. 8:9ff) and baptized the Ethiopian courtier (cf. 8:26ff).

21:9. Virginity is a gift of God which Paul discusses in his letters (cf. 1 Cor 7:25– 40). In his apostolic exhortation on the family, John Paul II devotes a section to this form of self-dedication to God: "Virginity or celibacy for the sake of the Kingdom of God not only does not contradict the dignity of marriage but presupposes it and confirms it. Marriage and virginity or celibacy are two ways of expressing and living the one mystery of the covenant of God with his people [...].

"Virginity or celibacy, by liberating the human heart in a unique way (1 Cor 7:32–35), bears witness that the Kingdom of God and his justice is that pearl of great price which is preferred to every other value no matter how great, and hence must be sought as the only definitive value. It is for this reason that the Church, throughout her history, has always defended the superiority of this charism to that of marriage, by reason of the wholly singular link which it has with

the Kingdom of God (cf. *Sacra virginitas*, 2).

"In spite of having renounced physical fecundity, the celibate person becomes spiritually fruitful, the father and mother of many, cooperating in the realization of the family according to God's plan" (*Familiaris consortio*, 16).

21:10–11. Agabus was the Christian prophet who, years earlier, warned of forthcoming famine and privation (cf. 11:27–28). In his present prophecy he uses symbolic gestures—like Old Testament prophets, particularly Jeremiah (cf. Jer 18:3ff; 19:1ff; 27:2ff)). His action is somewhat reminiscent of our Lord's prophecy about St Peter in John 21:18: "Truly, truly, I say to you, when you were young, you girded yourself and walked where you would; but when you are old, you will stretch out your hands, and another will gird you and carry you where you do not wish to go."

21:12–14. The Spirit's words and warnings (cf. 20:23; 21:4) confirm Paul's readiness to accept the will of God and bear the trials which they foretell (cf. 20:25, 27ff). His serenity contrasts with

Jesus." [14]And when he would not be persuaded, we ceased and Mt 6:10; 26:42
said, "The will of the Lord be done."

Paul arrives in Jerusalem and meets the Christians

[15]After these days we made ready and went up to Jerusalem.
[16]And some of the disciples from Caesarea went with us, bringing
us to the house of Mnason of Cyprus, an early disciple, with
whom we should lodge.

[17]When we had come to Jerusalem, the brethren received us
gladly. [18]On the following day Paul went in with us to James; and   Acts 12:17
all the elders were present. [19]After greeting them, he related one   Acts 15:4
by one the things that God had done among the Gentiles through
his ministry. [20]And when they heard it, they glorified God. And   Acts 15:1

---

the concern felt by those around him,
which stems from their affection for him.
His long life of self-surrender and self-
forgetfulness explains why he takes
things so calmly at this time: "This consists mainly or entirely in our ceasing to
care about ourselves and our own plea-
sures, for the least that anyone who is
beginning to serve the Lord can truly
offer him is his life. Once he has surren-
dered his will to him, what has he to
fear?" (St Teresa, *Way of Perfection*, 12).

"Accepting the will of God whole-
heartedly is a sure way of finding joy and
peace: happiness in the cross. Then we
realize that Christ's yoke is sweet and
that his burden is not heavy" (St
Josemaría Escrivá, *The Way*, 758).

Paul's example impresses the disciples and moves them to accept what God
has disposed, in words reminiscent of
Jesus' in the garden of Gethsemane (cf.
Lk 22:42).

21:18. Paul and his companions are received by James the Less, who was probably the head of the church of Jerusalem
during these years (cf. 12:17; 15:13; Gal
1:19; 1 Cor 15:7), and by the elders who
aided him in the government and spiritual care of the community. St Luke usually distinguishes elders from apostles.

Apparently the apostles, including Peter,
were no longer resident in the city.

The narrative here ceases to use the
first person plural and does not use it
again until the account of the journey to
Rome (cf. Acts 27:1). This indicates that
Luke accompanied Paul as far as
Jerusalem, and then was with him from
Caesarea to Rome.

21:19. Paul's apostolic ministry among
the Gentiles is readily accepted by the
Christians of the mother church of
Jerusalem because God has demonstrated
its legitimacy by blessing it with great
fruitfulness: God guides and plans the
mission to the Gentiles.

Paul in fact attributes all his success to
the Lord: "Neither he who plants nor he
who waters is anything, but only God who
gives the growth" (1 Cor 3:7). This conviction has guided every step he has
taken. "Everyone who prudently and
intelligently looks at the history of the
apostles of Jesus will clearly see", Origen
writes, "that they preached Christianity
with God-given strength and thereby were
able to attract men to the Word of God"
(*Against Celsus*, 1, 62).

21:20. The "zealous" Jews referred to by
St James should not be confused with

Rom 2:25–29
1 Cor 7:17–20

Acts 18:18

Acts 15:28–29

Num 6:1–20
1 Cor 9:20

they said to him, "You see, brother, how many thousands there are among the Jews of those who have believed; they are all zealous for the law, [21]and they have been told about you that you teach all the Jews who are among the Gentiles to forsake Moses, telling them not to circumcise their children or observe the customs. [22]What then is to be done? They will certainly hear that you have come. [23]Do therefore what we tell you. We have four men who are under a vow; [24]take these men and purify yourself along with them and pay their expenses, so that they may shave their heads. Thus all will know that there is nothing in what they have been told about you but that you yourself live in observance of the law. [25]But as for the Gentiles who have believed, we have sent a letter with our judgment that they should abstain from what has been sacrificed to idols and from blood and from what is strangled[y] and from unchastity." [26]Then Paul took the men, and the next day he purified himself with them and went into the temple, to give

---

"Zealots". Ardent attachment to the traditions of the fathers and hatred of the Romans had led to the development of a sect of Zealots, men of violence who played a key role in the rebellion of 66. This anti-Roman revolt, described in detail by Flavius Josephus in his book *The Jewish War* (written between 75 and 79) ended with the total destruction of the temple and of Jerusalem by the armies of Vespasian and Titus.

21:21. The rumours which observant Jews had heard about Paul's preaching were not without foundation, because the apostle regarded the Mosaic Law as something secondary as far as salvation was concerned: he did not accept circumcision as absolutely necessary (cf. Gal 4:9; 5:11; Rom 2:25–29). But the accusation was unjust. Paul never exhorted Christians of Jewish background not to circumcise their sons, and he himself ensured that Timothy was circumcised (cf. 16:3). In Corinth he came out in support of women following the Jewish custom of wearing the veil at liturgical

ceremonies (cf. 1 Cor 11:2–16); and he himself had no difficulty about taking a Nazirite vow (cf. 18:18).

"Paul was calumniated by those who did not understand the Spirit with which these customs should be kept by Jewish Christians, that is, in a spirit of homage to the divine authority and prophetic holiness of these signs — and not in order to attain salvation, which had been revealed with Christ and applied through the sacrament of Baptism. Those who calumniated were people who wanted to observe these customs as if believers in the Gospel could not attain salvation without them" (St Bede, *Super Act. expositio*, ad loc.).

21:23–24. This was a Nazirite vow (cf. Num 6). A Nazirite committed himself to abstaining from certain kinds of food and drink and not cutting his hair during the period of the vow (cf. the note on Acts 18:18). To end the vow the person arranged a sacrificial offering in the temple. St James suggests that Paul bear the expenses of this sacrifice — a common

---

y. Other early authorities omit *and from what is strangled*

notice when the days of purification would be fulfilled and the
offering presented for every one of them.

Paul is arrested in the temple

[27]When the seven days were almost completed, the Jews from
Asia, who had seen him in the temple, stirred up all the crowd,
and laid hands on him, [28]crying out, "Men of Israel, help! This is
the man who is teaching men everywhere against the people and
the law and this place; moreover he also brought Greeks into the
temple, and he has defiled this holy place." [29]For they had previously seen Trophimus the Ephesian with him in the city, and they
supposed that Paul had brought him into the temple. [30]Then all the
city was aroused, and the people ran together; they seized Paul
and dragged him out of the temple, and at once the gates were
shut. [31]And as they were trying to kill him, word came to the tri-

Ezek 44:9
Acts 6:13

Acts 20:4

type of pious act. This will show to all
who know him his respect for the Law
and the temple. Paul is putting into practice here the advice he gave to Christians
in Corinth: "To the Jews I became as a
Jew, in order to win Jews; to those under
the law I became as one under the law—
though not being myself under the law—
that I might win those under the law"
(1 Cor 9:20).

21:25. St James quotes the decisions of
the Council of Jerusalem, with which
Paul was very familiar. Presumably he
does this for the benefit of the apostle's
companions, who were not required, naturally, to go with Paul to the temple.

21:27–29. Paul's action, which should
have reassured these Jews, has in fact the
contrary effect and leads to the kind of
violent reaction typical of the fanatic.
Jews come as pilgrims to Jerusalem for
the Jewish feast of Pentecost and attack
Paul as a loathsome man: everywhere he
goes, they say, he speaks against the
Jewish people, the Law and the temple,
and now he has the effrontery to profane
the sacred precincts.

These accusations are similar to those

laid against our Lord in his time (cf. Mt
26:61; 27:40) and against Stephen (cf.
Acts 6:11–14). They start shouting and
soon bring everyone along with them—
the crowd only too ready to indulge their
prejudices by believing anything said
against Paul. The (groundless) accusation
that he has brought Gentiles into the
inner courtyards of the temple was a very
serious charge because that type of
offence was punishable by death under
Jewish law, and usually the Roman
authorities did execute those found guilty
of it. Archaeologists have unearthed one
of the temple's stone plaques warning
Gentiles, under pain of death, not to cross
over the low wall marking off the court-
yard of the Gentiles; the notice is in
Greek and Latin.

21:30. It was probably not the main
gates that were closed, but those between
the court of the Gentiles and the other
courtyards.

21:31–36. Paul would certainly have
been killed if the Roman soldiers had not
intervened. They were able to arrive on
the scene so quickly because the Antonia
Tower, where the Jerusalem garrison was

bune of the cohort that all Jerusalem was in confusion. [32]He at once took soldiers and centurions, and ran down to them; and when they saw the tribune and the soldiers, they stopped beating Paul. [33]Then the tribune came up and arrested him, and ordered him to be bound with two chains. He inquired who he was and what he had done. [34]Some in the crowd shouted one thing, some another; and as he could not learn the facts because of the uproar, he ordered him to be brought into the barracks. [35]And when he came to the steps, he was actually carried by the soldiers because of the violence of the crowd; [36]for the mob of the people followed, crying, "Away with him!"

[37]As Paul was about to be brought into the barracks, he said to the tribune, "May I say something to you?" And he said, "Do you know Greek? [38]Are you not the Egyptian, then, who recently stirred up a revolt and led the four thousand men of the Assassins out into the wilderness?" [39]Paul replied, "I am a Jew, from Tarsus

Acts 21:11

Lk 23:28
Acts 22:22

---

based, was located at one corner of the temple, only two flights of steps from the court of the Gentiles.

Having arrested Paul, whom the Romans take to be the cause of the uproar, the tribune prudently decides to transfer him to the fortress. A new section of the book now begins, in which St Luke will describe in detail the apostle's imprisonment (cf. Acts 21:33—22:29), his trial at Jerusalem and Caesarea (cf. chaps. 23–26) and his journey to Rome (cf. Acts 27:1—28:16) to appear before an imperial tribunal. From this point onwards Paul is not so much a tireless missionary and founder of churches as an imprisoned witness to the Gospel: even in these new circumstances he will manage to proclaim Christ.

21:38. This Egyptian outlaw is also mentioned by Flavius Josephus as a leader of a group of bandits who tried to capture Jerusalem and were put to flight by Felix, the governor (cf. *The Jewish War*, 2, 261–263).

The "Assassins" referred to were *sicarii*, so named because they always car-

ried a dagger (Latin: *sica*). Together with the Zealots, they played a prominent and inglorious part in the Jewish rebellion against Rome.

21:39. Paul continues to say nothing about his Roman citizenship. He simply states that he comes from Tarsus, a city which enjoyed self-government and to which he was proud to belong. It would seem that from the time of Claudius onwards it was possible to hold dual citizenship—to be a Roman citizen and the citizen of a particular city.

In keeping with his courage and sense of mission, the apostle decides to address the threatening crowd. He is more interested in winning over his adversaries than in escaping from them; in taking them on he is supported by the Gospel's inner strength and his own firm dedication to the service of Christ. "There is nothing weaker in fact", comments Chrysostom, "than many sinners—and nothing stronger than a man who keeps the law of God" (*Hom. on Acts*, 26). "The soldiers of Christ, that is, those who pray," St Teresa writes, "do not think of the time

in Cilicia, a citizen of no mean city; I beg you, let me speak to the people." ⁴⁰And when he had given him leave, Paul, standing on the steps, motioned with his hand to the people; and when there was a great hush, he spoke to them in the Hebrew language, saying:

Paul defends himself before the crowd

22 ¹"Brethren and fathers, hear the defence which I now make before you."

²And when they heard that he addressed them in the Hebrew language, they were the more quiet. And he said:

³"I am a Jew, born at Tarsus in Cilicia, but brought up in this city at the feet of Gamaliel, educated according to the strict manner of the law of our fathers, being zealous for God as you all are this day. ⁴I persecuted this Way to the death, binding and

Acts 7:2

Acts 26:4–5
2 Cor 11:22
Gal 1:14
Phil 3:5–6

Acts 8:3

---

when they will have to fight, they never fear public enemies; for they already know them and they realize that nothing can withstand the strength the Lord has given them, and that they will always be victors and heaped with gain" (*Way of Perfection*, 38, 2).

Once again, Paul relies on God giving him the right things to say; he does not settle for simply reproaching them for their behaviour: he knows that "truth is not preached with swords and lances, or the aid of soldiers, but rather by means of persuasion and counsel" (St Athanasius, *Historia arianorum*, 33).

21:40. "In the Hebrew language": this must mean Aramaic, the language which, after the return of the Jews from the Babylonian captivity, gradually came into general use, due to the influence of the Persian empire.

22:1–21. St Luke gives us Paul's address to the Jews of Jerusalem, the first of three speeches in his own defence (cf. 24:10–21; 26:1–23) in which he tries to show that there is no reason why Christianity should be opposed by Jew or by Roman.

Here he presents himself as a pious Jew, full of respect for his people and their sacred traditions. He earnestly desires his brethren to realize that there are compelling reasons for his commitment to Jesus. He is convinced that they can experience in their souls the same kind of spiritual change as he did. However, this speech is not a closely-argued apologia. His main intention is not so much to answer the accusations levelled against him as to use this opportunity to bear witness to Jesus Christ, whose commandments validate Paul's actions. What he is really trying to do is to get his hearers to obey the voice of the Lord.

22:1. "Brethren and fathers": the "fathers" may refer to members of the Sanhedrin present in the crowd.

22:3. Gamaliel (cf. 5:34) belonged to the school of the rabbi Hillel, which was noted for a less rigorous interpretation of the Law than that of Shammai and his disciples.

22:4. The situation described by Paul is confirmed by 1 Corinthians 15:9: "I am

Acts 9:1–18;
26:9–18

delivering to prison both men and women, [5]as the high priest and the whole council of elders bear me witness. From them I received letters to the brethren, and I journeyed to Damascus to take those also who were there and bring them in bonds to Jerusalem to be punished.

[6]"As I made my journey and drew near to Damascus, about noon a great light from heaven suddenly shone about me. [7]And I fell to the ground and heard a voice saying to me, 'Saul, Saul,

Mt 2:23

why do you persecute me?' [8]And I answered, 'Who are you, Lord?' And he said to me, 'I am Jesus of Nazareth whom you are per-

Wis 18:1

secuting.' [9]Now those who were with me saw the light but did not hear the voice of the one who was speaking to me. [10]And I said, 'What shall I do, Lord?' And the Lord said to me, 'Rise, and go into Damascus, and there you will be told all that is appointed for you to do.' [11]And when I could not see because of the brightness of that light, I was led by the hand by those who were with me, and came into Damascus.

[12]"And one Ananias, a devout man according to the law, well spoken of by all the Jews who lived there, [13]came to me, and

---

the least of the apostles, unfit to be called an apostle, because I persecuted the church of God"; Galatians 1:13: "You have heard of my former life in Judaism, how I persecuted the church of God violently and tried to destroy it"; Philippians 3:5–6: "as to the law a Pharisee, as to zeal a persecutor of the church"; and 1 Timothy 1:13: "I formerly blasphemed and persecuted and insulted him [Christ]".

22:6–11. Paul describes in his own words what happened on the way to Damascus (cf. 9:3–9; 26:6–16). This account differs in some ways from—but does not contradict—the two other versions of the episode, especially that of chapter 9, which is told in St Luke's words.

Paul adds that the whole thing happened at midday (cf. 26:13), and he says that Jesus referred to himself as "Jesus of Nazareth". He also includes the question "What shall I do, Lord?", which is not given in chapter 9.

As far as Paul's companions were concerned, we know that they saw the light (cf. 22:9) but did not see anyone (cf. 9:7): they did not see the glorified Jesus; they heard a voice (cf. 9:7) but did not hear the voice of the one who was speaking to Paul (cf. 22:9), that is, did not understand what the voice said.

22:10. Paul addresses Jesus as "Lord", which shows that the vision has revealed to him the divinity of the One he was persecuting.

The divine voice orders him to get up from the ground and the future apostle of the Gentiles obeys immediately. The physical movement of getting up is a kind of symbol of the spiritual uplift his soul is given by God's call. "This was the first grace, that was given to the first Adam; but more powerful than it is the grace in the second Adam. The effect of the first grace was that a man might have justice, if he willed; the second grace, therefore, is more powerful, because it affects the will itself; it makes for a

standing by me said to me, 'Brother Saul, receive your sight.' And in that very hour I received my sight and saw him. [14]And he said, 'The God of our fathers appointed you to know his will, to see the Just One and to hear a voice from his mouth; [15]for you will be a witness for him to all men of what you have seen and heard.[16]And now why do you wait? Rise and be baptized, and wash away your sins, calling on his name.'

[17]"When I had returned to Jerusalem and was praying in the temple, I fell into a trance [18]and saw him saying to me, 'Make haste and get quickly out of Jerusalem, because they will not accept your testimony about me.' [19]And I said, 'Lord, they themselves know that in every synagogue I imprisoned and beat those who believed in thee. [20]And when the blood of Stephen thy witness* was shed, I also was standing by and approving, and keeping the garments of those who killed him.' [21]And he said to me, 'Depart; for I will send you far away to the Gentiles.'"

Acts 3:14

1 Jn 1:1–3

Acts 9:26
Gal 1:18
Acts 13:46–48;
18:6; 28:25–28

Acts 7:58; 8:1

Acts 9:15

---

strong will, a burning charity, so that by a contrary will the spirit overcomes the conflicting will of the flesh" (St Augustine, *De correptione et gratia*, 11, 31).

"Many have come to Christianity", Origen says, "as if against their will, for a certain spirit, appearing to them, in sleep or when they are awake, suddenly silences their mind, and they change from hating the Word to dying for him" (*Against Celsus*, I, 46).

Paul's conversion is an outstanding example of what divine grace and divine assistance in general can effect in a person's heart.

22:12–16. This account of Ananias and his role in Paul's conversion is much shorter than that given in chapter 9 (cf. vv. 10–19). St Paul adapts it here to suit his audience (who are all Jews). He presents Jesus as the one in whom the Old Testament prophecies are fulfilled. Like Peter (cf. 3:13ff) and Stephen (cf. 7:52) he speaks of the "God of our fathers" and the "Just One" when referring to God and to Jesus respectively.

22:17–18. Paul's return to Jerusalem took place three years after his conversion. Paul deliberately mentiond his custom of going to pray in the temple, which at that time was a normal place of prayer for Christians. He refers to an ecstasy not mentioned anywhere else and to a vision of Jesus Christ reminiscent of that described in Revelation 1:10.

22:19. Synagogues were also used for non-liturgical purposes, they usually had additional rooms for meeting (cf. Mt 10:17; 23:34; Mk 13:9).

22:20. The word "witness" is beginning to acquire the meaning of "martyr" as now used in the Church: martyrdom is the supreme form of bearing witness to the Christian faith.

St Paul refers to his presence at the martyrdom of St Stephen to emphasize the miraculous nature of his own conversion.

22:21. By promising that he will "send" him to the Gentiles, our Lord makes him an "apostle", on a par with the Twelve.

Paul, the Roman citizen

^{Acts 25:24}

²²Up to this word they listened to him; then they lifted up their voices and said, "Away with such a fellow from the earth! For he ought not to live." ²³And as they cried out and waved their garments and threw dust into the air, ²⁴the tribune commanded him to be brought into the barracks, and ordered him to be examined by scourging, to find out why they shouted thus against him. ²⁵But

^{Acts 16:22–37}

when they had tied him up with the thongs, Paul said to the centurion who was standing by, "Is it lawful for you to scourge a man who is a Roman citizen, and uncondemned?" ²⁶When the centurion heard that, he went to the tribune and said to him, "What are you about to do? For this man is a Roman citizen." ²⁷So the tribune came and said to him, "Tell me, are you a Roman citizen?" And he said, "Yes." ²⁸The tribune answered, "I bought this citizenship for a large sum." Paul said, "But I was born a citizen."

^{Acts 16:38–39}

²⁹So those who were about to examine him withdrew from him instantly; and the tribune also was afraid, for he realized that Paul was a Roman citizen and that he had bound him.

Speech before the Sanhedrin

³⁰But on the morrow, desiring to know the real reason why the Jews accused him, he unbound him, and commanded the chief

---

22:22. The mere mention of preaching to the Gentiles leads to interruption: his listeners are so bigoted, their fear is so irrational, that they cannot listen calmly to what Paul has to say, never mind take it all in.

22:24. Roman law allowed suspects and slaves to be put under the lash in order to extract confessions.

22:25. As at Philippi (cf. 16:37), Paul stands on his rights as a Roman citizen; but this time he does so at an earlier stage and avoids being scourged.

22:30. This does not seem to have been a regular session of the Sanhedrin; it is an informal one arranged by Lysias (Acts 23:26) to enable documentation to be prepared, now that "evidence" cannot be extracted from Paul by torture.

23:1. In response to the Jews' accusations, which St Luke here takes as read, Paul sums up his defence with this key statement. Having an upright conscience is a central point in Pauline spirituality. It comes up all the time in his letters (cf. 1 Cor 4:4; 2 Cor 1:12; 1 Tim 1:5, 19; 2 Tim 1:3) and is borne out by his own conduct: even when he was a persecutor of the Church he was always trying to do his best to serve God; his sincerity was never in question, even if his zeal was misdirected. In this terse remark he rejects any suggestion that he was disrespectful to the Law.

23:2. This Ananias should not be confused with Annas (cf. 4:6). He was appointed high priest in 47 and deposed around the year 58. In 66 he was assassinated by Jews in revolt against Rome. He orders that Paul be struck, undoubtedly

priests and all the council to meet, and he brought Paul down and set him before them.

23 ¹And Paul, looking intently at the council, said, "Brethren, I have lived before God in all good conscience up to this day." ²And the high priest Ananias commanded those who stood by him to strike him on the mouth. ³Then Paul said to him, "God shall strike you, you whitewashed wall! Are you sitting to judge me according to the law, and yet contrary to the law you order me to be struck?" ⁴Those who stood by said, "Would you revile God's high priest?" ⁵And Paul said, "I did not know, brethren, that he was the high priest; for it is written, 'You shall not speak evil of a ruler of your people.'"

⁶But when Paul perceived that one part were Sadducees and the other Pharisees, he cried out in the council, "Brethren, I am a Pharisee, a son of Pharisees; with respect to the hope and the resurrection of the dead I am on trial." ⁷And when he had said this, a dissension arose between the Pharisees and the Sadducees; and the assembly was divided. ⁸For the Sadducees say that there is no resurrection, nor angel, nor spirit; but the Pharisees acknowledge

Acts 24:16
Heb 13:18

Jn 18:22

Ezek 13:10–15
Mk 23:27

Ex 22:28

Acts 26:5

Mt 22:23

---

because he cannot answer what Paul says or because he feels personally offended. Josephus tells us that Ananias was an arrogant and hot-tempered man (cf. *Jewish Antiquities*, 20, 199).

23:3. Paul's harsh words are not due to his annoyance at being unjustly treated. We might have expected him, in imitation of Jesus (cf. Mt 27:12), to remain silent. However, Paul thinks that the right thing to do here is to speak out. His words are a deliberate prophecy of the fate that awaits Ananias.

23:5. Many scholars think that Paul is being sarcastic here, as if to say, "I would never have thought that anyone who gave an order against the Law like that could be the high priest." Others think that the apostle realizes that his words may have scandalized some of those present, and therefore he wants to make it clear that he respects Jewish institutions and the Law.

23:6–9. From St Luke's Gospel (cf. 20:27) we know that the Sadducees, unlike the Pharisees, did not believe in a future resurrection of the dead. This is the only place in the New Testament where it says that they also denied the existence of angels and spirits; however, this is confirmed by Jewish and secular sources.

In the course of his trial, Paul brings up a subject which sets his judges at each other. Personal advantage is not his main reason for doing this. He is obviously very shrewd, but he really does not expect to get an impartial hearing from the Sanhedrin. Therefore he tries to stir their consciences and awaken their love for the truth and thereby elicit some sympathy for Christians. Although Christian belief in the Resurrection was not the same thing as the Pharisees' belief, the two had this in common: they believed in the resurrection of the dead.

them all. ⁹Then a great clamour arose; and some of the scribes of the Pharisees' party stood up and contended, "We find nothing wrong in this man. What if a spirit or an angel spoke to him?" ¹⁰And when the dissension became violent, the tribune, afraid that Paul would be torn in pieces by them, commanded the soldiers to go down and take him by force from among them and bring him into the barracks.

Acts 18:9–10; 27:24

¹¹The following night the Lord stood by him and said, "Take courage, for as you have testified about me at Jerusalem, so you must bear witness also at Rome."

A Jewish plot against Paul

Acts 9:23; 20:3 ¹²When it was day, the Jews made a plot and bound themselves by an oath neither to eat nor drink till they had killed Paul. ¹³There were more than forty who made this conspiracy. ¹⁴And they went to the chief priests and elders, and said, "We have strictly bound ourselves by an oath to taste no food till we have killed Paul. ¹⁵You therefore, along with the council, give notice now to the tribune to bring him down to you, as though you were going to determine his case more exactly. And we are ready to kill him before he comes near."

¹⁶Now the son of Paul's sister heard of their ambush; so he went and entered the barracks and told Paul. ¹⁷And Paul called one of the centurions and said, "Bring this young man to the tri-

23:9. They are referring to his vision on the road to Damascus. They are not going as far as to say that it was Jesus who spoke to Paul, but they do not rule out the possibility that he had a genuine spiritual experience.

23:11. The Lord is Jesus. These words of consolation to Paul show him that God will guide him all along, right up to his court appearance in Rome. From this point onwards the prisoner is seeking primarily to bear witness to the Gospel and not just to defend himself. In imprisonment he will continue to do the same work as he did when free. "Keep alert with all perseverance," he tells the Ephesians, "making supplication for all the saints, and also for me, that utterance may be given me in opening my mouth boldly to proclaim the mystery of the gospel, for which I am an ambassador in chains; that I may declare it boldly, as I ought to speak" (6:18–20).

23:12–22. Blinded by fanaticism, a small group of Jews take an oath to do away with Paul. Their promise not to eat or drink until they fulfil their intention is in line with similar vows taken in the service of better causes (cf. 1 Sam 14:24). Hatred has misdirected their piety, and what was originally religious conviction has changed into resistance to the Holy Spirit. "The Lord says, 'Blessed are those who hunger and thirst after justice'. These Jews, on the contrary, hunger after iniquity and thirst after blood. [...] But there is no wisdom or

bune; for he has something to tell him." [18]So he took him and brought him to the tribune and said, "Paul the prisoner called me and asked me to bring this young man to you, as he has something to say to you." [19]The tribune took him by the hand, and going aside asked him privately, "What is it that you have to tell me?" [20]And he said, "The Jews have agreed to ask you to bring Paul down to the council tomorrow, as though they were going to inquire somewhat more closely about him. [21]But do not yield to them; for more than forty of their men lie in ambush for him, having bound themselves by an oath neither to eat nor drink till they have killed him; and now they are ready, waiting for the promise from you."

13. FROM JERUSALEM TO ROME

Paul is moved to Caesarea

[22]So the tribune dismissed the young man, charging him, "Tell no one that you have informed me of this."

[23]Then he called two of the centurions and said, "At the third hour of the night get ready two hundred soldiers with seventy horsemen and two hundred spearmen to go as far as Caesarea. [24]Also provide mounts for Paul to ride, and bring him safely to Felix the governor." [25]And he wrote a letter to this effect:

---

prudence or counsel that can prevent God's will. For, although Paul, a Jew with the Jews, offered sacrifices, shaving his head and going barefoot, he did not escape the chains which had been foretold. And although these men make plans and swear an oath and prepare an ambush, the apostle will receive protection to enable him, as he had already been told, to bear witness to Christ in Rome" (St Bede, *Super Act. expositio*, ad loc.).

23:16. This is the only reference in this book or the letters (with the exception of Rom 16:7–11) to Paul's relatives.

23:23–24. The information brought by Paul's nephew must have led Lysias to advance his plans for the transfer of the

prisoner to the governor; besides, the Sanhedrin had only limited powers to detain a prisoner pending trial.

Felix had been governor or procurator of Judea since the year 52. He was a freedman who had risen remarkably high, but according to Tacitus he "exerted royal power with the mind of a slave". Felix was successful in repressing various riots which heralded the great Jewish uprising in the year 66, but he was recalled in 60 on account of his harsh and cruel rule (cf. 24:27).

23:25–30. This letter from Claudius Lysias is the only secular letter recorded in the New Testament. Lysias gives the governor a brief report on the detainee. He bends the facts a little in that he does not mention that at an early stage he planned

Act 22:25–29

Acts 25:18–19; 26:31

26"Claudius Lysias to his Excellency the governor Felix, greeting. 27This man was seized by the Jews, and was about to be killed by them, when I came upon them with the soldiers and rescued him, having learned that he was a Roman citizen. 28And desiring to know the charge on which they accused him, I brought him down to their council. 29I found that he was accused about questions of their law, but charged with nothing deserving death or imprisonment. 30And when it was disclosed to me that there would be a plot against the man, I sent him to you at once, ordering his accusers also to state before you what they have against him."

31So the soldiers, according to their instructions, took Paul and brought him by night to Antipatris. 32And on the morrow they returned to the barracks, leaving the horsemen to go on with him. 33When they came to Caesarea and delivered the letter to the governor, they presented Paul also before him. 34On reading the letter, he asked to what province he belonged. When he learned that he was from Cilicia 35he said, "I will hear you when your accusers arrive." And he commanded him to be guarded in Herod's praetorium.

---

to have Paul scourged: significantly the letter only mentions the Jews' religious accusation to the effect that Paul was speaking against the Law (cf. 21:28) and does not give weight to the charge that he brought Gentiles into the temple (cf. 21:28b).

23:31. Antipatris was 60 kilometres (40 miles) from Jerusalem and 40 kilometres from Caesarea. It had been founded by Herod the Great in honour of his father, Antipater.

23:33–35. Felix acts in line with what the law lays down. He acquaints himself firsthand with Paul's case and decides to try him as soon as his accusers arrive. The governor could have remitted the case to the legate of the province of Syria, which at that time included Cilicia, but he prefers to deal with the matter himself.

Herod's praetorium was a palace built by Herod the Great, which later became the residence of the Roman governor.

24:1–21. By being sent to Caesarea by the tribune, Paul has entered the jurisdiction of Roman law. The Jews fail to change things so that he can be tried by the Sanhedrin. The judicial hearing now begins. Here we have an instance of the Roman judicial process known as *cognitio extra ordinem*, or extraordinary procedure, to distinguish it from the *cognitio ordinaria*, the normal kind of trial. The former was marked by more flexible procedures. In the *cognitio ordinaria* the magistrate allowed charges to be brought against the accused according to established legal procedures which did not allow much flexibility in the way the trial was conducted or in the type of sentence that could be passed. The *cognitio extra ordinem* allowed a judge more initiative; it had five stages: 1) private accusation; 2) a formal *pro tribunali* hearing; 3) use by the judge of expert legal advice; 4) hearing of evidence from the parties concerned; and 5) assessment of this evidence by the judge.

The trial before Felix

24 [1]And after five days the high priest Ananias came down with some elders and a spokesman, one Tertullus. They laid before the governor their case against Paul; [2]and when he was called, Tertullus began to accuse him, saying:

Acts 23:2

"Since through you we enjoy much peace, and since by your provision, most excellent Felix, reforms are introduced on behalf of this nation, [3]in every way and everywhere we accept this with all gratitude. [4]But, to detain you no further, I beg you in your kindness to hear us briefly. [5]For we have found this man a pestilent fellow, an agitator among all the Jews throughout the world, and a ringleader of the sect of the Nazarenes. [6]He even tried to profane the temple, but we seized him.[z] [8]By examining him yourself you will be able to learn from him about everything of which we accuse him."

Acts 17:6

Acts 21:28

[9]The Jews also joined in the charge, affirming that all this was so.

[10]And when the governor had motioned to him to speak, Paul replied:

Chapters 24 and 25 of Acts are in fact an important source of information about the use of extraordinary procedures in criminal cases. The narrative tells us about Paul's being accused privately by Jews (cf. 23:35; 24:1). It uses the correct legal terminology when referring to hearings by the judge (cf. 25:6, 17). It mentions the committee of experts who assist the judge (cf. 25:9, 12). It describes the charges in some detail and shows the kind of discretion the magistrates (Felix and Festus) had in the way they handled the case and approached the evidence.

24:1. The charge had to be presented by a professional lawyer. Tertullus may have been a Jew skilled in Hebrew and Roman law. His language, at any rate, shows that he shares his clients' point of view.

24:2–4. Tertullus' opening words are sheer flattery. Felix's administration was

in fact notoriously inefficient and had disastrous effects.

24:5–9. The Jews make a timid effort to have Paul transferred back into their own jurisdiction. They see him as a kind of Jewish heretic, and Christianity as just a Jewish sect. They level four charges against the apostle: Paul is a social undesirable, an agitator and a leader of a dangerous sect. These three vague charges frame a fourth charge, which is much more specific: he has tried to profane the temple, the symbol of the Jewish nation. Even though the charge is basically religious in character, Tertullus tries to present Paul as a politically dangerous type.

24:10–21. In his defence Paul points out that the Jews, by failing to recognize Jesus, have failed to understand the true religious tradition of Israel, and also that their charges about creating a disturbance

---

z. Other ancient authorities add *and we would have judged him according to our law. [7]But the chief captain Lysias came and with great violence took him out of our hands, [8]commanding his accusers to come before you*

Acts 20:16

Mt 5:17
Rom 3:31; 16:26

Jn 15:29

Acts 23:1
Rom 15:25
Acts 21:27

"Realizing that for many years you have been judge over this nation, I cheerfully make my defence. [11]As you may ascertain, it is not more than twelve days since I went up to worship at Jerusalem; [12]and they did not find me disputing with any one or stirring up a crowd, either in the temple or in the synagogues, or in the city. [13]Neither can they prove to you what they now bring up against me. [14]But this I admit to you, that according to the Way, which they call a sect, I worship the God of our fathers, believing everything laid down by the law or written in the prophets, [15]having a hope in God which these themselves accept, that there will be a resurrection of both the just and the unjust. [16]So I always take pains to have a clear conscience toward God and toward men. [17]Now after some years I came to bring to my nation alms and offerings. [18]As I was doing this, they found me purified in the temple, without any crowd or tumult. But some Jews from Asia— [19]they ought to be here before you and to make an accusation, if

and profaning the temple are groundless and they have no proof for them.

The tone of the address is serious and sober, as befits the authority by which he is being judged. This is in keeping with what the Gospel teaches us about the respect due to civil authorities: they should be obeyed by all citizens because they are designed to protect the common good. "A Christian", Tertullian will write, "is an enemy of no one, least of all the emperor. Since he knows him to be appointed by his own God, he must love, reverence, honour, and wish him well, together with the whole Roman Empire, as long as the world shall last. [...] In this way, then, do we honour the emperor, as is both lawful for us and expedient for him, as a man next to God: who has received whatever he is from God; who is inferior to God alone" (*To Scapula*, 2).

"The political community and public authority", Vatican II teaches, "are based on human nature, and therefore they belong to an order established by God; nevertheless, the choice of political regime and the appointment of rulers are left to the free decision of the citizens (cf. Rom 13:1–5).

"It follows that political authority, either within the political community as such or through organizations representing the State, must be exercised within the limits of the moral order and directed toward the common good (understood in the dynamic sense of the term) according to the juridical order legitimately established or due to be established. Citizens, then, are bound in conscience to obey (cf. Rom 13:5). Accordingly, the responsibilty, the dignity, and the importance of State rulers is clear" (*Gaudium et spes*, 74).

24:11–12. Paul did not go up to Jerusalem to preach but rather to worship God in the temple.

24:14–16. The apostle rejects the charge that Christianity is a Jewish sect. It is something much more than that. For St Paul the Old Testament finds its fulfilment in the Gospel, and without the Gospel Judaism is incomplete. The central beliefs of the Jewish religion can be summed up as belief in God and in a

they have anything against me. [20]Or else let these men themselves say what wrongdoing they found when I stood before the council, [21]except this one thing which I cried out while standing among them, 'With respect to the resurrection of the dead I am on trial before you this day.'"

[22]But Felix, having a rather accurate knowledge of the Way, put them off, saying, "When Lysias the tribune comes down, I will decide your case." [23]Then he gave orders to the centurion that he should be kept in custody but should have some liberty, and that none of his friends should be prevented from attending to his needs.

A further appearance before Felix

[24]After some days Felix came with his wife Drusilla, who was a Jewess; and he sent for Paul and heard him speak upon faith in Christ Jesus. [25]And as he argued about justice and self-control and

Mk 6:17–20
Jn 16:8

future life and also upright conduct in line with the dictates of conscience; all this, Paul says, is also at the centre of Christian preaching.

The apostle establishes a direct connexion between hope in the resurrection and good deeds in this present life. The *St Pius V Catechism* will say, many centuries later, that the thought of a future resurrection "must also prove a powerful incentive to the faithful to use every exertion to lead lives of rectitude and integrity, unsullied by the defilement of sin. For if they reflect that those boundless riches which will follow after the resurrection are now offered to them as rewards, they will be easily attracted to the pursuit of virtue and piety.

"On the other hand, nothing will have greater effect in subduing the passions and withdrawing souls from sin, than frequently to remind the sinner of the miseries and torments with which the reprobate will be visited, who on the last day will come forth unto the resurrection of judgment.

"An ardent desire of the promised rewards of eternal life will always be one

of the most effective encouragements in our Christian life. However sorely fidelity to our faith as Christians may be tried in certain circumstances, hope of this reward will lighten our burden and revive our spirit, and God will always find us prompt and cheerful in his divine service" (I, 12, 14; 13, 1).

St Paul says that both the just and the unjust will experience the resurrection of the body.

24:17. This is the only reference in Acts to the collection in aid of the Jerusalem community (cf. Rom 15:25).

24:19. Paul's objection carries great legal weight because Roman law laid down that those who brought charges had to appear before the tribunal.

24:24. Drusilla was a daughter of Herod Agrippa (cf. 12:1ff). She had left her lawful husband to marry the Roman governor.

24:25. It is very daring of Paul to speak about chastity to this couple living in

Acts 25:9

future judgment, Felix was alarmed and said, "Go away for the present; when I have an opportunity I will summon you." [26]At the same time he hoped that money would be given him by Paul. So he sent for him often and conversed with him. [27]But when two years had elapsed, Felix was succeeded by Porcius Festus; and desiring to do the Jews a favour, Felix left Paul in prison.

Festus resumes the trial. Paul appeals to Caesar

Acts 23:15

25 [1]Now when Festus had come into his province, after three days he went up to Jerusalem from Caesarea. [2]And the chief priests and the principal men of the Jews informed him against Paul; and they urged him, [3]asking as a favour to have the man sent to Jerusalem, planning an ambush to kill him on the way. [4]Festus replied that Paul was being kept at Caesarea, and that he himself intended to go there shortly. [5]"So," said he, "let the men of authority among you go down with me, and if there is anything wrong about the man, let them accuse him."

---

concubinage. "Observe", says St John Chrystostom, "that, when he has the opportunity to converse with the governor, Paul does not say anything which might influence his decision or flatter him: he says things which shock him and disturb his conscience" (*Hom. on Acts*, 51).

Felix's fear of future judgment has little to do with true fear of God, which is the beginning of wisdom and therefore of conversion. The governor's attitude shows that he does have remorse of conscience—but it does not make him change his lifestyle.

24:26. Felix may well have wanted to get some of the money Paul brought to Jerusalem, funds which Paul in fact has referred to (v. 17). Venal officials were common enough during this period.

24:27. "Two years": a biennium, a technical word used in Roman law for the maximum length a person could be detained without a trial (cf. 28:30).

It was normal practice for an outgo-

ing governor to leave to his successor the resolution of important cases pending.

25:1–12. Paul's case is now re-heard before Festus, following the same procedure as described in the previous chapter. The new governor wants to examine the matter for himself before making a definitive judgment. He probably realizes or suspects that Paul is innocent, but he will soon be as perplexed as Felix his predecessor and as subject to the same pressures from the Jews.

Porcius Festus seems to have been a good governor. He held this position for two or three years, until the year 62, when he died.

25:1–2. Festus' courtesy visit to Jerusalem would enable him to be briefed on all matters awaiting decision, including Paul's case.

25:9. The governor is not thinking of handing the prisoner over to the Jewish courts. But his political prudence leads him to take Paul's accusers' requests

⁶When he had stayed among them not more than eight or ten days, he went down to Caesarea; and the next day he took his seat on the tribunal and ordered Paul to be brought. ⁷And when he had come, the Jews who had gone down from Jerusalem stood about him, bringing against him many serious charges which they could not prove. ⁸Paul said in his defence, "Neither against the law of the Jews, nor against the temple, nor against Caesar have I offended at all." ⁹But Festus, wishing to do the Jews a favour, said to Paul, "Do you wish to go up to Jerusalem, and there be tried on these charges before me?" ¹⁰But Paul said, "I am standing before Caesar's tribunal, where I ought to be tried; to the Jews I have done no wrong, as you know very well. ¹¹If then I am a wrong-doer, and have committed anything for which I deserve to die, I do not seek to escape death; but if there is nothing in their charges against me, no one can give me up to them. I appeal to Caesar." ¹²Then Festus, when he had conferred with his council, answered, "You have appealed to Caesar; to Caesar you shall go."

Mt 26:59–60
Lk 23:14–15

Acts 24:14

Acts 24:27

---

partly into account and give the Sanhedrin a say in the trial. Festus can also use the Sanhedrin as a *consilium*, a source of expert advice. It is in this sense that he invites Paul to agree to be tried in Jerusalem. The governor's question is in fact a rhetorical one: he is simply notifying Paul of a decision he has already made.

25:10–11. Paul realizes what Festus intends to do, and he appeals to Caesar in order to avoid being tried in unfavourable circumstances. From a strictly judicial point of view, Paul's action is not an "appeal" but what is termed in Roman law a *provocatio*. An appeal only operated once a lower court had passed sentence. A *provocatio* meant insisting that the case be brought to a higher court, for that court to decide whether the accused was guilty or not.

Only Roman citizens could ask for their cases to be examined by the imperial tribunal in Rome.

These various legal proceedings, ordained and used by Providence, help

ensure that Paul fulfil the task God has marked out for him and foretold (cf. Acts 23:11). "He appeals to Caesar and hastens to Rome to persist still longer in preaching, and thereby go to Christ crowned with the many who thereby will come to believe, as well as those who already believe [through him]" (St Bede, *Super Act. expositio*, ad loc.).

Paul's characteristic generosity once again brings him to contemplate and accept the prospect of having to die. For him death would in the last analysis be God's will for him and not just the decision of a human court. But his sense of justice obliges him to ask that his actions be judged on the basis of his merits and demerits in the eyes of the law. "These are not the words of a man who condemns himself to death, but of a man who firmly believes in his own innocence" (St John Chrysostom, *Hom. on Acts*, 51).

25:12. Possibly Paul's appeal did not take automatic effect: the governor may not necessarily have been obliged by law

Festus briefs Agrippa

¹³Now when some days had passed, Agrippa the king and Bernice arrived at Caesarea to welcome Festus. ¹⁴And as they stayed there many days, Festus laid Paul's case before the king, saying, "There is a man left prisoner by Felix; ¹⁵and when I was at Jerusalem, the chief priests and the elders of the Jews gave information about him, asking for sentence against him. ¹⁶I answered them that it was not the custom of the Romans to give up any one before the accused met the accusers face to face, and had opportunity to make his defence concerning the charge laid against him. ¹⁷When therefore they came together here, I made no delay, but on the next day took my seat on the tribunal and ordered the man to be brought in. ¹⁸When the accusers stood up, they brought no charge in his case of such evils as I supposed; ¹⁹but they had certain points of dispute with him about their own superstition and about one Jesus, who was dead, but whom Paul asserted to be alive. ²⁰Being at a loss how to investigate these questions, I asked whether he wished to go to Jerusalem and be tried there regarding them. ²¹But when Paul had appealed to be kept in custody for the decision of the emperor, I commanded him to be held until I send him to Caesar." ²²And Agrippa said to Festus, "I should like to hear the man myself." "Tomorrow," said he, "you shall hear him."

Acts 24:1; 25:2

Acts 18:5; 23:29 1 Cor 15:14

Lk 23:8

---

to send the detainee to Rome. But once the latter invoked his right of appeal, Festus would be able to escape the dilemma he faced, by sending Paul to Rome. If he did not transfer the case to Rome, this might have been taken as an insult to Caesar—involving political risk (cf. 26:32)—and if he set Paul free he would be needlessly offending the Jews.

25:13. Herod Agrippa II was a son of Herod Agrippa I. He was born in the year 27. Like his father he had won favour with Rome and had been given various territories in northern Palestine, which he was allowed to rule with the title of king. Bernice was his sister.

25:19. Festus' words show his indifference towards Paul's beliefs and his religious controversy with the Jews. The conversation between the two politicians

reveals a typical attitude of worldly men to matters which they consider far-fetched and irrelevant as far as everyday affairs are concerned. This passage also shows us that in the course of his trial Paul must have had an opportunity to speak about Jesus and confess his faith in the Resurrection.

Jesus Christ is alive; he is the centre of history and the centre of each and every person's existence. "The Church believes that Christ, who died and was raised for the sake of all (cf. 2 Cor 5:15) can show man the way and strengthen him through the Spirit in order to be worthy of his destiny: nor is there any other name under heaven given among men by which they can be saved (cf. Acts 4:12). The Church likewise maintains that the key, the centre and the purpose of the whole of man's history is to be found in its Lord and Master. She also maintains that beneath all that changes there is

Paul before Agrippa

[23]So on the morrow Agrippa and Bernice came with great pomp, and they entered the audience hall with the military tribunes and the prominent men of the city. Then by command of Festus Paul was brought in. [24]And Festus said, "King Agrippa and all who are present with us, you see this man about whom the whole Jewish people petitioned me, both at Jerusalem and here, shouting that he ought not to live any longer. [25]But I found that he had done nothing deserving death; and as he himself appealed to the emperor, I decided to send him. [26]But I have nothing definite to write to my lord about him. Therefore I have brought him before you, and, especially before you, King Agrippa, that, after we have examined him, I may have something to write. [27]For it seems to me unreasonable, in sending a prisoner, not to indicate the charges against him."

Paul's speech in the presence of Agrippa

26 [1]Agrippa said to Paul, "You have permission to speak for yourself." Then Paul stretched out his hand and made his defence:

[2]"I think myself fortunate that it is before you, King Agrippa, I am to make my defence today against all the accusations of the Jews, [3]because you are especially familiar with all customs and

---

much that is unchanging, much that has its ultimate foundation in Christ, who is the same yesterday, and today, and forever (cf. Heb 13:8)" (Vatican II, *Gaudium et spes*, 10).

"Stir up that fire of faith. Christ is not a figure of the past. He is not a memory that is lost in history.

"He lives! '*Iesus Christus heri et hodie, ipse et in saecula*', says Saint Paul, 'Jesus Christ is the same today as he was yesterday and as he will be for ever'" (St Josemaría Escrivá, *The Way*, 584).

25:21. "Caesar" and "Augustus" were titles of the Roman emperor. At this time the emperor was Nero (54–68).

25:22. Agrippa's reply is reminiscent of a similar scene when his grand-uncle Herod Antipas expressed a desire to see Jesus (cf. Lk 9:9; 23:8). "His conversa-

tion with the governor awakens in Agrippa a strong desire to hear Paul. Festus meets his wish, and thereby Paul's glory is further enhanced. This is the outcome of the machinations against him: without them no judge would have deigned to listen to such things, nor would anyone have heard them with such rapt attention" (St John Chrysostom, *Hom. on Acts*, 51).

26:1–30. Paul has already defended himself before Festus, and his words (cf. 25:8ff) make it clear that he is innocent of any offence against Roman law. Now he will speak before Agrippa, in an address aimed mainly at Jews rather than Romans. He bears witness to the Gospel before a king—fulfilling the prophecy of Acts 9:15 and Luke 21:12.

26:2–3. "Observe", comments St John

controversies of the Jews; therefore I beg you to listen to me patiently.

Acts 22:3

⁴"My manner of life from my youth, spent from the beginning among my own nation and at Jerusalem, is known by all the Jews.

Gal 1:14
Phil 3:5

⁵They have known for a long time, if they are willing to testify, that according to the strictest party of our religion I have lived as

Acts 23:6

a Pharisee. ⁶And now I stand here on trial for hope in the promise

Dan 12:1–3
2 Mac 7

made by God to our fathers, ⁷to which our twelve tribes hope to attain, as they earnestly worship night and day. And for this hope I am accused by Jews, O king! ⁸Why is it thought incredible by any of you that God raises the dead?

⁹"I myself was convinced that I ought to do many things in opposing the name of Jesus of Nazareth. ¹⁰And I did so in

Jn 16:2
Acts 9:13;
22:20

Jerusalem; I not only shut up many of the saints in prison, by authority from the chief priests, but when they were put to death I cast my vote against them. ¹¹And I punished them often in all the synagogues and tried to make them blaspheme; and in raging fury against them, I persecuted them even to foreign cities.

Chrysostom, "how Paul begins this exposition of his teaching not only about faith in the forgiveness of sin but also about the rules of human conduct. If his conscience had been heavy with any fault he would have been concerned about the idea of being judged by one who was in a position to know all the facts; but it is proper to a clear conscience not only not to reject as judge one who knows the facts but actually to rejoice at being judged by him" (*Hom. on Acts*, 52).

Paul wants to convince Agrippa, whom he regards as well versed in Jewish beliefs, that the Gospel is simply the fulfilment of the Holy Scriptures.

26:5. Paul uses the word "Pharisee" here to indicate his strict observance of the Law prior to becoming a Christian (cf. Phil 3:5).

25:6–8. In his addresses Paul frequently defends himself by referring to the fulfilment of the Old Testament prophecies and promises (cf. 23:6; 24:25; 28:20). In

addition to revealing his own attitudes and convictions, he is saying that the fundamental question at issue is whether the Jews really believe in these prophecies or not.

Although he is speaking about resurrection in general terms, Paul's words obviously refer to the resurrection of Jesus, which legitimates him as the Messiah. "Paul offers two proofs of resurrection. One is taken from the prophets. He does not quote any particular prophet; he simply says that this is what Jews believe. His second proof the apostle takes from the facts themselves. And what is it? That Christ, after rising from the dead, conversed with him" (*Hom. on Acts*, 52).

26:9–18. Paul once more gives an account of the circumstances of his conversion (cf. 9:3–9 and 22:6–11).

26:10. It is possible that Paul was involved in some way in Sanhedrin decisions to persecute the Church; or he may

¹²"Thus I journeyed to Damascus with the authority and commission of the chief priests. ¹³At midday, O king, I saw on the way a light from heaven, brighter than the sun, shining round me and those who journeyed with me. ¹⁴And when we had all fallen to the ground, I heard a voice saying to me in the Hebrew language, 'Saul, Saul, why do you persecute me? It hurts you to kick against the goads.' ¹⁵And I said, 'Who are you, Lord?' And the Lord said, 'I am Jesus whom you are persecuting. ¹⁶But rise and stand upon your feet; for I have appeared to you for this purpose, to appoint you to serve and bear witness to the things in which you have seen me and to those in which I will appear to you, ¹⁷delivering you from the people and from the Gentiles—to whom I send you ¹⁸to open their eyes, that they may turn from darkness to light and from the power of Satan to God, that they may receive forgiveness of sins and a place among those who are sanctified by faith in me.'

¹⁹"Wherefore, O King Agrippa, I was not disobedient to the heavenly vision, ²⁰but declared first to those at Damascus, then at

Ezek 2:1

Jer 1:7

Is 42:7, 16
Jn 8:12
Acts 9:17–18
Col 1:12–14

Mt 3:8
Gal 1:16

be referring to the part he played in the martyrdom of Stephen (cf. 8:1).

26:14. The final sentence in this verse is not given in Paul's two previous accounts of his conversion on the road to Damascus (cf. 9:4; 22:7). It is a Greek turn of phrase to describe useless resistance, but it was also known and used by Jews as a proverb (cf. *The Psalms of Solomon*, 16, 4).

26:16–18. Paul's calling and mission are described in terms similar to that of the calling of the prophets of Israel (cf. Ezek 2:1; Is 42:6f). God makes known his design in an imperious command which radically changes the whole life of his chosen one. He addresses the man's free will to get him to do what God wills simply because God wills it. But he also enlightens his mind to show him what his vocation means, so that he accept it in the conviction of being the recipient of a special grace to perform an important task.

26:19–23. This section is a summary of Paul's preaching, presenting Christianity as the fulfilment of the ancient prophecies.

26:19. The apostle asserts that he has not embraced Christianity blindly: he is totally convinced of its truth. He explains his change of heart in terms of docility and obedience to the divine voice he heard. Paul's experience is repeated in different (usually less dramatic) ways in the lives of every man and woman. At particular moments in life the Lord calls us and invites us to a new conversion which draws us out of sin or lukewarmness. What we have to do is to listen carefully to that calling and obey it. "We should let our Lord get involved in our lives, admitting him trustingly, removing from his way any obstacles or excuses. We tend to be on the defensive, to be attached to our selfishness. We always want to be in charge, even if it's only to be in charge of our wretchedness. That is why we must go to Jesus, so to have him

Acts 21:30–31

Acts 13:47; 17:3
1 Cor 15:20–23
Col 1:18

Jerusalem and throughout all the country of Judea, and also to the Gentiles, that they should repent and turn to God and perform deeds worthy of their repentance. [21]For this reason the Jews seized me in the temple and tried to kill me. [22]To this day I have had the help that comes from God, and so I stand here testifying both to small and great, saying nothing but what the prophets and Moses said would come to pass: [23]that the Christ must suffer, and that, by being the first to rise from the dead, he would proclaim light both to the people and to the Gentiles."

---

make us truly free. Only then will we be able to serve God and all men" (St J. Escrivá, *Christ Is Passing By*, 17).

Response to God's grace is a necessary pre-condition for being helped by God in the future. Accepting one grace is important for equipping us to accept the following one, a process which continues right through our life. "In this true perfection lies," St Gregory of Nyssa writes, "never stopping on the path towards the best and never putting limits on perfection" (*De perfecta christiani forma*).

"The grace of the Holy Spirit," Gregory says elsewhere, "is granted to every man with the idea that he ought to increase what he receives" (*De instituto christiano*). The same idea is expressed by St Teresa of Avila when she writes that "we must seek new strength with which to serve him, and endeavour not to be ungrateful, for that is the condition on which the Lord bestows his jewels. Unless we made good use of his treasures, and of the high estate to which he brings us, he will take those treasures back from us, and we shall be poorer than before, and His Majesty will give the jewels to some other person who can display them to advantage and to his own profit and that of others" (*Life*, 10, 6).

26:23. Paul identifies the Messiah with the suffering Servant of Yahweh (cf. Is 42:1ff; 49:1ff), and asserts that Jesus is the fulfilment of both these prophecies.

26:24. Festus cannot understand what Paul is saying; he thinks his mind is gone. He seems to have a certain sympathy for the apostle, but he cannot make him out. The fact is that divine wisdom does seem to make no sense humanly speaking. "He regarded it as madness for a man in chains not to deal with the calumnies that threatened him but, instead, to be speaking about the convictions which enlightened him from within" (St Bede, *Super Act. expositio*, in loc.).

26:27. Paul's only interest is in upholding the Gospel and bringing salvation to his hearers. He is trying to get Agrippa, who is presiding over this session and is Paul's main questioner, to react interiorly and allow grace to move his heart. "How admirably he behaves! Imprisoned for spreading the teachings of Christ, he misses no opportunity to preach the Gospel. Brought before Festus and Agrippa, he declares unflinchingly: 'To this day I have had the help that comes from God and so I stand here testifying to small and great ...' (Acts 26:22).

"The apostle does not silence or hide his faith, or his apostolic preaching that had brought down on him the hatred of his persecutors. He continues preaching salvation to everyone he meets. And, with marvellous daring, he boldly faces Agrippa [...]. Where did St Paul get all his strength from? *Omnia possum in eo qui me confortat!* (Phil 4:13). I can do all

Reactions to Paul's speech

[24] And as he thus made his defence, Festus said with a loud voice, "Paul, you are mad; your great learning is turning you mad." [25] But Paul said, "I am not mad, most excellent Festus, but I am speaking the sober truth. [26] For the king knows about these things, and to him I speak freely; for I am persuaded that none of these things has escaped his notice, for this was not done in a corner. [27] King Agrippa, do you believe the prophets? I know that you believe." [28] And Agrippa said to Paul, "In a short time you think to make me a Christian!" [29] And Paul said, "Whether short or long, I would to God that not only you but also all who hear me this day might become such as I am—except for these chains."

Jn 10:20
Jn 18:37
Jn 18:20
Acts 11:26
1 Pet 4:16

things in him who strengthens me. I can do all things, because God alone gives me this faith, this hope, this charity" (St Josemaría Escrivá, *Friends of God*, 270f).

Apostolate is a responsibility and a duty with which Christ charges every Christian at all times. "Nothing is more useless than a Christian who is not dedicated to saving his brethren. Do not appeal to your poverty: he whose alms amounted to only two little coins would rise up to accuse you, if you did; and so would Peter, who says, Silver and gold I have none; and Paul, who was so poor that he often went hungry. Do not appeal to your humble circumstances, because they too were humble people, of modest condition. Do not appeal to your lack of knowledge, for they too were unlettered. Are you a slave or a runaway? Onesimus was one also. [...] Are you unwell? So was Timothy" (St John Chrysostom, *Hom. on Acts*, 20).

26:28. The king's remark, which is angry yet serious, shows that Paul's words have touched him. He feels he cannot respond to the apostle's call, but his conscience and his position as a Jewish prince prevent him from denying that he has any faith in the prophecies God has given his people.

However, he resists the divine grace extended to him by what Paul has been saying and now by Paul's question. He lacks the inner dispositions which faith calls for—that is, the moral predisposition and attitude which allows someone to accept God's word and decide to give his life a new direction. He is not genuinely interested in seeking God. "If any man's will is to do his will, he shall know whether the teaching is from God or whether I am speaking on my own authority" (Jn 7:17).

26:29. Once again Paul shows his practical zeal for all souls; he is not overawed by the circumstances in which he finds himself.

"Charity with everyone means ... apostolate with everyone. It means we, for our part, must really translate into deeds the great desire of God 'who desires all men to be saved and to come to the knowledge of the truth' (1 Tim 2:4). [...] For Christians, loving means 'wanting to want', 'wanting to love', making up one's mind in Christ to work for the good of souls, without discrimination of any kind; trying to obtain for them, before any other good, the greatest good of all, that of knowing Christ and falling in love with him" (*Friends of God*, 230f).

³⁰Then the king rose, and the governor and Bernice and those who were sitting with them; ³¹and when they had withdrawn, they said to one another, "This man is doing nothing to deserve death or imprisonment." ³²And Agrippa said to Festus, "This man could have been set free if he had not appealed to Caesar."

Departure for Rome. Voyage to Crete

27 ¹And when it was decided that we should sail for Italy, they delivered Paul and some other prisoners to a centurion of the Augustan Cohort, named Julius. ²And embarking in a ship of Adramyttium, which was about to sail to the ports along the coast of Asia, we put to sea, accompanied by Aristarchus, a Macedonian from Thessalonica. ³The next day we put in at Sidon; and Julius treated Paul kindly, and gave him leave to go to his friends and be cared for. ⁴And putting to sea from there we sailed under the lee of Cyprus, because the winds were against us. ⁵And when we had sailed across the sea which is off Cilicia and Pamphylia, we came to Myra in Lycia. ⁶There the centurion found a ship of Alexandria sailing for Italy, and put us on board. ⁷We sailed slowly for a number of days, and arrived with difficulty off Cnidus, and as the wind did not allow us to go on, we sailed under the lee of Crete off Salmone. ⁸Coasting along it with difficulty, we

Acts 19:29

Acts 24:23; 28:16

26:32. To declare Paul innocent and set him free in spite of his appeal to Rome would have caused offence both to the emperor and to the Jews.

27:1—28:15. This account of St Paul's sea journey is so exact in its terminology that it is regarded as an important source of information on seafaring in ancient times. It gives a great deal of detail and describes things so vividly that it obviously is what it is—an account of an eyewitness, St Luke, who may even have made notes during the journey.

The narrative also shows how St Paul maintains supernatural outlook despite new difficulties; and how he keeps up his apostolic work and entrusts himself entirely to God's loving providence.

27:2. Prisoners were not sent on a special ship; instead, places were negotiated

for them on merchant ships. The centurion finds places for these prisoners on a ship which has to call into various ports on the coast of Asia Minor, in the hope of eventually finding a ship bound for Italy.

27:3. The centurion Julius sees the Christians of Sidon as "friends" of Paul. St Luke uses the word "friend" here, but it was not the normal thing for Christians to call each other "friend"; however, they are friends of God—"you are my friends" (Jn 15:14)—and from this friendship is born the loving friendship which binds them together. So it is quite understandable that pagans should see Christians as good friends of one another.

27:6. The ship of Alexandria on which they embark must have been a grain ship, one of many used to transport grain from Egypt to Rome. These broad, heavy

came to a place called Fair Havens, near which was the city of
Lasaea.

The voyage is resumed against Paul's advice

[9]As much time had been lost, and the voyage was already dangerous Lev 16:29–31
because the fast had already gone by, Paul advised them, [10]saying,
"Sirs, I perceive that the voyage will be with injury and much loss,
not only of the cargo and the ship, but also of our lives." [11]But the
centurion paid more attention to the captain and to the owner of the
ship than to what Paul said. [12]And because the harbour was not suitable to winter in, the majority advised to put to sea from there, on
the chance that somehow they could reach Phoenix, a harbour of
Crete, looking northeast and southeast,[a] and winter there.

A storm

[13]And when the south wind blew gently, supposing that they had
obtained their purpose, they weighed anchor and sailed along
Crete, close inshore. [14]But soon a tempestuous wind, called the
northeaster, struck down from the land; [15]and when the ship was
caught and could not face the wind, we gave way to it and were
driven. [16]And running under the lee of a small island called
Cauda,[b] we managed with difficulty to secure the boat; [17]after

---

boats had one mast amidship and another
forward; the hull was covered by a deck
which had openings or movable timbers
which gave access to the hold, where the
cargo was stored and where passengers
took shelter in bad weather.

27:9. By the time they reach Fair Havens
Paul and his companions have been travelling for almost forty days. At that time
travel on the high seas was considered
unsafe from the middle of September
onwards, and out of the question from
early November until March. The fast
was that prescribed for all Jews on the
Day of Atonement (cf. Lev 16:29–31). In
the year 60 it fell at the end of October.

27:10–13. Prior to this, Paul had suffered
shipwreck three times (cf. 2 Cor 11:25),
and he knew very well how risky the

voyage would be, but most of the people
on board were hoping to reach Sicily or
at least some port more suitable for win-
tering in. As soon as they got a suitable
wind they weighed anchor and went
along the coast in an easterly direction,
using a skiff (which doubled as a sort of
lifeboat) to take the ship out of harbour.

St John Chrysostom draws this lesson
from the passage: "Let us stay firm in the
faith, which is the safe port. Let us listen
to it rather than to the pilot we have
within, that is, our reason. Let us pay
attention to Paul rather than to the pilot
or the captain. If we do listen to experience we will not be injured or disdained"
(*Hom. on Acts*, 53).

27:17–18. They managed to haul up the
skiff, but due to the dark they were afraid
of going on to the dangerous Syrtis sand-

a. Or *southwest and northwest* **b.** Other ancient authorities read *Clauda*

hoisting it up, they took measures[c] to undergird the ship; then, fearing that they should run on the Syrtis, they lowered the gear, and so were driven. [18]As we were violently storm-tossed, they began next day to throw the cargo overboard; [19]and the third day they cast out with their own hands the tackle of the ship. [20]And when neither sun nor stars appeared for many a day, and no small tempest lay on us, all hope of our being saved was at last abandoned.

Jon 1:5

Paul's vision. He rallies his companions

Acts 27:33

[21]As they had been long without food, Paul then came forward among them and said, "Men, you should have listened to me, and should not have set sail from Crete and incurred this injury and loss. [22]I now bid you to take heart; for there will be no loss of life among you, but only of the ship. [23]For this very night there stood by me an angel of the God to whom I belong and whom I worship, [24]and he said, 'Do not be afraid, Paul; you must stand before Caesar; and lo, God has granted you all those who sail with you.' [25]So take heart, men, for I have faith in God that it will be exactly as I have been told. [26]But we shall have to run on some island."

Acts 23:11

[27]When the fourteenth night had come, as we were drifting across the sea of Adria, about midnight the sailors suspected that they were nearing land. [28]So they sounded and found twenty fath-

---

banks off the coast of Africa. To prevent this they put out a sea anchor to brake the progress of the ship. They also go to drastic lengths to lighten the vessel.

27:19–20. These perils at sea remind us of the difficulties a person can come up against in the course of his life as he makes his way towards eternity. If we are in danger of being shipwrecked, of losing supernatural life, we need to throw out everything which is in the way, even things which up to then were necessary, such as the tackle and the cargo, in order to save our life.

In moments of disorientation and darkness, which the Lord permits souls to experience, when we cannot see the stars to work out which way to go, we

need to use the resources God gives us for solving problems: "Christ has given his Church sureness in doctrine and a flow of grace in the sacraments. He has arranged things so that there will always be people to guide and lead us, to remind us constantly of our way" (St Josemaría Escrivá, *Christ Is Passing By*, 34). In particular, we have Mary, the Star of the Sea and the Morning Star, who has protected and will continue to protect and guide seafarers to their destination.

27:24. Paul prays to God for his own safety and that of his companions, and is made to understand that this prayer will definitely be granted. St John Chrysostom is very conscious of how apostolic Paul would have been in these circumstances

c. Greek *helps*

oms; a little farther on they sounded again and found fifteen fathoms. [29]And fearing that we might run on the rocks, they let out four anchors from the stern, and prayed for day to come. [30]And as the sailors were seeking to escape from the ship, and had lowered the boat into the sea, under pretence of laying out anchors from the bow, [31]Paul said to the centurion and the soldiers, "Unless these men stay in the ship, you cannot be saved." [32]Then the soldiers cut away the ropes of the boat, and let it go.

[33]As day was about to dawn, Paul urged them all to take some food, saying, "Today is the fourteenth day that you have continued in suspense and without food, having taken nothing. [34]Therefore I urge you to take some food; it will give you strength, since not a hair is to perish from the head of any of you." [35]And when he had said this, he took bread, and giving thanks to God in the presence of all he broke it and began to eat. [36]Then they all were encouraged and ate some food themselves. [37](We were in all two hundred and seventy-six[d] persons in the ship.) [38]And when they had eaten enough, they lightened the ship, throwing out the wheat into the sea.

Mt 10:30

Rom 14:5
1 Tim 4:4

Shipwreck and rescue
[39]Now when it was day, they did not recognize the land, but they noticed a bay with a beach, on which they planned if possible to

and, referring to his predictions about the fate of the ship, he says that "the apostle does not make them out of boasting; he wants to bring the seafarers to the faith and make them more receptive to what he has to teach" (*Hom. on Acts*, 53).

27:30–32. The sailors were trying to escape, but their skill was needed if everyone was to be saved. By letting the boat go, the centurion sees to it that all will contribute to ensuring that everyone on board reaches safety. This solidarity produces the desired result. In this we can see a symbol of what should happen in the ship of the Church: no one should leave the ship in an effort just to save himself, abandoning the others to their fate.

27:33. St John Chrysostom explains that "this long fast was not a miracle; it was that fear and danger took away their appetite completely. The miracle was that they escaped from the shipwreck. Despite all the misfortunes of the voyage, it gave Paul the chance to instruct the soldiers and crew, and how happy he would have been if all had embraced the faith" (*Hom. on Acts*, 53).

St Paul inspires the other seafarers with his own confidence; his serenity and initiative are in contrast with the despair felt by the others, who have no supernatural outlook of any kind.

27:35. This food which they eat is ordinary food, not the Eucharist or Christian *agape*; before the meal he gives thanks in

d. Other ancient authorities read *seventy-six* or *about seventy-six*

191

bring the ship ashore. [40]So they cast off the anchors and left them in the sea, at the same time loosening the ropes that tied the rudders; then hoisting the foresail to the wind they made for the beach. [41]But striking a shoal[e] they ran the vessel aground; the bow struck and remained immovable, and the stern was broken up by the surf. [42]The soldiers' plan was to kill the prisoners, lest any should swim away and escape; [43]but the centurion, wishing to save Paul, kept them from carrying out their purpose. He ordered those who could swim to throw themselves overboard first and make for the land, [44]and the rest on planks or on pieces of the ship. And so it was that all escaped to land.

Waiting in Malta

28 [1]After we had escaped, we then learned that the island was called Malta. [2]And the natives showed us unusual kindness, for they kindled a fire and welcomed us all, because it had begun to rain and was cold. [3]Paul had gathered a bundle of sticks and put them on the fire, when a viper came out because of the heat and fastened on his hand. [4]When the natives saw the creature hanging from his hand, they said to one another, "No doubt this

accordance with Jewish custom. Commenting on this, St Bede draws a lesson about our need of the bread of life to save us from the danger of this world: "Paul encourages those whom he has promised will come safe out of the shipwreck, to take some food. If four anchors had kept them afloat during the night, when the sun came up they were going to reach *terra firma*. But only he who eats the bread of life can avoid the storms of this world" (*Super Act. expositio*, ad loc.).

27:41. The present-day "St Paul's Bay" on the island of Malta exactly fits the description St Luke gives here. The sailors tried to steer the ship into the small inlet, but it ran aground on a sandbank before they could get there. Although they were within striking distance of the beach, the sea was so rough that it broke up the ship, whose prow was

trapped. "This is what happens to souls given to this world who do not strive to despise worldly things: the prow of their intentions is completely locked into the earth and the force of the waves completely demolishes all the work they have accomplished" (St Bede, *Super Act. expositio*, ad loc.).

"Why did God not save the boat from shipwreck? So that the travellers would realize the scale of the danger and that they were saved from it not by any human help but by God, who saved their lives after the boat broke up. In like manner the just are well off even in storms and tempests, on the high seas or in a rough bay, because they are protected from everything and even come to the rescue of others.

"Aboard a ship in danger of being engulfed by the waves, the enchained prisoners and the whole crew owe their

e. Greek *place of two seas*

man is a murderer. Though he has escaped from the sea, justice has not allowed him to live." [5]He, however, shook off the creature into the fire and suffered no harm. [6]They waited, expecting him to swell up or suddenly fall down dead; but when they had waited a long time and saw no misfortune come to him, they changed their minds and said that he was a god.

[7]Now in the neighbourhood of that place were lands belonging to the chief man of the island, named Publius, who received us and entertained us hospitably for three days. [8]It happened that the father of Publius lay sick with fever and dysentery; and Paul visited him and prayed, and putting his hands on him healed him. [9]And when this had taken place, the rest of the people on the island who had diseases also came and were cured. [10]They presented many gifts to us;[f] and when we sailed, they put on board whatever we needed.

Mk 16:18
Lk 10:19

Acts 14:11

Lk 4:38–40; 10:9

Arrival in Rome
[11]After three months we set sail in a ship which had wintered in the island, a ship of Alexandria, with the Twin Brothers as figureheads. [12]Putting in at Syracuse, we stayed there for three days.

safety to the presence of Paul. See how useful it is to live in the company of a devout and saintly person. Frequent and terrible storms buffet our souls. God can free us from them if we are as sensible as those sailors and pay attention to the saints' advice. [...] Not only were they saved from shipwreck but they embraced the faith.

"Let us believe St Paul. Even if we be in the midst of storms we shall be set free from dangers; even if we be fasting for forty days, we shall stay alive; even if we fall into darkness and obscurity, if we believe in him we shall be freed" (St John Chrysostom, *Hom. on Acts*, 53).

28:2. "Natives": literally "barbarians". The Maltese were Phoenicians by race and did not speak Greek—which is why Luke describes them in this way.

28:4. "Justice", here, is a proper name. The notion of justice was personified in a goddess of vengeance or vindictive justice.

28:5. This is a fulfilment of a promise made by our Lord: "These signs will accompany those who believe: in my name they will cast out demons; they will speak in new tongues; they will pick up serpents, and if they drink any deadly thing, it will not hurt them" (Mk 16:17–18).

28:12–14. Syracuse was then the main city of Sicily. From there they went along the eastern coast of the island and crossed the straits of Messina to reach Rhegium, where they stopped for a day. Finally, they disembarked at Pozzuoli, which was the principal port in the gulf of Naples. There Paul found a Christian community and stayed with them for a week, and they

f. Or *honoured us with many honours*

¹³And from there we made a circuit and arrived at Rhegium; and after one day a south wind sprang up, and on the second day we came to Puteoli. ¹⁴There we found brethren, and were invited to stay with them for seven days. And so we came to Rome. ¹⁵And the brethren there, when they heard of us, came as far as the Forum of Appius and Three Taverns to meet us. On seeing them Paul thanked God and took courage. ¹⁶And when we came into Rome, Paul was allowed to stay by himself, with the soldier that guarded him.

Paul and the Roman Jews

¹⁷After three days he called together the local leaders of the Jews; and when they had gathered, he said to them, "Brethren, though I had done nothing against the people or the customs of our fathers, yet I was delivered prisoner from Jerusalem into the hands of the Romans. ¹⁸When they had examined me, they wished to set me at liberty, because there was no reason for the death penalty in my case. ¹⁹But when the Jews objected, I was compelled to appeal to Caesar—though I had no charge to bring against my nation. ²⁰For

Acts 23:29

Acts 25:11; 26:32

---

would have sent word on to the Christians at Rome to tell them that Paul would soon be with them.

28:14. The text conveys the atmosphere of human and supernatural brotherhood that existed among the Christians. Paul would have been extremely happy to be received so affectionately by the brethren. Now at least he would have a chance to rest after his long journey.

"How well the early Christians practised this ardent charity which went beyond the limits of mere human solidarity or natural kindness. They love one another, through the heart of Christ, with a love both tender and strong. [...] The principal apostolate we Christians must carry out in the world, and the best witness we can give of our faith, is to help bring about a climate of genuine charity within the Church. For who indeed could feel attracted to the Gospel if those who say they preach the Good News do not really love one another, but spend their time attacking one another, spreading slander and rancour" (St Josemaría Escrivá, *Friends of God*, 225f).

28:15. The Forum of Appius and Three Taverns were 69 kilometres (about 40 miles) and 53 kilometres from Rome, respectively, on the Via Appia, which ran south from Rome to the port of Puteoli (modern Pozzuoli). We do not know anything about the Christian community in Rome at this time or how it came to be founded. The tradition is that it was founded by St Peter, which does not necessarily mean that no other Christians arrived there before him, or that there had not been conversions there of pagans or of Jewish residents. In fact, St Augustine (cf. *Letters*, 102, 8) quotes the philosopher Porphyry as saying that there were Jews in Rome shortly after the reign of Caligula (AD March 37 to January 41).

28:16. Paul must have arrived in Rome around the year 61. He was allowed to

this reason therefore I have asked to see you and speak with you, since it is because of the hope of Israel that I am bound with this chain." [21]And they said to him, "We have received no letters from Judea about you, and none of the brethren coming here has reported or spoken any evil about you. [22]But we desire to hear from you what your views are; for with regard to this sect we know that everywhere it is spoken against."

Acts 17:19

[23]When they had appointed a day for him, they came to him at his lodging in great numbers. And he expounded the matter to them from morning till evening, testifying to the kingdom of God and trying to convince them about Jesus both from the law of Moses and from the prophets. [24]And some were convinced by what he said, while others disbelieved. [25]So, as they disagreed among themselves, they departed, after Paul had made one statement: "The Holy Spirit was right in saying to your fathers through Isaiah the prophet:

Acts 13:15–41

Acts 13:46–47

[26]'Go to this people, and say,
You shall indeed hear but never understand,
and you shall indeed see but never perceive.

Is 6:9–10
Mt 13:14

---

stay in a private house; in other words, he was under *custodia militaris*, which meant that the only restriction was that he was guarded by a soldier at all times. This is the last verse where St Luke uses the first person plural.

28:17. In keeping with his missionary custom, Paul immediately addresses the Jews of Rome; in fact there is no further mention of his contact with the Christians in the city. The apostle wants to give his fellow Jews a kind of last opportunity to hear and understand the Gospel. He presents himself as a member of the Jewish community who wants to take a normal part in the life of that community and feels he has to explain his own position.

28:19. The use of Roman privileges by a Jew might have been regarded by Jews as a sign of disrespect towards their own beliefs and customs. Therefore, Paul tries to explain why he took the exceptional step of invoking his Roman citizenship and appealing to Caesar.

28:23. Paul speaks now not about his own salvation but about the Gospel, and, as he usually did in synagogues, he proclaims to his Jewish listeners that Jesus is the Messiah foretold by the prophets and promised to the people of Israel.

28:25–28. Since now, in Rome also, many Jews have rejected the Gospel, Paul announces that he is free of his self-imposed obligation to proclaim the Gospel first to the Jews. His words suggest that it is the Christians who have understood the meaning of the promises made by God to the chosen people, and that it is they who are really the true Israel. Christ's disciples have not abandoned the Law. It is, rather, the Jews who have renounced their position as the chosen people. "We are the true, spiritual people of Israel," St Justin writes, "the race of Judah, and of Jacob, and of Isaac and of

Jn 12:39
2 Cor 3:14

^{27}For this people's heart has grown dull,
and their ears are heavy of hearing,
and their eyes they have closed;
lest they should perceive with their eyes,
and hear with their ears,
and understand with their heart,
and turn for me to heal them.'
^{28}Let it be known to you then that this salvation of God has been
sent to the Gentiles; they will listen."[g]

Paul's ministry in Rome

Phil 1:14
2 Tim 2:9

^{30}And he lived there two whole years at his own expense,[h] and
welcomed all who came to him, ^{31}preaching the kingdom of God
and teaching about the Lord Jesus Christ quite openly and unhin-
dered.

Abraham, he who was testified to by God even while he was still uncircumcised, he who was blessed and named the father of many nations" (*Dialogue with Tryphon*, 11, 5).

28:30–31. "Not only was he not forbidden to preach in Rome", St Bede writes, "but despite the enormous power of Nero and all his crimes which history reports, he remained free to proclaim the Gospel of Christ to the furthest parts of the West, as he himself writes to the Romans: 'At present, however, I am going to Jerusalem with aid for the saints' (Rom 15:25); and a little later: 'When therefore I have completed this, and have delivered to them what has been raised, I shall go on by way of you to Spain' (v. 28). Finally he was crowned with martyrdom in the last years of Nero" (*Super Act. expositio*, ad loc.).

We do not know exactly what happened at the end of the two years. It may be that Paul's Jewish accusers did not appear, or they may have argued their case before the imperial tribunal and Paul was found not guilty. At any event, he was set free and Luke considers his task done—the work God gave him to do when he inspired him to write his book.

"If you ask me", St John Chrysostom observes, "why St Luke, who stayed with the apostle up to his martyrdom, did not bring his narrative up to that point, I will reply that the Book of the Acts, in the form that has come down to us, perfectly fulfils its author's purpose. For the evangelists' only aim was to write down the most essential things" (*Hom. on Acts*, 1).

The kind of conventional way the book concludes has led many commentators (from early times up to the present day) to think that it had already been finished before the end of Paul's first imprisonment in Rome. Christian tradition has nothing very concrete to say about exactly when the Acts of the Apostles was written.

---

g. Other ancient authorities add verse 29, *And when he had said these words, the Jews departed, holding much dispute among themselves* **h.** Or *in his own hired dwelling*

New Vulgate Text

LIBER ACTUUM APOSTOLORUM

[1] ¹Primum quidem sermonem feci de omnibus, o Theophile, quae coepit Iesus facere et docere, ²usque in diem, qua, cum praecepisset apostolis per Spiritum Sanctum, quos elegit, assumptus est; ³quibus et praebuit seipsum vivum post passionem suam in multis argumentis, per dies quadraginta apparens eis et loquens ea, quae sunt de regno Dei. ⁴Et convescens praecepit eis ab Hierosolymis ne discederent, sed exspectarent promissionem Patris: «Quam audistis a me, ⁵quia Ioannes quidem baptizavit aqua, vos autem baptizabimini in Spiritu Sancto non post multos hos dies». ⁶Igitur qui convenerant, interrogabant eum dicentes: «Domine, si in tempore hoc restitues regnum Israeli?». ⁷Dixit autem eis: «Non est vestrum nosse tempora vel momenta, quae Pater posuit in sua potestate, ⁸sed accipietis virtutem superveniente Sancto Spiritu in vos et eritis mihi testes et in Ierusalem et in omni Iudaea et Samaria et usque ad ultimum terrae». ⁹Et cum haec dixisset, videntibus illis, elevatus est, et nubes suscepit eum ab oculis eorum. ¹⁰Cumque intuerentur in caelum eunte illo, ecce duo viri astiterunt iuxta illos in vestibus albis, ¹¹qui et dixerunt: «Viri Galilaei, quid statis aspicientes in caelum? Hic Iesus, qui assumptus est a vobis in caelum, sic veniet quemadmodum vidistis eum euntem in caelum». ¹²Tunc reversi sunt in Ierusalem a monte, qui vocatur Oliveti, qui est iuxta Ierusalem sabbati habens iter. ¹³Et cum introissent, in cenaculum ascenderunt, ubi manebant et Petrus et Ioannes et Iacobus et Andreas, Philippus et Thomas, Bartholomaeus et Matthaeus, Iacobus Alphaei et Simon Zelotes et Iudas Iacobi. ¹⁴Hi omnes erant perseverantes unanimiter in oratione cum mulieribus et Maria matre Iesu et fratribus eius. ¹⁵Et in diebus illis exsurgens Petrus in medio fratrum dixit—erat autem turba hominum simul fere centum viginti—: ¹⁶«Viri fratres, oportebat impleri Scripturam, quam praedixit Spiritus Sanctus per os David de Iuda, qui fuit dux eorum, qui comprehenderunt Iesum, ¹⁷quia connumeratus erat in nobis et sortitus est sortem ministerii huius. ¹⁸Hic quidem possedit agrum de mercede iniquitatis et pronus factus crepuit medius, et diffusa sunt omnia viscera eius. ¹⁹Et notum factum est omnibus habitantibus Ierusalem, ita ut appellaretur ager ille lingua eorum Aceldamach, hoc est ager Sanguinis. ²⁰Scriptum est enim in libro Psalmorum: *"Fiat commoratio eius deserta, / et non sit qui inhabitet in ea"* / et: *"Episcopatum eius accipiat alius"*. ²¹Oportet ergo ex his viris, qui nobiscum congregati erant in omni tempore, quo intravit et exivit inter nos Dominus Iesus, ²²incipiens a baptismate Ioannis usque in diem, qua assumptus est a nobis, testem resurrectionis eius nobiscum fieri unum ex istis». ²³Et statuerunt duos, Ioseph, qui vocabatur Barsabbas, qui cognominatus est Iustus, et Matthiam. ²⁴Et orantes dixerunt: «Tu, Domine, qui corda nosti omnium, ostende quem elegeris ex his duobus unum ²⁵accipere locum ministerii huius et apostolatus, de quo praevaricatus est Iudas, ut abiret in locum suum». ²⁶Et dederunt sortes eis, et cecidit sors super Matthiam, et annumeratus est cum undecim apostolis. [2] ¹Et cum compleretur dies Pentecostes, erant omnes pariter in eodem loco. ²Et factus est repente de caelo sonus tamquam advenientis spiritus vehementis et replevit totam domum, ubi erant sedentes. ³Et apparuerunt illis dispertitae linguae tamquam ignis, seditque supra singulos eorum; ⁴et repleti sunt omnes Spiritu Sancto et coeperunt loqui aliis linguis, prout Spiritus dabat eloqui illis. ⁵Erant autem in Ierusalem habitantes Iudaei, viri religiosi ex omni natione, quae sub caelo est; ⁶facta autem hac voce, convenit multitudo et confusa est, quoniam audiebat unusquisque lingua sua illos loquentes. ⁷Stupebant autem et mirabantur dicentes: «Nonne ecce omnes isti, qui loquuntur, Galilaei sunt? ⁸Et quomodo nos audimus unusquisque propria lingua nostra, in qua nati sumus? ⁹Parthi et Medi et Elamitae, et qui habitant Mesopotamiam, Iudaeam quoque et Cappadociam, Pontum et Asiam, ¹⁰Phrygiam quoque et Pamphyliam, Aegyptum et partes Libyae, quae est circa Cyrenem, et advenae Romani, ¹¹Iudaei quoque et proselyti, Cretes et Arabes, audimus loquentes eos nostris linguis magnalia Dei». ¹²Stupebant autem omnes et haesitabant ad invicem dicentes: «Quidnam hoc vult esse?»; ¹³alii autem irridentes dicebant: «Musto pleni sunt isti». ¹⁴Stans autem Petrus cum Undecim levavit vocem suam et locutus est eis: «Viri Iudaei et, qui habitatis Ierusalem universi, hoc vobis notum sit, et auribus percipite verba mea. ¹⁵Non enim, sicut vos aestimatis, hi ebrii sunt, est enim hora diei tertia, ¹⁶sed hoc est, quod dictum est per prophetam Ioel:

[17]"*Et erit:* in novissimis diebus, dicit Deus, / *effundam de Spiritu meo super omnem carnem,* / *et prophetabunt filii vestri et filiae vestrae,* / *et iuvenes vestri visiones videbunt,* / *et seniores vestri somnia somniabunt;* / [18]*et quidem super servos meos et super ancillas meas* / *in diebus illis effundam de Spiritu meo,* / et prophetabunt. / [19]*Et dabo prodigia in caelo* sursum *et* signa *in terra* deorsum, / *sanguinem et ignem et vaporem fumi;* / [20]*sol convertetur in tenebras* / *et luna in sanguinem,* / *antequam veniat dies Domini* / *magnus et manifestus.* / [21]*Et erit:* / *omnis quicumque invocaverit nomen Domini, salvus erit".* [22]Viri Israelitae, audite verba haec: Iesum Nazarenum, virum approbatum a Deo apud vos virtutibus et prodigiis et signis, quae fecit per illum Deus in medio vestri, sicut ipsi scitis, [23]hunc definito consilio et praescientia Dei traditum per manum iniquorum affigentes interemistis, [24]quem Deus suscitavit solutis doloribus mortis, iuxta quod impossibile erat teneri illum ab ea. [25]David enim dicit circa eum: *"Providebam Dominum coram me semper,* / *quoniam a dextris meis est, ne commovear.* / [26]*Propter hoc laetatum est cor meum,* / *et exsultavit lingua mea;* / *insuper et caro mea requiescet in spe.* / [27]*Quoniam non derelinques animam meam in inferno* / *neque dabis Sanctum tuum videre corruptionem.* / [28]*Notas fecisti mihi vias vitae,* / *replebis me iucunditate cum facie tua".* [29]Viri fratres, liceat audenter dicere ad vos de patriarcha David quoniam et defunctus est et sepultus est et sepulcrum eius est apud nos usque in hodiernum diem; [30]propheta igitur cum esset et sciret quia iure iurando *iurasset illi* Deus *de fructu lumbi eius sedere super sedem eius,* [31]providens locutus est de resurrectione Christi quia *neque derelictus est in inferno, neque* caro eius *vidit corruptionem.* [32]Hunc Iesum resuscitavit Deus, cuius omnes nos testes sumus. [33]Dextera igitur Dei exaltatus et, promissione Spiritus Sancti accepta a Patre, effudit hunc, quem vos videtis et auditis. [34]Non enim David ascendit in caelos; dicit autem ipse: *"Dixit Dominus Domino meo: Sede a dextris meis,* / [35]*donec ponam inimicos tuos scabellum pedum tuorum".* [36]Certissime ergo sciat omnis domus Israel quia et Dominum eum et Christum Deus fecit, hunc, Iesum, quem vos crucifixistis». [37]His auditis, compuncti sunt corde et dixerunt ad Petrum et reliquos apostolos: «Quid faciemus, viri fratres?». [38]Petrus vero ad illos: «Paenitentiam, inquit, agite, et baptizetur unusquisque vestrum in nomine Iesu Christi in remissionem peccatorum vestrorum, et accipietis donum Sancti Spiritus; [39]vobis enim est repromissio et filiis vestris et omnibus, qui longe sunt, quoscumque advocaverit Dominus Deus noster». [40]Aliis etiam verbis pluribus testificatus est et exhortabatur eos dicens: «Salvamini a generatione ista prava». [41]Qui ergo, recepto sermone eius, baptizati sunt; et appositae sunt in illa die animae circiter tria milia. [42]Erant autem perseverantes in doctrina apostolorum et communicatione, in fractione panis et orationibus. [43]Fiebat autem omni animae timor; multa quoque prodigia et signa per apostolos fiebant. [44]Omnes autem, qui crediderant erant pariter et habebant omnia communia [45]et possessiones et substantias vendebant et dividebant illas omnibus, prout cuique opus erat; [46]cotidie quoque perdurantes unanimiter in templo et frangentes circa domos panem, sumebant cibum cum exsultatione et simplicitate cordis, [47]collaudantes Deum et habentes gratiam ad omnem plebem. Dominus autem augebat, qui salvi fierent cotidie in idipsum. [3] [1]Petrus autem et Ioannes ascendebant in templum ad horam orationis nonam. [2]Et quidam vir, qui erat claudus ex utero matris suae, baiulabatur, quem ponebant cotidie ad portam templi, quae dicitur Speciosa, ut peteret eleemosynam ab introeuntibus in templum; [3]is cum vidisset Petrum et Ioannem incipientes introire in templum, rogabat, ut eleemosynam acciperet. [4]Intuens autem in eum Petrus cum Ioanne dixit: «Respice in nos». [5]At ille intendebat in eos, sperans se aliquid accepturum ab eis. [6]Petrus autem dixit: «Argentum et aurum non est mihi; quod autem habeo, hoc tibi do: In nomine Iesu Christi Nazareni surge et ambula!». [7]Et apprehensa ei manu dextera, allevavit eum; et protinus consolidatae sunt bases eius et tali, [8]et exsiliens stetit et ambulabat et intravit cum illis in templum, ambulans et exsiliens et laudans Deum. [9]Et vidit omnis populus eum ambulantem et laudantem Deum; [10]cognoscebant autem illum quoniam ipse erat, qui ad eleemosynam sedebat ad Speciosam portam templi, et impleti sunt stupore et exstasi in eo, quod contigerat illi. [11]Cum teneret autem Petrum et Ioannem, concurrit omnis populus ad eos ad porticum, qui appellatur Salomonis, stupentes. [12]Videns autem Petrus respondit ad populum: «Viri Israelitae, quid miramini in hoc aut nos quid intuemini, quasi nostra virtute aut pietate fecerimus hunc ambulare? [13]*Deus Abraham et Deus Isaac et Deus Iacob, Deus patrum nostrorum* glorificavit puerum suum Iesum, quem vos quidem tradidistis et negastis ante faciem Pilati, iudicante illo dimitti; [14]vos autem Sanctum et Iustum negastis et petistis virum homicidam donari vobis, [15]ducem vero vitae interfecistis, quem Deus suscitavit a mortuis, cuius nos testes sumus. [16]Et in fide nominis eius hunc, quem videtis et nostis, confirmavit nomen eius, et fides, quae per eum est, dedit huic integritatem istam in conspectu omnium vestrum. [17]Et nunc, fratres, scio quia per ignorantiam fecistis, sicut et principes vestri; [18]Deus autem, quae praenuntiavit per os omnium prophetarum pati Christum suum, implevit sic. [19]Paenitemini igitur et convertimini, ut deleantur vestra peccata, [20]ut veniant tempora refrigerii a conspectu Domini, et mittat eum, qui praedestinatus est vobis Christus, Iesum, [21]quem oportet caelum

quidem suscipere usque in tempora restitutionis omnium, quae locutus est Deus per os sanctorum a saeculo suorum prophetarum. ²²Moyses quidem dixit: *"Prophetam vobis suscitabit Dominus Deus vester de fratribus vestris tamquam me; ipsum audietis iuxta omnia, quaecumque locutus fuerit* vobis. ²³*Erit autem: omnis anima, quae non audierit prophetam illum, exterminabitur de plebe".* ²⁴Et omnes prophetae a Samuel et deinceps quotquot locuti sunt, etiam annuntiaverunt dies istos. ²⁵Vos estis filii prophetarum et testamenti, quod disposuit Deus ad patres vestros dicens ad Abraham: *"Et in semine tuo benedicentur omnes familiae terrae".* ²⁶Vobis primum Deus suscitans Puerum suum, misit eum benedicentem vobis in avertendo unumquemque a nequitiis vestris». [4] ¹Loquentibus autem illis ad populum, supervenerunt eis sacerdotes et magistratus templi et sadducaei, ²dolentes quod docerent populum et annuntiarent in Iesu resurrectionem ex mortuis, ³et iniecerunt in eos manus et posuerunt in custodiam in crastinum; erat enim iam vespera. ⁴Multi autem eorum, qui audierant verbum, crediderunt; et factus est numerus virorum quinque milia. ⁵Factum est autem in crastinum, ut congregarentur principes eorum et seniores et scribae in Ierusalem, ⁶et Annas princeps sacerdotum et Caiphas et Ioannes et Alexander et quotquot erant de genere sacerdotali, ⁷et statuentes eos in medio interrogabant: «In qua virtute aut in quo nomine fecistis hoc vos?». ⁸Tunc Petrus repletus Spiritu Sancto dixit ad eos: «Principes populi et seniores, ⁹si nos hodie diiudicamur in benefacto hominis infirmi, in quo iste salvus factus est, ¹⁰notum sit omnibus vobis et omni plebi Israel quia in nomine Iesu Christi Nazareni, quem vos crucifixistis, quem Deus suscitavit a mortuis, in hoc iste astat coram vobis sanus. ¹¹Hic est *lapis, qui reprobatus est a vobis aedificatoribus, / qui factus est in caput anguli.* ¹²Et non est in alio aliquo salus, nec enim nomen aliud est sub caelo datum in hominibus, in quo oportet nos salvos fieri». ¹³Videntes autem Petri fiduciam et Ioannis, et comperto quod homines essent sine litteris et idiotae, admirabantur et cognoscebant eos quoniam cum Iesu fuerant; ¹⁴hominem quoque videntes stantem cum eis, qui curatus fuerat, nihil poterant contradicere. ¹⁵Iubentes autem eos foras extra concilium secedere, conferebant ad invicem ¹⁶dicentes: «Quid faciemus hominibus istis? Quoniam quidem notum signum factum est per eos omnibus habitantibus in Ierusalem manifestum, et non possumus negare; ¹⁷sed ne amplius divulgetur in populum, comminemur eis, ne ultra loquantur in nomine hoc ulli hominum». ¹⁸Et vocantes eos denuntiaverunt, ne omnino loquerentur neque docerent in nomine Iesu. ¹⁹Petrus vero et Ioannes respondentes dixerunt ad eos: «Si iustum est in conspectu Dei vos potius audire quam Deum, iudicate; ²⁰non enim possumus nos, quae vidimus et audivimus, non loqui». ²¹At illi ultra comminantes dimiserunt eos, nequaquam invenientes, quomodo punirent eos, propter populum, quia omnes glorificabant Deum in eo, quod acciderat; ²²annorum enim erat amplius quadraginta homo, in quo factum erat signum istud sanitatis. ²³Dimissi autem venerunt ad suos et annuntiaverunt quanta ad eos principes sacerdotum et seniores dixissent. ²⁴Qui cum audissent unanimiter levaverunt vocem ad Deum et dixerunt: «Domine, tu, qui *fecisti caelum et terram et mare et omnia, quae in eis sunt,* ²⁵qui Spiritu Sancto per os patris nostri David pueri tui dixisti: *"Quare fremuerunt gentes, / et populi meditati sunt inania? / ²⁶Astiterunt reges terrae, / et principes convenerunt in unum / adversus Dominum et adversus Christum eius".* ²⁷Convenerunt enim vere in civitate ista adversus sanctum puerum tuum Iesum, quem unxisti, Herodes et Pontius Pilatus cum gentibus et populis Israel ²⁸facere, quaecumque manus tua et consilium praedestinavit fieri. ²⁹Et nunc, Domine, respice in minas eorum et da servis tuis cum omni fiducia loqui verbum tuum, ³⁰in eo quod manum tuam extendas ad sanitatem et signa et prodigia facienda per nomen sancti pueri tui Iesu». ³¹Et cum orassent, motus est locus, in quo erant congregati, et repleti sunt omnes Sancto Spiritu et loquebantur verbum Dei cum fiducia. ³²Multitudinis autem credentium erat cor et anima una, nec quisquam eorum, quae possidebant, aliquid suum esse dicebat, sed erant illis omnia communia. ³³Et virtute magna reddebant apostoli testimonium resurrectionis Domini Iesu, et gratia magna erat super omnibus illis. ³⁴Neque enim quisquam egens erat inter illos; quotquot enim possessores agrorum aut domorum erant, vendentes afferebant pretia eorum, quae vendebant, ³⁵et ponebant ante pedes apostolorum; dividebatur autem singulis, prout cuique opus erat. ³⁶Ioseph autem, qui cognominatus est Barnabas ab apostolis—quod est interpretatum filius Consolationis—Levites, Cyprius genere, ³⁷cum haberet agrum, vendidit et attulit pecuniam et posuit ante pedes apostolorum. [5] ¹Vir autem quidam nomine Ananias cum Sapphira uxore sua vendidit agrum ²et subtraxit de pretio, conscia quoque uxore, et afferens partem quandam ad pedes apostolorum posuit. ³Dixit autem Petrus: «Anania, cur implevit Satanas cor tuum mentiri te Spiritui Sancto et subtrahere de pretio agri? ⁴Nonne manens tibi manebat et venumdatum in tua erat potestate? Quare posuisti in corde tuo hanc rem? Non es mentitus hominibus sed Deo!». ⁵Audiens autem Ananias haec verba cecidit et exspiravit; et factus est timor magnus in omnes audientes. ⁶Surgentes autem iuvenes involverunt eum et efferentes sepelierunt. ⁷Factum est autem quasi horarum trium spatium, et uxor ipsius nesciens, quod factum fuerat, introivit. ⁸Respondit autem ei Petrus: «Dic mihi si tanti agrum vendidistis?». At illa dixit: «Etiam, tanti». [9]Petrus autem ad eam: «Quid est quod convenit vobis tentare Spiritum Domini? Ecce pedes eorum, qui sepelierunt virum tuum, ad ostium et efferent te». [10]Confestim cecidit ante pedes eius et exspiravit; intrantes autem iuvenes invenerunt illam mortuam et efferentes sepelierunt ad virum suum. [11]Et factus est timor magnus super universam ecclesiam et in omnes, qui audierunt haec. [12]Per manus autem apostolorum fiebant signa et prodigia multa in plebe; et erant unanimiter omnes in porticu Salomonis. [13]Ceterorum autem nemo audebat coniungere se illis, sed magnificabat eos populus; [14]magis autem addebantur credentes Domino, multitudines virorum ac mulierum, [15]ita ut et in plateas efferrent infirmos et ponerent in lectulis et grabatis, ut, veniente Petro, saltem umbra illius obumbraret quemquam eorum. [16]Concurrebat autem et multitudo vicinarum civitatum Ierusalem, afferentes aegros et vexatos ab spiritibus immundis, qui curabantur omnes. [17]Exsurgens autem princeps sacerdotum et omnes, qui cum illo erant, quae est haeresis sadducaeorum, repleti sunt zelo [18]et iniecerunt manus in apostolos et posuerunt illos in custodia publica. [19]Angelus autem Domini per noctem aperuit ianuas carceris et educens eos dixit: [20]«Ite et stantes loquimini in templo plebi omnia verba vitae huius». [21]Qui cum audissent, intraverunt diluculo in templum et docebant. Adveniens autem princeps sacerdotum et, qui cum eo erant, convocaverunt concilium et omnes seniores filiorum Israel et miserunt in carcerem, ut adducerentur illi. [22]Cum venissent autem ministri, non invenerunt illos in carcere; reversi autem nuntiaverunt [23]dicentes: «Carcerem invenimus clausum cum omni diligentia et custodes stantes ad ianuas, aperientes autem intus neminem invenimus!». [24]Ut audierunt autem hos sermones, magistratus templi et principes sacerdotum ambigebant de illis quidnam fieret illud. [25]Adveniens autem quidam nuntiavit eis: «Ecce viri, quos posuistis in carcere, sunt in templo stantes et docentes populum». [26]Tunc abiens magistratus cum ministris adducebat illos, non per vim, timebant enim populum, ne lapidarentur. [27]Et cum adduxissent illos, statuerunt in concilio. Et interrogavit eos princeps sacerdotum [28]dicens: «Nonne praecipiendo praecepimus vobis, ne doceretis in nomine isto? Et ecce replevistis Ierusalem doctrina vestra et vultis inducere super nos sanguinem hominis istius». [29]Respondens autem Petrus et apostoli dixerunt: «Oboedire oportet Deo magis quam hominibus. [30]Deus patrum nostrorum suscitavit Iesum, quem vos interemistis suspendentes in ligno; [31]hunc Deus Ducem et Salvatorem exaltavit dextera sua ad dandam paenitentiam Israel et remissionem peccatorum. [32]Et nos sumus testes horum verborum, et Spiritus Sanctus, quem dedit Deus oboedientibus sibi». [33]Haec cum audissent, dissecabantur et volebant interficere illos. [34]Surgens autem quidam in concilio pharisaeus nomine Gamaliel, legis doctor honorabilis universae plebi, iussit foras ad breve homines fieri [35]dixitque ad illos: «Viri Israelitae, attendite vobis super hominibus istis quid acturi sitis. [36]Ante hos enim dies exstitit Theudas dicens esse se aliquem, cui consensit virorum numerus circiter quadringentorum; qui occisus est, et omnes, quicumque credebant ei, dissipati sunt et redacti sunt ad nihilum. [37]Post hunc exstitit Iudas Galilaeus in diebus census et avertit populum post se; et ipse periit, et omnes, quotquot consentiebant ei, dispersi sunt. [38]Et nunc dico vobis: Discedite ab hominibus istis et sinite illos. Quoniam si est ex hominibus consilium hoc aut opus hoc, dissolvetur; [39]si vero ex Deo est, non poteritis dissolvere eos, ne forte et adversus Deum pugnantes inveniamini!». Consenserunt autem illi [40]et convocantes apostolos, caesis denuntiaverunt, ne loquerentur in nomine Iesu, et dimiserunt eos. [41]Et illi quidem ibant gaudentes a conspectu concilii quoniam digni habiti sunt pro nomine contumeliam pati; [42]et omni die in templo et circa domos non cessabant docentes et evangelizantes Christum, Iesum. **[6]** [1]In diebus autem illis, crescente numero discipulorum, factus est murmur Graecorum adversus Hebraeos, eo quod neglegerentur in ministerio cotidiano viduae eorum. [2]Convocantes autem Duodecim multitudinem discipulorum, dixerunt: «Non est aequum nos derelinquentes verbum Dei ministrare mensis; [3]considerate vero, fratres, viros ex vobis boni testimonii septem plenos Spiritu et sapientia, quos constituemus super hoc opus; [4]nos vero orationi et ministerio verbi instantes erimus». [5]Et placuit sermo coram omni multitudine, et elegerunt Stephanum, virum plenum fide et Spiritu Sancto, et Philippum et Prochorum et Nicanorem et Timonem et Parmenam et Nicolaum proselytum Antiochenum, [6]quos statuerunt ante conspectum apostolorum, et orantes imposuerunt eis manus. [7]Et verbum Dei crescebat, et multiplicabatur numerus discipulorum in Ierusalem valde; multa etiam turba sacerdotum oboediebat fidei. [8]Stephanus autem plenus gratia et virtute faciebat prodigia et signa magna in populo. [9]Surrexerunt autem quidam de synagoga, quae appellatur Libertinorum et Cyrenensium et Alexandrinorum et eorum, qui erant a Cilicia et Asia, disputantes cum Stephano, [10]et non poterant resistere sapientiae et Spiritui, quo loquebatur. [11]Tunc submiserunt viros, qui dicerent: «Audivimus eum dicentem verba blasphemia in Moysen et Deum»; [12]et commoverunt plebem et seniores et scribas, et concurrentes rapuerunt eum et adduxerunt in concilium [13]et statuerunt testes falsos dicentes: «Homo iste non cessat loqui verba adversus locum sanctum et legem; [14]audivimus enim eum dicentem quoniam Iesus Nazarenus hic destruet locum istum et mutabit consuetudines, quas tradidit nobis Moyses». [15]Et intuentes eum omnes, qui sedebant in concilio, viderunt faciem eius tamquam faciem angeli. **[7]** [1]Dixit autem princeps sacerdotum: «Si haec ita se habent?». [2]Qui ait: «Viri fratres et patres, audite. Deus gloriae apparuit patri nostro Abraham, cum esset in Mesopotamia, priusquam moraretur in Charran, [3]*et dixit ad illum: "Exi de terra tua et de cognatione tua, et veni in terram, quam tibi monstravero"*. [4]Tunc egressus de terra Chaldaeorum habitavit in Charran. Et inde postquam mortuus est pater eius, transtulit illum in terram istam, in qua nunc vos habitatis, [5]et non dedit illi hereditatem in ea nec passum pedis et repromisit *dare illi eam in possessionem et semini eius post ipsum,* cum non haberet filium. [6]Locutus est autem sic Deus: *"Erit semen eius accola in terra aliena, et servituti eos subicient et male tractabunt annis quadringentis;* [7]*et gentem, cui servierint, iudicabo ego,* dixit Deus, *et post haec exibunt et deservient mihi in* loco *isto"*. [8]Et dedit illi testamentum circumcisionis; et sic genuit Isaac et circumcidit eum die octava, et Isaac Iacob, et Iacob duodecim patriarchas. [9]Et patriarchae aemulantes Ioseph vendiderunt in Aegyptum; et erat Deus cum eo, [10]et eripuit eum ex omnibus tribulationibus eius, et *dedit ei gratiam* et sapientiam *in conspectu pharaonis regis Aegypti, et constituit eum praepositum super Aegyptum et super omnem domum suam.* [11]*Venit autem fames in universam Aegyptum et Chanaan* et tribulatio magna, et non inveniebant cibos patres nostri. [12]Cum audisset autem Iacob esse frumentum in Aegypto, misit patres nostros primum; [13]et in secundo cognitus est Ioseph a fratribus suis, et manifestatum est pharaoni genus Ioseph. [14]Mittens autem Ioseph accersivit Iacob patrem suum et omnem cognationem in animabus septuaginta quinque, [15]et descendit Iacob in Aegyptum. Et defunctus est ipse et patres nostri, [16]et translati sunt in Sichem et positi sunt in sepulcro, quod emit Abraham pretio argenti a filiis Hemmor in Sichem. [17]Cum appropinquaret autem tempus repromissionis, quam confessus erat Deus Abrahae, crevit populus et multiplicatus est in Aegypto, [18]quoadusque *surrexit rex alius super Aegypto, qui non sciebat Ioseph.* [19]Hic circumveniens genus nostrum, afflixit patres, ut exponerent infantes suos, ne vivi servarentur. [20]Eodem tempore natus est Moyses et erat formosus coram Deo; qui nutritus est tribus mensibus in domo patris. [21]Exposito autem illo, sustulit eum filia pharaonis et enutrivit eum sibi in filium; [22]et eruditus est Moyses in omni sapientia Aegyptiorum et erat potens in verbis et in operibus suis. [23]Cum autem impleretur ei quadraginta annorum tempus, ascendit in cor eius, ut visitaret fratres suos filios Israel. [24]Et cum vidisset quendam iniuriam patientem, vindicavit et fecit ultionem ei, qui opprimebatur, percusso Aegyptio. [25]Existimabat autem intellegere fratres quoniam Deus per manum ipsius daret salutem illis, at illi non intellexerunt. [26]Atque sequenti die apparuit illis litigantibus et reconciliabat eos in pacem dicens: "Viri, fratres estis; ut quid nocetis alterutrum?". [27]Qui autem iniuriam faciebat proximo, reppulit eum dicens: *"Quis te constituit principem et iudicem super nos?* [28]*Numquid interficere me tu vis, quemadmodum interfecisti heri Aegyptium?"*. [29]Fugit autem Moyses propter verbum istud et factus est advena in terra Madian, ubi generavit filios duos. [30]Et expletis annis quadraginta, *apparuit illi in deserto montis* Sinai *angelus in ignis flamma rubi.* [31]Moyses autem videns admirabatur visum; accedente autem illo, ut consideraret, facta est vox Domini: [32]*"Ego Deus patrum tuorum, Deus Abraham et Isaac et Iacob"*. Tremefactus autem Moyses non audebat considerare. [33]*Dixit autem illi Dominus: "Solve calceamentum pedum tuorum; locus enim, in quo stas, terra sancta est.* [34]*Videns vidi afflictionem populi mei, qui est in Aegypto, et gemitum eorum audivi et descendi liberare eos; et nunc veni, mittam te in Aegyptum".* [35]Hunc Moysen, quem negaverunt dicentes: *"Quis te constituit principem et iudicem?",* hunc Deus et principem et redemptorem misit cum manu angeli, qui apparuit illi in rubo. [36]Hic eduxit illos faciens prodigia et signa in terra Aegypti et in Rubro mari et in deserto annis quadraginta. [37]Hic est Moyses, qui dixit filiis Israel: *"Prophetam vobis suscitabit Deus de fratribus vestris tamquam me".* [38]Hic est qui fuit in ecclesia in solitudine cum angelo, qui loquebatur ei in monte Sinai et cum patribus nostris, qui accepit verba viva dare nobis, [39]cui noluerunt oboedire patres nostri, sed reppulerunt et aversi sunt in cordibus suis in Aegyptum [40]dicentes ad Aaron: *"Fac nobis deos, qui praecedant nos; Moyses enim hic, qui eduxit nos de terra Aegypti, nescimus quid factum sit ei".* [41]Et vitulum fecerunt in illis diebus et obtulerunt hostiam simulacro et laetabantur in operibus manuum suarum. [42]Convertit autem Deus et tradidit eos servire militiae caeli, sicut scriptum est in libro Prophetarum: *"Numquid victimas et hostias obtulistis mihi / annis quadraginta in deserto, domus Israel? /* [43]*Et suscepistis tabernaculum Moloch / et sidus dei vestri Rhaephan, / figuras, quas fecistis* ad adorandum eas. / *Et transferam vos trans Babylonem".* [44]Tabernaculum testimonii erat patribus nostris in deserto, sicut disposuit, qui loquebatur ad Moysen, ut faceret illud secundum formam, quam viderat; [45]quod et induxerunt suscipientes patres nostri cum Iesu in possessionem gentium, quas expulit Deus a facie patrum nostrorum usque in diebus David, [46]qui invenit gratiam ante Deum et petiit, ut inveniret tabernaculum domui Iacob. [47]Salomon autem aedificavit illi domum. [48]Sed non Altissimus in manufactis habitat, sicut propheta dicit: [49]*"Caelum mihi thronus est, / terra autem scabellum pedum* *meorum. / Quam domum aedificabitis mihi, dicit Dominus, / aut quis locus requietionis meae? /* [50]*Nonne manus mea fecit haec omnia?"*. [51]Duri cervice et incircumcisi cordibus et auribus, vos semper Spiritui Sancto resistitis, sicut patres vestri et vos. [52]Quem prophetarum non sunt persecuti patres vestri? Et occiderunt eos, qui praenuntiabant de adventu Iusti, cuius vos nunc proditores et homicidae fuistis, [53]qui accepistis legem in dispositionibus angelorum et non custodistis». [54]Audientes autem haec, dissecabantur cordibus suis et stridebant dentibus in eum. [55]Cum autem esset plenus Spiritu Sancto, intendens in caelum vidit gloriam Dei et Iesum stantem a dextris Dei [56]et ait: «Ecce video caelos apertos et Filium hominis a dextris stantem Dei». [57]Exclamantes autem voce magna continuerunt aures suas et impetum fecerunt unanimiter in eum [58]et eicientes extra civitatem lapidabant. Et testes deposuerunt vestimenta sua secus pedes adulescentis, qui vocabatur Saulus. [59]Et lapidabant Stephanum invocantem et dicentem: «Domine Iesu, suscipe spiritum meum». [60]Positis autem genibus clamavit voce magna: «Domine, ne statuas illis hoc peccatum»; et cum hoc dixisset, obdormivit. [8] [1]Saulus autem erat consentiens neci eius. Facta est autem in illa die persecutio magna in ecclesiam, quae erat Hierosolymis; et omnes dispersi sunt per regiones Iudaeae et Samariae praeter apostolos. [2]Sepelierunt autem Stephanum viri timorati et fecerunt planctum magnum super illum. [3]Saulus vero devastabat ecclesiam per domos intrans et trahens viros ac mulieres tradebat in custodiam. [4]Igitur qui dispersi erant, pertransierunt evangelizantes verbum. [5]Philippus autem descendens in civitatem Samariae praedicabat illis Christum. [6]Intendebant autem turbae his, quae a Philippo dicebantur, unanimiter, audientes et videntes signa, quae faciebat: [7]ex multis enim eorum, qui habebant spiritus immundos clamantes voce magna exibant; multi autem paralytici et claudi curati sunt. [8]Factum est autem magnum gaudium in illa civitate. [9]Vir autem quidem nomine Simon iampridem erat in civitate magias faciens et dementans gentem Samariae, dicens esse se aliquem magnum, [10]cui attendebant omnes a minimo usque ad maximum dicentes: «Hic est virtus Dei, quae vocatur Magna». [11]Attendebant autem eum propter quod multo tempore magiis dementasset eos. [12]Cum vero credidissent Philippo evangelizanti de regno Dei et nomine Iesu Christi, baptizabantur viri ac mulieres. [13]Tunc Simon et ipse credidit et, cum baptizatus esset, adhaerebat Philippo; videns etiam signa et virtutes magnas fieri stupens admirabatur. [14]Cum autem audissent apostoli, qui erant Hierosolymis, quia recepit Samaria verbum Dei, miserunt ad illos Petrum et Ioannem, [15]qui cum descendissent, oraverunt pro ipsis, ut acciperent Spiritum Sanctum; [16]nondum enim super quemquam illorum venerat, sed baptizati tantum erant in nomine Domini Iesu. [17]Tunc imposuerunt manus super illos, et accipiebant Spiritum Sanctum. [18]Cum vidisset autem Simon quia per impositionem manuum apostolorum daretur Spiritus, obtulit eis pecuniam [19]dicens: «Date et mihi hanc potestatem, ut cuicumque imposuero manus, accipiat Spiritum Sanctum». [20]Petrus autem dixit ad eum: «Argentum tuum tecum sit in perditionem, quoniam donum Dei existimasti pecunia possideri! [21]Non est tibi pars neque sors in verbo isto, cor enim tuum non est rectum coram Deo. [22]Paenitentiam itaque age ab hac nequitia tua et roga Dominum, si forte remittatur tibi haec cogitatio cordis tui; [23]in felle enim amaritudinis et obligatione iniquitatis video te esse». [24]Respondens autem Simon dixit: «Precamini vos pro me ad Dominum, ut nihil veniat super me horum, quae dixistis». [25]Et illi quidem testificati et locuti verbum Domini, redibant Hierosolymam, et multis vicis Samaritanorum evangelizabant. [26]Angelus autem Domini locutus est ad Philippum dicens: «Surge et vade contra meridianum ad viam, quae descendit ab Ierusalem in Gazam; haec est deserta». [27]Et surgens abiit; et ecce vir Aethiops eunuchus potens Candacis reginae Aethiopum, qui erat super omnem gazam eius, qui venerat adorare in Ierusalem [28]et revertebatur sedens super currum suum et legebat prophetam Isaiam. [29]Dixit autem Spiritus Philippo: «Accede et adiunge te ad currum istum». [30]Accurrens autem Philippus audivit illum legentem Isaiam prophetam et dixit: «Putasne intellegis, quae legis?». [31]Qui ait: «Et quomodo possum, si non aliquis ostenderit mihi?». Rogavitque Philippum, ut ascenderet et sederet secum. [32]Locus autem Scripturae, quem legebat, erat hic: *«Tamquam ovis ad occisionem ductus est / et sicut agnus coram tondente se sine voce, / sic non aperit os suum. / [33]In humilitate eius iudicium eius sublatum est. / Generationem illius quis enarrabit? / Quoniam tollitur de terra vita eius».* [34]Respondens autem eunuchus Philippo dixit: «Obsecro te, de quo propheta dicit hoc? De se an de alio aliquo?». [35]Aperiens autem Philippus os suum et incipiens a Scriptura ista, evangelizavit illi Iesum. [36]Et dum irent per viam, venerunt ad quandam aquam, et ait eunuchus: «Ecce aqua; quid prohibet me baptizari?». [38]Et iussit stare currum, et descenderunt uterque in aquam Philippus et eunuchus, et baptizavit eum. [39]Cum autem ascendissent de aqua, Spiritus Domini rapuit Philippum, et amplius non vidit eum eunuchus; ibat autem per viam suam gaudens. [40]Philippus autem inventus est in Azoto et pertransiens evangelizabat civitatibus cunctis, donec veniret Caesaream. [9] [1]Saulus autem, adhuc spirans minarum et caedis in discipulos Domini, accessit ad principem sacerdotum [2]et petiit ab eo epistulas in Damascum ad synagogas, ut si quos invenisset huius viae, viros ac mulieres, vinctos perduceret in Ierusalem. [3]Et cum iter faceret, contigit ut appropinquaret Damasco, et subito circumfulsit eum lux de caelo, [4]et cadens in terram audivit vocem dicentem sibi: «Saul, Saul, quid me persequeris?». [5]Qui dixit: «Quis es, Domine?». Et ille: «Ego sum Iesus, quem tu persequeris! [6]Sed surge et ingredere civitatem, et dicetur tibi quid te oporteat facere». [7]Viri autem illi, qui comitabantur cum eo, stabant stupefacti, audientes quidem vocem, neminem autem videntes. [8]Surrexit autem Saulus de terra apertisque oculis nihil videbat; ad manus autem illum trahentes introduxerunt Damascum. [9]Et erat tribus diebus non videns et non manducavit, neque bibit. [10]Erat autem quidam discipulus Damasci nomine Ananias, et dixit ad illum in visu Dominus: «Anania». At ille ait: «Ecce ego, Domine». [11]Et Dominus ad illum: «Surgens vade in vicum, qui vocatur Rectus, et quaere in domo Iudae Saulum nomine Tarsensem; ecce enim orat [12]et vidit virum Ananiam nomine introeuntem et imponentem sibi manus, ut visum recipiat». [13]Respondit autem Ananias: «Domine, audivi a multis de viro hoc, quanta mala sanctis tuis fecerit in Ierusalem; [14]et hic habet potestatem a principibus sacerdotum alligandi omnes, qui invocant nomen tuum». [15]Dixit autem ad eum Dominus: «Vade, quoniam vas electionis est mihi iste, ut portet nomen meum coram gentibus et regibus et filiis Israel; [16]ego enim ostendam illi quanta oporteat eum pro nomine meo pati». [17]Et abiit Ananias et introivit in domum et imponens ei manus dixit: «Saul frater, Dominus misit me, Iesus qui apparuit tibi in via, qua veniebas, ut videas et implearis Spiritu Sancto». [18]Et confestim ceciderunt ab oculis eius tamquam squamae, et visum recepit. Et surgens baptizatus est [19]et, cum accepisset cibum, confortatus est. Fuit autem cum discipulis, qui erant Damasci, per dies aliquot [20]et continuo in synagogis praedicabat Iesum, quoniam hic est Filius Dei. [21]Stupebant autem omnes, qui audiebant et dicebant: «Nonne hic est, qui expugnabat in Ierusalem eos, qui invocabant nomen istud, et huc ad hoc venerat, ut vinctos illos duceret ad principes sacerdotum?». [22]Saulus autem magis convalescebat et confundebat Iudaeos, qui habitabant Damasci, affirmans quoniam hic est Christus. [23]Cum implerentur autem dies multi, consilium fecerunt Iudaei, ut eum interficerent; [24]notae autem factae sunt Saulo insidiae eorum. Custodiebant autem et portas die ac nocte, ut eum interficerent; [25]accipientes autem discipuli eius nocte per murum dimiserunt eum submittentes in sporta. [26]Cum autem venisset in Ierusalem, tentabat iungere se discipulis; et omnes timebant eum, non credentes quia esset discipulus. [27]Barnabas autem apprehensum illum duxit ad apostolos, et narravit illis quomodo in via vidisset Dominum et quia locutus est ei, et quomodo in Damasco fiducialiter egerit in nomine Iesu. [28]Et erat cum illis intrans et exiens in Ierusalem, fiducialiter agens in nomine Domini. [29]Loquebatur quoque et disputabat cum Graecis; illi autem quaerebant occidere eum. [30]Quod cum cognovissent, fratres deduxerunt eum Caesaream et dimiserunt Tarsum. [31]Ecclesia quidem per totam Iudaeam et Galilaeam et Samariam habebat pacem, aedificabatur et ambulabat in timore Domini et consolatione Sancti Spiritus crescebat. [32]Factum est autem Petrum, dum pertransiret universos, devenire et ad sanctos, qui habitabant Lyddae. [33]Invenit autem ibi hominem quendam nomine Aeneam ab annis octo iacentem in grabato, qui erat paralyticus. [34]Et ait illi Petrus: «Aenea, sanat te Iesus Christus; surge et sterne tibi». Et continuo surrexit. [35]Et viderunt illum omnes, qui inhabitabant Lyddam et Saron, qui conversi sunt ad Dominum. [36]In Ioppe autem erat quaedam discipula nomine Tabitha, quae interpretata dicitur Dorcas; haec erat plena operibus bonis et eleemosynis, quas faciebat. [37]Factum est autem in diebus illis ut infirmata moreretur; quam cum lavissent posuerunt in cenaculo. [38]Cum autem prope esset Lydda ab Ioppe, discipuli audientes quia Petrus esset in ea, miserunt duos viros ad eum rogantes: «Ne pigriteris venire usque ad nos!». [39]Exsurgens autem Petrus venit cum illis; et cum advenisset, duxerunt illum in cenaculum et circumsteterunt illum omnes viduae flentes et ostendentes tunicas et vestes, quas faciebat Dorcas, cum esset cum illis. [40]Eiectis autem omnibus foras Petrus, et ponens genua oravit et conversus ad corpus dixit: «Tabitha, surge!». At illa aperuit oculos suos et, viso Petro, resedit. [41]Dans autem illi manum erexit eam et, cum vocasset sanctos et viduas, exhibuit eam vivam. [42]Notum autem factum est per universam Ioppen, et crediderunt multi in Domino. [43]Factum est autem ut dies multos moraretur in Ioppe apud quendam Simonem coriarium. **[10]** [1]Vir autem quidam in Caesarea nomine Cornelius, centurio cohortis, quae dicitur Italica, [2]religiosus et timens Deum cum omni domo sua, faciens eleemosynas multas plebi et deprecans Deum semper, [3]vidit in visu manifeste quasi hora nona diei angelum Dei introeuntem ad se et dicentem sibi: «Corneli». [4]At ille intuens eum et timore correptus dixit: «Quid est, domine?». Dixit autem illi: «Orationes tuae et eleemosynae tuae ascenderunt in memoriam in conspectu Dei. [5]Et nunc mitte viros in Ioppen et accersi Simonem quendam, qui cognominatur Petrus; [6]hic hospitatur apud Simonem quendam coriarium, cui est domus iuxta mare». [7]Ut autem discessit angelus, qui loquebatur illi, cum vocasset duos domesticos suos et militem religiosum ex his, qui illi parebant, [8]et narrasset illis omnia, misit illos in Ioppen. [9]Postera autem die iter illis facientibus et appropinquantibus civitati, ascendit Petrus super tectum, ut oraret circa horam sextam. [10]Et cum esuriret, voluit gustare; parantibus autem eis, cecidit super eum mentis excessus, [11]et videt caelum apertum et descendens vas quoddam velut linteum magnum quattuor initiis submitti in terram, [12]in quo erant omnia quadrupedia et serpentia terrae et volatilia caeli. [13]Et facta est vox ad eum: «Surge, Petre, occide et manduca!». [14]Ait autem Petrus: «Nequaquam, Domine, quia numquam manducavi omne commune et immundum». [15]Et vox iterum secundo ad eum: «Quae Deus purificavit, ne tu commune dixeris». [16]Hoc autem factum est per ter, et statim receptum est vas in caelum. [17]Et dum intra se haesitaret Petrus quidnam esset visio, quam vidisset, ecce viri, qui missi erant a Cornelio, inquirentes domum Simonis astiterunt ad ianuam [18]et, cum vocassent, interrogabant si Simon, qui cognominatur Petrus, illic haberet hospitium. [19]Petro autem cogitante de visione, dixit Spiritus ei: «Ecce viri tres quaerunt te; [20]surge itaque et descende et vade cum eis nihil dubitans, quia ego misi illos». [21]Descendens autem Petrus ad viros dixit: «Ecce ego sum, quem quaeritis; quae causa est, propter quam venistis?». [22]Qui dixerunt: «Cornelius centurio, vir iustus et timens Deum et testimonium habens ab universa gente Iudaeorum, responsum accepit ab angelo sancto accersire te in domum suam et audire verba abs te». [23]Invitans igitur eos recepit hospitio. Sequenti autem die surgens profectus est cum eis, et quidam ex fratribus ab Ioppe comitati sunt eum. [24]Altera autem die introivit Caesaream; Cornelius vero exspectabat illos, convocatis cognatis suis et necessariis amicis. [25]Et factum est cum introisset Petrus, obvius ei Cornelius procidens ad pedes adoravit. [26]Petrus vero levavit eum dicens: «Surge, et ego ipse homo sum». [27]Et loquens cum illo intravit et invenit multos, qui convenerant, [28]dixitque ad illos: «Vos scitis quomodo illicitum sit viro Iudaeo coniungi aut accedere ad alienigenam. Et mihi ostendit Deus neminem communem aut immundum dicere hominem; [29]propter quod sine dubitatione veni accersitus. Interrogo ergo quam ob causam accersistis me». [30]Et Cornelius ait: «A nudius quarta die usque in hanc horam orans eram hora nona in domo mea, et ecce vir stetit ante me in veste candida [31]et ait: "Corneli, exaudita est oratio tua, et eleemosynae tuae commemoratae sunt in conspectu Dei. [32]Mitte ergo in Ioppen et accersi Simonem, qui cognominatur Petrus; hic hospitatur in domo Simonis coriarii iuxta mare". [33]Confestim igitur misi ad te, et tu bene fecisti veniendo. Nunc ergo omnes nos in conspectu Dei adsumus audire omnia, quaecumque tibi praecepta sunt a Domino». [34]Aperiens autem Petrus os dixit: «In veritate comperio quoniam non est personarum acceptor Deus, [35]sed in omni gente, qui timet eum et operatur iustitiam, acceptus est illi. [36]Verbum misit filiis Israel evangelizans pacem per Iesum Christum; hic est omnium Dominus. [37]Vos scitis quod factum est verbum per universam Iudaeam incipiens a Galilaea post baptismum, quod praedicavit Ioannes: [38]Iesum a Nazareth, quomodo unxit eum Deus Spiritu Sancto et virtute, qui pertransivit benefaciendo et sanando omnes oppressos a Diabolo, quoniam Deus erat cum illo. [39]Et nos testes sumus omnium, quae fecit in regione Iudaeorum et Ierusalem; quem et occiderunt suspendentes in ligno. [40]Hunc Deus suscitavit tertia die et dedit eum manifestum fieri [41]non omni populo, sed testibus praeordinatis a Deo, nobis, qui manducavimus et bibimus cum illo postquam resurrexit a mortuis; [42]et praecepit nobis praedicare populo et testificari quia ipse est, qui constitutus est a Deo iudex vivorum et mortuorum. [43]Huic omnes Prophetae testimonium perhibent remissionem peccatorum accipere per nomen eius omnes, qui credunt in eum». [44]Adhuc loquente Petro verba haec, cecidit Spiritus Sanctus super omnes, qui audiebant verbum. [45]Et obstupuerunt, qui ex circumcisione fideles, qui venerant cum Petro, quia et in nationes gratia Spiritus Sancti effusa est; [46]audiebant enim illos loquentes linguis et magnificantes Deum. Tunc respondit Petrus: [47]«Numquid aquam quis prohibere potest, ut non baptizentur hi, qui Spiritum Sanctum acceperunt sicut et nos?». [48]Et iussit eos in nomine Iesu Christi baptizari. Tunc rogaverunt eum, ut maneret aliquot diebus. **[11]** [1]Audierunt autem apostoli et fratres, qui erant in Iudaea, quoniam et gentes receperunt verbum Dei. [2]Cum ascendisset autem Petrus in Ierusalem, disceptabant adversus illum, qui erant ex circumcisione, [3]dicentes: «Introisti ad viros praeputium habentes et manducasti cum illis!». [4]Incipiens autem Petrus exponebat illis ex ordine dicens: [5]«Ego eram in civitate Ioppe orans et vidi in excessu mentis visionem, descendens vas quoddam velut linteum magnum quattuor initiis submitti de caelo, et venit usque ad me; [6]in quod intuens considerabam et vidi quadrupedia terrae et bestias et reptilia et volatilia caeli. [7]Audivi autem et vocem dicentem mihi: "Surgens, Petre, occide et manduca!". [8]Dixi autem: Nequaquam, Domine, quia commune aut immundum numquam introivit in os meum. [9]Respondit autem vox secundo de caelo: "Quae Deus mundavit, tu ne commune dixeris". [10]Hoc autem factum est per ter, et retracta sunt rursum omnia in caelum. [11]Et ecce confestim tres viri astiterunt in domo, in qua eramus, missi a Caesarea ad me. [12]Dixit autem Spiritus mihi, ut irem cum illis nihil haesitans. Venerunt autem mecum et sex fratres isti, et ingressi sumus in domum viri. [13]Narravit autem nobis quomodo vidisset angelum ad domum suam stantem et dicentem: "Mitte in Ioppen et accersi Simonem, qui cognominatur Petrus, [14]qui loquetur tibi verba, in quibus salvus eris tu et universa domus tua". [15]Cum autem coepissem loqui, decidit Spiritus Sanctus super eos sicut et super nos in initio. [16]Recordatus sum autem verbi Domini sicut dicebat: "Ioannes quidem baptizavit aqua, vos autem baptizabimini in Spiritu Sancto". ¹⁷Si ergo aequale donum dedit illis Deus sicut et nobis, qui credidimus in Dominum Iesum Christum, ego quis eram qui possem prohibere Deum?». ¹⁸His autem auditis acquieverunt et glorificaverunt Deum dicentes: «Ergo et gentibus Deus paenitentiam ad vitam dedit». ¹⁹Et illi quidem, qui dispersi fuerant a tribulatione, quae facta fuerat sub Stephano, perambulaverunt usque Phoenicen et Cyprum et Antiochiam, nemini loquentes verbum nisi solis Iudaeis. ²⁰Erant autem quidam ex eis viri Cyprii et Cyrenaei, qui cum introissent Antiochiam, loquebantur et ad Graecos evangelizantes Dominum Iesum. ²¹Et erat manus Domini cum eis; multusque numerus credentium conversus est ad Dominum. ²²Auditus est autem sermo in auribus ecclesiae, quae erat in Ierusalem, super istis, et miserunt Barnabam usque Antiochiam; ²³qui cum pervenisset et vidisset gratiam Dei, gavisus est et hortabatur omnes proposito cordis permanere in Domino, ²⁴quia erat vir bonus et plenus Spiritu Sancto et fide. Et apposita est turba multa Domino. ²⁵Profectus est autem Tarsum, ut quaereret Saulum; ²⁶quem cum invenisset, perduxit Antiochiam. Factum est autem eis ut annum totum conversarentur in ecclesia et docerent turbam multam, et cognominarentur primum Antiochiae discipuli Christiani. ²⁷In his autem diebus supervenerunt ab Hierosolymis prophetae Antiochiam; ²⁸et surgens unus ex eis nomine Agabus, significavit per Spiritum famem magnam futuram in universo orbe terrarum; quae facta est sub Claudio. ²⁹Discipuli autem, prout quis habebat, proposuerunt singuli eorum in ministerium mittere habitantibus in Iudaea fratribus; ³⁰quod et fecerunt, mittentes ad presbyteros per manum Barnabae et Sauli. [12] ¹Illo autem tempore misit Herodes rex manus, ut affligeret quosdam de ecclesia. ²Occidit autem Iacobum fratrem Ioannis gladio. ³Videns autem quia placeret Iudaeis, apposuit apprehendere et Petrum—erant autem dies Azymorum—⁴quem cum apprehendisset, misit in carcerem tradens quattuor quaternionibus militum custodire eum, volens post Pascha producere eum populo. ⁵Et Petrus quidem servabatur in carcere; oratio autem fiebat sine intermissione ab ecclesia ad Deum pro eo. ⁶Cum autem producturus eum esset Herodes, in ipsa nocte erat Petrus dormiens inter duos milites vinctus catenis duabus, et custodes ante ostium custodiebant carcerem. ⁷Et ecce angelus Domini astitit, et lumen refulsit in habitaculo; percusso autem latere Petri, suscitavit eum dicens: «Surge velociter!». Et ceciderunt catenae de manibus eius. ⁸Dixit autem angelus ad eum: «Praecingere et calcea te sandalia tua!». Et fecit sic. Et dicit illi: «Circumda tibi vestimentum tuum et sequere me!». ⁹Et exiens sequebatur et nesciebat quia verum est, quod fiebat per angelum; aestimabat autem se visum videre. ¹⁰Transeuntes autem primam custodiam et secundam venerunt ad portam ferream, quae ducit ad civitatem, quae ultro aperta est eis, et exeuntes processerunt vicum unum, et continuo discessit angelus ab eo. ¹¹Et Petrus ad se reversus dixit: «Nunc scio vere quia misit Dominus angelum suum et eripuit me de manu Herodis et de omni exspectatione plebis Iudaeorum». ¹²Consideransque venit ad domum Mariae matris Ioannis, qui cognominatur Marcus, ubi erant multi congregati et orantes. ¹³Pulsante autem eo ostium ianuae, processit puella ad audiendum, nomine Rhode; ¹⁴et ut cognovit vocem Petri prae gaudio non aperuit ianuam, sed intro currens nuntiavit stare Petrum ante ianuam. ¹⁵At illi dixerunt ad eam: «Insanis!». Illa autem affirmabat sic se habere. Illi autem dicebant: «Angelus eius est». ¹⁶Petrus autem perseverabat pulsans; cum autem aperuissent, viderunt eum et obstupuerunt. ¹⁷Annuens autem eis manu, ut tacerent, enarravit quomodo Dominus eduxisset eum de carcere dixitque: «Nuntiate Iacobo et fratribus haec». Et egressus abiit in alium locum. ¹⁸Facta autem die erat non parva turbatio inter milites, quidnam de Petro factum esset. ¹⁹Herodes autem cum requisisset eum et non invenisset, interrogatis custodibus iussit eos abduci; descendensque a Iudaea in Caesaream ibi commorabatur. ²⁰Erat autem iratus Tyriis et Sidoniis; at illi unanimes venerunt ad eum et persuaso Blasto, qui erat super cubiculum regis, postulabant pacem, eo quod aleretur regio eorum ab annona regis. ²¹Statuto autem die, Herodes, vestitus veste regia, sedens pro tribunali, contionabatur ad eos; ²²populus autem acclamabat: «Dei vox et non hominis!». ²³Confestim autem percussit eum angelus Domini, eo quod non dedisset gloriam Deo, et consumptus a vermibus exspiravit. ²⁴Verbum autem Dei crescebat et multiplicabatur. ²⁵Barnabas autem et Saulus reversi sunt in Ierusalem expleto ministerio, assumpto Ioanne, qui cognominatus est Marcus. [13] ¹Erant autem in ecclesia, quae erat Antiochiae, prophetae et doctores: Barnabas et Simeon, qui vocabatur Niger, et Lucius Cyrenensis, et Manaen, qui erat Herodis tetrarchae collactaneus, et Saulus. ²Ministrantibus autem illis Domino et ieiunantibus, dixit Spiritus Sanctus: «Separate mihi Barnabam et Saulum in opus, ad quod vocavi eos». ³Tunc ieiunantes et orantes imponentesque eis manus dimiserunt illos. ⁴Et ipsi quidem missi ab Spiritu Sancto devenerunt Seleuciam et inde navigaverunt Cyprum ⁵et, cum venissent Salamina, praedicabant verbum Dei in synagogis Iudaeorum; habebant autem et Ioannem ministrum. ⁶Et cum perambulassent universam insulam usque Paphum, invenerunt quendam virum magum pseudoprophetam Iudaeum, cui nomen Bariesu, ⁷qui erat cum proconsule Sergio Paulo, viro prudente. Hic accitis Barnaba et Saulo, quaesivit audire verbum Dei; ⁸resistebat autem illis Elymas, magus, sic enim interpretatur nomen eius, quaerens avertere proconsulem a fide. [9]Saulus autem, qui et Paulus, repletus Spiritu Sancto, intuens in eum [10]dixit: «O plene omni dolo et omni fallacia, fili Diaboli, inimice omnis iustitiae, non desines subvertere vias Domini rectas? [11]Et nunc ecce manus Domini super te: et eris caecus, non videns solem usque ad tempus». Et confestim cecidit in eum caligo et tenebrae, et circumiens quaerebat, qui eum manum darent. [12]Tunc proconsul, cum vidisset factum, credidit admirans super doctrinam Domini. [13]Et cum a Papho navigassent, qui erant cum Paulo, venerunt Pergen Pamphyliae; Ioannes autem discedens ab eis reversus est Hierosolymam. [14]Illi vero pertranseuntes, a Perge venerunt Antiochiam Pisidiae, et ingressi synagogam die sabbatorum sederunt. [15]Post lectionem autem Legis et Prophetarum, miserunt principes synagogae ad eos dicentes: «Viri fratres, si quis est in vobis sermo exhortationis ad plebem, dicite!». [16]Surgens autem Paulus et manu silentium indicens ait: «Viri Israelitae et qui timetis Deum, audite. [17]Deus plebis huius Israel elegit patres nostros et plebem exaltavit, cum essent incolae in terra Aegypti, et in brachio excelso eduxit eos ex ea [18]et per quadraginta fere annorum tempus mores eorum sustinuit in deserto [19]et destruens gentes septem in terra Chanaan sorte distribuit terram eorum, [20]quasi quadringentos et quinquaginta annos. Et post haec dedit iudices usque ad Samuel prophetam. [21]Et exinde postulaverunt regem, et dedit illis Deus Saul filium Cis, virum de tribu Beniamin, annis quadraginta. [22]Et amoto illo, suscitavit illis David in regem, cui et testimonium perhibens dixit: "*Inveni David* filium Iesse, *virum secundum cor meum*, qui faciet omnes voluntates meas". [23]Huius Deus ex semine secundum promissionem eduxit Israel salvatorem Iesum, [24]praedicante Ioanne ante adventum eius baptismum paenitentiae omni populo Israel. [25]Cum impleret autem Ioannes cursum suum, dicebat: "Quid me arbitramini esse? Non sum ego; sed ecce venit post me, cuius non sum dignus calceamenta pedum solvere". [26]Viri fratres, filii generis Abraham et qui in vobis timent Deum, nobis verbum salutis huius missum est. [27]Qui enim habitabant Ierusalem et principes eorum, hunc ignorantes et voces Prophetarum, quae per omne sabbatum leguntur, iudicantes impleverunt, [28]et nullam causam mortis invenientes petierunt a Pilato, ut interficeretur; [29]cumque consummassent omnia, quae de eo scripta erant, deponentes eum de ligno posuerunt in monumento. [30]Deus vero suscitavit eum a mortuis; [31]qui visus est per dies multos his, qui simul ascenderant cum eo de Galilaea in Ierusalem, qui nunc sunt testes eius ad plebem. [32]Et nos vobis evangelizamus eam, quae ad patres promissio facta est, [33]quoniam hanc Deus adimplevit filiis eorum, nobis resuscitans Iesum, sicut et in Psalmo secundo scriptum est: "*Filius meus es tu; ego hodie genui te*". [34]Quod autem suscitaverit eum a mortuis, amplius iam non reversurum in corruptionem, ita dixit: "*Dabo vobis sancta David fidelia*". [35]Ideoque et in alio dicit: "*Non dabis Sanctum tuum videre corruptionem*". [36]David enim sua generatione cum administrasset voluntati Dei, dormivit et appositus est ad patres suos et vidit corruptionem; [37]quem vero Deus suscitavit, non vidit corruptionem. [38]Notum igitur sit vobis, viri fratres, quia per hunc vobis remissio peccatorum annuntiatur; ab omnibus, quibus non potuistis in lege Moysi iustificari, [39]in hoc omnis, qui credit, iustificatur. [40]Videte ergo, ne superveniat, quod dictum est in Prophetis: [41]"*Videte, contemptores, / et admiramini et disperdimini, / quia opus operor ego in diebus vestris, / opus, quod non credetis, si quis enarraverit vobis!*"». [42]Exeuntibus autem illis, rogabant, ut sequenti sabbato loquerentur sibi verba haec. [43]Cumque dimissa esset synagoga, secuti sunt multi Iudaeorum et colentium proselytorum Paulum et Barnabam, qui loquentes suadebant eis, ut permanerent in gratia Dei. [44]Sequenti vero sabbato paene universa civitas convenit audire verbum Domini. [45]Videntes autem turbas Iudaei repleti sunt zelo et contradicebant his, quae a Paulo dicebantur, blasphemantes. [46]Tunc audenter Paulus et Barnabas dixerunt: «Vobis oportebat primum loqui verbum Dei; sed quoniam repellitis illud et indignos vos iudicatis aeternae vitae, ecce convertimur ad gentes. [47]Sic enim praecepit nobis Dominus: "*Posui te in lumen gentium, / ut sis in salutem usque ad extremum terrae*"». [48]Audientes autem gentes gaudebant et glorificabant verbum Domini, et crediderunt, quotquot erant praeordinati ad vitam aeternam; [49]ferebatur autem verbum Domini per universam regionem. [50]Iudaei autem concitaverunt honestas inter colentes mulieres et primos civitatis et excitaverunt persecutionem in Paulum et Barnabam et eiecerunt eos de finibus suis. [51]At illi, excusso pulvere pedum in eos, venerunt Iconium; [52]discipuli quoque replebantur gaudio et Spiritu Sancto. [14] [1]Factum est autem Iconii, ut eodem modo introirent synagogam Iudaeorum et ita loquerentur, ut crederet Iudaeorum et Graecorum copiosa multitudo. [2]Qui vero increduli fuerunt Iudaei, suscitaverunt et exacerbaverunt animas gentium adversus fratres. [3]Multo igitur tempore demorati sunt, fiducialiter agentes in Domino, testimonium perhibente verbo gratiae suae, dante signa et prodigia fieri per manus eorum. [4]Divisa est autem multitudo civitatis: et quidam quidem erant cum Iudaeis, quidam vero cum apostolis. [5]Cum autem factus esset impetus gentilium et Iudaeorum cum principibus suis, ut contumeliis afficerent et lapidarent eos, [6]intellegentes confugerunt ad civitates Lycaoniae, Lystram et Derben et ad regionem in circuitu, [7]et ibi evangelizantes erant. [8]Et quidam vir in Lystris infirmus pedibus sedebat, claudus ex utero matris suae, qui numquam ambulaverat. [9]Hic audivit

Paulum loquentem; qui intuitus eum et videns quia haberet fidem, ut salvus fieret, [10]dixit magna voce: «Surge super pedes tuos rectus!». Et exsilivit et ambulabat. [11]Turbae autem cum vidissent, quod fecerat Paulus, levaverunt vocem suam Lycaonice dicentes: «Dii similes facti hominibus descenderunt ad nos!»; [12]et vocabant Barnabam Iovem, Paulum vero Mercurium, quoniam ipse erat dux verbi. [13]Sacerdos quoque templi Iovis, quod erat ante civitatem, tauros et coronas ad ianuas afferens cum populis, volebat sacrificare. [14]Quod ubi audierunt apostoli Barnabas et Paulus, conscissis tunicis suis, exsilierunt in turbam clamantes [15]et dicentes: «Viri, quid haec facitis? Et nos mortales sumus similes vobis homines, evangelizantes vobis ab his vanis converti ad Deum vivum, *qui fecit caelum et terram et mare et omnia, quae in eis sunt.* [16]Qui in praeteritis generationibus permisit omnes gentes ambulare in viis suis; [17]et quidem non sine testimonio semetipsum reliquit benefaciens, de caelo dans vobis pluvias et tempora fructifera, implens cibo et laetitia corda vestra». [18]Et haec dicentes vix sedaverunt turbas, ne sibi immolarent. [19]Supervenerunt autem ab Antiochia et Iconio Iudaei et persuasis turbis lapidantesque Paulum trahebant extra civitatem aestimantes eum mortuum esse. [20]Circumdantibus autem eum discipulis, surgens intravit civitatem. Et postera die profectus est cum Barnaba in Derben. [21]Cumque evangelizassent civitati illi et docuissent multos, reversi sunt Lystram et Iconium et Antiochiam [22]confirmantes animas discipulorum, exhortantes, ut permanerent in fide, et quoniam per multas tribulationes oportet nos intrare in regnum Dei. [23]Et cum ordinassent illis per singulas ecclesias presbyteros et orassent cum ieiunationibus, commendaverunt eos Domino, in quem crediderant. [24]Transeuntesque Pisidiam venerunt Pamphyliam, [25]et loquentes in Perge verbum descenderunt in Attaliam. [26]Et inde navigaverunt Antiochiam, unde erant traditi gratiae Dei in opus, quod compleverunt. [27]Cum autem venissent et congregassent ecclesiam, rettulerunt quanta fecisset Deus cum illis et quia aperuisset gentibus ostium fidei. [28]Morati sunt autem tempus non modicum cum discipulis. **[15]** [1]Et quidam descendentes de Iudaea docebant fratres: «Nisi circumcidamini secundum morem Moysis, non potestis salvi fieri». [2]Facta autem seditione et conquisitione non minima Paulo et Barnabae adversum illos, statuerunt, ut ascenderent Paulus et Barnabas et quidam alii ex illis ad apostolos et presbyteros in Ierusalem super hac quaestione. [3]Illi igitur deducti ab ecclesia pertransiebant Phoenicen et Samariam narrantes conversionem gentium et faciebant gaudium magnum omnibus fratribus. [4]Cum autem venissent Hierosolymam, suscepti sunt ab ecclesia et apostolis et presbyteris et annuntiaverunt quanta Deus fecisset cum illis. [5]Surrexerunt autem quidam de haeresi pharisaeorum, qui crediderant, dicentes: «Oportet circumcidere eos, praecipere quoque servare legem Moysis!». [6]Conveneruntque apostoli et presbyteri videre de verbo hoc. [7]Cum autem magna conquisitio fieret, surgens Petrus dixit ad eos: «Viri fratres, vos scitis quoniam ab antiquis diebus in vobis elegit Deus per os meum audire gentes verbum evangelii et credere; [8]et qui novit corda, Deus testimonium perhibuit illis dans Spiritum Sanctum sicut et nobis [9]et nihil discrevit inter nos et illos fide purificans corda eorum. [10]Nunc ergo quid tentatis Deum imponere iugum super cervicem discipulorum, quod neque patres nostri neque nos portare potuimus? [11]Sed per gratiam Domini Iesu credimus salvari quemadmodum et illi». [12]Tacuit autem omnis multitudo, et audiebant Barnabam et Paulum narrantes quanta fecisset Deus signa et prodigia in gentibus per eos. [13]Et postquam tacuerunt, respondit Iacobus dicens: «Viri fratres, audite me. [14]Simeon narravit quemadmodum primum Deus visitavit sumere ex gentibus populum nomini suo, [15]et huic concordant verba Prophetarum, sicut scriptum est: [16]"*Post haec revertar / et reaedificabo tabernaculum David, quod decidit, / et diruta eius reaedificabo et erigam illud, / [17]ut requirant reliqui hominum Dominum / et omnes gentes, super quas invocatum est nomen meum, / dicit Dominus faciens haec [18]nota a saeculo".* [19]Propter quod ego iudico non inquietari eos, qui ex gentibus convertuntur ad Deum, [20]sed scribere ad eos, ut abstineant se a contaminationibus simulacrorum et fornicatione et suffocato et sanguine. [21]Moyses enim a generationibus antiquis habet in singulis civitatibus, qui eum praedicent in synagogis, ubi per omne sabbatum legitur». [22]Tunc placuit apostolis et presbyteris cum omni ecclesia electos viros ex eis mittere Antiochiam cum Paulo et Barnaba: Iudam, qui cognominatur Barsabbas, et Silam, viros primos in fratribus, [23]scribentes per manum eorum: «Apostoli et presbyteri fratres his, qui sunt Antiochiae et Syriae et Ciliciae fratribus ex gentibus, salutem! [24]Quoniam audivimus quia quidam ex nobis quibus non mandavimus, exeuntes turbaverunt vos verbis evertentes animas vestras, [25]placuit nobis collectis in unum eligere viros et mittere ad vos cum carissimis nobis Barnaba et Paulo, [26]hominibus, qui tradiderunt animas suas pro nomine Domini nostri Iesu Christi. [27]Misimus ergo Iudam et Silam, qui et ipsi verbis referent eadem. [28]Visum est enim Spiritui Sancto et nobis nihil ultra imponere vobis oneris quam haec necessario: [29]abstinere ab idolothytis et sanguine et suffocatis et fornicatione; a quibus custodientes vos bene agetis. Valete». [30]Illi igitur dimissi descenderunt Antiochiam et, congregata multitudine, tradiderunt epistulam; [31]quam cum legissent, gavisi sunt super consolatione. [32]Iudas quoque et Silas, cum et ipsi essent prophetae, verbo plurimo consolati sunt fratres et confirmaverunt. ³³Facto autem tempore, dimissi sunt cum pace a fratribus ad eos, qui miserant illos. ³⁵Paulus autem et Barnabas demorabantur Antiochiae docentes et evangelizantes cum aliis pluribus verbum Domini. ³⁶Post aliquot autem dies dixit ad Barnabam Paulus: «Revertentes visitemus fratres per universas civitates, in quibus praedicavimus verbum Domini, quomodo se habeant». ³⁷Barnabas autem volebat secum assumere et Ioannem, qui cognominatur Marcus; ³⁸Paulus autem iudicabat eum, qui discessisset ab eis a Pamphylia et non isset cum eis in opus, non debere recipi eum. ³⁹Facta est autem exacerbatio, ita ut discederent ab invicem, et Barnabas assumpto Marco navigaret Cyprum. ⁴⁰Paulus vero, electo Sila, profectus est traditus gratiae Domini a fratribus; ⁴¹perambulabat autem Syriam et Ciliciam confirmans ecclesias. **[16]** ¹Pervenit autem in Derben et Lystram. Et ecce discipulus quidam erat ibi nomine Timotheus, filius mulieris Iudaeae fidelis, patre autem Graeco; ²huic testimonium reddebant, qui in Lystris erant et Iconii fratres. ³Hunc voluit Paulus secum proficisci et assumens circumcidit eum propter Iudaeos, qui erant in illis locis; sciebant enim omnes quod pater eius Graecus esset. ⁴Cum autem pertransirent civitates, tradebant eis custodire dogmata, quae erant decreta ab apostolis et presbyteris, qui essent Hierosolymis. ⁵Ecclesiae quidem confirmabantur fide et abundabant numero cotidie. ⁶Transierunt autem Phrygiam et Galatiae regionem, vetati a Sancto Spiritu loqui verbum in Asia; ⁷cum venissent autem circa Mysiam, tentabant ire Bithyniam, et non permisit eos Spiritus Iesu; ⁸cum autem praeterissent Mysiam, descenderunt Troadem. ⁹Et visio per noctem Paulo ostensa est: vir Macedo quidam erat stans et deprecans eum et dicens: «Transiens in Macedoniam, adiuva nos!». ¹⁰Ut autem visum vidit, statim quaesivimus proficisci in Macedoniam, certi facti quia vocasset nos Deus evangelizare eis. ¹¹Navigantes autem a Troade recto cursu venimus Samothraciam et sequenti die Neapolim ¹²et inde Philippos, quae est prima partis Macedoniae civitas, colonia. Eramus autem in hac urbe diebus aliquot commorantes. ¹³Die autem sabbatorum egressi sumus foras portam iuxta flumen, ubi putabamus orationem esse, et sedentes loquebamur mulieribus, quae convenerant. ¹⁴Et quaedam mulier nomine Lydia, purpuraria civitatis Thyatirenorum colens Deum, audiebat, cuius Dominus aperuit cor intendere his, quae dicebantur a Paulo. ¹⁵Cum autem baptizata esset et domus eius, deprecata est dicens: «Si iudicastis me fidelem Domino esse, introite in domum meam et manete»; et coegit nos. ¹⁶Factum est autem euntibus nobis ad orationem, puellam quandam habentem spiritum pythonem obviare nobis, quae quaestum magnum praestabat dominis suis divinando. ¹⁷Haec subsecuta Paulum et nos clamabat dicens: «Isti homines servi Dei Altissimi sunt, qui annuntiant vobis viam salutis». ¹⁸Hoc autem faciebat multis diebus. Dolens autem Paulus et conversus spiritui dixit: «Praecipio tibi in nomine Iesu Christi exire ab ea»; et exiit eadem hora. ¹⁹Videntes autem domini eius quia exivit spes quaestus eorum, apprehendentes Paulum et Silam traxerunt in forum ad principes ²⁰et producentes eos magistratibus dixerunt: «Hi homines conturbant civitatem nostram, cum sint Iudaei, ²¹et annuntiant mores, quos non licet nobis suscipere neque facere cum simus Romani». ²²Et concurrit plebs adversus eos, et magistratus scissis tunicis eorum iusserunt virgis caedi ²³et, cum multas plagas eis imposuissent, miserunt eos in carcerem, praecipientes custodi, ut caute custodiret eos; ²⁴qui cum tale praeceptum accepisset, misit eos in interiorem carcerem et pedes eorum strinxit in ligno. ²⁵Media autem nocte Paulus et Silas orantes laudabant Deum, et audiebant eos, qui in custodia erant; ²⁶subito vero terraemotus factus est magnus, ita ut moverentur fundamenta carceris, et aperta sunt statim ostia omnia, et universorum vincula soluta sunt. ²⁷Expergefactus autem custos carceris et videns apertas ianuas carceris, evaginato gladio volebat se interficere, aestimans fugisse vinctos. ²⁸Clamavit autem Paulus magna voce dicens: «Nihil feceris tibi mali; universi enim hic sumus». ²⁹Petitoque lumine intro cucurrit et tremefactus procidit Paulo et Silae ³⁰et producens eos foras ait: «Domini, quid me oportet facere, ut salvus fiam?». ³¹At illi dixerunt: «Crede in Domino Iesu et salvus eris tu et domus tua». ³²Et locuti sunt ei verbum Domini cum omnibus, qui erant in domo eius. ³³Et tollens eos in illa hora noctis lavit eos a plagis, et baptizatus est ipse et omnes eius continuo; ³⁴cumque perduxisset eos in domum, apposuit mensam et laetatus est cum omni domo sua credens Deo. ³⁵Et cum dies factus esset, miserunt magistratus lictores dicentes: «Dimitte homines illos!». ³⁶Nuntiavit autem custos carceris verba haec Paulo: «Miserunt magistratus, ut dimittamini; nunc igitur exeuntes ite in pace». ³⁷Paulus autem dixit eis: «Caesos nos publice indemnatos, cum homines Romani essemus, miserunt in carcerem; et nunc occulte nos eiciunt? Non ita, sed veniant et ipsi nos educant». ³⁸Nuntiaverunt autem magistratibus lictores verba haec. Timueruntque audito quod Romani essent, ³⁹et venientes deprecati sunt eos et educentes rogabant, ut egrederentur urbem. ⁴⁰Exeuntes autem de carcere introierunt ad Lydiam et, visis fratribus, consolati sunt eos et profecti sunt. **[17]** ¹Cum autem perambulassent Amphipolim et Apolloniam, venerunt Thessalonicam, ubi erat synagoga Iudaeorum. ²Secundum consuetudinem autem suam Paulus introivit ad eos et per sabbata tria disserebat eis de Scripturis ³adaperiens et comprobans quia Christum oportebat pati et resurgere a mortuis, et: «Hic est Christus, Iesus, quem ego annuntio vobis». [4]Et quidam ex eis crediderunt et adiuncti sunt Paulo et Silae et de colentibus Graecis multitudo magna et mulieres nobiles non paucae. [5]Zelantes autem Iudaei assumentesque de foro viros quosdam malos et turba facta concitaverunt civitatem, et assistentes domui Iasonis quaerebant eos producere in populum. [6]Et cum non invenissent eos, trahebant Iasonem et quosdam fratres ad politarchas clamantes: «Qui orbem concitaverunt, isti et huc venerunt, [7]quos suscepit Iason; et hi omnes contra decreta Caesaris faciunt, regem alium dicentes esse, Iesum». [8]Concitaverunt autem plebem et politarchas audientes haec; [9]et accepto satis ab Iasone et a ceteris, dimiserunt eos. [10]Fratres vero confestim per noctem dimiserunt Paulum et Silam in Beroeam; qui cum advenissent, in synagogam Iudaeorum introierunt. [11]Hi autem erant nobiliores eorum, qui sunt Thessalonicae, qui susceperunt verbum cum omni aviditate, cotidie scrutantes Scripturas si haec ita se haberent. [12]Et multi quidem crediderunt ex eis et Graecarum mulierum honestarum et virorum non pauci. [13]Cum autem cognovissent in Thessalonica Iudaei quia et Beroeae annuntiatum est a Paulo verbum Dei, venerunt et illuc commoventes et turbantes multitudinem. [14]Statimque tunc Paulum dimiserunt fratres, ut iret usque ad mare; Silas autem et Timotheus remanserunt ibi. [15]Qui autem deducebant Paulum, perduxerunt usque Athenas, et accepto mandato ad Silam et Timotheum, ut quam celerrime venirent ad illum, profecti sunt. [16]Paulus autem cum Athenis eos exspectaret, irritabatur spiritus eius in ipso videns idololatriae deditam civitatem. [17]Disputabat igitur in synagoga cum Iudaeis et colentibus et in foro per omnes dies ad eos, qui aderant. [18]Quidam autem ex Epicureis et Stoicis philosophi disserebant cum eo. Et quidam dicebant: «Quid vult seminiverbius hic dicere?»; alii vero: «Novorum daemoniorum videtur annuntiator esse», quia Iesum et resurrectionem evangelizabat. [19]Et apprehensum eum ad Areopagum duxerunt dicentes: «Possumus scire quae est haec nova, quae a te dicitur doctrina? [20]Mira enim quaedam infers auribus nostris; volumus ergo scire quidnam velint haec esse». [21]Athenienses autem omnes et advenae hospites ad nihil aliud vacabant nisi aut dicere aut audire aliquid novi. [22]Stans autem Paulus in medio Areopagi ait: «Viri Athenienses, per omnia quasi superstitiosiores vos video; [23]praeteriens enim et videns simulacra vestra inveni et aram in qua scriptum erat: "Ignoto deo". Quod ergo ignorantes colitis, hoc ego annuntio vobis. [24]Deus, qui fecit mundum et omnia, quae in eo sunt, hic, caeli et terrae cum sit Dominus, non in manufactis templis inhabitat, [25]nec manibus humanis colitur indigens aliquo, cum ipse det omnibus vitam et inspirationem et omnia; [26]fecitque ex uno omne genus hominum inhabitare super universam faciem terrae, definiens statuta tempora et terminos habitationis eorum, [27]quaerere Deum si forte attrectent eum et inveniant, quamvis non longe sit ab unoquoque nostrum. [28]In ipso enim vivimus et movemur et sumus, sicut et quidam vestrum poetarum dixerunt: "Ipsius enim et genus sumus". [29]Genus ergo cum simus Dei, non debemus aestimare auro aut argento aut lapidi, sculpturae artis et cogitationis hominis, divinum esse simile. [30]Et tempora quidem ignorantiae despiciens Deus, nunc annuntiat hominibus, ut omnes ubique paenitentiam agant, [31]eo quod statuit diem, in qua iudicaturus est orbem in iustitia in viro, quem constituit, fidem praebens omnibus suscitans eum a mortuis». [32]Cum audissent autem resurrectionem mortuorum, quidam quidem irridebant, quidam vero dixerunt: «Audiemus te de hoc iterum». [33]Sic Paulus exivit de medio eorum. [34]Quidam vero viri adhaerentes ei crediderunt, in quibus et Dionysius Areopagita et mulier nomine Damaris et alii cum eis.   [18] [1]Post haec discedens ab Athenis venit Corinthum. [2]Et inveniens quendam Iudaeum nomine Aquilam, Ponticum genere, qui nuper venerat ab Italia, et Priscillam uxorem eius, eo quod praecepisset Claudius discedere omnes Iudaeos a Roma, accessit ad eos [3]et, quia eiusdem erat artis, manebat apud eos et operabatur; erant autem scenofactoriae artis. [4]Disputabat autem in synagoga per omne sabbatum suadebatque Iudaeis et Graecis. [5]Cum venissent autem de Macedonia Silas et Timotheus, instabat verbo Paulus testificans Iudaeis esse Christum Iesum. [6]Contradicentibus autem eis et blasphemantibus, excutiens vestimenta dixit ad eos: «Sanguis vester super caput vestrum! Mundus ego. Ex hoc nunc ad gentes vadam». [7]Et migrans inde intravit in domum cuiusdam nomine Titi Iusti, colentis Deum, cuius domus erat coniuncta synagogae. [8]Crispus autem archisynagogus credidit Domino cum omni domo sua, et multi Corinthiorum audientes credebant et baptizabantur. [9]Dixit autem Dominus nocte per visionem Paulo: «Noli timere, sed loquere et ne taceas, [10]quia ego sum tecum, et nemo apponetur tibi, ut noceat te, quoniam populus est mihi multus in hac civitate». [11]Sedit autem annum et sex menses docens apud eos verbum Dei. [12]Gallione autem proconsule Achaiae, insurrexerunt uno animo Iudaei in Paulum et adduxerunt eum ad tribunal [13]dicentes: «Contra legem hic persuadet hominibus colere Deum». [14]Incipiente autem Paulo aperire os, dixit Gallio ad Iudaeos: «Si quidem esset iniquum aliquid aut facinus pessimum, o Iudaei, merito vos sustinerem; [15]si vero quaestiones sunt de verbo et nominibus et lege vestra, vos ipsi videritis; iudex ego horum nolo esse». [16]Et minavit eos a tribunali. [17]Apprehendentes autem omnes Sosthenen, principem synagogae, percutiebant ante tribunal; et nihil horum Gallioni curae erat. [18]Paulus vero, cum adhuc sustinuisset dies multos, fratribus valefaciens navigabat Syriam, et cum eo Priscilla et Aquila, qui sibi totonderat in Cenchreis caput; habebat enim votum. [19]Deveneruntque Ephesum, et illos ibi reliquit, ipse vero ingressus synagogam disputabat cum Iudaeis. [20]Rogantibus autem eis, ut ampliore tempore maneret, non consensit, [21]sed valefaciens et dicens: «Iterum revertar ad vos Deo volente», navigavit ab Epheso; [22]et descendens Caesaream ascendit et salutavit ecclesiam et descendit Antiochiam. [23]Et facto ibi aliquanto tempore, profectus est perambulans ex ordine Galaticam regionem et Phrygiam, confirmans omnes discipulos. [24]Iudaeus autem quidam Apollo nomine, Alexandrinus natione, vir eloquens, devenit Ephesum, potens in Scripturis. [25]Hic erat catechizatus viam Domini et fervens spiritu loquebatur et docebat diligenter ea, quae sunt de Iesu, sciens tantum baptisma Ioannis. [26]Hic ergo coepit fiducialiter agere in synagoga; quem cum audissent Priscilla et Aquila, assumpserunt eum et diligentius exposuerunt ei viam Dei. [27]Cum autem vellet transire in Achaiam, exhortati fratres scripserunt discipulis, ut susciperent eum; qui cum venisset, contulit multum his, qui crediderant per gratiam; [28]vehementer enim Iudaeos revincebat publice ostendens per Scripturas esse Christum Iesum.   [19] [1]Factum est autem cum Apollo esset Corinthi, ut Paulus, peragratis superioribus partibus, veniret Ephesum et inveniret quosdam discipulos, [2]dixitque ad eos: «Si Spiritum Sanctum accepistis credentes?». At illi ad eum: «Sed neque si Spiritus Sanctus est audivimus». [3]Ille vero ait: «In quo ergo baptizati estis?». Qui dixerunt: «In Ioannis baptismate». [4]Dixit autem Paulus: «Ioannes baptizavit baptisma paenitentiae, populo dicens in eum, qui venturus esset post ipsum ut crederent, hoc est in Iesum». [5]His auditis, baptizati sunt in nomine Domini Iesu; [6]et cum imposuisset illis manus Paulus, venit Spiritus Sanctus super eos, et loquebantur linguis et prophetabant. [7]Erant autem omnes viri fere duodecim. [8]Introgressus autem synagogam cum fiducia loquebatur per tres menses disputans et suadens de regno Dei. [9]Cum autem quidam indurarentur et non crederent maledicentes viam coram multitudine, discedens ab eis segregavit discipulos, cotidie disputans in schola Tyranni. [10]Hoc autem factum est per biennium, ita ut omnes, qui habitabant in Asia, audirent verbum Domini, Iudaei atque Graeci. [11]Virtutesque non quaslibet Deus faciebat per manus Pauli, [12]ita ut etiam super languidos deferrentur a corpore eius sudaria vel semicinctia, et recederent ab eis languores, et spiritus nequam egrederentur. [13]Tentaverunt autem quidam et de circumeuntibus Iudaeis exorcistis invocare super eos, qui habebant spiritus malos, nomen Domini Iesu dicentes: «Adiuro vos per Iesum, quem Paulus praedicat». [14]Erant autem cuiusdam Scevae Iudaei principis sacerdotum septem filii, qui hoc faciebant. [15]Respondens autem spiritus nequam dixit eis: «Iesum novi et Paulum scio, vos autem qui estis?». [16]Et insiliens homo in eos, in quo erat spiritus malus, dominatus amborum invaluit contra eos, ita ut nudi et vulnerati effugerent de domo illa. [17]Hoc autem notum factum est omnibus Iudaeis atque Graecis, qui habitabant Ephesi, et cecidit timor super omnes illos, et magnificabatur nomen Domini Iesu. [18]Multique credentium veniebant confitentes et annuntiantes actus suos. [19]Multi autem ex his, qui fuerant curiosa sectati, conferentes libros combusserunt coram omnibus; et computaverunt pretia illorum et invenerunt argenti quinquaginta milia. [20]Ita fortiter verbum Domini crescebat et convalescebat. [21]His autem expletis, proposuit Paulus in Spiritu, transita Macedonia et Achaia, ire Hierosolymam, dicens: «Postquam fuero ibi, oportet me et Romam videre». [22]Mittens autem in Macedoniam duos ex ministrantibus sibi, Timotheum et Erastum, ipse remansit ad tempus in Asia. [23]Facta est autem in illo tempore turbatio non minima de via. [24]Demetrius enim quidam nomine, argentarius, faciens aedes argenteas Dianae praestabat artificibus non modicum quaestum; [25]quos congregans et eos, qui eiusmodi erant opifices, dixit: «Viri, scitis quia de hoc artificio acquisitio est nobis [26]et videtis et auditis quia non solum Ephesi, sed paene totius Asiae Paulus hic suadens avertit multam turbam dicens quoniam non sunt dii, qui manibus fiunt. [27]Non solum autem haec periclitatur nobis pars in redargutionem venire, sed et magnae deae Dianae templum in nihilum reputari, et destrui incipiet maiestas eius, quam tota Asia et orbis colit». [28]His auditis, repleti sunt ira et clamabant dicentes: «Magna Diana Ephesiorum!», [29]et impleta est civitas confusione, et impetum fecerunt uno animo in theatrum, rapto Gaio et Aristarcho Macedonibus, comitibus Pauli. [30]Paulo autem volente intrare in populum, non permiserunt discipuli; [31]quidam autem de Asiarchis, qui erant amici eius, miserunt ad eum rogantes, ne se daret in theatrum. [32]Alii autem aliud clamabant; erat enim ecclesia confusa, et plures nesciebant qua ex causa convenissent. [33]De turba autem instruxerunt Alexandrum, propellentibus eum Iudaeis; Alexander ergo, manu silentio postulato, volebat rationem reddere populo. [34]Quem ut cognoverunt Iudaeum esse, vox facta est una omnium quasi per horas duas clamantium: «Magna Diana Ephesiorum!». [35]Et cum sedasset scriba turbam dixit: «Viri Ephesii, quis enim est hominum, qui nesciat Ephesiorum civitatem cultricem esse magnae Dianae et simulacri a Iove delapsi? [36]Cum ergo his contradici non possit, oportet vos sedatos esse et nihil temere agere. [37]Adduxistis enim homines istos neque sacrilegos neque blasphemantes deam nostram. [38]Quod si Demetrius et, qui cum eo sunt, artifices habent adversus aliquem causam, conventus forenses aguntur, et proconsules sunt: accusent invicem.

[39]Si quid autem ulterius quaeritis, in legitima ecclesia poterit absolvi. [40]Nam et periclitamur argui seditionis hodiernae, cum nullus obnoxius sit, de quo non possimus reddere rationem concursus istius». Et cum haec dixisset, dimisit ecclesiam. [20] [1]Postquam autem cessavit tumultus, accersitis Paulus discipulis et exhortatus eos, valedixit et profectus est, ut iret in Macedoniam. [2]Cum autem perambulasset partes illas et exhortatus eos fuisset multo sermone, venit ad Graeciam; [3]cumque fecisset menses tres, factae sunt illi insidiae a Iudaeis navigaturo in Syriam, habuitque consilium, ut reverteretur per Macedoniam. [4]Comitabatur autem eum Sopater Pyrrhi Beroeensis, Thessalonicensium vero Aristarchus et Secundus et Gaius Derbeus et Timotheus, Asiani vero Tychicus et Trophimus. [5]Hi cum praecessissent, sustinebant nos Troade; [6]nos vero navigavimus post dies Azymorum a Philippis, et venimus ad eos Troadem in diebus quinque, ubi demorati sumus diebus septem. [7]In una autem sabbatorum cum convenissemus ad frangendum panem, Paulus disputabat eis, profecturus in crastinum, protraxitque sermonem usque in mediam noctem. [8]Erant autem lampades copiosae in cenaculo, ubi eramus congregati; [9]sedens autem quidam adulescens nomine Eutychus super fenestram, cum mergeretur somno gravi disputante diutius Paulo, eductus somno cecidit de tertio cenaculo deorsum et sublatus est mortuus. [10]Cum descendisset autem Paulus incubuit super eum et complexus dixit: «Nolite turbari, anima enim ipsius in eo est!». [11]Ascendens autem frangensque panem et gustans satisque allocutus usque in lucem, sic profectus est. [12]Adduxerunt autem puerum viventem et consolati sunt non minime. [13]Nos autem praecedentes navi enavigavimus in Asson, inde suscepturi Paulum, sic enim disposuerat volens ipse per terram iter facere. [14]Cum autem convenisset nos in Asson, assumpto eo, venimus Mitylenen [15]et inde navigantes sequenti die pervenimus contra Chium et alia applicuimus Samum et sequenti venimus Miletum. [16]Proposuerat enim Paulus transnavigare Ephesum, ne qua mora illi fieret in Asia; festinabat enim, si possibile sibi esset, ut diem Pentecosten faceret Hierosolymis. [17]A Mileto autem mittens Ephesum convocavit presbyteros ecclesiae. [18]Qui cum venissent ad eum, dixit eis: «Vos scitis a prima die, qua ingressus sum in Asiam, qualiter vobiscum per omne tempus fuerim, [19]serviens Domino cum omni humilitate et lacrimis et tentationibus, quae mihi acciderunt in insidiis Iudaeorum; [20]quomodo nihil subtraxerim utilium, quominus annuntiarem vobis et docerem vos publice et per domos, [21]testificans Iudaeis atque Graecis in Deum paenitentiam et fidem in Dominum nostrum Iesum. [22]Et nunc ecce alligatus ego Spiritu vado in Ierusalem, quae in ea eventura sint mihi ignorans, [23]nisi quod Spiritus Sanctus per omnes civitates protestatur mihi dicens quoniam vincula et tribulationes me manent. [24]Sed nihili facio animam meam pretiosam mihi, dummodo consummem cursum meum et ministerium, quod accepi a Domino Iesu, testificari evangelium gratiae Dei. [25]Et nunc ecce ego scio quia amplius non videbitis faciem meam vos omnes, per quos transivi praedicans regnum; [26]quapropter contestor vos hodierna die quia mundus sum a sanguine omnium, [27]non enim subterfugi, quominus annuntiarem omne consilium Dei vobis. [28]Attendite vobis et universo gregi, in quo vos Spiritus Sanctus posuit episcopos, pascere ecclesiam Dei, quam acquisivit sanguine suo. [29]Ego scio quoniam intrabunt post discessionem meam lupi graves in vos non parcentes gregi, [30]et ex vobis ipsis exsurgent viri loquentes perversa, ut abstrahant discipulos post se. [31]Propter quod vigilate memoria retinentes quoniam per triennium nocte et die non cessavi cum lacrimis monens unumquemque vestrum. [32]Et nunc commendo vos Deo et verbo gratiae ipsius, qui potens est aedificare et dare hereditatem in sanctificatis omnibus. [33]Argentum aut aurum aut vestem nullius concupivi; [34]ipsi scitis quoniam ad ea, quae mihi opus erant et his, qui mecum sunt, ministraverunt manus istae. [35]Omnia ostendi vobis quoniam sic laborantes oportet suscipere infirmos, ac meminisse verborum Domini Iesu, quoniam ipse dixit: "Beatius est magis dare quam accipere!"». [36]Et cum haec dixisset, positis genibus suis, cum omnibus illis oravit. [37]Magnus autem fletus factus est omnium, et procumbentes super collum Pauli osculabantur eum [38]dolentes maxime in verbo, quod dixerat, quoniam amplius faciem eius non essent visuri. Et deducebant eum ad navem. [21] [1]Cum autem factum esset ut navigaremus abstracti ab eis, recto cursu venimus Cho et sequenti die Rhodum et inde Patara; [2]et cum invenissemus navem transfretantem in Phoenicen, ascendentes navigavimus. [3]Cum paruissemus autem Cypro, et relinquentes eam ad sinistram navigabamus in Syriam et venimus Tyrum, ibi enim navis erat expositura onus. [4]Inventis autem discipulis, mansimus ibi diebus septem; qui Paulo dicebant per Spiritum, ne iret Hierosolymam. [5]Et explicitis diebus, profecti ibamus, deducentibus nos omnibus cum uxoribus et filiis usque foras civitatem; et positis genibus in litore orantes, [6]valefecimus invicem et ascendimus in navem, illi autem redierunt in sua. [7]Nos vero navigatione explicita, a Tyro devenimus Ptolemaida et salutatis fratribus mansimus die una apud illos. [8]Alia autem die profecti venimus Caesaream et intrantes in domum Philippi evangelistae, qui erat de septem, mansimus apud eum. [9]Huic autem erant filiae quattuor virgines prophetantes. [10]Et cum moraremur plures dies, supervenit quidam a Iudaea propheta nomine Agabus; [11]is cum venisset ad nos et tulisset zonam Pauli, alligans sibi pedes et manus dixit: «Haec dicit

Spiritus Sanctus: Virum, cuius est zona haec, sic alligabunt in Ierusalem Iudaei et tradent in manus gentium». [12]Quod cum audissemus, rogabamus nos et, qui loci illius erant, ne ipse ascenderet Ierusalem. [13]Tunc respondit Paulus: «Quid facitis flentes et affligentes cor meum? Ego enim non solum alligari sed et mori in Ierusalem paratus sum propter nomen Domini Iesu». [14]Et cum ei suadere non possemus, quievimus dicentes: «Domini voluntas fiat!». [15]Post dies autem istos praeparati ascendebamus Hierosolymam; [16]venerunt autem et ex discipulis a Caesarea nobiscum adducentes apud quem hospitaremur, Mnasonem quendam Cyprium, antiquum discipulum. [17]Et cum venissemus Hierosolymam, libenter exceperunt nos fratres. [18]Sequenti autem die introibat Paulus nobiscum ad Iacobum, omnesque collecti sunt presbyteri. [19]Quos cum salutasset, narrabat per singula, quae fecisset Deus in gentibus per ministerium ipsius. [20]At illi cum audissent, glorificabant Deum dixeruntque ei: «Vides, frater, quot milia sint in Iudaeis, qui crediderunt, et omnes aemulatores sunt legis; [21]audierunt autem de te quia discessionem doceas a Moyse omnes, qui per gentes sunt, Iudaeos, dicens non debere circumcidere eos filios suos, neque secundum consuetudines ambulare. [22]Quid ergo est? Utique audient te supervenisse. [23]Hoc ergo fac, quod tibi dicimus. Sunt nobis viri quattuor votum habentes super se; [24]his assumptis, sanctifica te cum illis et impende pro illis, ut radant capita, et scient omnes quia, quae de te audierunt, nihil sunt, sed ambulas et ipse custodiens legem. [25]De his autem, qui crediderunt, gentibus nos scripsimus iudicantes, ut abstineant ab idolothyto et sanguine et suffocato et fornicatione». [26]Tunc Paulus, assumptis viris, postera die purificatus cum illis intravit in templum annuntians expletionem dierum purificationis, donec offerretur pro unoquoque eorum oblatio. [27]Dum autem septem dies consummarentur, hi, qui de Asia erant, Iudaei cum vidissent eum in templo, concitaverunt omnem turbam et iniecerunt ei manus [28]clamantes: «Viri Israelitae, adiuvate! Hic est homo, qui adversus populum et legem et locum hunc omnes ubique docens, insuper et Graecos induxit in templum et polluit sanctum locum istum». [29]Viderant enim Trophimum Ephesium in civitate cum ipso, quem aestimabant quoniam in templum induxisset Paulus. [30]Commotaque est civitas tota, et facta est concursio populi, et apprehendentes Paulum trahebant eum extra templum, et statim clausae sunt ianuae. [31]Quaerentibus autem eum occidere, nuntiatum est tribuno cohortis quia tota confunditur Ierusalem, [32]qui statim, assumptis militibus et centurionibus, decucurrit ad illos; qui cum vidissent tribunum et milites, cessaverunt percutere Paulum. [33]Tunc accedens tribunus apprehendit eum et iussit alligari catenis duabus et interrogabat quis esset et quid fecisset. [34]Alii autem aliud clamabant in turba; et cum non posset certum cognoscere prae tumultu, iussit duci eum in castra. [35]Et cum venisset ad gradus, contigit ut portaretur a militibus propter vim turbae; [36]sequebatur enim multitudo populi clamantes: «Tolle eum!». [37]Et cum coepisset induci in castra, Paulus dicit tribuno: «Si licet mihi loqui aliquid ad te?». Qui dixit: «Graece nosti? [38]Nonne tu es Aegyptius, qui ante hos dies tumultum concitasti et eduxisti in desertum quattuor milia virorum sicariorum?». [39]Et dixit Paulus: «Ego homo sum quidem Iudaeus a Tarso Ciliciae, non ignotae civitatis municeps; rogo autem te, permitte mihi loqui ad populum». [40]Et cum ille permisisset, Paulus stans in gradibus annuit manu ad plebem et, magno silentio facto, allocutus est Hebraea lingua dicens: **[22]** [1]«Viri fratres et patres, audite a me, quam ad vos nunc reddo, rationem». [2]Cum audissent autem quia Hebraea lingua loquebatur ad illos, magis praestiterunt silentium. Et dixit: [3]«Ego sum vir Iudaeus, natus Tarso Ciliciae, enutritus autem in ista civitate, secus pedes Gamaliel eruditus iuxta veritatem paternae legis, aemulator Dei sicut et vos omnes estis hodie. [4]Qui hanc viam persecutus sum usque ad mortem, alligans et tradens in custodias viros ac mulieres, [5]sicut et princeps sacerdotum testimonium mihi reddit et omne concilium; a quibus et epistulas accipiens ad fratres, Damascum pergebam, ut adducerem et eos, qui ibi essent, vinctos in Ierusalem, uti punirentur. [6]Factum est autem eunte me et appropinquante Damasco, circa mediam diem subito de caelo circumfulsit me lux copiosa, [7]et decidi in terram et audivi vocem dicentem mihi: "Saul, Saul, quid me persequeris?". [8]Ego autem respondi: "Quis es, Domine?". Dixitque ad me: "Ego sum Iesus Nazarenus, quem tu persequeris". [9]Et qui mecum erant, lumen quidem viderunt, vocem autem non audierunt eius, qui loquebatur mecum. [10]Et dixi: "Quid faciam, Domine?". Dominus autem dixit ad me: "Surgens vade Damascum, et ibi tibi dicetur de omnibus, quae statutum est tibi, ut faceres". [11]Et cum non viderem prae claritate luminis illius, ad manum deductus a comitibus veni Damascum. [12]Ananias autem quidam vir religiosus secundum legem testimonium habens ab omnibus habitantibus Iudaeis, [13]veniens ad me et astans dixit mihi: "Saul frater, respice!". Et ego eadem hora respexi in eum. [14]At ille dixit: "Deus patrum nostrorum praeordinavit te, ut cognosceres voluntatem eius et videres Iustum et audires vocem ex ore eius, [15]quia eris testis illi ad omnes homines eorum, quae vidisti et audisti. [16]Et nunc quid moraris? Exsurgens baptizare et ablue peccata tua, invocato nomine ipsius". [17]Factum est autem revertenti mihi in Ierusalem et oranti in templo fieri me in stupore mentis [18]et videre illum dicentem mihi: "Festina et exi velociter ex Ierusalem, quoniam non recipient testimonium tuum de me". [19]Et ego dixi: "Domine, ipsi sciunt quia ego eram concludens in carcerem et caedens per synagogas eos, qui credebant in te; [20]et cum funderetur sanguis Stephani testis tui, et ipse astabam et consentiebam et custodiebam vestimenta interficientium illum". [21]Et dixit ad me: "Vade, quoniam ego in nationes longe mittam te"». [22]Audiebant autem eum usque ad hoc verbum et levaverunt vocem suam dicentes: «Tolle de terra eiusmodi, non enim fas est eum vivere!». [23]Vociferantibus autem eis et proicientibus vestimenta sua et pulverem iactantibus in aerem, [24]iussit tribunus induci eum in castra dicens flagellis eum interrogari, ut sciret propter quam causam sic acclamarent ei. [25]Et cum astrinxissent eum loris, dixit astanti centurioni Paulus: «Si hominem Romanum et indemnatum licet vobis flagellare?». [26]Quo audito, centurio accedens ad tribunum nuntiavit dicens: «Quid acturus es? Hic enim homo Romanus est». [27]Accedens autem tribunus dixit illi: «Dic mihi, tu Romanus es?». At ille dixit: «Etiam». [28]Et respondit tribunus: «Ego multa summa civitatem hanc consecutus sum». Et Paulus ait: «Ego autem et natus sum». [29]Protinus ergo discesserunt ab illo, qui eum interrogaturi erant; tribunus quoque timuit, postquam rescivit quia Romanus esset et quia alligasset eum. [30]Postera autem die volens scire diligenter qua ex causa accusaretur a Iudaeis, solvit eum et iussit principes sacerdotum convenire et omne concilium et producens Paulum statuit coram illis. [23] [1]Intendens autem concilium Paulus ait: «Viri fratres, ego omni conscientia bona conversatus sum ante Deum usque in hodiernum diem». [2]Princeps autem sacerdotum Ananias praecepit astantibus sibi percutere os eius. [3]Tunc Paulus ad eum dixit: «Percutiet te Deus, paries dealbate! Et tu sedes iudicans me secundum legem et contra legem iubes me percuti?». [4]Et qui astabant, dixerunt: «Summum sacerdotem Dei maledicis?». [5]Dixit autem Paulus: «Nesciebam, fratres, quia princeps est sacerdotum; scriptum est enim: *"Principem populi tui non maledices"*». [6]Sciens autem Paulus quia una pars esset sadducaeorum et altera pharisaeorum, exclamabat in concilio: «Viri fratres, ego pharisaeus sum, filius pharisaeorum; de spe et resurrectione mortuorum ego iudicor». [7]Et cum haec diceret, facta est dissensio inter pharisaeos et sadducaeos, et divisa est multitudo. [8]Sadducaei enim dicunt non esse resurrectionem neque angelum neque spiritum; pharisaei autem utrumque confitentur. [9]Factus est autem clamor magnus, et surgentes scribae quidam partis pharisaeorum pugnabant dicentes: «Nihil mali invenimus in homine isto: quod si spiritus locutus est ei aut angelus»; [10]et cum magna dissensio facta esset, timens tribunus ne discerperetur Paulus ab ipsis, iussit milites descendere, ut raperent eum de medio eorum ac deducerent in castra. [11]Sequenti autem nocte assistens ei Dominus ait: «Constans esto! Sicut enim testificatus es, quae sunt de me in Ierusalem, sic te oportet et Romae testificari». [12]Facta autem die, faciebant concursum Iudaei et devoverunt se dicentes neque manducaturos neque bibituros, donec occiderent Paulum. [13]Erant autem plus quam quadraginta, qui hanc coniurationem fecerant; [14]qui accedentes ad principes sacerdotum et seniores dixerunt: «Devotione devovimus nos nihil gustaturos, donec occidamus Paulum. [15]Nunc ergo vos notum facite tribuno cum concilio, ut producat illum ad vos, tamquam aliquid certius cognituri de eo; nos vero priusquam appropiet, parati sumus interficere illum». [16]Quod cum audisset filius sororis Pauli insidias, venit et intravit in castra nuntiavitque Paulo. [17]Vocans autem Paulus ad se unum ex centurionibus ait: Adulescentem hunc perduc ad tribunum, habet enim aliquid indicare illi». [18]Et ille quidem assumens eum duxit ad tribunum et ait: «Vinctus Paulus vocans rogavit me hunc adulescentem perducere ad te habentem aliquid loqui tibi». [19]Apprehendens autem tribunus manum illius, secessit cum eo seorsum et interrogabat: «Quid est quod habes indicare mihi?». [20]Ille autem dixit: «Iudaei constituerunt rogare te, ut crastina die Paulum producas in concilium, quasi aliquid certius inquisiturum sit de illo. [21]Tu ergo ne credideris illis; insidiantur enim ei ex eis viri amplius quadraginta, qui se devoverunt non manducare neque bibere, donec interficiant eum, et nunc parati sunt exspectantes promissum tuum». [22]Tribunus igitur dimisit adulescentem praecipiens, ne cui eloqueretur quoniam «haec nota mihi fecisti». [23]Et vocatis duobus centurionibus, dixit: «Parate milites ducentos, ut eant usque Caesaream, et equites septuaginta et lancearios ducentos, a tertia hora noctis, [24]et iumenta praeparate», ut imponentes Paulum salvum perducerent ad Felicem praesidem, [25]scribens epistulam habentem formam hanc: [26]«Claudius Lysias optimo praesidi Felici salutem. [27]Virum hunc comprehensum a Iudaeis et incipientem interfici ab eis, superveniens cum exercitu eripui, cognito quia Romanus est. [28]Volensque scire causam, propter quam accusabant illum, deduxi in concilium eorum; [29]quem inveni accusari de quaestionibus legis ipsorum, nihil vero dignum morte aut vinculis habentem crimen. [30]Et cum mihi perlatum esset de insidiis, quae in virum pararentur, confestim misi ad te denuntians et accusatoribus, ut dicant adversum eum apud te». [31]Milites ergo, secundum praeceptum sibi assumentes Paulum, duxerunt per noctem in Antipatridem; [32]et postera die dimissis equitibus, ut abirent cum eo, reversi sunt ad castra. [33]Qui cum venissent Caesaream et tradidissent epistulam praesidi, statuerunt ante illum et Paulum. [34]Cum legisset autem et interrogasset de qua provincia esset et cognoscens quia de Cilicia: [35]«Audiam te, inquit, cum et accusatores tui venerint»; iussitque in praetorio Herodis custodiri eum. [24] [1]Post quinque autem dies descendit princeps sacerdotum Ananias cum senioribus quibusdam et Tertullo quodam oratore, qui adierunt praesidem adversus Paulum. [2]Et citato eo coepit accusare Tertullus dicens: «Cum in multa pace agamus per te, et multa corrigantur genti huic per tuam providentiam, [3]semper et ubique suscipimus, optime Felix, cum omni gratiarum actione. [4]Ne diutius autem te protraham, oro breviter audias nos pro tua clementia. [5]Invenimus enim hunc hominem pestiferum et concitantem seditiones omnibus Iudaeis, qui sunt in universo orbe, et auctorem seditionis sectae Nazarenorum, [6]qui etiam templum violare conatus est, quem et apprehendimus, [8]a quo poteris ipse diiudicans de omnibus istis cognoscere, de quibus nos accusamus eum». [9]Adiecerunt autem et Iudaei dicentes haec ita se habere. [10]Respondit autem Paulus, annuente sibi praeside dicere: «Ex multis annis esse te iudicem genti huic sciens bono animo de causa mea rationem reddam, [11]cum possis cognoscere quia non plus sunt dies mihi quam duodecim, ex quo ascendi adorare in Ierusalem, [12]et neque in templo invenerunt me cum aliquo disputantem aut concursum facientem turbae neque in synagogis neque in civitate, [13]neque probare possunt tibi, de quibus nunc accusant me. [14]Confiteor autem hoc tibi quod secundum viam, quam dicunt haeresim, sic deservio patrio Deo credens omnibus, quae secundum Legem sunt et in Prophetis scripta, [15]spem habens in Deum, quam et hi ipsi exspectant, resurrectionem futuram iustorum et iniquorum. [16]In hoc et ipse studeo sine offendiculo conscientiam habere ad Deum et ad homines semper. [17]Post annos autem plures eleemosynas facturus in gentem meam veni et oblationes, [18]in quibus invenerunt me purificatum in templo, non cum turba neque cum tumultu; [19]quidam autem ex Asia Iudaei, quos oportebat apud te praesto esse et accusare si quid haberent adversum me [20]aut hi ipsi dicant quid invenerint iniquitatis, cum starem in concilio, [21]nisi de una hac voce, qua clamavi inter eos stans: De resurrectione mortuorum ego iudicor hodie apud vos!». [22]Distulit autem illos Felix certissime sciens ea, quae de hac via sunt, dicens: «Cum tribunus Lysias descenderit, cognoscam causam vestram», [23]iubens centurioni custodiri eum et habere mitigationem, nec quemquam prohibere de suis ministrare ei. [24]Post aliquot autem dies adveniens Felix cum Drusilla uxore sua, quae erat Iudaea, vocavit Paulum et audivit ab eo de fide, quae est in Christum Iesum. [25]Disputante autem illo de iustitia et continentia et de iudicio futuro, timefactus Felix respondit: «Quod nunc attinet, vade; tempore autem opportuno accersiam te», [26]simul et sperans quia pecunia daretur sibi a Paulo; propter quod et frequenter accersiens eum loquebatur cum eo. [27]Biennio autem expleto, accepit successorem Felix Porcium Festum; volensque gratiam praestare Iudaeis, Felix reliquit Paulum vinctum. **[25]** [1]Festus ergo cum venisset in provinciam, post triduum ascendit Hierosolymam a Caesarea; [2]adieruntque eum principes sacerdotum et primi Iudaeorum adversus Paulum, et rogabant eum [3]postulantes gratiam adversum eum, ut iuberet perduci eum in Ierusalem, insidias tendentes, ut eum interficerent in via. [4]Festus igitur respondit servari Paulum in Caesarea, se autem maturius profecturum: [5]«Qui ergo in vobis, ait, potentes sunt, descendentes simul, si quod est in viro crimen, accusent eum». [6]Demoratus autem inter eos dies non amplius quam octo aut decem, descendit Caesaream, et altera die sedit pro tribunali et iussit Paulum adduci. [7]Qui cum perductus esset, circumsteterunt eum, qui ab Hierosolyma descenderant, Iudaei, multas et graves causas obicientes, quas non poterant probare, [8]Paulo rationem reddente: «Neque in legem Iudaeorum neque in templum neque in Caesarem quidquam peccavi». [9]Festus autem volens Iudaeis gratiam praestare, respondens Paulo dixit: «Vis Hierosolymam ascendere et ibi de his iudicari apud me?». [10]Dixit autem Paulus: «Ad tribunal Caesaris sto, ubi me oportet iudicari. Iudaeis nihil nocui, sicut et tu melius nosti. [11]Si ergo iniuste egi et dignum morte aliquid feci, non recuso mori; si vero nihil est eorum, quae hi accusant me, nemo potest me illis donare. Caesarem appello!». [12]Tunc Festus cum consilio locutus respondit: «Caesarem appellasti; ad Caesarem ibis». [13]Et cum dies aliquot transacti essent, Agrippa rex et Berenice descenderunt Caesaream et salutaverunt Festum. [14]Et cum dies plures ibi demorarentur, Festus regi indicavit de Paulo dicens: «Vir quidam est derelictus a Felice vinctus, [15]de quo cum essem Hierosolymis, adierunt me principes sacerdotum et seniores Iudaeorum postulantes adversus illum damnationem; [16]ad quos respondi quia non est consuetudo Romanis donare aliquem hominem, priusquam is, qui accusatur, praesentes habeat accusatores locumque defendendi se ab accusatione accipiat. [17]Cum ergo huc convenissent, sine ulla dilatione sequenti die sedens pro tribunali iussi adduci virum; [18]de quo cum stetissent accusatores, nullam causam deferebant, de quibus ego suspicabar malis, [19]quaestiones vero quasdam de sua superstitione habebant adversus eum et de quodam Iesu defuncto, quem affirmabat Paulus vivere. [20]Haesitans autem ego de huiusmodi quaestione, dicebam si vellet ire Hierosolymam et ibi iudicari de istis. [21]Paulo autem appellante, ut servaretur ad Augusti cognitionem, iussi servari eum, donec mittam eum ad Caesarem». [22]Agrippa autem ad Festum: «Volebam et ipse hominem audire!». «Cras, inquit, audies eum». [23]Altera autem die, cum venisset Agrippa et Berenice cum multa ambitione, et introissent in auditorium cum tribunis et viris principalibus civitatis, et iubente Festo, adductus est Paulus. [24]Et dicit Festus: «Agrippa rex et omnes, qui simul adestis nobiscum viri, videtis hunc, de quo omnis multitudo Iudaeorum interpellavit me Hierosolymis et hic, clamantes non oportere eum vivere amplius. [25]Ego vero comperi nihil dignum eum morte fecisse, ipso autem hoc appellante Augustum, iudicavi mittere. [26]De quo quid certum scribam domino, non habeo; propter quod produxi eum ad vos et maxime ad te, rex Agrippa, ut, interrogatione facta, habeam quid scribam: [27]sine ratione enim mihi videtur mittere vinctum et causas eius non significare». [26] [1]Agrippa vero ad Paulum ait: «Permittitur tibi loqui pro temetipso». Tunc Paulus, extenta manu, coepit rationem reddere: [2]«De omnibus, quibus accusor a Iudaeis, rex Agrippa, aestimo me beatum, apud te cum sim defensurus me hodie, [3]maxime te sciente omnia, quae apud Iudaeos sunt consuetudines et quaestiones; propter quod obsecro patienter me audias. [4]Et quidem vitam meam a iuventute, quae ab initio fuit in gente mea et in Hierosolymis, noverunt omnes Iudaei, [5]praescientes me ab initio, si velint testimonium perhibere, quoniam secundum diligentissimam sectam nostrae religionis vixi pharisaeus. [6]Et nunc propter spem eius, quae ad patres nostros repromissionis facta est a Deo, sto iudicio subiectus, [7]in quam duodecim tribus nostrae cum perseverantia nocte ac die deservientes sperant devenire; de qua spe accusor a Iudaeis, rex! [8]Quid incredibile iudicatur apud vos, si Deus mortuos suscitat? [9]Et ego quidem existimaveram me adversus nomen Iesu Nazareni debere multa contraria agere; [10]quod et feci Hierosolymis, et multos sanctorum ego in carceribus inclusi, a principibus sacerdotum potestate accepta, et cum occiderentur, detuli sententiam, [11]et per omnes synagogas frequenter puniens eos compellebam blasphemare, et abundantius insaniens in eos persequebar usque in exteras civitates. [12]In quibus dum irem Damascum cum potestate et permissu principum sacerdotum, [13]die media in via vidi, rex, de caelo supra splendorem solis circumfulgens me lumen et eos, qui mecum simul ibant; [14]omnesque nos cum decidissemus in terram, audivi vocem loquentem mihi Hebraica lingua: "Saul, Saul, quid me persequeris? Durum est tibi contra stimulum calcitrare". [15]Ego autem dixi: "Quis es, Domine?". Dominus autem dixit: "Ego sum Iesus, quem tu persequeris. [16]Sed exsurge et sta super pedes tuos; ad hoc enim apparui tibi, ut constituam te ministrum et testem eorum, quae vidisti, et eorum, quibus apparebo tibi, [17]eripiens te de populo et de gentibus, in quas ego mitto te [18]aperire oculos eorum, ut convertantur a tenebris ad lucem et de potestate Satanae ad Deum, ut accipiant remissionem peccatorum et sortem inter sanctificatos per fidem, quae est in me". [19]Unde, rex Agrippa, non fui incredulus caelestis visionis, [20]sed his, qui sunt Damasci primum et Hierosolymis, et in omnem regionem Iudaeae et gentibus annuntiabam, ut paenitentiam agerent et converterentur ad Deum digna paenitentiae opera facientes. [21]Hac ex causa me Iudaei, cum essem in templo comprehensum, tentabant interficere. [22]Auxilium igitur assecutus a Deo usque in hodiernum diem sto testificans minori atque maiori, nihil extra dicens quam ea, quae prophetae sunt locuti futura esse et Moyses, [23]si passibilis Christus, si primus ex resurrectione mortuorum lumen annuntiaturus est populo et gentibus». [24]Sic autem eo rationem reddente, Festus magna voce dixit: «Insanis, Paule; multae te litterae ad insaniam convertunt!». [25]At Paulus: «Non insanio, inquit, optime Feste, sed veritatis et sobrietatis verba eloquor. [26]Scit enim de his rex, ad quem et audenter loquor; latere enim eum nihil horum arbitror, neque enim in angulo hoc gestum est. [27]Credis, rex Agrippa, prophetis? Scio quia credis». [28]Agrippa autem ad Paulum: «In modico suades me Christianum fieri!». [29]Et Paulus: «Optarem apud Deum et in modico et in magno non tantum te sed et omnes hos, qui audiunt me hodie, fieri tales, qualis et ego sum, exceptis vinculis his!». [30]Et exsurrexit rex et praeses et Berenice et, qui assidebant eis, [31]et cum secessissent, loquebantur ad invicem dicentes: «Nihil morte aut vinculis dignum quid facit homo iste». [32]Agrippa autem Festo dixit: «Dimitti poterat homo hic, si non appellasset Caesarem». [27] [1]Ut autem iudicatum est navigare nos in Italiam, tradiderunt et Paulum et quosdam alios vinctos centurioni nomine Iulio, cohortis Augustae. [2]Ascendentes autem navem Hadramyttenam, incipientem navigare circa Asiae loca, sustulimus, perseverante nobiscum Aristarcho Macedone Thessalonicensi; [3]sequenti autem die devenimus Sidonem, et humane tractans Iulius Paulum permisit ad amicos ire et curam sui agere. [4]Et inde cum sustulissemus, subnavigavimus Cypro, propterea quod essent venti contrarii, [5]et pelagus Ciliciae et Pamphyliae navigantes venimus Myram, quae est Lyciae. [6]Et ibi inveniens centurio navem Alexandrinam navigantem in Italiam transposuit nos in eam. [7]Et cum multis diebus tarde navigaremus et vix devenissemus contra Cnidum, prohibente nos vento, subnavigavimus Cretae secundum Salmonem, [8]et vix iuxta eam navigantes venimus in locum quendam, qui vocatur Boni Portus, cui iuxta erat civitas Lasaea. [9]Multo autem tempore peracto, et cum iam non esset tuta navigatio, eo quod et ieiunium iam praeterisset, monebat Paulus [10]dicens eis: «Viri, video quoniam cum iniuria et multo damno non solum oneris et navis sed etiam animarum nostrarum incipit esse navigatio». [11]Centurio autem gubernatori et nauclero magis credebat quam his, quae a Paulo dicebantur. [12]Et cum aptus portus non esset ad hiemandum, plurimi statuerunt consilium enavigare inde, si quo modo possent devenientes Phoenicen hiemare, portum Cretae respicientem ad africum et ad caurum. [13]Aspirante autem austro, aestimantes propositum se tenere, cum sustulissent, propius legebant Cretam. [14]Non post multum autem misit se contra ipsam ventus typhonicus, qui vocatur euroaquilo; [15]cumque arrepta esset navis et non posset conari in ventum, data nave flatibus, ferebamur. [16]Insulam autem quandam decurrentes, quae vocatur Cauda, potuimus vix obtinere scapham, [17]qua sublata, adiutoriis utebantur accingentes navem; et timentes, ne in Syrtim inciderent, submisso vase, sic ferebantur. [18]Valide autem nobis tempestate iactatis, sequenti die iactum fecerunt [19]et tertia die suis manibus armamenta navis proiecerunt. [20]Neque sole autem neque sideribus apparentibus per plures dies, et tempestate non exigua imminente, iam auferebatur spes omnis salutis nostrae. [21]Et cum multa ieiunatio fuisset, tunc stans Paulus in medio eorum dixit: «Oportebat quidem, o viri, audito me, non tollere a Creta lucrique facere iniuriam hanc et iacturam. [22]Et nunc suadeo vobis bono animo esse, nulla enim amissio animae erit ex vobis praeterquam navis; [23]astitit enim mihi hac nocte angelus Dei, cuius sum ego, cui et deservio, [24]dicens: "Ne timeas, Paule; Caesari te oportet assistere, et ecce donavit tibi Deus omnes, qui navigant tecum". [25]Propter quod bono animo estote, viri; credo enim Deo quia sic erit, quemadmodum dictum est mihi. [26]In insulam autem quandam oportet nos incidere». [27]Sed posteaquam quarta decima nox supervenit, cum ferremur in Hadria, circa mediam noctem suspicabantur nautae apparere sibi aliquam regionem. [28]Qui submittentes bolidem invenerunt passus viginti et pusillum inde separati et rursum submittentes invenerunt passus quindecim; [29]timentes autem, ne in aspera loca incideremus, de puppi mittentes ancoras quattuor optabant diem fieri. [30]Nautis vero quaerentibus fugere de navi, cum demisissent scapham in mare sub obtentu, quasi a prora inciperent ancoras extendere, [31]dixit Paulus centurioni et militibus: «Nisi hi in navi manserint, vos salvi fieri non potestis». [32]Tunc absciderunt milites funes scaphae et passi sunt eam excidere. [33]Donec autem lux inciperet fieri, rogabat Paulus omnes sumere cibum dicens: «Quarta decima hodie die exspectantes ieiuni permanetis nihil accipientes; [34]propter quod rogo vos accipere cibum, hoc enim pro salute vestra est, quia nullius vestrum capillus de capite peribit». [35]Et cum haec dixisset et sumpsisset panem, gratias egit Deo in conspectu omnium et, cum fregisset, coepit manducare. [36]Animaequiores autem facti omnes et ipsi assumpserunt cibum. [37]Eramus vero universae animae in navi ducentae septuaginta sex. [38]Et satiati cibo alleviabant navem iactantes triticum in mare. [39]Cum autem dies factus esset, terram non agnoscebant, sinum vero quendam considerabant habentem litus, in quem cogitabant si possent eicere navem. [40]Et cum ancoras abstulissent, committebant mari simul laxantes iuncturas gubernaculorum et, levato artemone, secundum flatum aurae tendebant ad litus. [41]Et cum incidissent in locum dithalassum, impegerunt navem; et prora quidem fixa manebat immobilis, puppis vero solvebatur a vi fluctuum. [42]Militum autem consilium fuit, ut custodias occiderent, ne quis, cum enatasset, effugeret; [43]centurio autem volens servare Paulum prohibuit eos a consilio, iussitque eos, qui possent natare, mittere se primos et ad terram exire [44]et ceteros, quosdam in tabulis, quosdam vero super ea, quae de navi essent; et sic factum est ut omnes evaderent ad terram. [28] [1]Et cum evasissemus, tunc cognovimus quia Melita insula vocatur. [2]Barbari vero praestabant non modicam humanitatem nobis; accensa enim pyra suscipiebant nos omnes propter imbrem, qui imminebat et frigus. [3]Cum congregasset autem Paulus sarmentorum aliquantam multitudinem et imposuisset super ignem, vipera, a calore cum processisset, invasit manum eius. [4]Ut vero viderunt barbari pendentem bestiam de manu eius, ad invicem dicebant: «Utique homicida est homo hic, qui cum evaserit de mari, Ultio non permisit vivere». [5]Et ille quidem excutiens bestiam in ignem, nihil mali passus est; [6]at illi exspectabant eum in tumorem convertendum aut subito casurum et mori. Diu autem illis exspectantibus et videntibus nihil mali in eo fieri, convertentes se dicebant eum esse deum. [7]In locis autem illis erant praedia principis insulae nomine Publii, qui nos suscipiens triduo benigne hospitio recepit. [8]Contigit autem patrem Publii febribus et dysenteria vexatum iacere, ad quem Paulus intravit et, cum orasset et imposuisset ei manus, sanavit eum. [9]Quo facto et ceteri, qui in insula habebant infirmitates, accedebant et curabantur; [10]qui etiam multis honoribus nos honoraverunt et navigantibus imposuerunt, quae necessaria erant. [11]Post menses autem tres navigavimus in navi Alexandrina, quae in insula hiemaverat, cui erat insigne Castorum. [12]Et cum venissemus Syracusam, mansimus ibi triduo; [13]inde solventes devenimus Rhegium. Et post unum diem, superveniente austro, secunda die venimus Puteolos, [14]ubi inventis fratribus rogati sumus manere apud eos dies septem; et sic venimus Romam. [15]Et inde cum audissent de nobis fratres, occurrerunt nobis usque ad Appii Forum et Tres Tabernas; quos cum vidisset Paulus, gratias agens Deo, accepit fiduciam. [16]Cum introissemus autem Romam, permissum est Paulo manere sibimet cum custodiente se milite. [17]Factum est autem ut post tertium diem convocaret primos Iudaeorum; cumque convenissent dicebat eis: «Ego, viri fratres, nihil adversus plebem faciens aut mores paternos, vinctus ab Hierosolymis traditus sum in manus Romanorum, [18]qui cum interrogationem de me habuissent, volebant dimittere eo quod nulla causa esset mortis in me; [19]contradicentibus autem Iudaeis, coactus sum appellare Caesarem, non quasi gentem meam habens aliquid accusare. [20]Propter hanc igitur causam rogavi vos videre et alloqui; propter spem enim Israel catena hac circumdatus sum». [21]At illi dixerunt ad eum: «Nos neque litteras accepimus de te a Iudaea, neque adveniens aliquis fratrum nuntiavit aut locutus est quid de te malum. [22]Rogamus autem a te audire quae sentis, nam de secta hac notum est nobis quia ubique ei contradicitur». [23]Cum constituissent autem illi diem, venerunt ad eum in hospitium plures, quibus exponebat testificans regnum Dei, suadensque eos de Iesu ex Lege Moysis et Prophetis a mane usque ad vesperam. [24]Et quidam credebant his quae dicebantur, quidam vero non credebant; [25]cumque invicem non essent consentientes, discedebant, dicente Paulo unum verbum: «Bene Spiritus Sanctus locutus est per Isaiam prophetam ad patres vestros [26]dicens: *"Vade ad populum istum et dic: / Auditu audietis et non intellegetis, / et videntes videbitis et non perspicietis. /* [27]*Incrassatum est enim cor populi huius, / et auribus graviter audierunt, / et oculos suos compresserunt, / ne forte videant oculis / et auribus audiant / et corde intellegant et convertantur, / et sanabo illos"*. [28]Notum ergo sit vobis quoniam gentibus missum est hoc salutare Dei; ipsi et audient!».(29) [30]Mansit autem biennio toto in suo conducto; et suscipiebat omnes qui ingrediebantur ad eum, [31]praedicans regnum Dei et docens quae sunt de Domino Iesu Christo cum omni fiducia sine prohibitione.

Explanatory Notes

Asterisks in the text of the New Testament refer to these "Explanatory Notes" in the RSVCE.

THE ACTS OF THE APOSTLES

1:1, *the first book*: i.e., St Luke's Gospel.

1:14, *brethren*: See note on Mt 12:46.

1:22: An apostle must be a witness to Christ's resurrection.

2:14: Peter assumes the leadership in public. In this discourse we have the earliest form of the apostolic preaching.

3:1: In the early days, the first Christians observed the prescriptions of the Jewish law.

4:2: The Sadducees did not believe in the resurrection of the dead.

4:32, *everything in common*: They freely shared what was theirs individually; cf. Acts 5:4.

5:11 *church*: i.e., the Christian and Messianic community, a term borrowed from the Old Testament.

5:20, *Life*: cf. Acts 9:2, "the Way". These terms recall the words of Jesus, "I am the way, and the truth, and the life" (Jn 14:6).

5:34, *Gamaliel*: teacher of St Paul; cf. Acts 22:3.

6:1, *Hellenists*: Greek-speaking Jews of the Dispersion, who had their own synagogues in Jerusalem and read the scriptures in Greek.

8:20: Hence the word "simony", meaning "buying and selling spiritual powers and privileges".

9:5: Jesus identifies himself with his followers.

9:13, *saints*: i.e., Christians, made holy by baptism.

10:16: The vision was to prepare Peter for his reception of Cornelius the Gentile and his household into the church; cf. also Acts 15.

12:1: The second wave of persecution; cf. Acts 8:1.

13:16–41: This first recorded sermon of Paul is similar to that of Peter in Acts 2:14–36.

16:10: This is the first of the passages in Acts in which the story is told in the first person plural, indicating that Luke, the author, was there. The manuscript Codex Bezae, however, has a "we" passage in 11:28.

16:13: Being a Roman colony, Philippi had no synagogue within its walls.

19:35, *the sacred stone* or statue of the goddess which according to legend came down from heaven. Possibly a meteorite.

20:7: Celebration of the Eucharist on the Lord's day, i.e. Saturday evening, according to the Jewish way of reckoning a day from sunset to sunset.

20:34: Paul insisted on working for his living, though recognizing the apostle's right to support by the faithful; cf. 1 Cor 9:4–7.

21:4, *told Paul not to go*: This was not a command. The Holy Spirit enlightened them about what lay before Paul and they naturally wished to spare him; cf. verse 11.

22:20, *thy witness*: Greek, "martyr". Witnessing by one's death (i.e., martyrdom) is the supreme example.

Changes in the RSV for the Catholic Edition

| | TEXT | | FOOTNOTES | |
	RSV	RSVCE	RSV	RSVCE
Acts 1:14	brothers	brethren		

Headings added to the Biblical Text

Prologue 1:1
The Ascension 1:6

Part One: The Church in Jerusalem

1. THE DISCIPLES IN JERUSALEM
The apostolic college 1:12
The election of Matthias 1:15

2. PENTECOST
The coming of the Holy Spirit 2:1
Peter's address 2:14
Many baptisms 2:37
The early Christians 2:42

3. THE APOSTLES' WORK IN JERUSALEM
Curing of a man lame from birth 3:1
Peter's address in the temple 3:11
Peter and John are arrested 4:1
Address to the Sanhedrin 4:5

The Church's thanksgiving prayer 4:23
The way of life of the early Christians 4:32
Deception by Ananias and Sapphira 5:1
Growth of the Church 5:12
The apostles are arrested and miraculously freed 5:17
The apostles before the Sanhedrin 5:26
Gamaliel's intervention 5:34
The apostles are flogged 5:40

4. THE "DEACONS". ST STEPHEN
Appointment of the seven deacons 6:1
Stephen's arrest 6:8
Stephen's address to the Sanhedrin 7:1
Martyrdom of St Stephen 7:54

Part Two: The Church spreads beyond Jerusalem

5. THE CHURCH IN SAMARIA
Persecution of the Church 8:1b
Philip's preaching in Samaria 8:5
Simon the magician 8:9
Peter and John in Samaria 8:14
The sin of simony 8:18
Philip baptizes an Ethiopian official 8:26

6. THE CONVERSION OF ST PAUL
Saul on his way to Damascus 9:1
Ananias baptizes Saul 9:10
Paul begins his apostolate 9:19
Paul flees from Damascus 9:23
Barnabas and Paul in Jerusalem 9:26
Growth of the Church 9:31

7. ST PETER'S ACTIVITY
Curing of a paralyzed man at Lydda 9:32
Peter raises Tabitha to life 9:36
The vision of the centurion Cornelius 10:1
Peter's vision 10:9
Peter in the house of Cornelius 10:23
Peter preaches to Cornelius 10:34
The baptism of Cornelius and his household 10:44
In Jerusalem Peter justifies his conduct 11:1
Beginning of the Church in Antioch 11:19
Antioch helps the Church in Judea 11:27
Persecution by Herod. Peter's arrest and miraculous
    deliverance 12:1
Death of Herod 12:20
Barnabas and Paul return 12:24

Part Three: The spread of the Church among the Gentiles. Missionary journeys of St Paul

8. ST PAUL'S FIRST APOSTOLIC JOURNEY
Paul and Barnabas are sent on a mission 13:1
Paul and Barnabas in Cyprus 13:4
Paul and Barnabas cross into Asia Minor 13:13
Preaching in the synagogue of Antioch of Pisidia 13:14
Paul and Barnabas preach to the pagans 13:44
Iconium evangelized. Persecution 14:1
Curing of a cripple at Lystra 14:8
Paul is stoned 14:19
Return journey to Antioch 14:21

9. THE COUNCIL OF JERUSALEM
Dissension at Antioch; Judaizers 15:1

Paul and Barnabas go to Jerusalem 15:3
Peter's address to the council 15:6
James' speech 15:12
The council's decision 15:22
Reception of the council's decree 15:30

10. ST PAUL'S SECOND APOSTOLIC JOURNEY
Silas, Paul's new companion 15:36
Timothy joins Paul 16:1
Tour of the churches of Asia Minor 16:4
Macedonia 16:11
The conversion of Lydia 16:12
Curing of a possessed girl. Imprisonment of Paul 16:16

221

Headings added to the Biblical Text

Part Four: St Paul, in imprisonment, bears witness to Christ

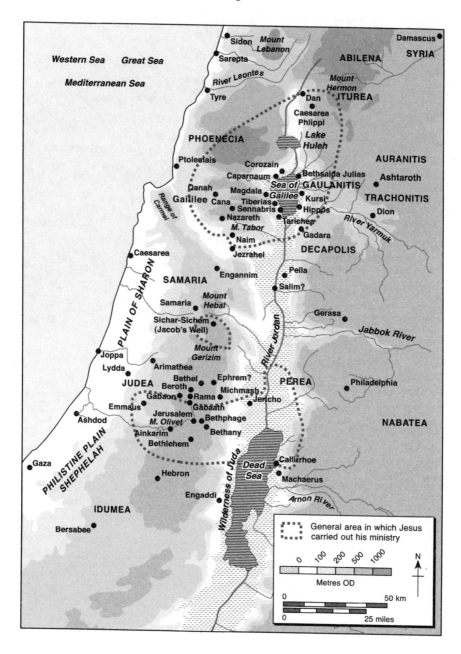

Palestine in the time of Jesus

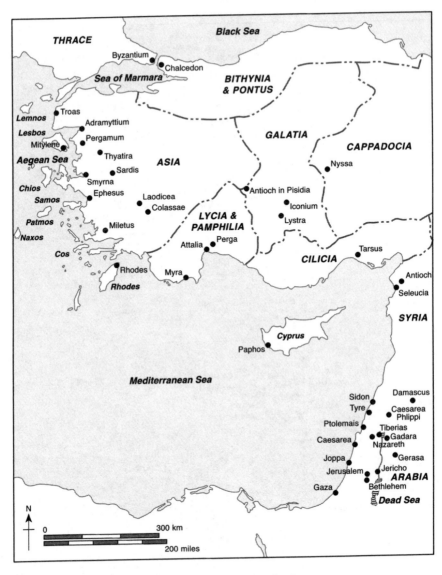

The Eastern Mediterranean Sea in the first century AD

Maps

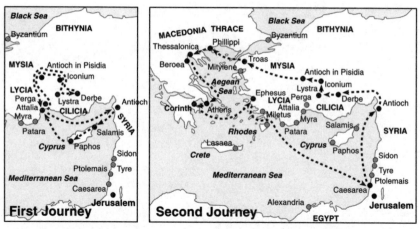

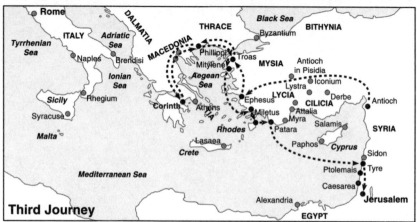

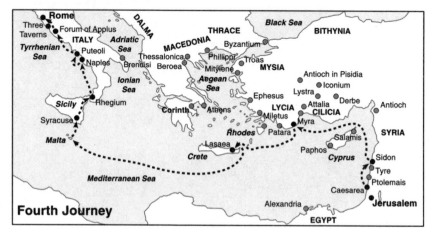

Missionary journeys of St Paul

225

Sources quoted in the Navarre Bible New Testament Commentary

1. DOCUMENTS OF THE CHURCH AND OF POPES

Benedict XII
Const. *Benedictus Deus*, 29 January 1336
Benedict XV
Enc. *Humani generis redemptionem*, 15 June 1917
Enc. *Spiritus Paraclitus*, 1 September 1920
Clement of Rome, St
Letter to the Corinthians
Constantinople, First Council of
Nicene-Constantinopolitan Creed
Constantinople, Third Council of
Definitio de duabus
　　in Christo voluntatibus et operationibus
Florence, Council of
Decree *Pro Jacobitis*
Laetentur coeli
Decree *Pro Armeniis*
John Paul II
Addresses and homilies
Apos. Exhort. *Catechesi tradendae*, 16 October 1979
Apos. Exhort. *Familiaris consortio*, 22 November 1981
Apos. Exhort. *Reconciliatio et paenitentia*, 2 December 1984
Apos. Letter. *Salvifici doloris*, 11 February 1984
Bull, *Aperite portas*, 6 January 1983
Enc. *Redemptor hominis*, 4 March 1979
Enc. *Dives in misericordia*, 30 November 1980
Enc. *Dominum et Vivificantem*, 30 May 1986
Enc. *Laborem exercens*, 14 September 1981
Letter to all priests, 8 April 1979
Letter to all bishops, 24 February 1980
Gelasius I
Ne forte
Gregory the Great, St
Epistula ad Theodorum medicum contra Fabianum
Exposition on the Seven Penitential
Ne forte
In Evangelia homiliae
In Ezechielem homiliae
Moralia in Job

Regulae pastoralis liber
Innocent III
Letter *Eius exemplo*, 18 December 1208
John XXIII
Pacem in terris, 11 April 1963
Enc. *Ad Petri cathedram*, 29 June 1959
Lateran Council (649)
Canons
Leo the Great, St
Homilies and sermons
Licet per nostros
Promisisse mememeni
Leo IX
Creed
Leo XIII
Enc. *Aeterni Patris*, 4 August 1879
Enc. *Immortale Dei*, 1 November 1885
Enc. *Libertas praestantissimum*, 20 June 1888
Enc. *Sapientiae christianae*, 18 January 1890
Enc. *Rerum novarum*, 15 May 1891
Enc. *Providentissimus Deus*, 18 November 1893
Enc. *Divinum illud munus*, 9 May 1897
Lateran, Fourth Council of (1215)
De fide catholica
Lyons, Second Council of (1274)
Doctrina de gratia
Profession of faith of Michael Palaeologue
Orange, Second Council of (529)
De gratia
Paul IV
Const. *Cum quorumdam*, 7 August 1555
Paul VI
Enc. *Ecclesiam suam*, 6 August 1964
Enc. *Mysterium fidei*, 9 September 1965
Apos. Exhort. *Marialis cultus*, 2 February 1967
Apos. Letter *Petrum et Paulum*, 27 February 1967
Enc. *Populorum progressio*, 26 March 1967
Enc. *Sacerdotalis coelibatus*, 24 June 1967
Creed of the People of God: Solemn Profession of Faith, 30 June 1968
Apos. Letter *Octagesima adveniens*, 14 June 1971

Sources quoted in the Commentary

Apos. Exhort. *Gaudete in Domino*, 9 May 1975
Apos. Exhort. *Evangelii nuntiandi*, 8 Dec. 1975
Homilies and addresses
Pius V, St
*Catechism of the Council of Trent for Parish
  Priests* or *Pius V Catechism*
Pius IX, Bl.
Bull *Ineffabilis Deus*, 8 December 1854
Syllabus of Errors
Pius X, St
Enc. *E supreme apostolatus*, 4 October 1903
Enc. *Ad Diem illum*, 2 February 1904
Enc. *Acerbo nimis*, 15 April 1905
Catechism of Christian Doctrine, 15 July 1905
Decree *Lamentabili*, 3 July 1907
Enc. *Haerent animo*, 4 August 1908
Pius XI
Enc. *Quas primas*, 11 December 1925
Enc. *Divini illius magistri*, 31 December 1929
Enc. *Mens nostra*, 20 December 1929
Enc. *Casti connubii*, 31 December 1930
Enc. *Quadragesimo anno*, 15 May 1931
Enc. *Ad catholici sacerdotii*, 20 December 1935
Pius XII
Enc. *Mystici Corporis*, 29 June 1943
Enc. *Mediator Dei*, 20 November 1947
Enc. *Divino afflante Spiritu*, 30 September 1943
Enc. *Humani generis*, 12 August 1950
Apost. Const. *Menti nostrae*, 23 September 1950
Enc. *Sacra virginitas*, 25 March 1954
Enc. *Ad caeli Reginam*, 11 October 1954
Homilies and addresses
Quierzy, Council of (833)
*Doctrina de libero arbitrio hominis et de
  praedestinatione*
Trent, Council of (1545–1563)
De sacris imaginibus

De Purgatorio
De reformatione
De sacramento ordinis
De libris sacris
De peccato originale
De SS. Eucharistia
De iustificatione
De SS. Missae sacrificio
De sacramento matrimonio
Doctrina de peccato originali
Doctrina de sacramento extremae unctionis
Doctrina de sacramento paenitentiae
Toledo, Ninth Council of (655)
De Redemptione
Toledo, Eleventh Council of (675)
De Trinitate Creed
Valence, Third Council of (855)
De praedestinatione
Vatican, First Council of the (1869–1870)
Dogm. Const. *Dei Filius*
Dogm. Const. *Pastor aeternus*
Vatican, Second Council of the   (1963–
  1965)
Const. *Sacrosanctum Concilium*
Decree *Christus Dominus*
Decl. *Dignitatis humanae*
Decl. *Gravissimum educationis*
Decl. *Nostrae aetate*
Decree *Optatam totius*
Decree *Ad gentes*
Decree *Apostolicam actuositatem*
Decree *Perfectae caritatis*
Decree *Presbyterorum ordinis*
Decree *Unitatis redintegratio*
Dogm. Const. *Dei Verbum*
Dogm. Const. *Lumen gentium*
Past. Const. *Gaudium et spes*

Liturgical Texts

Roman Missal: Missale Romanum, editio typica altera (Vatican City, 1975)
The Divine Office (London, Sydney, Dublin, 1974)

Other Church Documents

Code of Canon Law
Codex Iuris Canonici (Vatican City, 1983)
Congregation for the Doctrine of the Faith
Declaration concerning Sexual Ethics,
  December 1975
Instruction on Infant Baptism, 20 October 1980
Inter insigniores, 15 October 1976
*Letter on certain questions concerning
  Eschatology*, 17 May 1979

Libertatis conscientia, 22 March 1986
Sacerdotium ministeriale, 6 August 1983
Libertatis nuntius, 6 August 1984
Mysterium Filii Dei, 21 February 1972
Pontifical Biblical Commission
Replies
New Vulgate
*Nova Vulgata Bibliorum Sacrorum editio typica
  altera* (Vatican City, 1986)

Sources quoted in the Commentary

2. THE FATHERS, ECCLESIASTICAL WRITERS AND OTHER AUTHORS

Alphonsus Mary Liguori, St
Christmas Novena
*The Love of Our Lord Jesus Christ reduced to
    practice*
Meditations for Advent
Thoughts on the Passion
Shorter Sermons
Sunday Sermons
Treasury of Teaching Material
Ambrose, St
De sacramentis
De mysteriis
De officiis ministrorum
Exameron
Expositio Evangelii secundum Lucam
Expositio in Ps 118
Treatise on the Mysteries
Anastasius of Sinai, St
Sermon on the Holy Synaxis
Anon.
Apostolic Constitutions
Didache, or *Teaching of the Twelve Apostles*
Letter to Diognetus
Shepherd of Hermas
Anselm, St
Prayers and Meditations
Aphraates
Demonstratio
Athanasius, St
Adversus Antigonum
De decretis nicaenae synodi
De Incarnatio contra arianos
Historia arianorum
Oratio I contra arianos
Oratio II contra arianos
Oratio contra gentes
Augustine, St
The City of God
Confessions
Contra Adimantum Manichaei discipulum
De Actis cum Felice Manicheo
De agone christiano
De bono matrimonii
De bono viduitatis
De catechizandis rudibus
De civitate Dei
De coniugiis adulterinis
De consensu Evangelistarum
De correptione et gratia
De doctrina christiana
De dono perseverantiae
De fide et operibus

De fide et symbolo
De Genesi ad litteram
De gratia et libero arbitrio
De natura et gratia
De praedestinatione sanctorum
De sermo Domini in monte
De spiritu et littera
De Trinitate
De verbis Domini sermones
Enarrationes in Psalmos
Enchiridion
Expositio epistulae ad Galatas
In I Epist. Ioann. ad Parthos
In Ioannis Evangelium tractatus
Letters
Quaestiones in Heptateuchum
Sermo ad Cassariensis Ecclesiae plebem
Sermo de Nativitate Domini
Sermons
Basil, St
De Spiritu Sancto
Homilia in Julittam martyrem
In Psalmos homiliae
Bede, St
Explanatio Apocalypsis
In Ioannis Evangelium expositio
In Lucae Evangelium expositio
In Marci Evangelium expositio
In primam Epistolam Petri
In primam Epistolam S. Ioanis
Sermo super Qui audientes gavisi sunt
Super Acta Apostolorum expositio
Super divi Iacobi Epistolam
Bernal, Salvador
Monsignor Josemaría Escrivá de Balaguer,
    Dublin, 1977
Bernard, St
Book of Consideration
De Beata Virgine
De fallacia et brevitate vitae
De laudibus novae militiae
Divine amoris
*Meditationes piissimae de cognitionis humanae
    conditionis*
Sermons on Psalm 90
Sermon on Song of Songs
Sermons
Bonaventure, St
In IV Libri sententiarum
Speculum Beatae Virgine
Borromeo, St Charles
Homilies

Sources quoted in the Commentary

Catherine of Siena, St
Dialogue
Cano, Melchor
De locis
Cassian, John
Collationes
De institutis coenobiorum
Clement of Alexandria
Catechesis III, De Baptismo
Commentary on Luke
Quis dives salvetur?
Stromata
Cyprian, St
De bono patientiae
De dominica oratione
De mortalitate
De opere et eleemosynis
De unitate Ecclesiae
De zelo et livore
Epist. ad Fortunatum
Quod idola dii non sint
Cyril of Alexandria, St
Commentarium in Lucam
Explanation of Hebrews
Homilia XXVIII in Mattheum
Cyril of Jerusalem, St
Catecheses
Mystagogical Catechesis
Diadochus of Photike
Chapters on Spiritual Perfection
Ephrem, St
Armenian Commentary on Acts
Commentarium in Epistolam ad Haebreos
Eusebius of Caesarea
Ecclesiastical History
Francis de Sales, St
Introduction to the Devout Life
Treatise on the Love of God
Francis of Assisi, St
Little Flowers
Reflections on Christ's Wounds
Fulgentius of Ruspe
Contra Fabianum libri decem
De fide ad Petrum
Gregory Nazianzen, St
Orationes theologicae
Sermons
Gregory of Nyssa, St
De instituto christiano
De perfecta christiana forma
On the Life of Moses
Oratio catechetica magna
Oratio I in beatitudinibus
Oratio I in Christi resurrectionem

Hippolytus, St
De consummatione saeculi
Ignatius of Antioch, St
Letter to Polycarp
Letters to various churches
Ignatius, Loyola, St
Spiritual Exercises
Irenaeus, St
Against Heresies
Proof of Apostolic Preaching
Jerome, St
Ad Nepotianum
Adversus Helvidium
Comm. in Ionam
Commentary on Galatians
Commentary on St Mark's Gospel
Contra Luciferianos
Dialogus contra pelagianos
Expositio in Evangelium secundum Lucam
Homilies to neophytes on Psalm 41
Letters
On Famous Men
John of Avila, St
Audi, filia
Lecciones sobre Gálatas
Sermons
John Chrysostom, St
Ante exilium homilia
Adversus Iudaeos
Baptismal Catechesis
De coemeterio et de cruce
De incomprehensibile Dei natura
De sacerdotio
De virginitate
Fifth homily on Anna
Hom. De Cruce et latrone
Homilies on St Matthew's Gospel, St John's
  Gospel, Acts of the Apostles, Romans,
  Ephesians, 1 and 2 Corinthians, Colossians,
  1 and 2 Timothy, 1 and 2 Thessalonians,
  Philippians, Philemon, Hebrews
II Hom. De proditione Iudae
Paraeneses ad Theodorum lapsum
Second homily in praise of St Paul
Sermon recorded by Metaphrastus
John of the Cross, St
A Prayer of the Soul enkindled by Love
Ascent of Mount Carmel
Dark Night of the Soul
Spiritual Canticle
John Damascene, St
De fide orthodoxa
John Mary Vianney, St
Sermons

Sources quoted in the Commentary

Josemaría Escrivá, St
Christ Is Passing By
Conversations
The Forge
Friends of God
Furrow
Holy Rosary
In Love with the Church
The Way
The Way of the Cross
Josephus, Flavius
Against Apion
Jewish Antiquities
The Jewish War
Justin Martyr, St
Dialogue with Tryphon
First and Second Apologies
à Kempis, Thomas
The Imitation of Christ
Luis de Granada, Fray
Book of Prayer and Meditation
Guide for Sinners
Introducción al símbolo de la fe
Life of Jesus Christ
Sermon on Public Sins
Suma de la vida cristiana
Luis de Léon, Fray
Exposición del Libro de Job
Minucius Felix
Octavius
Newman, J.H.
Biglietto Speech
Discourses to Mixed Congregations
Historical Sketches
Origen
Contra Celsum
Homilies on Genesis
Homilies on St John
In Exodum homiliae
Homiliae in Iesu nave
In Leviticum homiliae
In Matth. comm.
In Rom. comm.
Philo of Alexandria
De sacrificio Abel
Photius
Ad Amphilochium
Polycarp, St
Letter to the Philippians
del Portillo, A.
On Priesthood, Chicago, 1974
Primasius
Commentariorum super Apocalypsim B. Ioannis libri quinque
Prosper of Aquitaine, St
De vita contemplativa

Pseudo-Dionysius
De divinis nominibus
Pseudo-Macarius
Homilies
Severian of Gabala
Commentary on 1 Thessalonians
Teresa of Avila, St
Book of Foundations
Exclamations of the Soul to God
Interior Castle
Life
Poems
Way of Perfection
Tertullian
Against Marcion
Apologeticum
De baptismo
De oratione
Theodore the Studite, St
Oratio in adorationis crucis
Theodoret of Cyrrhus
Interpretatio Ep. ad Haebreos
Theophylact
Enarratio in Evangelium Marci
Thérèse de Lisieux, St
The Autobiography of a Saint
Thomas Aquinas, St
Adoro te devote
Commentary on St John = Super Evangelium S. Ioannis lectura
Commentaries on St Matthew's Gospel, Romans, 1 and 2 Corinthians, Galatians, Ephesians, Colossians, Philippians, 1 and 2 Timothy, 1 and 2 Thessalonians, Titus, Hebrews
De veritate
Expositio quorumdam propositionum ex Epistola ad Romanos
On the Lord's Prayer
On the two commandments of Love and the ten commandments of the Law
Summa contra gentiles
Summa theologiae
Super Symbolum Apostolorum
Thomas More, St
De tristitia Christi
Victorinus of Pettau
Commentary on the Apocalypse
Vincent Ferrer, St
Treatise on the Spiritual Life
Vincent of Lerins, St
Commonitorium
Zosimus, St
Epist. Enc. "Tractoria" ad Ecclesias Orientales